PRIMARY CARE SERIES: PERIPHERAL ARTERIAL DISEASE AND INTERMITTENT CLAUDICATION

A compilation of
The American Journal of Medicine®
Continuing Education Series

An Office-Based Approach to the Diagnosis and Treatment of Peripheral Arterial Disease

Parts I through VIII

SERIES EDITOR
ALAN T. HIRSCH, MD

PUBLISHER'S NOTE:

This is a compilation of a Continuing Medical Education Series on the diagnosis and treatment of peripheral arterial disease (PAD). The series was sponsored by the Excerpta Medica Office of Continuing Medical Education under the auspices of *The American Journal of Medicine*®. The opinions expressed in these pages are those of the authors and are not attributable to the sponsor or grantor, or to the publisher, editor, or editorial board of *The American Journal of Medicine*®.

Librarians please note: The original series was not part of the regular numbered sequence of issues or supplements to *The American Journal of Medicine*®.

The program was developed for primary care physicians, vascular internists, vascular specialists, and other clinicians who treat PAD. The series was planned and implemented in accordance with the Essentials and Standards of the Accreditation Council for Continuing Medical Education (ACCME) through the joint sponsorship of the Excerpta Medica Office of Continuing Medical Education and the Society for Vascular Medicine and Biology. The Excerpta Medica Office of Continuing Medical Education is accredited by the ACCME to sponsor continuing medical education for physicians.

The series was originally published between September 1998 and December 2000 and subsequently reprinted between September 2000 and November 2001. The Excerpta Medica Office of Continuing Medical Education had designated this educational activity for a maximum of 3 hours in Category 1 credit toward the AMA Physician's Recognition Award. Each physician was instructed to claim only those hours of credit that he/she actually spent in the educational activity.

SERIES EDUCATIONAL OBJECTIVES:

At the conclusion of this series, the participants should have been able to:
- Understand the prevalence of PAD and associated cardiovascular diseases, the clinical evaluation of PAD patients, and the role of the ankle-brachial index in office-based disease detection and vascular laboratory in the assessment of PAD.
- Understand the mortality of PAD, including the risk factors for the development of PAD; the impact of lipid lowering, tobacco cessation, and antiplatelet therapies; the consequences of atherosclerosis, thrombosis, myocardial infarction, and stroke; and issues regarding emerging atherosclerosis risk factors.
- Define and interpret severe PAD and critical limb ischemia (CLI), with an emphasis on the functional status of CLI patients; the role of angioplasty and stents for claudication and CLI, and thrombolytic therapy for acute arterial occlusion, vascular surgery, and limb salvage; and amputation, rehabilitation, and mortality.
- Understand the morbidity of PAD, including the functional status of PAD patients, quality of life for PAD patients, medical therapy for claudication, and the future of claudication pharmacotherapies.

The publication series and this compilation were supported by an unrestricted educational grant from Otsuka America Pharmaceutical, Inc. and Pharmacia Corporation.

ISBN 0-444-01858-1
Date of release: March 2001.

Society for Vascular Medicine and Biology

The Society for Vascular Medicine and Biology (SVMB) is a professional organization that was founded in 1989 to promote a vision of vascular medicine that encompasses the totality of vascular disease prevention, diagnosis, treatment, and rehabilitation. Our goals are to improve the integration of vascular biologic advances into medical practice, and to maintain high standards of clinical vascular medicine.

Our mission includes:

- The formation of vascular medicine training programs;
- Fostering formal vascular research and educational activities;
- Promulgating standards for postgraduate continuing medical educational (CME) curricula;
- Promoting the establishment of clinical centers-of-excellence for the diagnosis and treatment of vascular diseases; and
- Serving in an advisory capacity to educational institutions, government agencies, and health care policy makers.

Distinguished by our emphasis on clinical approaches to vascular disorders, it is our fundamental philosophy that optimal vascular care is best accomplished by the collegial interaction of a community of vascular professionals—including individuals with expertise in vascular medicine, vascular surgery, interventional radiology, vascular nursing, vascular technology—and other disciplines. The long-term care of patients with peripheral arterial disease also requires the devoted care of primary care physicians and their dedicated support staff. We recognize the importance of individuals with diverse backgrounds in achieving ideal standards of research and clinical practice.

Over the past decade, we have developed a wide array of educational programs for specialists in vascular medicine, as well as for primary care physicians, to improve the care of patients with arterial and venous diseases. It is our goal to serve as a national resource for such information by our ongoing efforts to publish monographs, create new audiovisual materials including slide sets and CD ROM–based learning, and by sponsorship of national audio-conferences on vascular topics.

The official journal of our organization, *Vascular Medicine*, provides peer-reviewed literature to an international audience. Our presence on the World Wide Web (www.svmb.org) provides a much needed resource for medical professionals with features such as CME and news about events, as well as offering vital information to patients and their families, including links to other sites to enhance public access to vascular educational material. We are also proud to be a cosponsor of the Vascular Disease Foundation, whose goal is to provide vascular educational information to the public.

We sincerely hope that you find the material presented in this compilation useful and informative.

Please consider joining us. Besides the many resources you can use, our Annual Scientific Meeting provides an ideal setting for all health care professionals to explore the newest frontiers in vascular biology or vascular practice, and to establish the professional liaisons that support the continuous improvement of vascular health. For further information, please contact us at:

Society for Vascular Medicine and Biology
13 Elm Street
Manchester, Massachusetts 01944
Telephone: (978) 526-8330
Fax: (978) 526-4018
E-mail: svmb@prri.com
Web site: www.svmb.org

Dear Colleague,

The transition from disease to health, from silence to communication, and from ignorance to wisdom is facilitated by the passion of health care professionals who are dedicated to a common mission. This compilation of an 8-monograph Continuing Medical Education series originally published under the auspices of *The American Journal of Medicine*® reflects the spirit of the Society for Vascular Medicine and Biology (SVMB), a professional society that is committed to vascular health and to professional camaraderie on behalf of public health.

My heartfelt thanks are due to all of my colleagues who generously offered their time to research and write the monographs in this compilation. I would also like to gratefully acknowledge Otsuka America Pharmaceutical, Inc. and Pharmacia Corporation for their generous support of these efforts.

Thanks are also due to the source of my inspiration, my wife, children, and family, who share my goals and foster these efforts.

It is my sincere hope, as well as the intention of the SVMB, that this work will aid your efforts to improve the long-term vascular and global health of your patients.

Sincerely,

Alan T. Hirsch, MD
Associate Professor of Medicine
Director, Vascular Medicine Program
Minnesota Vascular Diseases Center
University of Minnesota Medical School
Minneapolis, Minnesota USA

Introduction

Mark A. Creager, MD
Associate Professor of Medicine
Harvard Medical School
Director of the Vascular Center
Brigham and Women's Hospital
Boston, Massachusetts

Peripheral arterial disease (PAD) is an important and common clinical manifestation of atherosclerosis that affects >8 million persons in the United States. Its prevalence is greatest among those ≥60 years of age. PAD is the diagnosis applied to atherosclerotic involvement of a limb artery in which plaque is causing a flow-limiting lesion. PAD is but one manifestation of systemic atherosclerosis, and often is a harbinger of myocardial infarction or stroke. In addition, the quality of life of patients with PAD may be affected by symptoms of claudication, including walking impairment and even amputation. Early recognition of PAD should prompt therapeutic interventions that improve patients' prognosis, increase functional capabilities, and preserve limb viability.

The primary care physician and nurse practitioner are ideally situated to identify the patient with PAD and begin the treatment process. The diagnosis is not difficult to make. It requires a fundamental understanding of the disease, incorporation of a relevant history and vascular examination into the patient's evaluation, and knowledge of the ancillary diagnostic tests that can be utilized to establish the diagnosis. Perhaps it is lack of knowledge, lack of time, or both that contribute to the underdiagnosis of this problem and the loss of opportunity for treatment. Thus, the purpose of this book is to raise awareness of PAD among primary care physicians, who represent the first line in its diagnosis and treatment.

This book began as a continuing education series developed by the Society for Vascular Medicine and Biology (SVMB) and directed by the book's editor, Alan T. Hirsch, MD. Developing educational activity for physicians to learn about vascular diseases is one of the SVMB's most important missions. This series of 8 monographs was distributed widely to primary care physicians, many of whom participated in educational teleconferences based on the material. Given extremely favorable feedback, a decision was made to incorporate these monographs into a single text. The editors and authors are preeminent vascular clinicians and educa-tors; the book captures all of the major clinical aspects of PAD, ranging from epidemiology to diagnosis, medical therapies, and interventional treatments.

Part I includes articles on the epidemiology and practical detection of PAD. It provides information regarding the overall prevalence of PAD and the prognostic implications of coexisting cardiovascular and cerebrovascular diseases. There is also a discussion of the functional limitations imposed on walking ability, even in the absence of classic symptoms of claudication. Of great importance to primary care physicians is the article focusing on the office-based recognition and detection of PAD.

Part II extends these themes and focuses on recognizing and treating systemic atherosclerosis in the patient with PAD. There is a comprehensive discussion of the risk factors relevant for PAD development and potential benefits of risk-factor modification. The concept of atherothrombosis (ie, the thrombotic complication of atherosclerosis) is discussed in detail as is the efficacy of antithrombotic therapy, particularly with antiplatelet agents. There is also an article on PAD in women, an area that has not received sufficient emphasis in training or in the literature.

Part III provides fundamental information regarding the identification and treatment of patients with severe PAD, including those with critical limb ischemia. There is an article discussing pathogenetic factors leading to disease progression and another focusing on specific anatomic abnormalities that contribute to disabling and limb-threatening manifestations of PAD. Interventional approaches, including catheter-based procedures such as balloon angioplasty and stenting, surgical treatment such as bypass grafting, and thrombolysis are reviewed.

Part IV shifts our attention to the claudicant. One article focuses on the pathophysiology of claudication and its profound impact on daily activities and exercise performance. Methods to assess functional capacity, including the use of treadmill testing and questionnaires, are reviewed in another article. Of particular relevance to primary care physicians is the article dedicated to pharmacotherapy and supervised exercise rehabilitation in the management of the patient with intermittent claudication.

Part V extends the discussion to case management of the patient with moderate claudication. The indications and potential benefits of catheter-based endovascular treatment of claudication are presented. Also, in this section is a cogent review of the indications and potential benefits and risks of surgical bypass of patients with claudication to improve their quality of life. The roles of pharmacotherapy and exercise are explained as central features of effective claudication treatment.

The noninvasive vascular laboratory is an unfamiliar arena to most primary care physicians; the potential tests and their utility in diagnosing PAD are not understood. Thus, Part VI is a primer to the vascular laboratory for the primary care physician. One article is dedicated to the physiologic tests used to diagnose PAD, whereas another discusses the principles and utility of duplex ultrasound, a technique that permits direct visualization of the limb circulation. The role of the vascular diagnostic laboratory is exemplified by presenting specific clinical scenarios in vascular medicine, emphasizing the appropriate use of specific tests that would be available in a noninvasive laboratory. In addition, this part includes an article on arterial aneurysms, reviewing the imaging tests that are available to assist in the diagnosis of this disorder.

Women and PAD, an issue touched on in Part II, is covered more extensively in Part VII. One article in this section discusses the epidemiology of PAD in women, emphasizing its important impact on mobility and quality of life. Another article underscores the fact that PAD in women is largely unrecognized, despite its high prevalence and associated mortality. The effect of hormone replacement therapy, based on data from the Heart and Estrogen/Progestin Replacement Study (HERS) (the first prospective clinical trial to assess efficacy of hormonal replacement therapy in women with established coronary disease), is the topic of yet another article in this section.

Part VIII looks at specific risk factors and their management as they apply to patients with PAD. There are articles on diabetes mellitus, dyslipidemia, and other notable risk factors such as lipoprotein(a), triglycerides, high-density lipoproteins, and hyperhomocysteinemia.

The editors believe that primary care physicians must take a leading role in the care of patients with vascular diseases, including PAD. Taken together, the articles included herein can provide the cognitive and practical information that is most useful to the practicing physician. It is anticipated that familiarity with the principles and concepts discussed in this book will raise awareness of PAD among primary care physicians, nurses and nurse practitioners, and trainees. Possessing the knowledge and skills to diagnose PAD with confidence and initiate treatment adds credibility to the role of the primary care provider and has important dividends for the patients. Equally important is recognizing when additional expertise is needed and referral to a vascular specialist is indicated. Questions often arise in the course of a patient's evaluation. Hopefully, the book will provide many of the answers. ■

Acknowledgments

Excerpta Medica, Inc., a Reed Elsevier Company

Kevin R. Connolly
President

Janice Van Deusen
Senior Editorial Director, Office of Continuing Medical Education

Louis S. Revesz
Managing Editor, Office of Continuing Medical Education

Vanessa Fendt
Editorial Project Coordinator, Office of Continuing Medical Education

Donna Opperman
Editorial Assistant, Office of Continuing Medical Education

Chancey A. Wesner
Senior Operations Manager

James C. Adamczyk
Senior Director of Quality Control

Judy Galvach
Manager of Quality Control

Robert N. Mancuso
Senior Art Director

Jane Baxter
Associate Art Director

Charles N. Shaheen
Account Director

Editorial Offices
105 Raider Boulevard, Suite 101
Hillsborough, NJ 08844-1528
Telephone: 908-874-8550
Facsimile: 908-874-5633

An Office-Based Approach to the Diagnosis and Treatment of Peripheral Arterial Disease

Alan T. Hirsch, MD, Series Editor

Contents

Part I: The Epidemiology and Practical Detection of PAD
Jeffrey W. Olin, DO, Guest Editor

Part II: Recognizing and Treating Systemic Atherosclerosis
Mark A. Creager, MD, Guest Editor

continued on next page

Part III: Severe PAD: Limb Salvage and Revascularization Failure
J. Michael Bacharach, MD, MPH, Guest Editor

Part IV: Morbidity of PAD: Medical Approaches to Claudication
William R. Hiatt, MD, Guest Editor

continued on next page

Part V: Management of Peripheral Arterial Disease: Moderate Claudication

Emile R. Mohler III, MD, Guest Editor

Part VI: A Primer to the Vascular Laboratory for the Primary Care Physician

Michael R. Jaff, DO, FACP, FACC, Guest Editor

continued on next page

Part VII: Women and PAD
Marie D. Gerhard-Herman, MD, MMSc, and Judith G. Regensteiner, PhD, Guest Co-Editors

Part VIII: PAD and Risk-Factor Management
Jonathan L. Halperin, MD, Guest Editor

Index

The American Journal of Medicine®

CONTINUING EDUCATION SERIES

AN OFFICE-BASED APPROACH TO THE DIAGNOSIS AND TREATMENT OF PERIPHERAL ARTERIAL DISEASE

PART I: The Epidemiology and Practical Detection of PAD

SERIES EDITOR
ALAN T. HIRSCH, MD
GUEST EDITOR
JEFFREY W. OLIN, DO

Jointly sponsored by
The Excerpta Medica Office of Continuing Medical Education and the Society for Vascular Medicine and Biology

Dear Colleague:

Peripheral arterial disease (PAD) is a common health problem that we will increasingly recognize in our patients, our families, our friends. Unfortunately, patients with PAD have often received less than optimal medical care because it was thought that primary care physicians could offer little to ameliorate this condition. This earlier pattern of "conservative" management permitted the atherosclerotic disease to progress, claudication to go untreated, and cardiovascular ischemic events to supervene. This pattern of care is not appropriate in the current era.

The Society for Vascular Medicine and Biology, as a central feature of our educational missions, has initiated an array of programs designed to raise both professional and community awareness of the morbidity and mortality of PAD. One of our most important efforts is the PAD Primary Care Series, which is being launched with this monograph. This is the first national program to date by any national professional society to describe current data regarding the prevalence and natural history of PAD, with attention to those diagnostic and therapeutic modalities that should be available in every primary care office in our nation. A series of national experts on PAD have been assembled so that you can be assured of receiving the most accurate and advanced data available regarding this complex atherosclerotic disease. This educational effort has been made possible through an unrestricted educational grant from Otsuka America Pharmaceutical, Inc.

This monograph is the first in a series of four publications developed by our society to aid you in the delivery of effective, efficient, state-of-the-art care to patients with PAD. Published by Excerpta Medica, Inc., this monograph has been designated for up to 3 Category 1 CME credits. In addition to these written materials, which you will be able to share with your peers, a series of 15 live CME audioconferences will follow distribution of each monograph.

The PAD Primary Care Series will include subjects from the following four clinically important topic areas:
• The Epidemiology and Practical Detection of PAD
• Mortality of PAD: Consequences of Systemic Atherosclerosis
• Severe PAD: Limb Salvage Therapeutic Interventions
• Morbidity of PAD: Claudication and a Medical Therapeutic Approach

We hope you enjoy the information that will be presented in each bound monograph and that you will also join with your peers and accept our invitation to participate in the national PAD audioconferences. Together, we hope these efforts lead to improved PAD recognition, fuller access to care, and effective medical interventions in primary care offices across the country.

A goal of all national educational efforts is to provide benefits to both you and your patients. The primary care community of practitioners must play a leading role in the care of prevalent vascular diseases, such as PAD. It is our responsibility to provide each patient with an accurate vascular diagnosis and a comprehensive array of therapeutic options tailored to that individual's specific needs. To accomplish this task, collaboration must occur between primary care physicians, vascular internists, and other vascular specialty colleagues.

Please take an activist *educational* role on behalf of your patients with PAD by working with your partners in practice and with those critical members of the nursing, rehabilitation, and vascular technology communities whose skills are also central to excellence in vascular care. If you would like any additional information about the medical care of vascular diseases, please call the Society for Vascular Medicine and Biology (1-978-526-8330) or consider joining the Society as a member in support of the mission of improving future vascular care in our nation.

Sincerely,

Alan T. Hirsch, MD
President, Society for Vascular Medicine and Biology
On behalf of the Education Committee, Officers, and Trustees
Associate Professor of Medicine
Vascular Medicine Program
Minnesota Vascular Diseases Center
University of Minnesota Medical School
Minneapolis, Minnesota

Introduction

Jeffrey W. Olin, DO
Chairman, Department of Vascular Medicine
The Cleveland Clinic Foundation
Cleveland, Ohio

The realization that peripheral arterial disease (PAD) is a manifestation of systemic atherosclerosis, and therefore a predictor of cardiovascular and cerebrovascular disease, has generated a strong impetus for enhanced understanding of PAD and its pathophysiologic implications, as well as a need for improved methods of diagnosis and treatment.

However, the symptoms of PAD may be subtle—intermittent claudication is not always present—and diagnosis may be challenging. To optimize management of PAD, the primary care physician must develop a comprehensive understanding of the condition, including etiology, pathophysiology, and the benefits of recent progress in vascular technology.

To this end, the Society for Vascular Medicine and Biology and the Society for General Internal Medicine have developed a PAD educational program that includes a eight-part series of Continuing Medical Education (CME) publications under the auspices of *The American Journal of Medicine*®; this volume on the Epidemiology and Practical Detection of PAD is the first. These monographs are to be followed by live CME audioconferences featuring presentations by authors of these chapters covering the same curriculum.

To introduce the topic of this monograph, Michael H. Criqui, MD, MPH, discusses the epidemiology of PAD, endeavoring to make clear that the high mortality and morbidity of PAD is a reflection of the overlap between PAD and cardiovascular and cerebrovascular disease. He then points out that PAD risk can be reduced by aggressive risk-factor modification.

My chapter focuses on office-based recognition and detection of PAD, emphasizing that an intensive medical program can help prevent many of the complications of PAD. I detail what the clinician should look for during history-taking and physical examination and describe noninvasive laboratory tests that have advanced PAD assessment.

Finally, Mary M. McDermott, MD, and Philip Greenland, MD, review a program for intensive atherosclerotic risk-factor therapy, which they stress is greatly undertreated in PAD, thereby emphasizing the point that appropriate risk prevention in PAD is equivalent to risk prevention in systemic atherosclerotic disease, including cardiovascular disease.

Later publications in this series will include discussions of Mortality of PAD: Consequences of Systemic Atherosclerosis; Severe PAD: Limb Salvage Therapeutic Interventions; and Morbidity of PAD: Claudication.

The authors hope and expect that the information in this and future issues will go a long way toward enabling the primary care practitioner to manage PAD in an optimal fashion, thereby helping to preserve many lives—and limbs. ■

Epidemiology and Prognostic Significance of Peripheral Arterial Disease

Michael H. Criqui, MD, MPH
Professor, Departments of Family and Preventive Medicine and Medicine
University of California, San Diego School of Medicine
San Diego, California

Objective: To review the incidence, prevalence, and risk factors for PAD and its implications for cardio- and cerebrovascular disease.

Incidence data for peripheral arterial disease (PAD) are limited to intermittent claudication (IC). Prevalence data show a sharp increase in PAD with age from <3% at age <60 years to >20% at ages 75 years and older. The strongest cardiovascular disease (CVD) risk factors for PAD are cigarette smoking and diabetes, although several "newer" risk factors have recently been shown to be associated with PAD. Evaluation of atherosclerosis in multiple arterial beds has revealed it to be a systemic disease. Because of this systemic nature, persons with PAD are at sharply increased risk of subsequent CVD morbidity and mortality and can benefit from aggressive risk-factor modification.

The reported prevalence of PAD has varied considerably, largely because of different definitions of the disease. Older studies typically defined PAD by IC or pulse palpitation (Ludbrook et al, 1962; Reid et al, 1974; Hughson et al, 1978; Reunanen et al, 1982); in men 50 to 59 years of age, IC rates have ranged from 1% to 3%, but abnormal pulse findings have been reported in as many as 21%. Noninvasive testing can give a reliable estimate of PAD prevalence; in a population study we found that IC underestimated and pulse palpitation overestimated the true rate of PAD (Criqui et al, 1985a). We used a battery of noninvasive tests to assess PAD: segmental blood pressures above the knee, below the knee, at the ankle, and at the toe, divided by the brachial pressure, and three measures of flow velocity in each of the femoral and posterior tibial arteries. PAD rates by noninvasive testing were 2.5% at ages 40 to 59, 8.3% at ages 60 to 69, and 18.8% at ages 70 to 79. Prevalence data consistent with these estimates using only an abnormal ankle-brachial ratio or index (ABI) to define PAD have been reported (Hiatt et al, 1995; Vogt et al, 1993). The best incidence data for PAD came from the Framingham Study, but were based only on IC (Kannel et al, 1970). Annual IC incidence per 10,000 persons at risk rose from 6 in men and 3 in women aged 30 to 44, to 61 in men and 54 in women aged 65 to 74. Thus, PAD becomes quite common with increasing age, and as the US population continues to age, overall PAD prevalence will increase, even if age-specific rates are stable.

RISK FACTORS FOR PAD

In general, risk factors for PAD are the same as those that predict atherosclerotic events in the coronary and cerebrovascular arterial systems. However, some risk factors, such as cigarette smoking, diabetes mellitus, and the "syndrome X" lipid pattern appear to be especially important in PAD. Table I is based on our population study, where there were 408 men and women without evidence of PAD; 49 with moderate PAD, defined as abnormal segmental pressure ratios or flow velocity abnormalities, but not both; and 18 persons with severe PAD, defined as abnormalities of both ratios and flow velocities (Criqui et al, 1991a). After adjustment for age and sex, those with moderate PAD, mostly (89.8%) asymptomatic, had elevations in most CVD risk factors, but only the finding for body

Table I. Age- and Sex-Adjusted Mean Levels of CVD Risk Factors in Subjects Without Versus Subjects With Moderate and Severe PAD

Risk Factor	No PAD (n = 408)	Moderate PAD (n = 49)	Severe PAD (n = 18)
Cigarettes (pack-years)	18.7	25.8	39.2*
Triglycerides (mg/dL)	134.5	153.7	176.2*
HDL cholesterol (mg/dL)	55.5	55.6	49.5
LDL cholesterol (mg/dL)	158.5	153.6	159.5
Systolic BP (mm Hg)	129.6	131.0	137.7*
Diastolic BP (mm Hg)	76.8	78.7	82.9*
BMI (kg/m²)	24.5	27.1*	25.9
Fasting glucose (mg/dL)	94.9	Men 95.2 Women 96.4	122.5* 95.7

CVD = cardiovascular disease; PAD = peripheral arterial disease; HDL = high-density lipoprotein; LDL = low-density lipoprotein; BP = blood pressure; BMI = body mass index.
*P <0.05 compared with normals.

mass index (BMI) reached a conventional level of statistical significance. In those with severe PAD, mostly (72.2%) symptomatic, despite their smaller numbers, significant associations (P <0.05) were found for pack-years of cigarettes, triglycerides, systolic and diastolic blood pressure, and, in men only, fasting plasma glucose. The data for glucose are presented sex-specific because of the interaction shown. Low-density lipoprotein cholesterol (LDL-C) was not elevated in persons with severe PAD, but the lower high-density lipoprotein cholesterol (HDL-C) level approached statistical significance. Similar to our findings, other studies have suggested that cigarette smoking and/or diabetes are the strongest risk factors for PAD (Kannel and McGee, 1985; Fowkes et al, 1992b; Goldhaber et al, 1992; Hiatt et al, 1995). The dyslipidemia most frequently found in PAD is not elevated total or LDL-C, but a combination of elevated triglycerides and low HDL-C and a decreased LDL-C particle size, or "pattern B" (Davignon et al, 1977; Bradby et al, 1978; Senti et al, 1992; Ogren et al, 1993b). The severity of pattern B appears to be a direct function of the level of triglycerides (Austin et al, 1988). Since high triglycerides and low HDL-C are the most frequent lipid/lipoprotein pattern in syndrome X (Reaven, 1988), where insulin resistance is thought to be central, this is

consistent with the high risk of diabetes and/or insulin resistance for PAD.

Newer CVD risk factors have shown significant correlations with PAD as well, including apolipoprotein B (Valentine et al, 1994), lipoprotein(a) (Tyrrell et al, 1992; Valentine et al, 1994), homocysteine (Malinow et al, 1989), fibrinogen (Lowe et al, 1993) and fibrinogen genotype (Fowkes et al, 1992a), blood viscosity (Lowe et al, 1993), and C-reactive protein (Ridker et al, 1998).

Limited evidence exists for risk-factor intervention reducing incident PAD. Four lipid-lowering trials have reported a favorable effect on PAD incidence or progression (Blankenhorn et al, 1991; Lipid Research Clinics Program, 1984; Buchwald et al, 1990; Pedersen et al, 1998). Antiplatelet agents have been reported to reduce PAD progression and reduce the need for invasive intervention (De Felice et al, 1990; Goldhaber et al, 1992; Balsano et al, 1993).

THE OVERLAP BETWEEN PAD AND CAD PREVALENCE

In our population study, participants with noninvasively determined PAD had a higher CVD prevalence than those free of PAD—29.4% versus 11.5% for men and 21.2% versus 9.3% for women (Criqui et al, 1997). We defined prevalent CVD as a history of myocardial infarction (MI), coronary artery bypass graft, stroke, or stroke surgery. We did not separate these events because of the relatively small numbers. A study of 1,886 patients ≥62 years of age in a long-term care facility reported extensive overlap among PAD, coronary artery disease (CAD), and stroke (Aronow and Ahn, 1994), as did data for the 19,185 patients in the Clopidogrel Versus Aspirin in Patients at Risk of Ischaemic Events (CAPRIE) trial (CAPRIE Steering Committee, 1996). In the Cardiovascular Health Study (CHS), there was a graded response between the ABI and prevalence of MI, angina, and congestive heart failure (Newman et al, 1993a). In addition, significant correlations were found between ABI and major electrocardiogram (ECG) abnormalities, ECG left ventricular hypertrophy, and regional and global wall motion abnormalities. Dormandy et al (1989) have reviewed the literature for the prevalence of CAD in patients presenting with PAD. In seven studies, CAD was defined by "clinical history and electrocardiogram," and in these studies PAD patients had an average CAD prevalence of 39%. Two studies utilized stress tests and found a 62% and 63% prevalence of CAD in PAD patients. Finally, one study used angiography and found a 90% prevalence of CAD in PAD patients. These results illustrate two important points. First, atherosclerosis is a systemic disease. Second, the degree of overlap of atheroscle-

Table II. Mortality (%) Over 10 Years and RR by PAD Status in Men and Women, Average Age 66 Years at Baseline

	Men			Women		
	No PAD	**PAD**	**RR†**	**No PAD**	**PAD**	**RR†**
Number	183	34	—	225	33	—
All-cause	16.9	61.8	3.3*	11.6	33.3	2.5*
CVD	7.7	41.7	5.1*	3.6	18.2	4.8*
CAD	5.5	35.3	5.8*	2.2	9.1	4.8*
Other	9.3	14.7	1.6	8.0	15.2	1.6

PAD = peripheral arterial disease; RR = relative risk; CVD = cardiovascular disease; CAD = coronary artery disease.
*$P < 0.05$.
†Age-adjusted.

rosis across various vascular beds is a direct function of the sensitivity of the assessment instruments for CAD (and PAD); that is, the higher the sensitivity, the greater the overlap.

THE OVERLAP BETWEEN PAD AND CEREBROVASCULAR DISEASE

In the CHS, stroke and transient ischemic attack were both related to ABI level, as well as the presence of carotid plaque (Newman et al, 1993a). The review by Dormandy et al (1989) looked at the prevalence of cerebrovascular disease in PAD patients. The findings showed somewhat less overlap than for CAD, but again the results were a function of the sensitivity of the assessment for cerebrovascular disease. In four studies relying primarily on history of clinical events, the prevalence of cerebrovascular disease in PAD patients ranged from 0.5% to 15%. However, in three studies where a cervical bruit or abnormal Doppler testing was used to define cerebrovascular disease, the prevalence in PAD patients ranged from 44% to 52%. Thus, these findings again demonstrate that atherosclerosis is a systemic disease. A recent study has also shown that not only is the presence of PAD correlated with carotid disease, but also that the severity of the PAD correlates with the severity of carotid disease (Long et al, unpublished).

PAD AND INCIDENT NONFATAL CVD

Since PAD prevalence correlates with both the prevalence of CAD and cerebrovascular disease, it seems reasonable to assume that PAD patients experience a high rate of incident nonfatal CAD and cerebrovascular disease.

Three studies have reported CVD morbidity combined with CVD mortality in persons with PAD. In our population study, we found a relative risk (RR) in men of 2.4 for CAD and 3.3 for cerebrovascular disease, and in women 3.6 for CAD and 9.0 for cerebrovascular disease (Criqui et al, 1991b). Focusing on morbidity

alone, the excess in men was limited to baseline morbidity, while in women both baseline and incident morbidity were increased. A substudy of a hypertension trial showed that in participants with an ABI ≤0.9 versus others, the RR for CAD was 1.9 and for all CVD (including cerebrovascular disease) was 2.5 (Newman et al, 1993b). Morbidity was not evaluated separately from mortality. A study from Sweden reported that the cardiac event rate, including nonfatal and fatal events, was doubled in participants with an ABI <0.9 (Ogren et al, 1993a). Neither nonfatal cardiac events nor cerebrovascular events were reported separately.

PAD AND SUBSEQUENT CAD, CVD, AND ALL-CAUSE MORTALITY

A 1989 review concluded that in studies of patients with PAD, 50% of deaths were due to CAD, 15% to stroke, and 10% to abdominal vascular disease, leaving only 1 in 4 deaths due to non-CVD causes (Dormandy et al, 1989). This review also concluded that total mortality risk in PAD patients was doubled or tripled after about 5 years.

Recent epidemiologic studies have confirmed, extended, and refined these earlier observations. In 1992, we published 10-year mortality findings in our community cohort, which underwent a battery of noninvasive tests for PAD at baseline (Criqui et al, 1992). Table II shows mortality findings by PAD status at baseline separately for men and women who on average were 66 years old. CVD mortality is a subset of total mortality, and CAD mortality is a subset of CVD mortality. Among men without PAD, 16.9% died over 10 years of follow-up compared with a death rate of 61.8% in those with PAD, for an age-adjusted RR of 3.3. This increase in total mortality was due to a 5.8 RR for CAD mortality and a fivefold increased risk for CVD mortality; other causes of mortality were not significantly increased (RR = 1.6). In women, although the absolute death rates were lower (11.6% in women

Table III. RR (95% Confidence Interval) for Mortality, Adjusted for Multiple Covariates

	All Subjects (n = 474)	Subjects Free of CVD Baseline (n = 415)
Total mortality	3.1 (1.9–4.9)	3.1 (1.8–5.3)
CVD mortality	5.9 (3.0–11.4)	6.3 (2.6–15.0)
CAD mortality	6.6 (2.9–14.9)	4.3 (1.4–2.8)

RR = relative risk; CVD = cardiovascular disease; CAD = coronary artery disease.

Table IV. RR (95% Confidence Interval) for Mortality, Stratified by PAD Symptoms and Adjusted for Multiple Covariates

	Asymptomatic PAD (n = 49)	Symptomatic PAD (n = 18)
Total mortality	2.7 (1.6–4.5)	4.7 (2.3–9.6)
CVD mortality	4.7 (2.3–9.8)	11.2 (4.5–27.9)
CAD mortality	5.6 (2.3–11.6)	11.4 (3.6–35.8)

RR = relative risk; PAD = peripheral arterial disease; CVD = cardiovascular disease; CAD = coronary artery disease.

without PAD vs 33.3% in women with PAD), the relative increase in mortality associated with PAD was similar, and, like men, was limited to cardiovascular causes. Table III shows data for both sexes combined after adjusting for multiple potential covariates; specifically age, sex, cigarettes per day, systolic blood pressure, HDL-C, LDL-C, natural log triglycerides, fasting plasma glucose, BMI, and selection criteria (random sample or hyperlipidemic). It seemed appropriate to combine both sexes (and adjust for sex), since the proportional increase in risk in both sexes was similar. The first column shows the data for all subjects. The second column shows the data after excluding 59 subjects (31 men and 28 women) who had a history of CVD at baseline as defined earlier. Both columns were adjusted for the multiple risk factors noted above. The first column for all subjects shows that despite multivariate adjustment for multiple potentially confounding risk factors, the RRs for all-cause, CVD, and CAD mortality were essentially unchanged from the RRs in Table II, which were only age-adjusted. This indicates that the prognostic significance of PAD for CVD mortality is largely independent of risk factors that may influence both the development of PAD and the probability of CVD death. The second column shows that the risk of PAD for total and CVD mortality is not dependent upon a baseline diagnosis of CAD or cerebrovascular disease; that is, the RRs for total and CVD mortality were essentially unchanged after excluding subjects with known CVD at baseline. For CAD, there was a decrease in the RR from 6.6 before exclusion to 4.3 after exclusion, indicating some attenuation of the prognostic significance of PAD for CAD mortality in subjects free of clinical CVD at baseline. Nonetheless, a fourfold risk remained, and the 95% confidence interval excluded one.

The fact that PAD as a marker for future CVD mortality was largely independent of both CVD risk factors and baseline clinical CVD seems somewhat surprising since CVD risk factors predict not only CVD but PAD. However, much of the variance in atherosclerotic disease occurrence remains unexplained by traditional CVD risk factors. In addition, extant CVD at base-

line was assessed by clinical events, and obviously many participants "free of CVD" at baseline probably had, in this older group, considerable atherosclerosis in the coronary and cerebrovascular beds, and as reviewed earlier, such atherosclerosis is much more likely in patients with PAD. Thus, the presence of PAD can be conceptualized as an independent marker of an individual's propensity to develop atherosclerosis at any given level of traditional cardiovascular risk factors, and largely independent of previous clinical CVD, although previous CVD did influence the PAD–CAD mortality association somewhat.

PAD SYMPTOMS, SEVERITY, AND OUTCOME
In our population study, subjects were classified by asymptomatic and symptomatic PAD. IC was defined as exercise calf pain not present at rest. We also subdivided PAD into moderate or severe, as defined earlier. Symptoms correlated strongly with disease severity. Thirteen of 18 PAD subjects (72.2%) with IC had severe disease versus severe disease in only 5 of 49 subjects (10.2%) without IC. Table IV shows the RRs of asymptomatic versus symptomatic PAD for mortality. For total, CVD, and CAD mortality, each considered separately, the RRs are about twice as great for symptomatic (mostly severe) PAD than for asymptomatic (mostly moderate) PAD. Thus, a dose-response relation exists between the severity of PAD and mortality. Figure 1 illustrates these findings graphically with Kaplan–Meier curves. There was a graded correlation between survival and PAD severity. In the subjects with severe and symptomatic PAD (a subset of symptomatic PAD), only one in four survived 10 years. It is important to note the sharply reduced survival in subjects without symptoms of IC but with subclinical PAD.

Figure 2 is adapted from a follow-up study of 744 patients studied with noninvasive tests for PAD at a hospital vascular laboratory (McKenna et al, 1991). This group of patients had the same average age as our community cohort, 66 years. Survival was stratified by the finding on a single noninvasive test, the ABI, using the lowest value for the two limbs. The results indicate

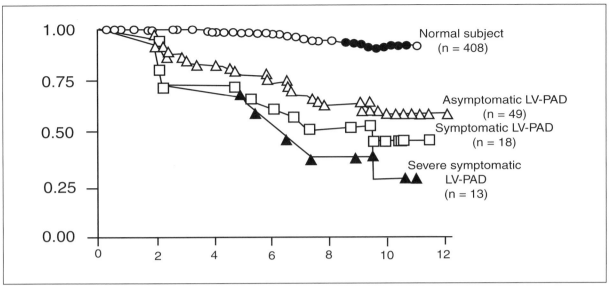

Figure 1. Kaplan–Meier survival curves for a defined population, stratified by presence and extent of PAD. (From Criqui et al, 1992) LV-PAD = large-vessel peripheral arterial disease.

Key Points

- Neither IC nor pulse palpitation can be relied upon for the diagnosis of PAD. Noninvasive testing is accurate and reliable.

- The ABI is a valid, simple, noninvasive assessment for PAD.

- PAD prevalence increases sharply with age, from <3% at age <60 years to >20% at age 75 years and older. Only a minority of patients are symptomatic.

- Risk factors for PAD are similar to those for CAD, although cigarette smoking and diabetes mellitus and/or insulin resistance are especially important in PAD.

- Atherosclerosis is a systemic disease, and PAD patients have an increased prevalence of CAD and cerebrovascular disease.

- PAD patients are at very high risk for subsequent CVD morbidity and mortality, and the risk is proportional to the severity of PAD. This risk can be reduced by aggressive risk-factor modification.

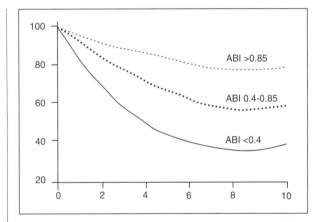

Figure 2. Survival curves for noninvasive vascular hospital laboratory examinees, stratified by ABI level. (From McKenna et al, 1991) ABI = ankle-brachial index.

a dose-response gradient between PAD severity, as assessed by the ABI, and mortality over 10 years—very similar to our findings.

A study of ABI level and mortality in older (≥65 years) women revealed a sharp stepwise mortality gradient for ABI >1.0, 0.9 to 1.0, and 0.8 to 0.9, but no additional mortality gradient below 0.8 (Vogt et al, 1993). Survival in a group of PAD patients has been reported (McDermott et al, 1994). Unlike the above three studies, there were no patients with bilateral normal ABIs. All 422 patients had at least one ABI (either right or left) <0.92. Follow-up time was shorter than in the above two studies, about 4.3 years. The findings were strikingly similar to earlier studies, with a clear and early separation of survival probability based on ABI level.

It is interesting to compare these results with earlier studies showing a two- to threefold increase in mortality in persons with reported IC (Peabody et al, 1974; Hughson et al, 1978; Reunanen et al, 1982; Jelnes et al, 1986; Dormandy et al, 1989; Smith et al, 1990). Since IC is symptomatic PAD, why weren't the relative risks even higher? Part of the answer may be in the unexpectedly low positive predictive value of classic IC; that is, only about 50% of persons with classic IC complaints in epidemiologic studies have PAD on noninvasive assessment (Criqui et al, 1985b). Thus, this substantial number of false positives biases the RR downward, compared with studies where noninvasive test results are employed (Criqui et al, 1992).

These mortality findings reflect the coprevalence of PAD with atherosclerosis in other vascular beds, and the highly significant prognostic importance of the presence of symptomatic and asymptomatic PAD for subsequent mortality, with a graded correlation between PAD severity and mortality.

BIBLIOGRAPHY

Aronow WS, Ahn C. Prevalence of coexistence of coronary artery disease, peripheral arterial disease, and atherothrombotic brain infarction in men and women ≥62 years of age. Am J Cardiol 1994;74:64–5.

Austin MA, Breslow JL, Hennekens CH, et al. Low-density lipoprotein subclass patterns and risk of myocardial infarction. JAMA 1988;260:1917–21.

Balsano F, Violi F, and the ADEP Group. Effect of picotamide on the clinical progression of peripheral vascular disease. Circulation 1993;87:1563–9.

Blankenhorn DH, Azen SP, Crawford DW, et al. Effects of colestipol-niacin therapy on human femoral atherosclerosis. Circulation 1991;83:438–47.

Bradby GVH, Valente AJ, Walton KW. Serum high-density lipoproteins in peripheral vascular disease. Lancet 1978;2:1271–4.

Buchwald H, Varco RL, Matts JP, et al. Effect of partial ileal bypass surgery on mortality and morbidity from coronary heart disease in patients with hypercholesterolemia. N Engl J Med 1990;323:946–55.

CAPRIE Steering Committee. A randomized, blinded trial of Clopidogrel Versus Aspirin in Patients at Risk of Ischaemic Events (CAPRIE). Lancet 1996;348:1329–39.

Criqui MH, Denenberg JO, Langer RD, et al. The epidemiology of peripheral arterial disease: importance of identifying the population at risk. Vasc Med 1997;2:221–6.

Criqui MH, Fronek A, Barrett-Connor E, et al. The prevalence of peripheral arterial disease in a defined population. Circulation 1985a;71:510–15.

Criqui MH, Fronek A, Klauber MR, et al. The sensitivity, specificity, and predictive value of traditional clinical evaluation of peripheral arterial disease: results from noninvasive testing in a defined population. Circulation 1985b;71:516–21.

Criqui MH, Langer RD, Fronek A, et al. Large vessel and isolated small vessel disease. In: Fowkes FGR, ed. Epidemiology of Peripheral Vascular Disease. London: Springer-Verlag; 1991a:85–96.

Criqui MH, Langer RD, Fronek A, et al. Coronary disease and stroke in patients with large vessel peripheral arterial disease. Drugs 1991b;42(suppl 5):16–21.

Criqui MH, Langer RD, Fronek A, et al. Mortality over a period of 10 years in patients with peripheral arterial disease. N Engl J Med 1992;326:381–6.

Davignon J, Lussier-Cacan S, Ortin-George M, et al. Plasma lipids and lipoprotein patterns in angiographically graded atherosclerosis of the legs and in coronary heart disease. Can Med Assoc J 1977;116:1245–50.

De Felice M, Gallo P, Masotti G. Current therapy of peripheral obstructive arterial disease. The non-surgical approach. Angiology 1990;41:1–11.

Dormandy J, Mahir M, Ascada G, et al. Fate of the patient with chronic leg ischaemia. J Cardiovasc Surg 1989;30:50–7.

Fowkes FGR, Connor JM, Smith FB, et al. Fibrinogen genotype and risk of peripheral atherosclerosis. Lancet 1992a;339:693–6.

Fowkes FGR, Housley E, Riemersma RA, et al. Smoking, lipids, glucose intolerance, and blood pressure as risk factors for peripheral atherosclerosis compared with ischemic heart disease in the Edinburgh Artery Study. Am J Epidemiol 1992b;135:331–40.

Goldhaber SZ, Manson JE, Stampfer MJ, et al. Low-dose aspirin and subsequent peripheral arterial surgery in the Physicians' Health Study. Lancet 1992;340:143–5.

Hiatt WR, Hoag S, Hamman RF. Effect of diagnostic criteria on the prevalence of peripheral arterial disease. The San Luis Valley Diabetes Study. Circulation 1995;91:1472–9.

Hughson WG, Mann JI, Garrod A. Intermittent claudication: prevalence and risk factors. Br Med J 1978;i:1379–81.

Jelnes R, Gaardsting O, Hougaard-Jensen K, et al. Fate in intermittent claudication: outcome and risk factors. Br Med J 1986;293:1137–40.

Kannel WB, McGee DL. Update on some epidemiologic features of intermittent claudication: The Framingham Study. J Am Geriatr Soc 1985;33:13–8.

Kannel WB, Skinner JJ Jr, Schwartz MJ, et al. Intermittent claudication: incidence in the Framingham Study. Circulation 1970;41:875–83.

Lipid Research Clinics Program. The Lipid Research Clinics Primary Prevention Trial results. JAMA 1984;251:351–64.

Lowe GDO, Fowkes FGR, Dawes J, et al. Blood viscosity, fibrinogen, and activation of coagulation and leukocytes in peripheral arterial disease and the normal population in the Edinburgh Artery Study. Circulation 1993;87:1915-20.

Ludbrook J, Clarke AM, McKenzie JK. Significance of absent ankle pulse. Br Med J 1962;i:1724–6.

Malinow MR, Kang SS, Taylor LM, et al. Prevalence of hyperhomocyst(e)inemia in patients with peripheral arterial occlusive disease. Circulation 1989;79:1180–8.

McDermott MM, Feinglass J, Slavensky R, et al. The ankle-brachial index as a predictor of survival in patients with peripheral vascular disease. J Gen Intern Med 1994;9:445–9.

McKenna M, Wolfson S, Kuller L. The ratio of ankle and arm arterial pressure as an independent predictor of mortality. Atherosclerosis 1991;87:119–28.

Newman AB, Siscovick DS, Manolio TA, et al. Ankle-arm index as a marker of atherosclerosis in the Cardiovascular Health Study. Circulation 1993a;88:837–45.

Newman AB, Sutton-Tyrrell K, Vogt MT, et al. Morbidity and mortality in hypertensive adults with a low ankle/arm blood pressure index. JAMA 1993b;270:487–9.

Ogren M, Hedblad B, Isacsson S-O, et al. Non-invasively detected carotid stenosis and ischaemic heart disease in men with leg arteriosclerosis. Lancet 1993a;342:1138–41.

Ogren M, Hedblad B, Jungquist G, et al. Low ankle-brachial pressure index in 68-year-old men: prevalence, risk factors and prognosis. Eur J Vasc Surg 1993b;7:500–6.

Peabody CN, Kannel WB, McNamara PM. Intermittent claudication: surgical significance. Arch Surg 1974;109:693–7.

Pedersen TR, Kjekshus J, Pyorala K, et al. Effect of simvastatin on ischemic signs and symptoms in the Scandinavian Simvastatin Survival Study (4S). Am J Cardiol 1998;81:333–5.

Reaven G. Role of insulin resistance in human disease. Diabetes 1988;37:1595–1607.

Reid DD, Brett GZ, Hamilton PJS, et al. Cardiorespiratory disease and diabetes among middle-aged male civil servants: a study of screening and intervention. Lancet 1974;i:469–73.

Reunanen A, Takkunen H, Aroma A. Prevalence of intermittent claudication and its effect on mortality. Acta Med Scand 1982;211:249–56.

Ridker PM, Cushman M, Stampfer MJ, et al. Plasma concentration of C-reactive protein and risk of developing peripheral vascular disease. Circulation 1998;97:425–8.

Senti M, Nogues X, Pedro-Botet J, et al. Lipoprotein profile in men with peripheral vascular disease. Role of intermediate density lipoproteins and apoprotein E phenotypes. Circulation 1992;85:30–6.

Smith GD, Shipley MJ, Rose G. Intermittent claudication, heart disease risk factors and mortality: The Whitehall Study. Circulation 1990;82:1925–31.

Tyrrell J, Cooke T, Reilly M, et al. Lipoprotein [Lp(a)] and peripheral vascular disease. J Intern Med 1992;232:349–52.

Valentine JR, Grayburn PA, Vega GL, et al. Lp(a) lipoprotein is an independent, discriminating risk factor for premature peripheral atherosclerosis among white men. Arch Intern Med 1994;154:801–6.

Vogt MT, Cauley JA, Newman AB, et al. Decreased ankle/arm blood pressure index and mortality in elderly women. JAMA 1993;270:465–9.

Clinical Evaluation and Office-Based Detection of Peripheral Arterial Disease

Jeffrey W. Olin, DO
Chairman, Department of Vascular Medicine
The Cleveland Clinic Foundation
Cleveland, Ohio

Objective:
To review the procedures, including history-taking, physical examination, and laboratory tests, that enhance the ability to detect and evaluate peripheral arterial disease.

Patients with peripheral arterial disease (PAD) may experience decreased exercise capacity, impaired functional status, and poor quality of life. Some patients progress to a more severe degree of limb ischemia, requiring revascularization or amputation. Besides limb-related complications, patients with PAD have an increased rate of mortality from cardiovascular disease. Early office-based recognition and detection and an aggressive medical program can help to prevent many of these complications.

Atherosclerosis of the abdominal aorta and arteries of the lower extremity is referred to as peripheral arterial disease (PAD). Patients with PAD most commonly present with intermittent claudication and less often with ischemic rest pain and/or gangrene. However, the incidence of asymptomatic PAD is higher than previously believed (Newman et al, 1993b; Vogt et al, 1993). The ankle-brachial index (ABI) was ≤0.90 in 25.5% of the 1,537 participants in the Systolic Hypertension in the Elderly Study (Newman et al, 1993b) and 5.5% of 1,492 asymptomatic women entered into the Multicenter Study of Osteoporotic Fractures (Vogt et al, 1993). These studies also demonstrated that in the asymptomatic patient with a low ABI, there is an increased cardiovascular mortality rate.

Weitz and colleagues (1996) suggested that in a population of individuals >55 years of age, approximately 5% will have intermittent claudication, 10% will have asymptomatic PAD (ABI <0.90), and 1% will develop critical leg ischemia (Figure 1). There are two major sequelae of PAD: limb-related complications and increased cardiovascular morbidity and mortality. While many patients with PAD remain asymptomatic,

others may have atherosclerotic involvement of one or more arterial segments. However, in most instances, there is adequate collateral circulation and no jeopardy to the limb (Hertzer, 1991). Most subjects with more severe degrees of limb-threatening ischemia have tandem lesions and/or multisegment disease. A compilation of data suggest that in patients with intermittent claudication, worsening claudication occurs in approximately 16%, lower extremity bypass surgery is required in approximately 7%, and primary major amputation in approximately 4% (Figure 1). Of those undergoing bypass surgery, 26% may require repeat revascularization and an additional 20% may require amputation. The late incidence of amputation, severe ischemia, and/or operation in patients with claudication from three different series are shown in Table I. It is estimated that in patients with claudication, approximately 1.4% per year will develop ischemic rest pain and/or gangrene. This progression rate is higher in the diabetic population and in patients who continue to smoke (Jonason and Ringqvist, 1985; Jonason and Bergstrom, 1987). Gangrene occurred in approximately 31% of diabetics as opposed to 5% of patients without diabetes (P <0.001), and rest pain and/or

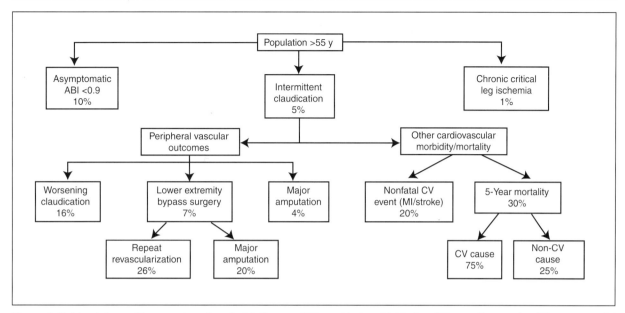

Figure 1. Epidemiology of lower extremity arterial disease. ABI = ankle-brachial index; CV = cardiovascular; MI = myocardial infarction. Weitz JI, et al. Circulation 1996;94:3026–49. Reprinted with permission.

Table I. Late Incidence of Amputation, Severe Ischemia, and/or Operation in Patients with Claudication

Series	No.	Follow-up Years	Severe Ischemia and/or Operation (%)	Amputation (%)
Juergens, et al (1960)	336	5	NA	3
Humphries, et al (1963)	1,552		23	7
Stable claudication	661	4 (mean)	26	8
Progressive claudication	891		21	6
McDaniel, Cronenwett (1989)				
History and PE	2,469	7	19	7
Vascular laboratory and/or angiography	1,624	5	27	4

PE = physical examination. Adapted from Hertzer NR. Circulation 1991;83(suppl I):I-12–I-19.

gangrene occurred in 40% of patients with diabetes mellitus and 18% of those without (P <0.001). In a large series of patients with PAD, ischemic rest pain occurred in 16% of patients who continued to smoke compared with none who discontinued smoking (Jonason and Bergstrom, 1987).

In addition to the limb complications associated with PAD, there is a markedly decreased survival in this patient population. PAD is a marker for atherosclerosis elsewhere. Population-based studies and follow-up studies of surgically treated patients indicate that those with PAD have a mortality rate of approximately 30% at 5 years, 50% at 10 years, and 70% to 75% at 15 years (Coffman, 1986). Hertzer and colleagues (1987) showed that patients with abdominal aortic aneurysm, PAD, or extracranial cerebrovascular disease have an increased prevalence of significant asymptomatic coronary artery disease. In a prospective study of patients followed for 10 years, Criqui and associates (1992) reported a 10-year mortality of 61.7% in men and 33.3% in women with large-vessel PAD compared with 16.9% of men and 11.6% of women without evidence of PAD. The relative risk of dying from coronary artery disease in patients with PAD was 6.6, cardiovascular disease 5.9, and all-cause mortality 3.1 compared with patients without PAD.

Patients with asymptomatic PAD also have a markedly increased mortality from cardiovascular disease. Vogt and associates (1993) demonstrated that the 4-year mortality rate is approximately 25% in patients with an ABI <0.80. The lower the ABI, the greater the likelihood of dying from cardiovascular disease.

Table II. Differentiating True Claudication from Pseudoclaudication

	Claudication	Pseudoclaudication
Character of discomfort	Cramping, tightness, tiredness, aching	Same or tingling, weakness, clumsiness
Location of discomfort	Buttock, hip, thigh, calf, foot	Same
Exercise induced	Yes	Yes or no
Distance to claudication	Same each time	Variable
Occurs with standing	No	Yes
Relief	Stop walking	Often must sit or change body positions

Krajewski LP, Olin JW. Atherosclerosis of the aorta and lower extremity arteries. In: Young JR, Olin JW, Bartholomew JR, eds. Peripheral Vascular Diseases. 2nd ed. St. Louis:Yearbook; 1996:208–33.

CLINICAL MANIFESTATIONS OF PAD

History

The primary symptom of PAD is intermittent claudication (Latin *claudicare*, to limp); its current definition is pain or discomfort in the lower extremity brought on by walking, which ceases when stopping (hence intermittent). Onset is usually gradual and may go unrecognized for years by patients and physicians who may attribute the symptoms to arthritis, muscular pain, or simply aging. The extent of disease may become quite severe involving multiple arterial segments before the patient is aware that a problem exists. Claudication may be further described as aching, cramping, tightness, tiredness, or pain that occurs when walking. The discomfort often occurs in the muscle group immediately distal to the arterial obstruction. Most characteristically, it occurs in the calf as a result of superficial femoral artery atherosclerosis. Claudication may also occur in the hip, thigh, or buttock when aortoiliac occlusive disease is present. Claudication rarely occurs in the foot alone, except in small-vessel occlusive disease that occurs in patients with thromboangiitis obliterans (Buerger's disease). Foot or arch claudication may then be the presenting manifestation in this disease.

As a general rule, patients experience claudication each time they walk a particular distance, as long as the speed of walking and grade of the terrain remain the same. The discomfort often resolves in 2 to 5 minutes after stopping. Once the discomfort goes away, the patient can again walk the same distance before experiencing discomfort again. If the patient continues to walk until severe or excruciating leg pain occurs, it may take longer for the discomfort to disappear and the patient may have to sit down to get relief. This is due to accumulation of lactic acid in the ischemic muscle. The triad of discomfort brought on by exercise, relief within 2 to 5 minutes of stopping, and the ability to walk again the same distance once the discomfort has disappeared are classic symptoms for patients with vascular claudication. This should be differentiated from patients who have pseudoclaudication due to lumbar canal stenosis or lumbar radiculopathy (Table II). Since many patients who develop pseudoclaudication are elderly, there is also an increased prevalence of PAD in this subgroup of patients. Therefore, the history is extremely important in helping to differentiate which disease entity is, in fact, causing the symptoms. It is notable that patients with pseudoclaudication have a variable level of exercise required to bring on the discomfort. One day they may be able to walk several blocks and the next day only half a block. In addition, it often takes 10 to 20 minutes for the discomfort to disappear, and the patients must sit down, take weight off the extremity, or change body position to get relief. True claudication secondary to PAD never occurs just with standing while pseudoclaudication may (Krajewski and Olin, 1996).

Many patients can provide an accurate description of their walking distance before claudication occurs. Walking upgrade or at an increased speed brings on the discomfort more rapidly. In those patients who are poor observers, the treadmill exercise test is an excellent means to determine their functional disability. Others have used the Walking Impairment Questionnaire (WIQ) to determine the functional disability in patients with claudication (Regensteiner et al, 1990).

The following should be ascertained and documented in all patients with claudication: the character of the discomfort or pain as well as its location; the duration of symptoms; the distance the patient can walk before developing symptoms in relation to the speed of walking and the grade; the time it takes for the discomfort to disappear after cessation of exercise; the position required to get relief (ie, sitting, standing, etc.); and whether the discomfort returns after the same time and distance when walking is resumed.

Progression to critical limb ischemia is evidenced by the onset of ischemic rest pain or the presence of ischemic ulcerations or gangrene. Pain at rest indicates severe arterial disease. It characteristically occurs at night with the patient lying supine. It may be described as a dull, aching sensation in the toes or forefoot, or as a severe, burning, nagging type of pain. The patient may hang the affected foot or leg over the side of the bed or get up and walk around to obtain relief. Some patients with severe rest pain will sleep sitting in a chair with the legs in a dependent position. This may help to relieve the rest pain; however, it often results in a moderate-to-severe degree of lower extremity edema. Patients who experience rest pain usually have multi-level arterial occlusive disease.

Trauma to or pressure on one of the toes or bony prominences in patients with severe PAD may result in ischemic ulceration and the onset of gangrene. Ischemic ulcers most often occur on the tips of the toes or over bony pressure points, and may begin after minor trauma such as nail trimming or wearing ill-fitting shoes.

Some patients with severe degrees of lower extremity ischemia develop ischemic neuropathy (ischemic monomelic neuropathy); this may occur in the absence of ulceration or gangrene (Wilbourn et al, 1983). Patients often describe a numb, painful, or burning sensation of the forefoot and toes. Whether or not this will be reversible after revascularization depends on the degree and duration of ischemia. Patients with severe arterial ischemia may also develop other abnormalities such as sensory disturbances (coldness of the feet), muscular weakness, joint stiffness, and disuse atrophy of the involved limb.

The presence of ischemic rest pain and/or ischemic ulceration and gangrene necessitates a more aggressive approach to management. Endovascular or surgical revascularization should be considered in this group of patients.

In addition to eliciting a history of claudication, it is also important to take a complete cardiovascular history for all patients who have PAD. Because of the association of PAD with concomitant coronary and cerebrovascular involvement, clues for atherosclerosis in these vascular beds should be searched for. A careful history of transient ischemic attacks or prior strokes should be obtained. The patient should be questioned about the presence of chest discomfort or angina, prior myocardial infarction, or cardiac revascularization. In addition, a history of past or present cigarette smoking, the presence or absence of diabetes, hypertension, and hyperlipidemia should be obtained.

Physical Examination

A complete vascular examination should be performed in all patients who have PAD (Krajewski and Olin, 1996; Olin, 1998). Blood pressure (BP) should be measured in both arms. A discrepancy in BP between the arms often indicates the presence of subclavian or innominate artery disease. The *higher* of the two BPs should always be used. The carotid arteries should be palpated low in the neck. The presence of subclavian and cervical bruits should be carefully searched for and noted. Palpation of the superficial temporal, axillary, brachial, radial, and ulnar arteries should be obtained bilaterally.

A complete abdominal examination should be performed and the abdominal aorta palpated for the presence of an aneurysm and normal pulse. If the aorta is enlarged, its size should be estimated from the physical examination and an ultrasound of the aorta should be obtained.

In patients with relatively mild occlusive PAD, the physical diagnostic findings may be minimal. It is helpful to compare the involved lower extremity with the other. The physician should evaluate the color and skin nutrition of both lower extremities. Physical findings such as gangrene, ulceration, edema, and atrophy are usually readily apparent. The toes should be inspected, especially for the presence of underlying tinea infection or ulcerations between the toes (kissing ulcers).

It is important to palpate the femoral, popliteal, posterior tibial, and dorsalis pedis pulses. A systematic approach should be used in examining the relative strength and quality of the arterial pulse. The pulses on each side should be compared with each other and each pulse should be compared with the radial pulse. There are several different grading methods for pulses, but we find it useful to grade pulses as normal, diminished or absent. It is also important to recognize that some individuals may have nonpalpable dorsalis pedis pulses with essentially normal lower extremity arterial perfusion. This may be a result of an anomaly of the below-knee arterial anatomy. However, it is never normal to have an absent posterior tibial pulse.

There are patients who may have a typical history of claudication yet have normal pulses on physical examination. These patients should undergo a treadmill exercise test to rule out the presence of significant PAD.

NONINVASIVE VASCULAR LABORATORY TESTS

There have been dramatic advances in the noninvasive assessment of the peripheral circulation over the last several decades. The ABI may be performed at the bedside or in the office, providing information about the presence or absence of vascular disease and its severity. However, segmental Doppler systolic blood pressures (SBPs) and pulse waveform analysis by plethysmography provide more objective evidence about the level and severity of occlusive disease.

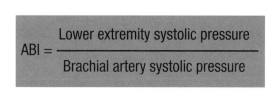

$$ABI = \frac{\text{Lower extremity systolic pressure}}{\text{Brachial artery systolic pressure}}$$

Figure 2. Ankle-brachial index (ABI).

Arteriography is not necessary to make a diagnosis of PAD. An arteriogram should be performed only when considering some form of intervention such as surgical revascularization or catheter-based intervention (percutaneous transluminal angioplasty or stent placement). Arteriography provides an anatomic assessment, but it does not provide a physiologic assessment of the degree of circulatory impairment. It is always important to assess both inflow and outflow when performing arteriography. Therefore, an aortogram with runoffs should be obtained in all patients in whom an arteriogram is obtained.

Doppler Ankle-Brachial Index

The simplest vascular laboratory test to assess the lower extremity circulation is the ABI (Figure 2). This test can be performed in the office by primary care providers or at the bedside for hospitalized patients. The equipment necessary is inexpensive and consists of an ordinary BP cuff and a Doppler ultrasonic velocity detector (Newman et al, 1993a). A BP cuff is placed over the upper arm and inflated above SBP. Resumption of blood flow is detected with the Doppler probe over the brachial artery. If there is a discrepancy in the readings between the two arms, the *higher* of the two arm SBPs is used to calculate the ABI. The BP cuff is then moved to the ankle and inflated above SBP. The Doppler ultrasonic velocity detector is placed alternately over the posterior tibial artery at the ankle and the dorsalis pedis artery. The ABI is obtained by dividing the ankle SBP by the brachial SBP (Figure 2). The higher of the two readings between the posterior tibial and dorsalis pedis arteries should be used in calculating the ABI. The ABI should be measured in each leg.

Usually the ABI correlates well with functional symptoms. Thus, the ABI is a useful guide to determine the severity of disease. While many of these categories are arbitrarily defined, they do provide the clinician with some guidelines as to whether the patient is normal or has mild, moderate, or severe disease (Table III). In a normal individual, the ABI ranges from 0.90 to 1.30. Patients experiencing ischemic rest pain or those with ischemic ulcerations will usually have an ABI of <0.40.

Table III. Ankle-Brachial Index (ABI) Severity of Disease

ABI	Severity
0.90–1.30	Normal
0.70–0.89	Mild
0.40–0.69	Moderate
≤0.40	Severe

The ABI can also be used to assess the circulation in patients with normal pulses at rest but who have typical claudication symptoms. These individuals should exercise and the systolic ABI be measured following exercise. If the symptoms are reproduced during treadmill exercise testing, and there is no significant drop in the systolic ABI following exercise, the cause of the symptoms is something other than PAD. Measurement of the ABI can also be used to follow patients who have undergone surgical bypass reconstruction or endovascular procedures such as balloon angioplasty or stent implantation. The degree of improvement following intervention can be compared with future measurements during follow-up visits. This method of surveillance may detect functional deterioration of the bypass before limb-threatening ischemia occurs.

The absolute ankle pressure may be erroneous in diabetics with calcified, noncompressible arteries (Ramsey et al, 1983). Calcification of the arteries should be suspected when the ankle pressure is much higher than the brachial pressure. In this situation, pulse volume waveform analysis or obtaining a toe-brachial index is necessary to accurately evaluate the circulation (Ramsey et al, 1983; Carter, 1985). These tests should be performed in an accredited vascular laboratory.

There is no uniformity of opinion as to which patients should have an ABI measured. We believe that an ABI should be measured in all individuals with claudication, rest pain, or gangrene. It should also be measured in a patient with exercise-induced leg pain or leg or foot pain when the history is not clear. Some investigators would argue that an ABI should be obtained in patients with one or more cardiovascular risk factors to provide the clinician with a more detailed analysis of cardiovascular risk.

Segmental Pressures

Segmental pressures can be measured by placing BP cuffs at the thigh, calf, and ankle to determine the level of occlusive disease. This examination is usually performed in combination with segmental volume plethysmography or analysis of Doppler-derived pulse waveforms (Yao, 1993). Vascular stress testing with

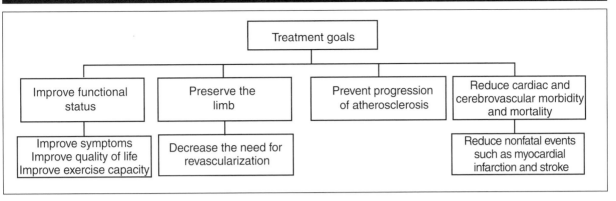

Figure 3. Treatment goals in patients with peripheral arterial disease.

Table IV. Pulse-Volume Recordings and Segmental Blood Pressures

- Confirm or rule out the presence of peripheral arterial disease
  - When pulses and resting pressures are normal, perform treadmill exercise test
- Determine the level of vascular involvement
- Determine the severity of disease
  - Ankle-brachial index
  - Pulse-volume waveforms
- Quantify functional impairment (questionnaires and treadmill exercise test)
- Predict level of amputation
- Provide objective evidence of improvement or worsening after an intervention (percutaneous transluminal angioplasty/stent/surgery)

treadmill walking exercise may be used to unmask subcritical stenoses or marginally significant stenotic lesions. In addition, treadmill exercise testing provides a functional evaluation of the patient's symptoms. Standard stress measurements (fixed treadmill test) are used, such as walking at 2 miles per hour on a 12% grade for 5 minutes. Postexercise ankle pressures and recovery at 2 minutes after exercise are recorded. Some investigators (Hiatt et al, 1997; Gardner et al, 1991) suggested that a progressive treadmill test is more reproducible than a single-stage treadmill test. In the progressive or graded treadmill test, there is a fixed speed (2 miles per hour), but the grade increases over time to produce an increased workload. Practically speaking, most vascular laboratories use the fixed treadmill test (2 miles per hour, 12% grade). However, in the last several years, multicenter clinical trials evaluating different therapies to treat patients with claudication have used the graded treadmill test (Hiatt et al, 1997).

Segmental Volume Plethysmography
Pulse volume waveform analysis can be performed with a system that incorporates mercury strain gauges or the pneumoplethysmograph (pulse volume recorder [PVR]; Life Sciences, Greenwich, Conn) (Raines, 1993). We prefer the PVR as the method of evaluation along with segmental pressure measurements and treadmill walking exercise. The advantages of this system are outlined in Table IV. A combination of segmental limb pressure measurements and PVR waveform analysis has been accurate to the 97th percentile, predicting the level and extent of occlusive disease (Rutherford et al, 1979).

Duplex Ultrasonography
Duplex ultrasonography (DUS) has been increasingly used in evaluation of patients with PAD (Kohler et al, 1990). DUS can assess both the arterial anatomy and physiology. By using spectral analysis, the hemodynamic effects of localized stenoses can be accurately gauged. In addition, measurement of velocity profiles can be compared before and after endovascular procedures. DUS has proved to be an extremely useful tool in following patients after endovascular procedures or lower extremity arterial bypass operations. By periodically studying the patient with "surveillance" ultrasound examinations, one can accurately detect restenosis or a failing saphenous vein bypass graft. This abnormality can then be corrected before graft thrombosis or native artery thrombosis occurs (Bandyk, 1993).

Other noninvasive tests such as transcutaneous oximetry and magnetic resonance angiography are beyond the scope of this article.

MANAGEMENT OF PAD
The management of patients with PAD will be discussed in more detail in future monographs. Figure 3 illustrates the treatment goals that should be considered in patients with PAD. The ideal treatment should improve the functional status of the patient. Therefore,

Table V. Factors Important in Affecting the Natural History of Peripheral Arterial Disease

- Smoking cessation
- Exercise
- Blood pressure control
- Lipid control
- Diabetes control
- Antiplatelet therapy

the patient's symptoms, quality of life, and exercise capacity should all improve. In addition, ideal treatment should preserve the limb and decrease the need for endovascular or surgical revascularization. A comprehensive treatment program should also prevent the progression of atherosclerosis and allow regression

to occur. Lastly, any treatment instituted should result in a reduction in cardiac and cerebrovascular morbidity and mortality in addition to nonfatal events such as MI and stroke. Such a program should include the factors outlined in Table V. Patients should be advised to stop smoking. A structured exercise program has been shown not only to improve symptoms but to decrease all-cause mortality as well (Hiatt et al, 1990; Regensteiner et al, 1996). An aggressive program of risk factor modification should be undertaken to control BP, lipids, and diabetes. All patients should be placed on antiplatelet therapy since this has been shown to decrease MI, stroke, and vascular deaths in this high-risk population (Jansen et al, 1990; CAPRIE Steering Committee, 1996). ■

Key Points

- Patients with PAD may suffer lower extremity complications requiring revascularization or amputation.

- Patients with PAD have an increased rate of mortality from cardio- and cerebrovascular disease. PAD is a marker for atherosclerosis elsewhere.

- Early detection and evaluation of PAD coupled with an aggressive medical program can help prevent complications.

- Intermittent claudication is the primary symptom of PAD. This is currently defined as pain or discomfort in the lower extremity when walking, which ceases on stopping.

- Careful claudication and cardio- and cerebrovascular history-taking, as well as smoking, hypertension, diabetes, and hyperlipidemia history, are important in evaluation.

- Also important is a complete physical examination, including relative limb blood pressures, notably the ankle-brachial index.

- If necessary, segmental Doppler systolic blood pressures and pulse waveform analysis by plethysmography provide more objective evidence about the limb level and severity of disease.

BIBLIOGRAPHY

Bandyk DF. Essentials of graft surveillance. Semin Vasc Surg 1993;6:92–102.

CAPRIE Steering Committee. A randomized blinded trial of Clopidogrel versus Aspirin in Patients at Risk of Ischemic Events (CAPRIE). Lancet 1996; 348:1329–39.

Carter SA. The role of pressure measurements in vascular disease. In: Bernstein EF, ed. Non-invasive Diagnostic Techniques in Vascular Disease. St. Louis: Mosby; 1985:513–44.

Coffman JD. Intermittent claudication: not so benign. Am Heart J 1986;112:1127–8.

Criqui MH, Langer RD, Fronek A, et al. Mortality over a period of ten years in patients with peripheral arterial disease. New Engl J Med 1992;326:381–6.

Gardner AW, Skinner JS, Cantwell BW, Smith LK. Progressive versus single-stage treadmill test for evaluation of claudication. Med Sci Sports Exerc 1991; 23:402–8.

Hertzer NR. The natural history of peripheral vascular disease. Implications for its management. Circulation 1991;83(suppl I):I-12–I-19.

Hertzer NR, Young JR, Beven EG, et al. Late results of coronary bypass in patients presenting with lower extremity ischemia: The Cleveland Clinic Study. Ann Vasc Surg 1987;1:411–9.

Hiatt WR, Hirsch AT, Regensteiner JG, Bress EP. Clinical trials for claudication. Assessment of exercise performance, functional status and clinical endpoints. Vascular Clinical Trialists. Circulation 1997;92:614–21.

Hiatt WR, Regensteiner JG, Hargarten ME, et al. Benefit of exercise conditioning for patients with peripheral arterial disease. Circulation 1990; 81:602–9.

Humphries AW, et al. Evaluation of the natural history

and results of treatment in occlusive arteriosclerosis involving the lower extremities in 1,850 patients. In: Wesolowski SA, Dennis C, eds. Fundamentals of Vascular Grafting. New York:McGraw-Hill; 1963.

Jansen L, Berqvist D, Boberg J, et al. Prevention of myocardial infarction and stroke in patients with intermittent claudication: effects of ticlopidine. Results from STIMS, the Swedish Ticlopidine Multi-center Study. J Intern Med 1990;227:301–8.

Jonason T, Bergstrom R. Cessation of smoking in patients with intermittent claudication: effects on the risk of peripheral vascular complications, myocardial infarction and mortality. Acta Med Scand 1987;21:253–60.

Jonason T, Ringqvist I. Diabetes mellitus and intermittent claudication. Relation between peripheral vascular complications and location of occlusive atherosclerosis of the legs. Acta Med Scand 1985;218:217–21.

Juergens JL, Barker NW, Hines EA Jr. Arteriosclerosis obliterans: review of 520 cases with special reference to pathogenetic and prognostic factors. Circulation 1960;21:118.

Kohler TR, Andros G, Porter JM, et al. Can duplex scanning replace arteriography for lower extremity arterial disease? Ann Vasc Surg 1990;4:280–7.

Krajewski LP, Olin JW. Atherosclerosis of the aorta and lower extremity arteries. In: Young JR, Olin JW, Bartholomew JR, eds. Peripheral Vascular Diseases. 2nd ed. St. Louis: Yearbook; 1996:208–33.

McDaniel MD, Cronenwett JL. Basic data related to the natural history of intermittent claudication. Ann Vasc Surg 1989;3:273–7.

Newman AB, Siscovick DS, Manolio TA, et al. Ankle-arm index as a marker of atherosclerosis in the Cardiovascular Health Study. Circulation 1993a; 88:837–45.

Newman AB, Sutton-Tyrrell K, Vogt MT, Kuller LH. Morbidity and mortality in hypertensive adults with low ankle/arm blood pressure index. JAMA 1993b;28:487–9.

Olin JW. Evaluation of the peripheral circulation. In: Izzo JL, Black HR, eds. Hypertension Primer. 2nd ed. Dallas: American Heart Association; 1998. In press.

Raines JK. The pulse volume recorder in peripheral arterial disease. In: Bernstein EF, ed. Non-invasive Diagnostic Techniques in Vascular Disease. St. Louis: Mosby; 1993:534–43.

Ramsey DE, Manke DA, Sumner DS. Toe blood pressure: a valuable adjunct to ankle pressure measurement for assessing peripheral arterial disease. J Cardiovasc Surg 1983;24:43–8.

Regensteiner JG, Steiner JF, Hiatt WR. Exercise training improves functional status in patients with peripheral arterial disease. J Vasc Surg 1996;23:104–15.

Regensteiner JG, Steiner JF, Panzer RJ, Hiatt WR. Evaluation of walking impairment by questionnaire in patients with peripheral arterial disease. J Vasc Med Biol 1990;2:142–50.

Rutherford RB, Lowenstein DH, Klein MF. Combining segmental systolic pressures and plethysmography to diagnose arterial disease in the legs. Am J Surg 1979;38:211–8.

Vogt MT, Cauley JA, Newman AB, et al. Decreased ankle/arm brachial arm blood pressure index and mortality in elderly women. JAMA 1993;270:465–9.

Weitz JI, Byrne J, Clagett P, et al. Diagnosis and treatment of chronic arterial insufficiency of the lower extremities: a critical review. Circulation 1996; 94:3026–49.

Wilbourn AJ, Furlan AJ, Hulley W, Ruschhaupt WF. Ischemic monomelic neuropathy. Neurology 1983;33:447–51.

Yao JST. Pressure measurement in the extremity. In: Bernstein EF, ed. Vascular Diagnosis. 4th ed. St. Louis:Mosby; 1993:169–75.

Clinical Significance and Functional Implications of Peripheral Arterial Disease

Mary McGrae McDermott, MD
Assistant Professor
Division of General Internal Medicine
Department of Medicine
Department of Preventive Medicine
Northwestern University Medical School
Chicago, Illinois

Philip Greenland, MD
Dingman Professor of Cardiology
Chairman, Department of Preventive Medicine
Northwestern University Medical School
Chicago, Illinois

Objective: To alert clinicians to the association between peripheral arterial disease and increased risk of cardiovascular events. We review coronary heart disease risk-factor interventions and functional implications of peripheral arterial disease.

In general medical practice, lower extremity peripheral arterial disease (PAD) affects 18% to 23% of men and women aged 55 and older, and may be difficult to diagnose with traditional history taking and physical examination. Patients with ankle-brachial index (ABI) ≤0.90 are at increased risk for cardiovascular events, and lower ABI levels are associated with higher risk of total mortality and cardiovascular events. Because of the association between low ABI and cardiovascular events, intensive atherosclerotic risk-factor therapy is recommended for PAD patients. Available data suggest that atherosclerotic risk factors are greatly undertreated in PAD. ABI ≤0.90 is associated with poorer activity levels, leg strength, and walking distance even among PAD patients without classic intermittent claudication symptoms. Further study is necessary to determine whether targeted interventions, such as atherosclerotic risk-factor therapy, could prevent mobility loss among men and women with PAD who do not have classic intermittent claudication symptoms.

Available data suggest that peripheral arterial disease (PAD) may go largely unrecognized by clinicians in the primary care setting. Published reports describe a high prevalence of PAD among both men and women patients in general medical practices (Fowkes et al, 1991; Farkouh et al, 1996). Fowkes et al assessed the prevalence of PAD in 1,582 men and women aged 55 to 74 years randomly selected from 11 general medical practices in Edinburgh, Scotland. Approximately 50% of study participants were women, all but two patients were Caucasian, and 38.6% had a history of ischemic heart disease. Eighteen percent of patients had an ankle-brachial index (ABI) ≤ 0.90, which is consistent with PAD. Only 15% of these had symptoms consistent with intermittent claudication. Farkouh et al assessed the prevalence of ABI ≤0.90 among both men and women patients aged 55 and older in 11 university-affiliated primary care practices in the United States and Canada. Those with amputations or acute leg pain were excluded. Of 218 patients studied, 23% had ABI ≤0.90, consistent with PAD. Thus, PAD is common in primary care settings. However, many PAD patients do not have typical intermittent claudication symptoms (Fowkes et al, 1991; Criqui et al, 1996; McDermott et al, in press), and therefore primary care clinicians may underappreciate the high prevalence of PAD in patients aged 55 and older. As discussed elsewhere in this monograph (see page 15), pulse palpitation is not very sensitive for diagnosing PAD (Criqui et al, 1985). Although PAD is common in patients regularly encountered by primary care clinicians, it may be difficult to recognize and diagnose.

ABI PREDICTS CARDIOVASCULAR EVENTS AMONG PATIENTS IN PRIMARY CARE SETTINGS

Prospective studies have shown that patients in

primary care settings with ABI ≤0.90 are at significantly increased risk of cardiovascular events (Leng et al, 1996). The Edinburgh patients described above (Fowkes et al, 1991) were followed prospectively for 5 years for incident fatal and nonfatal cardiovascular events. Cardiovascular event data were obtained from study participants, primary care physicians, and hospital medical records. At 5-year follow-up, ABI ≤0.90 was a significant, independent predictor of stroke, death due to cardiovascular disease, and all-cause mortality. Among patients with ABI ≤0.90, 17.6% (95% confidence interval [CI] 13.1 to 22.1) had a cardiovascular event during follow-up compared with 9.6% (95% CI 8.0 to 11.2) among patients with ABI >0.90. The relative risk of cardiovascular death for patients with ABI ≤0.90 was 1.85 (95% CI 1.15 to 2.97, P ≤0.01) adjusting for age, sex, angina, myocardial infarction (MI), and diabetes mellitus. Thus, ABI ≤0.90 can identify patients in a general medical practice who are at increased risk of cardiovascular events and cardiovascular death (Leng et al, 1996).

Leng et al (1996) also studied the positive predictive value of ABI ≤0.90 for cardiovascular events among patients with and without a history of hypertension, cigarette smoking, and hypercholesterolemia. The ability to predict future cardiovascular events was increased when ABI ≤0.90 was combined with specific atherosclerotic risk factors. For example, among hypertensive smokers with a normal cholesterol level, the positive predictive value for cardiovascular events was 43.8% for patients with ABI ≤0.90 and 15.6% for patients with ABI >0.90. Among normotensive smokers with normal cholesterol levels, the positive predictive value for cardiovascular events was 20.8% for patients with ABI ≤0.90 compared with 8.9% for patients with ABI >0.90. Therefore, ABI ≤0.90 may be a particularly important prognostic indicator of future cardiovascular events among smokers without hypercholesterolemia.

ABI IS A PROGNOSTIC INDICATOR OF TOTAL MORTALITY IN PAD

Among PAD patients, the lower the ABI, the higher the risk of cardiovascular events and total mortality (Howell et al, 1989; McDermott et al, 1994). For example, PAD patients with ABI <0.30 have a higher mortality risk than PAD patients with ABI between 0.30 and 0.90. This correlation was illustrated by Howell et al (1989), who studied 247 consecutive patients undergoing noninvasive lower extremity arterial testing in a blood-flow laboratory. Of the 247 patients, 21% were diabetic, 47% were women, and the mean age was 65 ± 15 years. Patients were categorized at baseline by disease severity according to ABI, and followed for 6 years for mortality and cardiovascular morbidity. Severe PAD was defined

as ABI ≤0.30 (n = 25), moderate PAD as ABI 0.31–0.49 (n = 39); mild PAD as ABI 0.50–0.91 (n = 86), and absence of PAD as ABI ≥0.92 (n = 97). At follow-up, total mortality rates were 64% among patients with ABI ≤0.30, 31% with ABI 0.31–0.49, 26% with ABI 0.50–0.91, and 20% with ABI ≥0.92. Differences in total mortality rates between PAD patients with ABI <0.30 and each of the other ABI categories were statistically significant at P ≤0.01. Rates of cardiovascular morbidity, defined as MI, stroke, amputation, or vascular surgery, were highest among PAD patients with ABI ≤0.30 (92%) and progressively lower among patients with ABI 0.31–0.49 (68%), ABI 0.50–0.91 (64%), and ABI ≥0.92 (18%). Therefore, among PAD patients ABI level is an important prognostic indicator of total mortality and cardiovascular events (Howell et al, 1989).

The inverse relation between ABI level and total mortality among PAD patients was also demonstrated by McDermott et al (1994) in a study of 422 patients with ABI <0.92 identified from a blood-flow laboratory at an academic medical center. In this PAD cohort, 28% were diabetic, 54% were men, and 62% were age 65 and older. PAD patients were classified according to the methods of Howell et al (1989). A National Death Index search was performed to establish mortality rates within each ABI category at 4.3 years of follow-up. Figure 1 shows cumulative survival rates according to baseline ABI level. Increasingly severe PAD was associated with higher mortality rates. PAD patients with ABI ≤0.30 had an 84% increased risk of mortality compared with PAD patients with ABI 0.50–0.91, after controlling for age, sex, comorbid disease, and cardiovascular risk factors. Clinicians can therefore use ABI to assess future risk of total mortality and cardiovascular event rates in PAD patients.

RISK FACTORS IN PAD
Prospective cohort studies have shown an association

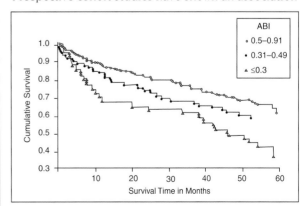

Figure 1. Survival by ankle-brachial index (ABI). From McDermott et al, 1994.

between (1) cigarette smoking, (2) hypertension, and (3) diabetes mellitus and PAD progression to limb loss, gangrene, and lower extremity ulcers (McDermott and McCarthy, 1995). Cigarette smoking has been consistently associated with progression of lower extremity ischemia. Cronenwett et al (1984) followed 91 men with intermittent claudication prospectively for 2.5 years. Patients with a history of lower extremity amputation or rest pain, and patients who underwent lower extremity revascularization during the first 6 months of the study were excluded. The mean age of participants was 58 ± 8 years; 11% were African American, 27% were diabetic, and 79% smoked cigarettes at study enrollment. All patients were advised to walk twice daily and cigarette smokers were urged to quit. During follow-up, 31% stopped smoking, 26% reduced cigarette use by 50%, and 43% continued smoking. At 2.5-year follow-up, patients who stopped or reduced their smoking had less progression of claudication symptoms than those who continued smoking at the same rate, though the difference was not statistically significant. Patients who exercised regularly were less likely to have progression of claudication symptoms compared with those who did not exercise regularly.

Jonason and Ringqvist (1985) studied 224 men and women with intermittent claudication referred for noninvasive vascular testing at a medical center. Patients aged 76 and older, or with diabetes mellitus, rest pain, gangrene, previous vascular surgery, or referral for amputation or vascular surgery within 1 month were excluded. Patients were enrolled between 1975 and 1978 and followed until the spring of 1983 for development of rest pain. Rest pain was defined as pain in the leg or foot when recumbent that was relieved with leg dependency. Of the 224 patients, 160 continued cigarette smoking for at least 1 year after baseline examination (smokers) and 64 had either never smoked, stopped smoking before study enrollment, or stopped smoking within 1 year after baseline examination (nonsmokers). The mean age of smokers was 62 ± 7 years and that of nonsmokers was 66 ± 6 years. Fifty-nine percent of smokers were men, as were 78% of nonsmokers. At 6-year follow-up, 92% of nonsmokers were without rest pain compared with only 79% of smokers (P <0.03). Cigarette smoking and multiple arterial stenoses at baseline were significantly associated with the development of rest pain, adjusting for sex, age, systolic blood pressure (SBP), participating in a supervised exercise program, duration of claudication, toe or ankle blood pressure, and treatment with β-blockers, in the Cox proportional analysis.

In a study of 257 consecutive patients referred for evaluation of intermittent claudication, higher systolic arterial blood pressure was independently and significantly associated with progression to rest pain or gangrene. The study population consisted of 100 women and 127 men with a mean age of 65 ± 8.8 years. None of the study patients had rest pain, ulcers, or lower extremity gangrene at enrollment. Patients were followed for a mean of 6.5 years. After adjusting for age, sex, ankle SBP, diabetes mellitus, toe SBP, and the character of femoral artery pulsation in the Cox proportional hazards analysis, each increase of 10 mm Hg in SBP was associated with a 33% increased risk of rest pain or gangrene (Jelnes et al, 1986). Lower ankle SBP was also associated independently with higher risk of rest pain or gangrene.

Finally, diabetes mellitus was associated with increased risk of amputation among 160 patients (61 women), mean age 68.6 years, followed for 8 years after first discharge from a hospitalization for PAD (Hughson et al, 1978).

ATHEROSCLEROTIC RISK-FACTOR THERAPY IN PAD

Clinical trials assessing the effects of intensive atherosclerotic risk-factor interventions on cardiovascular event rates or PAD progression have not been performed to our knowledge. However, because of the strong, independent correlation between PAD and cardiovascular events, intensive atherosclerotic risk-factor therapy is recommended for PAD subjects (Orchard and Strandness, 1993; NCEP, 1993). Associations between atherosclerotic risk factors and progression of lower extremity ischemia suggest that intensive atherosclerotic risk-factor therapy may prevent limb loss and other important lower extremity outcomes. The National Cholesterol Education Program Adult Treatment Panel II defines optimal low-density lipoprotein (LDL) values as <100 mg/dL for patients with PAD and recommends annual lipoprotein analyses to ensure that LDL levels remain optimal (NCEP, 1993). In the American Heart Association Scientific Statement on assessment of peripheral vascular disease in diabetes, intensive atherosclerotic risk-factor therapy is advised for patients with ABI <0.90 (Orchard and Strandness, 1993). Specific attention to LDL, high-density lipoprotein levels, triglycerides, blood pressure control, smoking cessation, weight control, and exercise is recommended. Aspirin therapy is also advised for diabetic patients with ABI <0.90.

Despite recommendations for intensive atherosclerotic risk-factor therapy in PAD, available data suggest that atherosclerotic risk factors are undertreated in PAD (McDermott et al, 1997). Undertreatment of risk factors has previously been documented for patients with coronary artery disease (CAD) (Cohen et al, 1991; CASS, 1983). However, preliminary data suggest that undertreatment of risk factors occurs to an even greater degree in PAD than in CAD (McDermott et al, 1997).

McDermott et al (1997) interviewed patients with established PAD or CAD at an academic medical center to compare rates of atherosclerotic risk-factor therapy. Participants were 202 PAD and 147 CAD patients. Average ages were 68 and 64 years, respectively. Fifty-five percent of PAD patients and 75% of CAD patients were men; 12% of PAD patients and 2% of CAD patients were African American. Among PAD patients, 99 (49%) had no history of CAD and were considered to have "exclusive" PAD. Among CAD patients, 104 (71%) had no history of PAD and were classified as having "exclusive" CAD. Patients unable to walk and those with amputations were excluded from the exercise analyses. No differences in rates of hypertensive therapy were observed among PAD and CAD patients with hypertension. Among PAD and CAD patients who smoked cigarettes, there were no differences in rates at which participants recalled physician advice to quit smoking. However, significant differences between PAD and CAD patients were identified for rates of hypercholesterolemia therapy and for the proportion of patients who recalled physician advice to exercise. Among hypercholesterolemic patients, 58% of CAD patients versus 46% of PAD patients were taking cholesterol-lowering drugs (P = 0.08), and 94% of CAD patients versus 83% of PAD patients recalled a physician's advice to follow a low-fat, low-cholesterol diet (P = 0.01). Among patients with exclusive PAD and exclusive CAD, these differences were even greater. Only 40% of hypercholesterolemic patients with exclusive PAD were taking cholesterol-lowering drugs versus 56% of hypercholesterolemic patients with exclusive CAD. Among all patients, 71% of CAD patients versus 50% of PAD patients exercised regularly (P <0.01). Among patients not exercising, 74% of CAD patients versus 47% of PAD patients recalled a physician's advice to exercise (P <0.01). Eighty-three percent of nonexercising patients with exclusive CAD recalled a physician's advice to exercise as compared with just 35% of nonexercising patients with exclusive PAD (P <0.01).

These data suggest that hypercholesterolemia is undertreated in PAD. Although exercise lowers cardiovascular risk and improves walking ability among patients with intermittent claudication, these data also suggest that physicians may not be effectively counseling PAD patients to exercise.

PAD CAUSES MOBILITY LOSS AND FUNCTIONAL DECLINE

Most PAD patients do not experience gangrene, amputation, or limb loss (Cronenwett et al, 1984; Weitz et al, 1996). However, the leg symptoms and lower extremity muscle fiber changes associated with PAD confer an increased risk of mobility loss and functional decline. Studies assessing lower extremity muscle fibers in PAD patients show diminished muscle fiber numbers and atrophy compared with non-PAD control patients (Hedberg et al, 1989; Farinon et al, 1984). Nerve demyelination has also been observed in muscle biopsies from PAD patients (Hedberg et al, 1989).

Lower Extremity Muscles in PAD

Hedberg et al (1989) compared gastrocnemius and soleus muscle fibers between 5 healthy men ages 66 to 81 years who died accidentally (controls) and amputated lower legs from 5 PAD patients ages 72 to 86 years. Two of the PAD patients were men. None had diabetes mellitus or documented neuromuscular disease. Comparisons showed that PAD patients had 47% of the total number of muscle fibers found in controls. In the gastrocnemius muscles, a preferential decrease in the proportion of type II fibers was observed among PAD patients. In contrast, a preferential decrease in the proportion of type I fibers was observed in the soleus muscle of PAD patients. Type II muscle fibers are "fast twitch," responsible for short, fast bursts of exertion. Type I muscle fibers are "slow twitch," responsible for prolonged exertion and walking endurance. Increased connective tissue and atrophy of muscle fibers were observed for gastrocnemius and soleus muscles obtained from PAD patients. Thus, lower extremity muscle fibers are smaller and fewer among PAD patients compared with controls. Muscle fibers responsible for both short bursts of energy and walking endurance may be affected by lower extremity arterial ischemia.

Farinon et al (1984) studied 80 muscle biopsy specimens from 40 PAD patients (36 men). The mean age of participants was 65.4 years; 10 had diabetes mellitus. Muscle biopsies were obtained from the gastrocnemius or the rectus femoris and were examined with both light and electron microscopy. Results showed smaller sizes of both type I and type II muscle fibers with greater arterial ischemia, while higher proportions of type I muscle fibers were observed with greater arterial ischemia. On electron microscopy, hyperplastic mitochondria and demyelination of nerve fibers were observed. These data suggest that muscle fibers are quantitatively and qualitatively affected by lower extremity arterial ischemia.

Defining the relationship between ABI level and lower extremity function should help clinicians more accurately gauge the functional capabilities of PAD patients. Specifically, if the degree of lower extremity arterial obstruction, as measured by ABI, correlates with leg function, clinicians could use the ABI as a means to gauge lower extremity function in PAD. If the baseline ABI predicts subsequent declines in lower extremity function, clinicians could use the ABI as a prognostic tool to predict change in lower extremity function over time. Ultimately, interventions might be developed to prevent functional decline in PAD.

Lower Extremity Function in PAD

Vogt et al (1994) assessed the correlation between ABI ≤0.90 and comprehensive measures of lower extremity function among Caucasian women participating in the Pittsburgh cohort of the Study of Osteoporotic Fractures. Of 1,492 participants who underwent ABI measurement, 82 (5.5%) had ABI ≤0.90, consistent with PAD. Objective measures of lower extremity function as well as patient reported activity levels were compared between PAD and non-PAD participants. All participants were age 65 and older. The average age of PAD subjects was 73.6 ± 5.4 years versus 70.6 ± 4.7 years for non-PAD subjects. In bivariate comparisons, 73% of PAD subjects versus 84% of non-PAD subjects left their home at least once daily (P <0.05), and 11% of PAD subjects versus 33% of non-PAD subjects reported sufficient exertion to work up a sweat at least once a week (P <0.05). Hip abduction and knee extension force were significantly reduced among women with ABI ≤0.90 as compared with women with ABI >0.90. After adjusting for age, body mass index (BMI), waist/hip ratio, smoking, SBP >140 mm Hg, diabetes mellitus, cardiovascular disease, and arthritis, ABI ≤0.90 was independently associated with fewer blocks walked for exercise per day, fewer episodes per week of sufficient exertion to generate a sweat, and lower knee extension force. Most women with PAD in this study did not have typical intermittent claudication symptoms. Results of this study suggest an independent correlation between ABI ≤0.90 and lower physical activity levels, as well as poorer lower extremity function. Further study is necessary, however, to determine whether the relation studied by Vogt et al exists in larger and more diverse cohorts of PAD patients. Study is also needed to determine whether greater PAD severity is associated with greater impairment in functioning, as suggested by the muscle biopsy studies. The correlation between PAD severity and lower extremity function could not be assessed in the study by Vogt et al, because the majority of participants had mild PAD.

In addition to potential deleterious effects of lower extremity arterial ischemia on lower extremity function in PAD, exertional leg symptoms associated with PAD may impair lower extremity function. Although the majority of PAD patients do not have typical symptoms of intermittent claudication, two studies suggest that most PAD patients have exertional leg symptoms (Criqui et al, 1996; McDermott et al, in press). Guralnik et al (1993) showed that exertional leg symptoms were associated with mobility loss among community-dwelling patients. Between 1981 and 1983, Guralnik et al studied 6,891 men and women aged 65 and older living in three US communities who had intact mobility at baseline. Mobility was defined as the ability to climb up and down stairs and walk a half mile without assistance. The mean age of study participants was 73.1 years and slightly more than 50% in each community were women. At 4-year follow-up, 8.7% had died. Of those still living, 36.2% were no longer able to climb up and down stairs and walk a half mile without assistance. Patients with exertional leg symptoms at baseline were significantly more likely to experience mobility loss during follow-up. Adjusting for age, income, education, and comorbid diseases, patients with exertional leg pain at baseline had a 1.3- to 1.6-fold higher risk of mobility loss at follow-up as compared with those without exertional leg pain. In addition, patients with higher physical activity levels were significantly less likely to lose mobility (relative risk 0.4–0.6) after adjusting for age, comorbid disease, alcohol consumption, cigarette smoking, and BMI (LaCroix et al, 1993). Physical activity was defined as taking frequent walks, gardening, and exercising vigorously. Among PAD patients, muscle atrophy resulting from inactivity may further contribute to mobility loss.

Atherosclerotic risk factors, such as cigarette smoking, diabetes mellitus, lack of exercise, and a low ABI are associated with progression of intermittent claudication symptoms, amputation, and lower extremity revascularization (Hughson et al, 1978; Cronenwett et al, 1984; Jelnes et al, 1986). However, relationships between atherosclerotic risk factors and comprehensive measures of lower extremity function, such as walking velocity, 6-minute walk performance, physical activity, and leg strength have not been well studied in a heterogeneous cohort of PAD patients, including PAD patients who are asymptomatic, or have exertional leg symptoms other than intermittent claudication. In a pilot study of 166 men and women identified from a blood-flow laboratory and a general medicine practice at an academic medical center, lack of regular exercise performed at least three times weekly and a BMI >27 kg/m^2 were associated indepen-

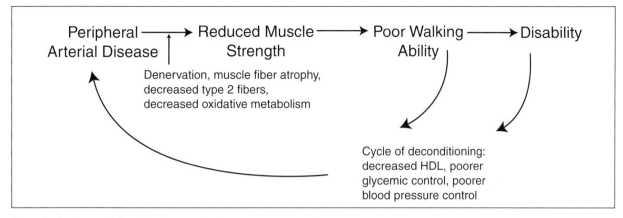

Figure 2. Pathway of disability in peripheral arterial disease. HDL = high-density lipoprotein.

dently with poorer walking endurance, as measured by the 6-minute walk, and slower walking velocity, as measured by the 4-meter walk (McDermott et al, 1998). Most of the PAD patients in this pilot study did not have classic intermittent claudication symptoms. Further study is necessary to determine whether weight loss or increased physical activity results in improved 6-minute walk performance and faster walking velocity in a heterogeneous population of PAD patients. PAD may result in a cycle of disability, in which disease-related lower extremity impairment leads to inactivity, which in turn worsens PAD severity (see Figure 2).

Key Points

• Lower extremity PAD is common in general medical practices.

• The ABI is an independent predictor of future cardiovascular events.

• Among PAD patients, the ABI is an important prognostic indicator of total mortality.

• Atherosclerotic risk factors are undertreated in PAD.

• PAD patients are at increased risk of mobility loss and functional decline.

• Intensive atherosclerotic risk-factor interventions in PAD are recommended by the American Heart Association and the National Cholesterol Education Program to prevent cardiovascular events.

SUMMARY AND CONCLUSION

Lower extremity PAD is common among men and women aged 55 and older in general medical practices. Because PAD is difficult to diagnose with traditional history taking and physical examination, clinicians should be alert to the possibility of PAD among patients aged 55 and older who are diabetic or who have other atherosclerotic risk factors. Although the majority of PAD patients do not have classic symptoms of intermittent claudication, many have exertional leg symptoms that are not typical for claudication. Therefore, clinicians should also consider noninvasive testing for PAD in older patients with atypical exertional leg symptoms.

Patients with ABI ≤0.90 are at increased risk for cardiovascular events. Furthermore, lower ABI levels are associated with higher total mortality and cardiovascular event rates among PAD patients. Because of the association between a low ABI and cardiovascular event rates, intensive atherosclerotic risk-factor therapy is recommended for PAD patients.

Finally, available data suggest that ABI ≤0.90 is associated with lower levels of activity, leg strength, and walking distance even among patients without classic symptoms of intermittent claudication. Further study is necessary to determine whether ABI ≤0.90 is associated with important outcomes such as social dependence, mobility loss, and nursing home placement, and whether targeted interventions might prevent mobility loss in PAD patients without classic symptoms of intermittent claudication.

BIBLIOGRAPHY

CASS Principal Investigators. Coronary Artery Surgery Study (CASS): a randomized trial of coronary artery bypass surgery. Quality of life in patients randomly assigned to treatment groups. Circulation 1983; 68:951-60.

Cohen MB, Byrne MJ, Levine B, et al. Low rate of treatment of hypercholesterolemia by cardiologists in patients with suspected and proven coronary artery disease. Circulation 1991;83:1294-304.

Criqui MH, Denenberg JO, Bird CE, et al. The correlation between symptoms and non-invasive test results in patients referred for peripheral arterial disease testing. Vasc Med 1996;1:65-71.

Criqui MH, Fronek A, Barrett-Connor E, et al. The sensitivity, specificity, and predictive value of traditional clinical evaluation of peripheral arterial disease: results from noninvasive testing in a defined population. Circulation 1985;71:516-22.

Cronenwett JL, Warner KG, Zelenock GB, et al. Intermittent claudication. Current results of nonoperative management. Arch Surg 1984;119:430-36.

Expert Panel on Detection, Evaluation, and Treatment of High Blood Cholesterol in Adults. Summary of the Second Report of the National Cholesterol Education Program (NCEP) Expert Panel on Detection, Evaluation, and Treatment of High Blood Cholesterol in Adults (Adult Treatment Panel II). JAMA 1993;269:3015-23.

Farinon AM, Marbini A, Gemignani F, et al. Skeletal muscle and peripheral nerve changes caused by chronic arterial insufficiency. Significance and clinical correlations—histological, histochemical and ultrastructural study. Clin Neuropathol 1984;3:240-52.

Farkouh ME, Oddone EZ, Simel DL, for the U.S.-Canadian Research Group on the Clinical Examination. The clinical examination for peripheral arterial disease. J Gen Intern Med 1996;11:46. Abstract.

Fowkes FGR, Housley E, Cawood EHH, et al. Edinburgh artery study: prevalence of asymptomatic and symptomatic peripheral arterial disease in the general population. Int J Epidemiol 1991;20:384-91.

Guralnik JM, LaCroix AZ, Abbott RD, et al. Maintaining mobility in late life. I. Demographic characteristics and chronic conditions. Am J Epidemiol 1993;137:845-57.

Hedberg B, Angquist KA, Henriksoon-Larsen K, Sjostrom M. Fibre loss and distribution in skeletal muscle from patients with severe peripheral arterial insufficiency. Eur J Vasc Surg 1989;3:315-22.

Howell MA, Colgan MP, Seeter RW, et al. Relationship of severity of lower limb peripheral vascular disease to mortality and morbidity: a six-year follow-up study. J Vasc Surg 1989;9:691-7.

Hughson G, Mann JI, Tibbs DJ, et al. Intermittent claudication: factors determining outcome. BMJ 1978;1:1377-9.

Jelnes R, Gaardsting O, Jenson KH, et al. Fate in intermittent claudication: outcome and risk factors. BMJ 1986;293:1137-40.

Jonason T, Ringqvist I. Factors of prognostic importance for subsequent rest pain in patients with intermittent claudication. Acta Med Scand 1985;218:27-33.

LaCroix AZ, Guralnik JM, Berkman LF, et al. Maintaining mobility in late life. II. Smoking, alcohol consumption, physical activity, and body mass index. Am J Epidemiol 1993;137:858-69.

Leng GC, Fowkes FGR, Lee AJ, et al. Use of ankle-brachial pressure index to predict cardiovascular events and death: a cohort study. BMJ 1996;313:1440-4.

McDermott MM, Feinglass J, Slavensky R, Pearce W. The ankle-brachial index as a predictor of survival in patients with peripheral vascular disease. J Gen Intern Med 1994;9:445-9.

McDermott MM, Liu K, Guralnik JM, et al. Modifiable risk factors are associated with impaired lower extremity function in peripheral arterial disease. J Gen Intern Med 1998;13:27. Abstract.

McDermott MM, McCarthy W. Intermittent claudication. The natural history. Surg Clin North Am 1995; 75:581-91.

McDermott MM, Mehta S, Ahn H, Greenland P. Atherosclerotic risk factors are less intensively treated in patients with peripheral arterial disease than in patients with coronary artery disease. J Gen Intern Med 1997;12:209-15.

McDermott MM, Mehta S, Greenland P. Exertional leg symptoms other than intermittent claudication are common in peripheral arterial disease. Arch Intern Med (in press).

Orchard TJ, Strandness DE. Assessment of peripheral vascular disease in diabetes. Report and recommendations of an International Workshop sponsored by the American Diabetes Association and the American Heart Association. September 18-20, 1992. Circulation 1993;88:819-28.

Vogt MT, Cauley JA, Kuller LH, Nevitt MC. Functional status and mobility among elderly women with lower extremity arterial disease: The Study of Osteoporotic Fractures. J Am Geriatr Soc 1994;42:923-9.

Weitz JI, Byrne J, Clagett P, et al. Diagnosis and treatment of chronic arterial insufficiency of the lower extremities: a critical review. Circulation 1996;94:3026-49.

The American Journal of Medicine®

CONTINUING EDUCATION SERIES

AN OFFICE-BASED APPROACH TO THE DIAGNOSIS AND TREATMENT OF PERIPHERAL ARTERIAL DISEASE

PART II: Recognizing and Treating Systemic Atherosclerosis

SERIES EDITOR
ALAN T. HIRSCH, MD
GUEST EDITOR
MARK A. CREAGER, MD

Jointly sponsored by
The Excerpta Medica Office of Continuing Medical Education, the Society for Vascular Medicine and Biology, and the Society of General Internal Medicine

SGIM Society of General Internal Medicine

Dear Colleague:

Atherosclerosis is a systemic disease, yet health care is divided into clinical specialties based on organ systems of interest to providers. Patients desire integrated care that is both preventive and therapeutic. Only primary care physicians and vascular medicine specialists are positioned to satisfactorily provide patients the integrated, long-term care that they desire, that is mandated by the systemic, lifelong nature of atherosclerotic disease, and that is likely to be effective in forestalling adverse atherosclerotic ischemic events.

The role of atherosclerosis risk factors in the etiology of both coronary artery disease (CAD) and stroke has long been recognized by both patient and physician alike, thanks to the efforts of epidemiologists, clinician-investigators, and health care advocacy groups. In contrast, our awareness that these same factors contribute to the development and the progression of peripheral arterial disease (PAD) has been extremely limited. Most patients with PAD are not aware that undertreated hypertension, smoking, and hypercholesterolemia have caused their claudication, nonhealing wound, gangrene, amputation, heart attack, or stroke, or that these factors, left inadequately treated, may claim their lives. Similarly, our public health database does not adequately code PAD as a cause of death or disability, attributing the fate of the patient instead to the final cardiac ischemic event that supervened in the last days of life. The link between atherosclerosis, PAD, and death is one that requires recognition by all physicians and all patients.

This monograph, the second in the PAD Primary Care Series, provides a succinct focus on the relation between atherosclerosis risk factors and the development and progression of PAD. Much is known about this association, especially with regard to the etiologic links between tobacco use, diabetes, and PAD. Unfortunately, the basis of current recommendations for treatment of hypertension and elevated lipids in the PAD population is extrapolated from recent data derived from clinical investigations of patients with CAD. Despite the continued, pressing demands of PAD clinician-investigators for resources to evaluate aggressive interventional strategies for patients with atherosclerotic PAD, the National Institutes of Health and the pharmaceutical industry have rarely created those major prospective clinical investigations that should guide our application of atherosclerosis treatment interventions in the fragile PAD population.

Current PAD care efforts certainly have proved to be efficient in detecting PAD in its earlier stages. Once PAD is a recognized diagnosis, medical interventional therapies to retard atherosclerosis and to prevent thrombosis are also known to be effective. The data in this monograph are intended to improve our care of the systemic manifestations of atherosclerosis in the PAD population.

The PAD Primary Care Series was created to offer you and all primary care practitioners an essential, office-based primer on current standards of care for patients with PAD. The Society for Vascular Medicine and Biology and the Society of General Internal Medicine are united to provide such practical vascular clinical educational material. Please consider joining or supporting your vascular and general medical professional societies, as our public health task cannot be accomplished when we work only as individual practitioners. For critical limb ischemia, our patients are truly "out-on-a-limb" and "dying to see us." Let us not let them down.

Sincerely,

Alan T. Hirsch, MD
President, Society for Vascular Medicine and Biology
On behalf of the Education Committee, Officers, and Trustees
Associate Professor of Medicine
Vascular Medicine Program
Minnesota Vascular Diseases Center
University of Minnesota Medical School
Minneapolis, Minnesota

Introduction

Mark A. Creager, MD
Clinical Director, Vascular Medicine Unit, Cardiovascular Division
Brigham and Women's Hospital
Associate Professor of Medicine
Harvard Medical School
Boston, Massachusetts

This volume is the second in a series of eight Continuing Medical Education (CME) publications on the clinical aspects of peripheral arterial disease (PAD) as it impacts office-based primary care. The first volume emphasized our understanding that PAD is a manifestation of systemic atherosclerosis, and thus a predictor of cardio- and cerebrovascular disease. This second volume focuses on the clinical consequences of this new awareness and stresses approaches to treatment that take into consideration the systemic implications of the PAD diagnosis. Subsequent volumes in this series will focus on more specific aspects of PAD. All in all, the authors and editors have endeavored to organize a comprehensive overview of current thinking on PAD.

The editors wish to acknowledge the role of the Society for Vascular Medicine and Biology and the Society of General Internal Medicine in the development of this publication. We remind the reader that these monographs, published under the auspices of *The American Journal of Medicine*®, will be published in conjunction with live CME audioconferences featuring presentations covering the same curriculum by the authors of these articles.

In the first article, I point out that the clinical manifestations of PAD are major causes of disability and, in keeping with the overall theme, that PAD is an important marker for future cardio- or cerebrovascular events. Modifiable risk factors including hypercholesterolemia, smoking, hypertension, diabetes, and hyperhomocystinemia are present in most patients with PAD. All of these can be treated at the primary care level.

In the second article, Jonathan L. Halperin, MD, points out that the clinical consequences of peripheral atherosclerosis, as in cardiac and cerebral atherosclerosis, are fundamentally thrombotic in nature; this results in arterial occlusion, that is, atherothrombosis and its ischemic sequelae. Available antithrombotic agents such as aspirin—inexpensive and effective—and the newer clopidogrel reduce adverse PAD cardiovascular events.

In the last article, Marie Gerhard-Herman, MD, MSc, and Avni Thakore, MS, BS, turn attention to PAD in women, noting that the higher proportion of females in the aging population and the increased rates of cigarette smoking in women portend a female majority among PAD patients in the coming years. In addition, the authors note an atherosclerotic syndrome associated with young women who smoke heavily. Likewise, diabetes mellitus is of particular interest for PAD in women where it is a greater risk factor for mortality than in men. Conservative therapy with reduction of risk factors remains the mainstay of PAD therapy in women as in men. Estrogen replacement therapy in postmenopausal women may be of significant benefit in the treatment of PAD.

Study of the information presented here should enable the primary care clinician to offer patients the latest in PAD care. This may actually be tantamount to primary prevention of cardio- and cerebrovascular disease. ∎

Risk-Factor Modification in Peripheral Arterial Disease

Mark A. Creager, MD
Clinical Director, Vascular Medicine Unit, Cardiovascular Division
Brigham and Women's Hospital
Associate Professor of Medicine
Harvard Medical School
Boston, Massachusetts

Objective: To describe the clinical consequences of risk-factor modification in peripheral arterial disease as a manifestation of systemic atherosclerosis.

Clinical manifestations of peripheral arterial disease (PAD), such as intermittent claudication and critical limb ischemia, are important causes of disability and adverse quality of life. The presence of PAD is also a major predictor for adverse cardiovascular events, such as myocardial infarction (MI) and death. Indeed, the risk of death from coronary artery disease (CAD) is increased more than 6-fold in patients with PAD (Criqui et al, 1992). This observation underscores the fact that atherosclerosis is a systemic problem, rarely confined to a single regional circulation. The risk factors contributing to atherosclerosis of the extremities, that is, PAD, are the same as those causing coronary and cerebral atherosclerosis. As such, the finding of PAD should prompt a careful search for modifiable risk factors and an evaluation for coexisting coronary artery and cerebrovascular disease in order to initiate timely therapeutic interventions that may reduce the incidence of MI and stroke. Among the treatable risk factors for atherosclerosis are hypercholesterolemia, cigarette smoking, hypertension, diabetes mellitus, and hyperhomocystinemia. This article focuses on the effect of treating these risk factors on the clinical consequences of atherosclerosis.

HYPERCHOLESTEROLEMIA

There should no longer be any debate over the importance of identifying and treating hypercholesterolemia in patients with atherosclerosis. The risk of death from CAD is proportional to the serum cholesterol level (Martin et al, 1986). To reduce this risk, the National Cholesterol Education Program recommends lowering the low-density lipoprotein cholesterol (LDL-C) level to <100 mg/dL in patients with atherosclerosis. Clinical trials of lipid-lowering therapy published over the past several years support this notion. Both the Scandinavian Simvastatin Survival Study (4S) and the Cholesterol and Recurrent Events (CARE) trial found that lipid-lowering therapy with hepatic 3-hydroxy-3-methylglutaryl coenzyme A (HMG-CoA) reductase inhibitors significantly reduces the incidence of death and fatal and nonfatal MI in patients with coronary atherosclerosis (Scandinavian Simvastatin Survival Study Group, 1994; Sacks et al, 1996). The benefits were substantial. In the 4S trial, involving patients whose total cholesterol levels averaged 260 mg/dL and ranged from 212 to 369 mg/dL, simvastatin reduced total mortality by 30% and nonfatal and fatal MI by 34%. In CARE, the total cholesterol level of the participants was lower than in 4S, averaging 209 mg/dL. In this trial, pravastatin reduced the incidence of fatal and nonfatal MI by 24%. It is not possible to know how many patients in these trials had PAD, since documentation of the clinical manifestations of PAD and ankle-brachial indices were limited. Nonetheless, it is reasonable to extrapolate these findings to patients with PAD since it is unlikely that a large clinical trial of lipid-lowering therapy in PAD will be conducted.

Lipid-lowering therapy may also benefit peripheral manifestations of atherosclerosis. In the Cholesterol Lowering Atherosclerosis Study (CLAS), lipid-lowering therapy with niacin and colestipol was associated with less progression of femoral artery atherosclerosis than placebo. In the Program on the Surgical Control of Hyperlipidemias (POSCH) study, reduction in LDL-C was achieved by partial ileal bypass (Buchwald et al, 1990). The incidence of intermittent claudication over the ensuing 10 years was less in patients who underwent ileal bypass than in the control group. Similarly, in the 4S trial, the risk of developing new or worsening claudication was decreased by 38% in the group of patients receiving simvastatin compared with the placebo group (Pedersen et al, 1998) (Figure 1). A beneficial effect of lipid-lowering therapy has also been observed in patients with cerebrovascular disease. One meta-analysis of 13 randomized, placebo-controlled trials found that treatment with an HMG-CoA reductase inhibitor was associated with a 31% risk reduction in the incidence of stroke compared with placebo (Blauw et al, 1997). Another review of 16 randomized trials of lipid-lowering therapy found that HMG-CoA reductase inhibitors reduced the risk of stroke by 29% compared with placebo (Hebert et al, 1997).

The mechanisms whereby lipid-lowering therapy reduce cardiovascular events require consideration since these may have important implications for the development and consequences of PAD as well. One important mechanism whereby lipid-lowering therapy is likely to reduce cardiovascular events is by stabilizing atherosclerotic plaque, thereby reducing the likelihood for plaque rupture and thrombosis. Clinical and pathologic studies have found that acute MI develops as a consequence of acute plaque rupture and thrombosis (Davies and Thomas, 1985; Gruppo Italiano per lo Studio della Streptochinasi nell'Infarto Miocardico, 1986). Several angiographic studies have found that the majority of thrombosed coronary arteries in patients presenting with acute MI occurred at a site of a previously non–flow-limiting lesion (Ambrose et al, 1988; Hackett et al, 1988). As reviewed recently by Fuster and Lewis (1994) and by Libby (1995), features predisposing to plaque rupture include a large lipid core, lipid-laden macrophages, a thin fibrous cap, and high stress at the plaque margins (Figure 2). Lipid-lowering therapy has the potential of transforming a fragile plaque to a stable one in which a lipid component is substantially reduced and the fibrous component increased.

Another mechanism whereby lipid-lowering therapy may favorably affect the clinical manifestations of CAD is by altering vasomotor activity. An important determinant of vasomotor tone is nitric oxide (NO). This molecule is synthesized in the endothelium and acts upon subjacent vascular smooth muscle to induce vasodilation. NO is released by a variety of biochemical

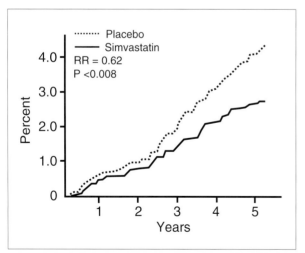

Figure 1. In the Scandinavian Simvastatin Survival Study, lipid-lowering therapy was associated with a 38% reduction in the risk for developing new or worsening claudication. RR = relative risk. Adapted from Pedersen et al (1998) and reproduced with permission.

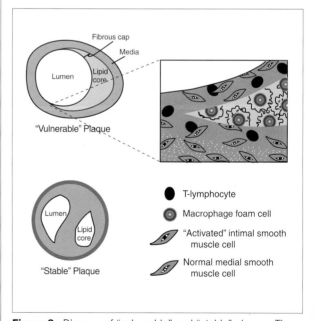

Figure 2. Diagram of "vulnerable" and "stable" plaque. The "vulnerable" plaque has features that predispose it to rupture including a large lipid core, lipid-laden macrophages (foam cells), activated smooth muscle cells, and a thin fibrous cap. Adapted from Libby (1995) and reproduced with permission from the American Heart Association.

stimuli, including acetylcholine, serotonin, thrombin, and bradykinin, as well as by physical stimuli such as shear stress. The bioavailability of endothelium-derived NO is reduced in patients with atherosclerosis. Clinical studies have found that infusion of acetylcholine causes vasodilation in nonatherosclerotic coronary arteries and vasoconstriction in atherosclerotic vessels (Ludmer et al, 1986). The vasoconstriction is caused by stimulation of muscarinic receptors on vascular smooth muscle, a response not modulated by NO in these vessels. Endogenous substances, such as serotonin and thrombin, might be anticipated to have similar effects. Therefore, platelet aggregation and release of platelet content in the vicinity of an atherosclerotic vessel are likely to cause vasoconstriction, since the protective effect of NO is not present. In addition, it has been shown that exercise causes coronary vasodilation in healthy individuals but coronary vasoconstriction in patients with atherosclerosis (Gordon et al, 1989). This phenomenon is likely to be related to the bioavailability of endothelium-derived NO also. Shear stress, resulting from the increase in coronary blood flow during exercise, is likely to release NO from the endothelium and obviate the vasoconstrictive effects of the sympathetic nervous system. In contrast, flow through atherosclerotic coronary arteries during exercise will not increase levels of NO, enabling the dominant vasomotor effects to be constriction-mediated by the sympathetic nervous system. Lipid-lowering therapy has been shown to improve endothelium-dependent vasodilation in atherosclerotic coronary arteries (Egashira et al, 1994; Anderson et al, 1995; Treasure et al, 1995). One might postulate, therefore, that improved endothelial function reduces coronary vasoconstriction and improves the myocardial oxygen supply/demand relation. Indeed, lipid-lowering therapy reduces the frequency of myocardial ischemia as assessed by ambulatory monitoring (Andrews et al, 1997). In addition, it is conceivable that reduction of coronary vasoconstriction may reduce the likelihood of forces at the margins of unstable plaque and reduce the potential for plaque rupture.

CIGARETTE SMOKING

Although cigarette smoking is recognized as an important risk factor for atherosclerosis, and particularly for the development of PAD, there are far fewer studies examining the benefits of smoking cessation on clinical manifestations of atherosclerosis than on hypercholesterolemia. For ethical reasons, there are no prospective controlled trials of smoking cessation; therefore, data relevant to PAD must be derived by

comparing populations that continue to smoke with populations that voluntarily stopped smoking. In one study, smokers with intermittent claudication were followed for up to 10 years (Jonason and Bergstrom, 1987). Of those who continued to smoke, 16% developed critical limb ischemia versus none of the patients who stopped smoking. Moreover, over a 10-year period, 53% of the smokers developed MI compared with 11% of those who stopped smoking, while cardiac death rates were 43% in the smokers versus 6% in the former smokers. In a study of patients who had undergone limb revascularization, 3-year survival rates were 40% and 65% in heavy (>15 cigarettes/day) and moderate (<15 cigarettes/day) smokers, respectively (Lassila and Lepantalo, 1988). Cigarette smoking has also been shown to have an adverse effect on infrainguinal bypass graft patency (Wiseman et al, 1989). One mechanism whereby smoking may contribute to development and progression of atherosclerosis is by reducing bioavailability of NO. Indeed, several clinical studies have shown that cigarette smoking is associated with abnormal endothelium-dependent vasodilation (Celermajer et al, 1993; Heitzer et al, 1996).

HYPERTENSION, DIABETES, HYPERHOMOCYSTINEMIA

Effective treatment of hypertension reduces mortality and the incidence of stroke. Meta-analyses of prospective, population-based observational studies conducted before 1990, including the Multiple Risk Factor Intervention Trial (MRFIT) and the Framingham, Whitehall, Honolulu, and Western Electric studies, have found that an approximately 7.5-mm Hg lower diastolic blood pressure predicts a 46% reduction in stroke and a 29% reduction in CAD (MacMahon et al, 1990). In patients treated for hypertension, meta-analyses of trials such as the Hypertension Detection and Follow-up Program, the Medical Research Council study, the European Working Party on Hypertension in the Elderly study, the Australian National Blood Pressure Study, and others have found that antihypertensive treatment is associated with an approximately 40% reduction in the risk of stroke and a 10% to 15% reduction in the risk of CAD (Collins et al, 1990). Data are lacking with respect to the importance of antihypertensive therapy in reducing the incidence and sequelae of peripheral atherosclerosis.

Diabetes mellitus substantially increases the risk of developing PAD and is associated with a higher prevalence of tibioperoneal artery atherosclerosis. Aggressive control of diabetes has been shown to reduce the incidence of microvascular complications such as retinopathy and nephropathy (Reichard et al, 1993; Diabetes Control and Complications Trial Research Group, 1993). In the Diabetes Control and Complications Trial (DCCT) (Diabetes Control and Complications Trial Research Group, 1995), intensive treatment was associated with approximately 50% fewer major macrovascular events, but the difference did not achieve statistical significance. The data to derive any conclusions regarding the efficacy of aggressive diabetes management on the progression and complications of peripheral atherosclerosis are nonsignificant.

Hyperhomocystinemia is also associated with peripheral atherosclerosis, and treatment with B complex vitamins including folic acid, pyridoxine, and cyanocobalamin reduces homocysteine levels (Naurath et al, 1995; Malinow et al, 1989; Clarke et al, 1991). Nonetheless, there are no findings to date with respect to the efficacy of treating hyperhomocystinemia on the clinical consequences of atherosclerosis.

CONCLUSION

Two important considerations emerge in the management of patients with PAD. The first is recognition of the possibility of coexisting CAD and cerebrovascular disease. Timely intervention may reduce the risk of MI, stroke, and death. Second, risk factors should be addressed and modified with particular attention to smoking cessation and lipid-lowering therapy. Aggressive risk-factor modification is likely to reduce the incidence of adverse cardiovascular events and may also have favorable effects on the clinical sequelae of PAD.

Key Points

• Clinical findings of PAD should prompt a careful search for modifiable risk factors and evaluation for coexisting coronary artery and cerebrovascular disease in order to initiate timely therapeutic interventions that may reduce the incidence of MI and stroke.

• Aggressive lipid-lowering therapy with HMG-CoA reductase inhibitors reduces the risk of adverse cardiovascular events such as nonfatal MI in patients with atherosclerosis.

• Lipid-lowering therapy also appears to reduce the incidence of developing new or worsening claudication, although prospective trials are needed to confirm this observation.

• Cessation of cigarette smoking is associated with improved long-term outcome in patients with intermittent claudication. Patients who stop smoking have a lower incidence of progression to critical limb ischemia and are less likely to develop MI.

• Hyperhomocystinemia is associated with PAD. Although treatment with B complex vitamins, including folic acid, pyridoxine, and cyanocobalamin reduces homocysteine levels, it is not yet known whether such treatment reduces the adverse complications of atherosclerosis.

BIBLIOGRAPHY

Ambrose JA, Tannenbaum MA, Alexopoulos D, et al. Angiographic progression of coronary artery disease and the development of myocardial infarction. J Am Coll Cardiol 1988;12:56–62.

Anderson TJ, Meredith IT, Yeung AC, et al. The effect of cholesterol-lowering and antioxidant therapy on endothelium-dependent coronary vasomotion. N Engl J Med 1995;332:488–93.

Andrews TC, Raby K, Barry J, et al. Effect of cholesterol reduction on myocardial ischemia in patients with coronary disease. Circulation 1997;95:324–28.

Blauw GJ, Lagaay AM, Smelt AHM, Westendorp RGJ. Stroke, statins, and cholesterol: a meta-analysis of randomized, placebo-controlled, double-blind trials with HMG-CoA reductase inhibitors. Stroke 1997; 28:946–50.

Buchwald H, Varco RL, Matts JP, et al. Effect of partial ileal bypass surgery on mortality and morbidity from coronary heart disease in patients with hypercholesterolemia. Report of the Program on the Surgical Control of the Hyperlipidemias (POSCH). N Engl J Med 1990;323:946–55.

Celermajer DS, Sorensen KE, Georgakopoulos D, et al. Cigarette smoking is associated with dose-related and potentially reversible impairment of endothelium-dependent dilation in healthy young adults. Circulation 1993;88:2149–55.

Clarke R, Daly L, Robinson K, et al. Hyperhomocysteinemia: an independent risk factor for vascular disease. N Engl J Med 1991;324:1149–55.

Collins R, Peto R, MacMahon S, et al. Blood pressure, stroke, and coronary heart disease. Part 2. Short-term reductions in blood pressure: overview of randomized drug trials in their epidemiological context. Lancet 1990;335:827–38.

Criqui M, Langer RD, Fronek A, et al. Mortality over a period of 10 years in patients with peripheral arterial disease. N Engl J Med 1992;326:381–86.

Davies MJ, Thomas AC. Plaque fissuring: the cause of acute myocardial infarction, sudden ischemic death, and crescendo angina. Br Heart J 1985;53:363–73.

Diabetes Control and Complications Trial Research Group. The effect of intensive treatment of diabetes on the development and progression of long-term complications in insulin-dependent diabetes mellitus. N Engl J Med 1993;329:977–86.

Diabetes Control and Complications Trial (DCCT) Research Group. Effect of intensive diabetes management on macrovascular events and risk factors in the diabetes control and complications trial. Am J Cardiol 1995;75:894–903.

Egashira K, Hirooka Y, Kai H, et al. Reduction in serum cholesterol with pravastatin improves endothelium-dependent coronary vasomotion in patients with hypercholesterolemia. Circulation 1994;89:2519–24.

Fuster V, Lewis A. Connor Memorial Lecture. Mechanisms leading to myocardial infarction: insights from studies of vascular biology. Circulation 1994;90:2126–46.

Gordon JB, Ganz P, Nabel EG, et al. Atherosclerosis and endothelial function influence the coronary vasomotor response to exercise. J Clin Invest 1989;83:1946.

Gruppo Italiano per lo Studio della Streptochinasi nell'Infarto Miocardico (GISSI). Effectiveness of intravenous thrombolytic treatment in acute myocardial infarction. Lancet 1986;1:397–402.

Hackett D, Davies G, Maseri A. Pre-existing coronary stenoses in patients with first myocardial infarction are not necessarily severe. Eur Heart J 1988;9:1317–23.

Hebert PR, Gaziano JM, Chan KS, Hennekens CH. Cholesterol lowering with statin drugs, risk of stroke, and total mortality: an overview of randomized trials. JAMA 1997;278:313–21.

Heitzer T, Just H, Münzel T. Antioxidant vitamin C improves endothelial dysfunction in chronic smokers. Circulation 1996;94:6–9.

Jonason T, Bergstrom R. Cessation of smoking in patients with intermittent claudication. Effects on the risk of peripheral vascular complications, myocardial infarction and mortality. Acta Med Scand 1987;221:253–60.

Lassila R, Lepantalo M. Cigarette smoking and the outcome after lower limb arterial surgery. Acta Chir Scand 1988;154:635–40.

Libby P. Molecular bases of the acute coronary syndromes. Circulation 1995;91:2844–50.

Ludmer PL, Selwyn AP, Shook TL, et al. Paradoxical vasoconstriction induced by acetylcholine in atherosclerotic coronary arteries. N Engl J Med 1986;315:1046–51.

MacMahon S, Peto S, Cutter J, et al. Blood pressure, stroke and coronary heart disease: Part 1. Prolonged differences in blood pressure: prospective observational studies corrected for the regression dilution bias. Lancet 1990;335:765–74.

Malinow MR, Kang SS, Taylor LM, et al. Prevalence of hyperhomocyst(e)inemia in patients with peripheral arterial occlusive disease. Circulation 1989;79:1180–88.

Martin MJ, Hulley SB, Browner WS, et al. Serum cholesterol, blood pressure, and mortality: implications from a cohort of 361,662 men. Lancet 1986;2:933–36.

Naurath HJ, Joosten E, Riezler R, et al. Effects of vitamin B_{12}, folate, and vitamin B_6 supplements in elderly people with normal serum vitamin concentrations. Lancet 1995;346:85–89.

Pedersen TR, Kjekshus J, Pyörälä K, et al. Effect of simvastatin on ischemic signs and symptoms in the Scandinavian Simvastatin Survival Study (4S). Am J Cardiol 1998;81:333–38.

Reichard P, Nilsson B-Y, Rosenqvist U. The effect of long-term intensified insulin treatment on the development of microvascular complications of diabetes mellitus. N Engl J Med 1993;329:304–09.

Sacks FM, Pfeffer MA, Moye LA, et al. The effect of pravastatin on coronary events after myocardial infarction in patients with average cholesterol levels. N Engl J Med 1996;335:1001–09.

Scandinavian Simvastatin Survival Study Group. Randomised trial of cholesterol lowering in 4444 patients with coronary heart disease: the Scandinavian Simvastastin Survival Study (4S). Lancet 1994;344:1383–89.

Treasure CB, Klein JL, Weintraub WS, et al. Beneficial effects of cholesterol-lowering therapy on the coronary endothelium in patients with coronary artery disease. N Engl J Med 1995;332:481–87.

Wiseman S, Kenchington G, Dain R, et al. Influence of smoking and plasma factors on patency of femoropopliteal vein grafts. BMJ 1989;299:643–46.

Antithrombotic Therapy for Peripheral Arterial Disease

Jonathan L. Halperin, MD
Robert and Harriet Heilbrunn Professor of Medicine (Cardiology)
Mount Sinai School of Medicine
Director, Cardiology Clinical Services
The Zena and Michael A. Wiener Cardiovascular Institute
Mount Sinai Medical Center
New York, New York

Objective: To describe current approaches to antithrombotic therapy in the management of peripheral arterial disease.

Patients with peripheral atherosclerosis are at ongoing risk of myocardial infarction (MI), ischemic stroke, and vascular death due predominantly to thrombotic arterial occlusion, reflected in the term *atherothrombosis*. The platelet cyclo-oxygenase inhibitor aspirin reduces the rate of these ischemic events in patients at risk, as do the platelet adenosine diphosphate-receptor inhibitors ticlopidine and clopidogrel. Chronic anticoagulation with warfarin and combinations of antithrombotic agents are generally reserved for patients at highest risk, such as those who have undergone complex revascularization procedures, to preserve graft patency.

Intermittent claudication due to peripheral arterial disease (PAD) is but one clinical presentation of atherosclerosis, a systemic disease that also affects the coronary and cerebral circulations, causing MI, ischemic stroke, and vascular death. These events are due predominantly to thrombosis, and the term *atherothrombosis* denotes the essential relation between atherosclerotic vascular stenosis and thrombotic arterial occlusion, which underlies most ischemic events (Fuster et al, 1992).

ASPIRIN FOR PREVENTION OF ISCHEMIC EVENTS

Arterial wall injury resulting from atherosclerosis leads to both platelet activation and production of thrombin and fibrin. Most cases of acute MI are caused by thrombotic coronary occlusion at the site of an advanced atherosclerotic lesion. Vessel recanalization can occur spontaneously or through the injection of thrombolytic medication, but the risk of thrombotic reocclusion remains high for several weeks after an acute ischemic episode. In patients with acute coronary syndromes like unstable angina pectoris, aspirin reduces the relative risk of acute MI by >50% compared with placebo. Beyond the acute phase of MI, morbidity

and mortality are related to other factors, such as left ventricular dysfunction and ventricular arrhythmia, which are not directly amenable to an antithrombotic prophylactic approach, so the long-term advantages of aspirin treatment given for secondary prevention of complications of ischemic heart disease have been harder to verify.

Available antithrombotic medications for prevention of ischemic syndromes in patients with atherosclerosis include platelet inhibitors, anticoagulants, and a recently introduced class of direct inhibitors of thrombin. A combination of approaches is warranted for high-risk patients with unstable angina, evolving acute MI, or in the early phase following angioplasty. In the chronic phase of coronary disease, patients with stable angina, remote MI angioplasty, or bypass surgery are more often managed with a platelet inhibitor alone rather than with an anticoagulant, for reasons of convenience, safety, and economy. Aspirin therapy has been convincingly demonstrated to reduce the risks of MI, ischemic stroke, and vascular death for many patients with manifest vascular disease. A meta-analysis of over 100 randomized clinical trials involving about 70,000 participants concluded that aspirin reduces these vascular events by about 25%, regardless of the aspirin dose. Nonfatal MI and strokes were reduced by about one third, while vascular deaths were reduced by about one sixth (Antiplatelet Trialists' Collaboration, 1994a).

Aspirin is also recommended for primary prevention in low-risk patients with such risk factors as family history, tobacco exposure, or hypercholesterolemia. In the US Physicians' Health Study, aspirin (325 mg every other day) reduced the incidence of MI by almost half in 22,071 male physicians over 40 years of age followed for 4.8 years (Steering Committee of the Physicians' Health Study Research Group, 1989). The rate of cardiovascular death was no different in those treated with aspirin than in those given placebo, but aspirin was associated with a statistically insignificant trend suggesting a slight increase in the number of severe hemorrhagic strokes (13 vs 6). Aspirin therapy was also associated with a lower relative risk of peripheral arterial surgery (0.54; 95% confidence interval [CI] 0.30–0.95; P = 0.03). For patients over 50 years of age who have risk factors for the development of coronary events, dosages as low as 80 mg/d have been proved effective. Direct randomized comparisons of different aspirin dosages on stroke have involved patients with transient cerebral ischemic attack or minor stroke (ie, manifest vascular disease). In the Dutch TIA trial, the adjusted relative risk of fatal or nonfatal stroke was 0.82 (95% CI 0.64–1.04) comparing aspirin dosages of 30 mg/d to 283 mg/d. Disregarding hemorrhagic strokes, it is likely that the difference between aspirin dosages on ischemic stroke approaches conventional statistical significance (the Dutch TIA Study Group, 1991). There were no trends to distinguish stroke rates between aspirin dosages of 300 mg/d versus 1,200 mg/d in the United Kingdom Transient Ischaemic Attack (UK-TIA) – aspirin trial (UK-TIA Study Group, 1991).

The toxicity of maintenance therapy with aspirin most commonly involves the gastrointestinal (GI) tract. Aspirin produces gastric mucosal erosion, and subjective digestive complaints have been reported about 3% to 5% more often per year in patients assigned to aspirin in double-blind trials than in those given placebo. In studies using relatively high dosages (over 1,000 mg/d), GI intolerance sufficient to require medication withdrawal occurs at a rate of about 2.5% per year in patients given aspirin compared with about 1.5% with placebo. Occult bleeding was detected by serial stool guaiac examinations in 17% of aspirin-treated patients and 13% of placebo-treated patients in one study, but symptomatic blood loss occurred in <1% of these patients. Clinically significant GI bleeding occurred at an average rate of about 1.8% yearly with aspirin and 0.7% with placebo. Enteric-coated preparations of aspirin display bioavailability comparable to conventional formulations, yet seem less frequently associated with gastroduodenal ulceration. Aspirin exerts clinically effective platelet inhibitory effects at a dosage of 1 mg/kg daily, which is about the 75 to 81 mg contained in aspirin tablets formulated for pediatric use. Such a dosage is associated with minimal GI toxicity when taken alone, and may be better tolerated than larger quantities when given in combination with an oral anticoagulant, though indications for long-term therapy with such a combination have not been established.

Thrombogenic effects of aspirin have been demonstrated experimentally, particularly at high dosages, possibly relating to inhibition of endothelial-derived prostacyclin (PGI_2) synthesis. In the absence of atherosclerotic vascular disease, for which the antiplatelet effect of aspirin reduces stroke, inhibition of PGI_2 may increase ischemic stroke. Hence, the low dosages of aspirin that reduce MI and enhance hemorrhagic stroke by virtue of the antiplatelet effect may be less likely to potentiate a separate competing prothrombotic effect based on PGI_2 inhibition. In patients with manifest vascular disease, the antiplatelet effect may dominate, causing a reduction in ischemic stroke, but potentially less so in low-risk populations. Paradoxically, increased platelet adhesiveness has been reported in some patients taking aspirin ("aspirin nonresponders"), but the clinical consequences and implications of these observations are uncertain.

OTHER PLATELET INHIBITORS

Combining aspirin with dipyridamole has delayed the angiographic progression of obstructive PAD and reduced the need for arterial reconstruction in a study of male patients, but the effects of dipyridamole alone are unclear. In a study of 199 patients, the angiographic severity of atherosclerotic lesions over 2 years was lower in those treated with a combination of aspirin (1 g/d) plus dipyridamole (225 mg/d), compared with patients treated with aspirin alone or with those given placebo. In a study of 300 patients with femoral artery stenosis, the rate of occlusion over 4.5 years was 58% with placebo compared with 20% among those given aspirin (1 g/d) and 34% with a combination of aspirin (1 g/d) plus dipyridamole (225 mg/d), significantly lower in the groups treated with platelet inhibitor medication (Schoop et al, 1993). Studies in animals suggest that dipyridamole augments the antithrombotic effect of aspirin on artificial prosthetic surfaces, and this forms the basis for the therapeutic use of the combination of aspirin plus dipyridamole in patients undergoing lower extremity revascularization with prosthetic bypass grafts.

Another class of platelet inhibitors, the thienopyridine derivatives ticlopidine and clopidogrel, antagonize the platelet adenosine diphosphate receptor. The randomized Swedish Ticlopidine Multicenter Study found no significant hemodynamic (ankle-brachial systolic blood pressure [SBP] index) or functional (walking distance) improvement with ticlopidine compared with placebo (Fagher, 1994). Ticlopidine reduced the rate of an event constellation consisting of sudden death, MI, and stroke in another stratified, randomized, multicenter trial compared with placebo, and the number of patients achieving >50% improvement in walking capacity was slightly greater in the group treated with ticlopidine (Blanchard et al, 1994). A meta-analysis of 5 studies has suggested that more improvement in walking capacity accrues during treatment with ticlopidine, but the mechanism of gain has not been clarified and hemorheologic factors may be more important than antithrombotic effects (Palareti et al, 1988). Ticlopidine therapy in a dosage of 250 mg twice daily was associated with less progression of angiographic lower extremity arterial disease over 1 year than occurred in a control group (n = 43), and in a French study, ticlopidine improved graft patency in patients with femoropopliteal or femorotibial saphenous venous bypass grafts from 63% to 82% over 2 years (Stiegler et al, 1984; Becquemin, 1997). Treatment with ticlopidine, however, is associated with a tangible risk of hematologic side effects including suppression of hematopoiesis and, more rarely, thrombotic thrombocytopenic purpura (Moloney, 1993).

In a recent large, multicenter trial, clopidogrel was compared with aspirin in over 19,000 patients with clinical atherosclerosis (CAPRIE steering committee, 1996). Participants included survivors of MI, nondisabling stroke, and symptomatic PAD. Specific entry criteria for patients with PAD were a history of intermittent claudication, as defined by the World Health Organization (leg pain of presumed atherosclerotic origin while walking that disappears after <10 minutes of standing still), and an ankle-arm SBP ratio ≤0.85 in either leg measured at rest on 2 separate occasions. Patients with a history of intermittent claudication who had undergone reconstructive surgery, angioplasty, or leg amputation without persisting complications were eligible. Patients were randomly assigned to take either aspirin (325 mg/d) or clopidogrel (75 mg/d). Anticoagulant and other antithrombotic medications were withdrawn prior to randomization. The treatment groups were well matched in terms of age, gender, race, and cardiovascular risk factors, including diabetes mellitus, hypertension, hypercholesterolemia, and cigarette smoking. In total, 19,185 enrolled patients

were followed for up to 3 years (mean, 1.5 years). The primary endpoint was a composite of ischemic stroke, MI, or vascular death. The principal finding was that patients treated with clopidogrel had a 5.32% annual risk of ischemic stroke, MI, or vascular death compared with 5.83% for those treated with aspirin (relative risk reduction 8.7%), a small but significant difference. Most of the benefit was confined to the 6,452 patients entered on the basis of PAD, in whom the relative risk reduction for occurrence of primary vascular events was 24% (P = 0.0028, Figure).

Cilostazol, an agent recently approved by the US Food and Drug Administration (FDA) for reduction of symptoms of intermittent claudication, possesses antiplatelet, antithrombotic, and vasodilatory properties. Cilostazol has been shown to inhibit smooth muscle cell proliferation, platelet aggregation, and prevent thrombotic death in animal models. Clinical trials with this compound have shown increases in walking distances and beneficial effects on plasma lipids in patients with intermittent claudication (Dawson et al, 1998). Studies are under way to assess cilostazol's potential benefit in secondary stroke prevention.

Prostaglandin E_1 (PGE_1) and PGI_2, potent vasodilators and inhibitors of platelet aggregation, have been

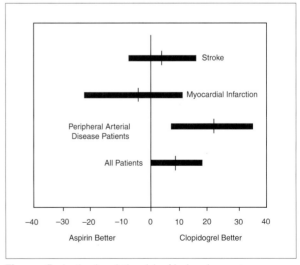

Figure. Reduction in relative risk of ischemic events (composite of myocardial infarction, ischemic stroke, or vascular death) among 19,185 patients assigned to treatment with clopidogrel (75 mg/d) or aspirin (325 mg/d), based on atherosclerotic criteria for entry into the Clopidogrel vs Aspirin in Patients at Risk of Ischemic Events (CAPRIE) study. For patients with PAD assigned to clopidogrel, the average event rate was 3.71% per year compared with 4.86% per year with aspirin, a relative risk reduction of 23.8% (95% confidence interval 8.9–36.2) favoring clopidogrel (P = 0.0028).

shown to improve claudication, relieve pain, and promote ulcer healing in short-term studies. Intravenous or intra-arterial infusions of PGE_1 and PGI_2 have persisting effects on blood flow and exercise capacity for weeks to months after treatment. The major drawback to this type of prostaglandin therapy is the short half-lives of these drugs; however, oral analogues are under development. Other antiplatelet compounds undergoing clinical evaluation include trapidil and picotamide. The last is an inhibitor of thromboxane A_2 synthesis and receptor activity with antiplatelet effects, but its efficacy and safety compared with aspirin have not been fully evaluated.

The methylxanthine derivative, pentoxifylline, is approved by the FDA for treatment of patients with intermittent claudication. Pentoxifylline has been reported to improve erythrocyte deformability, lower whole blood viscosity, and inhibit platelet reactivity and coagulation, and these properties may operate individually or in combination to produce the improvement in walking capacity described in some studies. Its antithrombotic effects are comparatively mild, and most clinicians favoring its use do so in addition to rather than as an alternative to aspirin.

ANTICOAGULANT THERAPY

Ever since Herrick (1912) first recognized the relation between acute MI and coronary thrombosis, anticoagulant therapy in patients prone to these events has been contemplated. The importance of activation of the coagulation system and fibrin formation in the pathogenesis of thrombotic events arising in the cardiac chambers and in atherosclerotic coronary arteries has made anticoagulation a routine component of treatment for patients with acute MI. The optimum duration of anticoagulation is still speculative, as the hemorrhage risks entailed accumulate with length of exposure and exceed those with aspirin. In patients with congestive heart failure, impaired hepatic metabolism might potentiate suppression of vitamin K-dependent coagulation factors, rendering dosage adjustment more difficult when agents like warfarin are given to achieve the currently recommended intensity for a therapeutic anticoagulant effect (international normalized ratio [INR] 2–3).

Chronic anticoagulation with warfarin is advocated for patients with cardiovascular disease when thromboembolism rates exceed 5% annually, but is clearly associated with considerable morbidity due to hemorrhage, particularly in elderly or hypertensive patients or when INR values >3.0 are sustained. In over 200 patient-centuries of observation, anticoagulation in patients with prosthetic heart valves carries a risk of

cerebral hemorrhage of about 0.2% annually, and an additional 2.2% yearly chance of major hemorrhage outside the central nervous system. On average, studies of patients receiving conventional doses of warfarin or related anticoagulants have found that major hemorrhages—those requiring hospital admission or blood transfusion or resulting in permanent disability—occur at a rate of 1% to 2% per year, and that hemorrhagic complications of lesser severity occur more than twice as often. Intracerebral hemorrhage occurs in about 0.5% annually of patients given conventional doses of anticoagulant medication on a long-term basis, and the risk rises up to 3-fold for those anticoagulated because of cerebrovascular disease. This complication is not entirely predictable, occurring in nonhypertensive patients and when prothrombin time is being maintained within the accepted therapeutic range. However, advanced age and anticoagulation in excess of the target range clearly increase the danger, as do uncontrolled hypertension, drug interactions, intercurrent surgery, alcoholism, and concomitant aspirin therapy.

Insufficient data have been forthcoming to validate an advantage to long-term anticoagulation for patients with PAD. Two Dutch trials found a lower incidence of ischemic events in patients with PAD given oral anticoagulants, and survival was greater among selected anticoagulated patients following femoropopliteal bypass surgery than in a control group (Hamming et al, 1965; DeSmit and van Urk, 1987). Ankle-brachial systolic pressure indices declined more gradually in the anticoagulated patients, and graft patency was prolonged out to 12 years, but this falls short of confirming delayed progression of atherosclerotic vascular disease (Kretschmer and Holzenbein, 1995). In contrast, a 3-year, 116-patient study in Sweden found no advantage to anticoagulation in terms of graft patency, limb salvage, or survival among anticoagulated patients compared with controls, and a 5% rate of major hemorrhagic complications (Arfidsson et al, 1990).

ANTITHROMBOTIC THERAPY FOLLOWING EXTREMITY REVASCULARIZATION

Beyond the intraoperative use of heparin, patients undergoing lower extremity revascularization surgery have shown benefit with platelet-inhibitor agents as well. A meta-analysis of 11 randomized trials involving over 2,000 patients found that platelet-inhibitor drugs reduced the incidence of graft occlusion by one third, from 24% to 16% during a mean follow-up interval of 19 months (P <0.0001; Antiplatelet Trialists' Collaboration, 1994b). A comparison of aspirin plus dipyridamole with low-molecular-weight heparin found graft patency better with the heparin compound over 3 months following femoropopliteal reconstruction (Edmondson et al, 1994). Whether suppression of neointimal hyperplasia or prevention of thrombus formation accounts for this difference remains to be determined.

Anticoagulant medication, alone or in combination with a platelet inhibitor, is reserved for patients undergoing arterial reconstructive surgery to enhance graft patency when synthetic prosthetic material such as Dacron® or polytetrafluoroethylene (Gore-tex®) is employed, when the anastomosis involves smaller arteries distal to the inguinal ligament, when complex or composite grafts or endarterectomy are involved, or when distal outflow is compromised. In other cases, aspirin or clopidogrel is justified generally for patients undergoing revascularization for lower extremity arterial disease to prevent coronary and cerebral ischemic events.

Prior to peripheral angioplasty, aspirin is conventionally given, and heparin is used during the procedure. Following angioplasty, aspirin or aspirin plus ticlopidine combination is used, pending completion of studies with clopidogrel. In the absence of contraindications, patients undergoing angioplasty for relief of atherosclerotic obstruction should receive aspirin or clopidogrel over the long-term for reduction of cardiovascular morbidity and mortality (Clagett and Krupiski, 1995).

Key Points

• The term *atherothrombosis* denotes the essential relation between atherosclerotic vascular stenosis and thrombotic arterial occlusion, which underlies most ischemic events in the coronary, cerebral, and peripheral arterial beds.

• Available antithrombotic medications for prevention of ischemic syndromes in patients with atherosclerosis include platelet inhibitors, anticoagulants, and a recently introduced class of direct inhibitors of thrombin; a combination of approaches is warranted for patients at highest risk.

• Aspirin therapy has been convincingly demonstrated to reduce the risks of MI, ischemic stroke, and vascular death for many patients with manifest vascular disease.

• Clopidogrel was compared with aspirin in a recent multicenter trial involving over 19,000 patients with clinical atherosclerosis. In a subgroup of 6,452 patients entered on the basis of PAD, the relative risk reduction for occurrence of primary vascular events (ischemic stroke, MI, or vascular death) was 24% compared with aspirin (P = 0.0028).

• Chronic anticoagulation with warfarin may be appropriate for patients with cardiovascular disease at especially high risk of thromboembolism, but is clearly associated with considerable morbidity due to hemorrhage. Available data are not sufficient to justify long-term anticoagulation for most patients with PAD.

• In the absence of contraindications, patients with atherosclerotic PAD should be treated with aspirin or clopidogrel to reduce cardiovascular morbidity and mortality.

BIBLIOGRAPHY

Antiplatelet Trialists' Collaboration. Collaborative overview of randomised trials of antiplatelet therapy. Prevention of death, myocardial infarction, and stroke by prolonged antiplatelet therapy in various categories of patients. Br Med J 1994a;308:81–101.

Antiplatelet Trialists' Collaboration. Collaborative overview of randomized trials of antiplatelet treatment. Part II. Maintenance of vascular graft patency by antiplatelet therapy. Br Med J 1994b;309:159–68.

Arfidsson B, Lundgren F, Drott C, et al. Influence of coumarin treatment on patency and limb salvage after peripheral arterial reconstructive surgery. Am J Surg 1990;159:556–60.

Becquemin JP. Effect of ticlopidine on the long-term patency of saphenous-vein bypass grafts in the legs. Etude de la Ticlopidine après Pontage Femoro-Poplite and the Association Universitaire de Recherche en Chirurgie. N Engl J Med 1997;337:1726–31.

Blanchard J, Carreras LO, Kindermans M, and the EMATAP group. Results of EMATAP: a double-blind placebo-controlled multicentre trial of ticlopidine in patients with peripheral arterial disease. Nouv Rev Fr Hematol 1994;35:523–28.

CAPRIE steering committee. A randomised, blinded trial of Clopidogrel versus Aspirin in Patients at Risk of Ischemic Events (CAPRIE). Lancet 1996;348:1329–39.

Clagett GP, Krupiski WC. Antithrombotic therapy in peripheral arterial occlusive disease. Chest 1995;108(suppl 4):431S–43S.

Dawson DL, Cutler BS, Meissner MH, Strandness DE.

Cilostazol has beneficial effects in treatment of intermittent claudication: results from a multi-center, randomized, prospective, double-blind trial. Circulation 1998;98:678–86.

DeSmit P, van Urk H. The effect of long-term treatment with oral anticoagulants in patients with peripheral vascular disease. In: Tilsner V, Mattias FR, eds. Arterielle Verschlusskrankheit und Blutgerinnung. Basel: Editiones Roche; 1987:211–17.

Dutch TIA Study Group. A comparison of two doses of aspirin (30 mg vs. 283 mg a day) in patients after a transient ischemic attack or minor ischemic stroke. N Engl J Med 1991;325:1261–66.

Edmondson RA, Cohen AT, Das SK, et al. Low-molecular-weight heparin versus aspirin and dipyridamole after femoropopliteal bypass grafting. Lancet 1994; 344:914–18.

Fagher B. Long-term effects of ticlopidine on lower limb blood flow, ankle/brachial index and symptoms in peripheral arteriosclerosis. A double-blind study. The STIMS Group in Lund. Swedish Ticlopidine Multicenter Study. Angiology 1994;45:777–88.

Fuster V, Badimon L, Badimon JJ, Chesebro JH. The pathogenesis of coronary artery disease and the acute coronary syndromes. N Engl J Med 1992;326: 242-50, 310–18.

Hamming JJ, Hensen A, Loeliger EA. The value of long-term coumarin treatment in peripheral sclerosis: clinical trial. Thromb Haemost 1965;21:405. Abstract.

Herrick JB. Clinical features of sudden obstruction of the coronary arteries. JAMA 1912;59:2015.

Kretschmer GJ, Holzenbein T. The role of anticoagulation in infrainguinal bypass surgery. In: Yao JST, Pearce WH, eds. The Ischemic Extremity: Advances in Treatment. East Norwalk, Conn: Appleton & Lange; 1995:447–54.

Moloney BA. An analysis of the side-effects of ticlopidine. In: Hass JD, Easton JD, eds. Ticlopidine, Platelets and Vascular Disease. New York: Springer-Verlag; 1993:117–39.

Palareti G, Poggi M, Toricelli P, et al. Long-term effects of ticlopidine on fibrinogen and hemorheology in patients with peripheral arterial disease. Thromb Res 1988;52:621–29.

Schoop W, Levy H, Schoop B, Gaentch A. Experimentelle und klinische studien zu der sekundaren prävention der peripheren arteriosklerose. In: Bollinger A, Rhyner K, eds. Thrombozytenfunktionshemmer. Stuttgart: Georg Thieme Verlag; 1993: 49–58.

Steering Committee of the Physicians' Health Study Research Group. Final report on the aspirin component of the ongoing Physicians' Health Study. N Engl J Med 1989;321:129–35.

Stiegler H, Hess H, Mietaschk A, et al. Einfluss von ticlopidine auf die perfere obliterierende arteriopathie. Dtsch Med Wochenschr 1984;109:1240–43.

UK-TIA Study Group. The United Kingdom Transient Ischaemic Attack (UK-TIA) aspirin trial. Final results. J Neurol Neurosurg Psychiatry 1991;54:1044–54.

Lower Extremity Arterial Occlusive Disease in Women

Marie Gerhard-Herman, MD, MMSc
Instructor in Medicine
Harvard Medical School
Medical Director Vascular Laboratory
Cardiovascular Division, Brigham and Women's Hospital
Boston, Massachusetts

Avni Thakore, MS, BS
Harvard Medical School
Boston, Massachusetts

Objective: To review current knowledge of prevalence, risk factors, prognosis, and treatment of peripheral atherosclerotic disease in women.

Lower extremity atherosclerosis results in significant morbidity, particularly in elderly women, ranging from loss of mobility to amputation. Up to 25% of women from 55 to 75 years of age are affected. The incidence of intermittent claudication is smaller for premenopausal women than for age-matched men, but the gap decreases with increasing age. However, few data are available to expand our knowledge of the relation between gender and peripheral atherosclerotic disease (PAD). Estimates from census figures indicate that with increasing life expectancy and declining fertility rate, approximately 15% to 20% of Americans will be women over age 65 by the middle of the next century. The trend of an aging female population combined with increased rates of female cigarette smoking predict that women will represent the majority of patients with PAD in the next century. This article summarizes current knowledge of prevalence, risk factors, prognosis, and therapy for PAD in women.

PREVALENCE

Much of the data on prevalence of peripheral atherosclerotic disease (PAD) comes from studies of claudication. Intermittent claudication is often the first manifestation of lower extremity arterial occlusive disease, and is characterized by cramping discomfort in the large muscle groups while walking that is relieved with rest. If the arterial occlusive disease is in the femoral popliteal system it often results in calf pain, while aortoiliac disease often causes pain in the buttock, hip, and thigh. As stenosis in these arteries progresses, blood flow is further limited and pain begins to occur even at rest. The prevalence of intermittent claudication is 1.2% to 14.1% for women as compared with 2.2% to 14.4% for men, and increases with age in both sexes. In the Framingham Study, the biennial incidence rate of intermittent claudication was measured over a 20-year follow-up period (Kannel and McGee, 1985). It was 3.5% per 1000 for women and 7.1% per 1000 for men. The incidence in women lagged 10 years behind that in men, but this gap decreased with increasing age. In the Edinburgh Artery Study (Figure 1), prevalence of claudication increased with increasing age; by age 65 to 69, claudication is more prevalent in women (Fowkes et al, 1991).

Prevalence of lower extremity PAD as determined by noninvasive testing is greater, and likely to be more accurate, than when determined by questionnaire. Objective noninvasive tests to diagnose PAD include ankle-brachial index (ABI), segmental systolic pressure determination in the legs, and plethysmography to determine distal blood flow. Mild PAD is often evident only after exercise or with reactive hyperemia following ischemia. In a defined population in the United States, 275 women were evaluated for PAD by noninvasive testing to determine if ABI was <0.80. Lower extremity PAD was present in 3% of women under 60

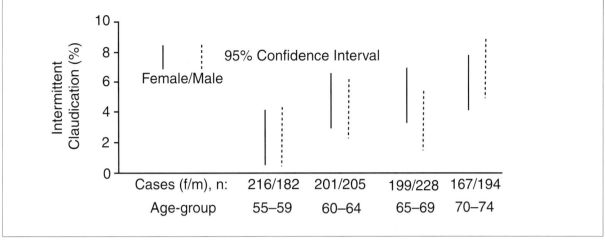

Figure 1. Prevalence of intermittent claudication by age and sex. The prevalence was the same in men and women and increased with age. (Adapted from Fowkes et al, 1991, with permission.)

and in 20% of women over 75 years of age. The ratio of male to female prevalence was 1.27 (Criqui et al, 1985). The definition of lower extremity PAD was more inclusive in the Edinburgh Artery Study, that is, ABI <0.90 or a reduction of >20% in ankle systolic pressure during reactive hyperemia. By this definition, 24.6% of those 55 to 74 years of age had lower extremity PAD, with men and women affected equally (Fowkes et al, 1991). Perhaps most importantly, the prevalence of PAD in elderly nursing home residents is quite high. In one screening program, 88% of a mostly female nursing home population had ABI <0.90. Only 5% of these patients had been previously diagnosed with PAD (Cammer Paris et al, 1988).

RISK FACTORS
Diabetes
Diabetes was a greater risk factor for intermittent claudication in women than in men in the Framingham Study. Women with impaired glucose tolerance had a 4-fold increase in risk compared with a 2.4-fold increase in men. In the presence of glycosuria, the risk of claudication rose 8.6-fold in women compared with 3.5-fold in men. There is greater morbidity from PAD in diabetics than in nondiabetics. Gangrene is up to 17 times more likely, and amputation occurs 5 times more often. While the incidence of PAD is 9 times greater in diabetics, the presence of diabetes does not necessarily imply increased progression of lower extremity PAD. Osmundson and colleagues (1990) looked at progression of lower extremity PAD in diabetic and nondiabetic women. They saw no significant change in postexercise ABI over 4 years. In comparing the patterns of infrainguinal PAD in diabetics and cigarette smokers, diabetics are more likely to present with gangrene and have

significantly more peroneal and posterior tibial disease (Menzoian et al, 1989). In contrast to the effect of diabetes, smokers appear to have less extensive occlusive disease in the large arteries of the calf.

Cigarette Smoking
The strong association between cigarette smoking and the incidence and progression of PAD is clearly demonstrated in many large epidemiologic studies. Despite the publicized health risks of smoking, the number of female smokers continues to increase. A distinct aortoiliac atherosclerotic syndrome has been reported in young females who are heavy smokers, hypoplastic aortoiliac syndrome (Jernigan et al, 1983). This syndrome was described in a series of 19 patients as "an entity peculiar to women," in which the distal aorta is narrowed to <14 mm in diameter and the iliac artery at the origin is <7 mm in diameter. The average age of claudication onset was 42 years. Morbidity associated with this syndrome was significant, with 75% having aortobifemoral bypass surgery because of disabling claudication and 20% requiring reoperation. The patients were all heavy smokers; the syndrome may be a variation of the pattern of PAD seen in most female smokers.

Large epidemiologic series show that women smokers present with more aortoiliac disease than nonsmokers and with lower extremity PAD 10 years earlier (Kannel and Shurtleff, 1973). Typical aortoiliac disease in a 57-year-old female smoker is seen in Figure 2, before and after stent placement. Of 75 consecutive women requiring vascular reconstruction for aortoiliac occlusive disease at the Dartmouth-Hitchcock Medical Center, 93% were smokers (Cronenwett et al, 1980). Of females <46 years of age seen at the Mayo Clinic for

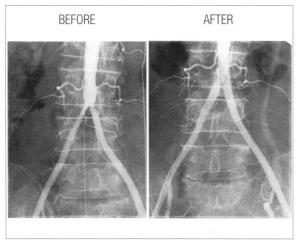

BEFORE   AFTER

Figure 2. Comparison of aortoiliac angiogram in a 57-year-old female smoker before and after stent placement.

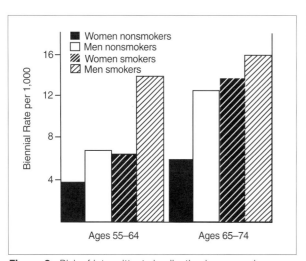

Figure 3. Risk of intermittent claudication in men and women by cigarette smoking status. Nonsmokers are represented by solid bars and smokers by hatched bars (data from 26-year follow-up of the Framingham Study). (Adapted from Kannel and McGee, 1985, with permission.)

peripheral angiography in preparation for revascularization, all were smokers (Holmes et al, 1979). Smoking increased risk of claudication much more dramatically in women than in men aged 65 to 74 in the Framingham Study (Figure 3). Both the Edinburgh Artery Study and a similar study in Oxford, United Kingdom, described an association between fibrinogen levels, smoking, and increased risk of intermittent claudication. In the Oxford study, the risk of developing claudication was 7 times greater in women who smoked than in those who had never smoked.

Smoking is also very influential in the progression of PAD. Jonason and Ringqvist (1986) studied progression of disease in nondiabetic females with intermittent claudication. The ABI of the affected leg was stable in nonsmokers over 5 years but decreased in smokers. Smoking status, initial ABI, number of stenoses, and duration of intermittent claudication were independent predictors of disease progression by multivariate analysis. Hughson and colleagues (1978) followed 60 patients (13 women) for up to 8 years after initial referral for intermittent claudication. The patients who reduced or stopped smoking after referral had a significantly improved prognosis compared with those with unchanged smoking habits.

Menopause

Menopausal status is clearly an important risk factor for cardiovascular disease, and there is evidence to suggest it is uniquely important in the development and progression of lower extremity PAD. As early as 1964, Friedman and colleagues had observed that in 12 consecutive women presenting with aortoiliac occlusions, 6 had undergone artificial (ie, surgical) menopause. Review of operative records for nondiabetic women undergoing lower extremity revascularization over 24 years demonstrated that atherosclerotic aortoiliac occlusion occurred twice as frequently among females in whom the onset of menopause was before age 43 (Weiss, 1972). Less-direct evidence also suggests that menopause is important in the development and progression of PAD. The incidence of claudication is smaller for women than for men at typically premenopausal ages, but begins to rise by the sixth decade until it is the same for men and women by the ninth decade. Premenopausal women, compared with men and postmenopausal women, have higher high-density lipoprotein cholesterol (HDL-C), lower low-density lipoprotein cholesterol (LDL-C), and higher estradiol levels. These differences are likely to contribute to their protection from atherosclerosis. Age, which correlates strongly with menopausal status, was the strongest clinical predictor of PAD in women in an analysis of risk factors in a defined population in the United States (Criqui et al, 1985).

Other Risk Factors

An association between initial cholesterol level and subsequent development of intermittent claudication or an ABI <0.9 was observed in longitudinal studies in Framingham and Denmark. Vitale and colleagues (1990) looked at lipoprotein profiles in men and women with extracoronary atherosclerosis. They found that elevated cholesterol levels were associated with angiographic evidence of lower extremity PAD in women but not in men. There is evidence to suggest that elderly women with elevated thyroid-stimulating hormone have increased risk of PAD, and this may also occur through elevation of cholesterol (Powell et al, 1987).

Hypertension may also increase the risk of lower extremity PAD. In the Framingham Study, elevated systolic blood pressure was an independent predictor of claudication. Diastolic pressure >85 mm Hg in women and >95 mm Hg in men was also a predictor of intermittent claudication. Elevated systolic and diastolic pressures have also been correlated with noninvasive evidence of PAD 10 years later. However, the association between hypertension and intermittent claudication has not been confirmed by all large epidemiologic trials. Novel risk factors for PAD continue to be described in men. For example, elevated levels of C-reactive protein at baseline predict risk of future development of intermittent claudication in men (Ridker et al, 1998). Whether this or other inflammatory markers will predict risk of future PAD in women is unknown.

PROGNOSIS

The presence of lower extremity PAD doubles the risk of mortality in both men and women, and there is a 5-fold increase in risk when lower extremity PAD is confirmed by noninvasive testing. In one 10-year longitudinal survey of 70- and 80-year-olds, women with intermittent claudication had greater total 10-year mortality than men (Agner, 1981). Female nursing home residents with an ABI <0.70 had greater morbidity and twice the mortality of women with less disease at 1-year follow-up (Cammer Paris, 1988).

TREATMENT

The majority of patients (70% to 80%) do not progress beyond stable intermittent claudication. Conservative therapy with risk-factor reduction, medical therapy, and exercise remains the management mainstay for stable intermittent claudication. Walking distance may increase 40% in female claudicants who stop smoking (Quick and Cotton, 1982). In 302 patients with intermittent claudication, none who stopped smoking developed rest pain (Jonason and Berstrom, 1987). Supervised exercise training for up to 6 months was studied in 47 women with intermittent claudication. Walking distance more than doubled from pretraining values. Smoking cessation can increase treadmill walking distance in a supervised program above the increment obtained with exercise alone. The keys to success in the walking program are active supervision, patient motivation, and instruction.

Lipid-Lowering Therapy

The risk of new or worsening intermittent claudication was decreased with lipid-lowering therapy in the Scandinavian Simvastatin Survival Study (4S) (Pedersen et al, 1998). In the Program on the Surgical Control of Hyperlipidemias (POSCH), effective lipid modification also decreased the onset of intermittent claudication (Buchwald et al, 1998). However, it is difficult to extrapolate these findings to women because there were very few in these trials. Further evidence of benefit from cholesterol lowering in PAD was demonstrated in a small regression study by Barndt and colleagues. They looked at 25 patients (6 women) with high cholesterol levels and PAD. There was regression of femoral atherosclerosis by angiography after 13 months of cholesterol-lowering therapy.

Estrogen Replacement Therapy

Hormone replacement therapy may have a role in the treatment of lower extremity PAD. Estrogen replacement raises HDL-C, lowers LDL-C and total cholesterol (Walsh et al, 1991), decreases lipoprotein(a) (Moliterno et al, 1995) and decreases homocysteine levels (van der Mooren et al, 1994). All these changes would be expected to decrease the likelihood of PAD development. In a double-blind, placebo-controlled crossover trial, improved arterial dilatation with reactive hyperemia was seen in postmenopausal women taking estradiol with and without micronized progesterone (Figure 4) (Gerhard et al, 1998). This observed improvement in endothelium-dependent vasodilation suggests that estradiol may improve bioavailability of nitric oxide, a potent antiatherogenic molecule. Postmenopausal women who have taken estrogen replace-

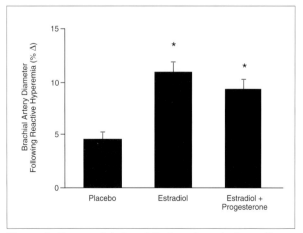

Figure 4. Flow-mediated, endothelium-dependent vasodilation of the brachial artery during placebo therapy, estradiol therapy, and estradiol-plus-progesterone therapy. Values are presented as mean ± standard error. *P <0.001 vs placebo.

ment therapy have improved cardiovascular outcomes, that is, fewer myocardial infarctions and strokes (Grady et al, 1992). The potential effect of estrogen therapy on atherosclerosis in the extremities is unknown; however, these data suggest estrogen replacement would be beneficial.

Revascularization

Invasive intervention may be necessary in women with rest pain, gangrene, ulcers, and possibly, disabling claudication. Surgical revascularization has been helpful in critical lower limb ischemia, resulting in dramatic reduction of amputation rates over the past 2 decades (Veith et al, 1990). Limb salvage rates were similar in men and women undergoing infrainguinal bypass at a single center (Magnant et al, 1993), despite the observation that graft patency rates were lower for all women, and survival was significantly lower for women with diabetes (Figure 5). Gender did not predict graft failure after infrainguinal saphenous vein bypass grafting in 2 other, smaller series of consecutive patients. Indications for surgery, the number of major complications, and reoperation rates were the same for men and women undergoing secondary infrainguinal bypass surgery (Belkin et al, 1995).

Peripheral percutaneous transluminal angioplasty (PTA) is another means of achieving revascularization in lower limb ischemia. Acceptable 5-year patency is achieved following PTA for iliac PAD; however, there are too few women in these series to be certain that the patency rates are the same in women and men (Tegt-meyer et al, 1991). Extent of dissection and free lumen area and diameter measured by intravascular ultrasound are predictive of 6-month patency after PTA (Gussenhoven et al, 1995). Since women have smaller vessels than men do, these findings suggest that patency after PTA is decreased in women. One concern has been that failed angioplasty could compromise

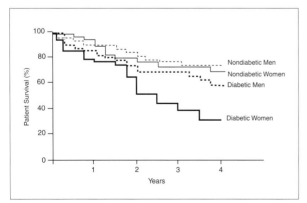

Figure 5. Life table analysis following infrainguinal bypass surgery. (From Magnant et al, 1993, with permission.)

Key Points

• The incidence of intermittent claudication is lower for women than for men until the seventh decade, when it becomes similar. In the aging population predicted for the next century, women could represent the majority of patients with PAD.

• The prevalence of PAD is higher when determined by objective testing than by questionnaire. Objective noninvasive tests to diagnose PAD include ankle-brachial index, segmental systolic pressure determination in the legs, and plethysmography to determine distal blood flow.

• Diabetes and cigarette smoking are risk factors of particular interest for PAD in women. Diabetes appears to be a greater risk factor for PAD in women than in men, and is often associated with tibial and peroneal atherosclerosis. Cigarette smoking is often associated with aortoiliac PAD. Hypoplastic aortoiliac syndrome is a distinct aortoiliac atherosclerotic syndrome associated with significant morbidity that has been described in young females who are heavy smokers.

• The incidence of intermittent claudication is less for women than for men at typically premenopausal ages, but begins to rise after menopause to approach the incidence in men. There is an association between early menopause and the diagnosis of aortoiliac PAD.

• Conservative therapy with reduction of risk factors remains the mainstay of management for stable intermittent claudication. Lipid-lowering therapy decreases intermittent claudication in men, but has not been adequately studied in women. Estrogen replacement therapy may improve the lipid profile and has direct vascular effects. These findings suggest that estrogen replacement could have a role in the treatment of lower extremity PAD.

• Men and nondiabetic women fare equally well following surgical revascularization for PAD. Aggressive revascularization for critical limb ischemia results in similar rates of limb salvage and functional outcome in men and women. There are data to suggest that women are offered peripheral revascularization at a lower rate.

subsequent surgical intervention. In 299 patients (135 women) with failed PTA, subsequent management was not compromised by the failed procedure. Taken together with the surgical series, these data support an interventional approach to save critically ischemic limbs.

In contrast to the above findings, a database study of all patients in Maryland undergoing invasive intervention for lower extremity PAD did not find an association between increasing use of revascularization and increasing limb salvage (Tunis et al, 1991). Instead, the study found that the use of PTA was associated with increased use of peripheral bypass operations and no change in the number of lower extremity amputations. One notable finding in this study was that a disproportionate number of the patients undergoing amputations were female, compared with those undergoing bypass surgery or PTA. These women may have presented with more advanced disease, or the pathogenesis may be somehow different in these patients. Traditionally, the results of infrainguinal bypass surgery have been evaluated as discussed above, in terms of limb salvage rates and graft patency. More recently, however, the focus has shifted to the functional status of patients before and after infrainguinal bypass operation. No significant difference has been detected between men and women for multiple functional outcome measures after revascularization.

BIBLIOGRAPHY

Agner E. Natural history of angina pectoris, possible intermittent claudication and intermittent claudication during the eighth decade. Acta Med Scand 1981;210:271–76.

Barndt R Jr, Blankenhorn DH, Crawford DW, Brooks SH. Regression and progression of early femoral atherosclerosis in treated hyperlipoproteinemic patients. Ann Intern Med 1977;86(2):139–46.

Belkin M, Conte MS, Donaldson MC, et al. Preferred strategies for secondary infrainguinal bypass: lessons learned from 300 consecutive reoperations. J Vasc Surg 1995;21:282–93.

Buchwald H, Varco RL, Boen J, et al. Effective lipid modification by partial ileal bypass reduced long-term coronary heart disease mortality and morbidity: five-year posttrial follow-up report from the POSCH. Arch Intern Med 1998;158:1253–61.

Cammer Paris BE, Libow LS, Halperin JL, Mulvihill MN. The prevalence and one year outcome of limb arterial obstructive disease in a nursing home population. J Am Geriatr Soc 1988;36:607–12.

Criqui MH, Fronek A, Barrett-Connor E, et al. The prevalence of peripheral arterial disease in a defined population. Circulation 1985;71:510–15.

Cronenwett JL, Davis JT, Gooch JB, Garrett HE. Aortoiliac occlusive disease in women. Surgery 1980;88:775–84.

Fowkes FGR, Housley E, Cawood EHH, et al. Edinburgh Artery Study: prevalence of asymptomatic and symptomatic peripheral arterial disease in the general population. Int J Epidemiol 1991;20:384–92.

Friedman SA, Holling HE, Roberts B. Etiologic factors in aortoiliac and femoropopliteal vascular disease. N Engl J Med 1964;271:1382–85.

Gerhard MD, Walsh BW, Tawakol A, et al. Estradiol therapy combined with progesterone and endothelium-dependent vasodilation in postmenopausal women. Circulation 1998;98:1158–63.

Grady D, Rubin SM, Petitti DB, et al. Hormone therapy to prevent disease and prolong life in postmenopausal women. Ann Intern Med 1992;117:1016–37.

Gussenhoven EJ, Van der Lugt A, Pasterkamp G, et al. Intravascular ultrasound predictors of outcome after peripheral balloon angioplasty. Eur J Vasc Endovasc Surg 1995;10:279–88.

Holmes DR, Burbank MK, Fulton RE, Bernatz PE. Arteriosclerosis obliterans in young women. Am J Med 1979;66:997–1000.

Hughson WG, Mann JI, Tibbs G, et al. Intermittent claudication: factors determining outcome. Br Med J 1978;1:1377–79.

Jernigan WR, Fallat ME, Hatfield DR. Hypoplastic aortoiliac syndrome: an entity peculiar to women. Surgery 1983;94:752–57.

Jonason T, Berstrom R. Cessation of smoking in patients with intermittent claudication. Acta Med Scand 1987;221:253–60.

Jonason T, Ringqvist I. Changes in peripheral blood pressures after five years of follow-up in non-operated patients with intermittent claudication. Acta Med Scand 1986;220:127–32.

Kannel WB, McGee DL. Update on some epidemiologic features of intermittent claudication: the Framingham Study. J Am Geriatr Soc 1985;33:13–18.

Kannel WB, Shurtleff D. The Framingham Study. Cigarettes and the development of intermittent claudication. Geriatrics 1973;28:61–68.

Magnant JG, Cronenwett JL, Walsh DB, et al. Surgical treatment of infrainguinal arterial occlusive disease in women. J Vasc Surg 1993;17:67–78.

Menzoian JO, LaMorte WW, Panisyn CC, et al. Symptomatology and anatomic patterns of peripheral vascular disease: differing impact of smoking and diabetes. Ann Vasc Surg 1989;3:224–28.

Moliterno DJ, Jokinen EV, Miserez AR, et al. No association between plasma lipoprotein(a) concentrations and the presence or absence of coronary atherosclerosis in African-Americans. Arterioscler Thromb Vasc Biol 1995;15:850–55.

Osmundson PJ, O'Fallon WM, Zimmerman BR, et al. Course of peripheral occlusive arterial disease in diabetes. Diabetes Care 1990;13:143–52.

Pedersen TR, Kjekshus J, Pyorala K, et al. Effect of simvastatin on ischemic signs and symptoms in the Scandinavian Simvastatin Survival Study (4S). Am J Cardiol 1998;81:333–38.

Powell J, Zadeh JA, Garter G, et al. Raised serum thyrotrophin in women with peripheral arterial disease. Br J Surg 1987;74:1139–41.

Quick CR, Cotton LT. The measured effect of stopping smoking on intermittent claudication. Br J Surg 1982;69(suppl):S24–S26.

Ridker PM, Cushman M, Stampfer MJ, et al. Plasma concentration of C-reactive protein and risk of developing peripheral vascular disease. Circulation 1998;97:425–28.

Tegtmeyer CJ, Hartwell GD, Selby JB, et al. Results and complications of angioplasty in aortoiliac disease. Circulation 1991;83:I-53–I-60.

Tunis SR, Bass EB, Steinberg EP. The use of angioplasty, bypass surgery, and amputation in the management of peripheral vascular disease. N Engl J Med 1991;325:556–62.

van der Mooren MJ, Wouters MG, Blom HJ, et al. Hormone replacement therapy may reduce high serum homocysteine in postmenopausal women. Eur J Clin Invest 1994;25:333–36.

Veith FJ, Gupta SK, Wengerter KR, et al. Changing arteriosclerotic disease patterns and management strategies in lower-limb-threatening ischemia. Ann Surg 1990;212:402–13.

Vitale E, Zuliani G, Baroni L, et al. Lipoprotein abnormalities in patients with extra-coronary atherosclerosis. Atherosclerosis 1990;81:95–102.

Walsh BW, Schiff I, Rosner R, et al. Effects of postmenopausal estrogen replacement on the concentrations and metabolism of plasma proteins. N Engl J Med 1991;325:1196–1204.

Weiss NS. Premature menopause and aortoiliac occlusive disease. J Chronic Dis 1972;25:133–38.

The American Journal of Medicine®

Jointly sponsored by
The Excerpta Medica Office of Continuing Medical Education, the Society for Vascular Medicine and Biology, and the Society of General Internal Medicine

CONTINUING EDUCATION SERIES

AN OFFICE-BASED APPROACH TO THE DIAGNOSIS AND TREATMENT OF PERIPHERAL ARTERIAL DISEASE

PART III: Severe PAD: Limb Salvage and Revascularization Failure

SERIES EDITOR
ALAN T. HIRSCH, MD
GUEST EDITOR
J. MICHAEL BACHARACH, MD, MPH

Society for Vascular Medicine and Biology

SVMB

SGIM Society of General Internal Medicine

Dear Colleague:

We become primary care physicians in order to take global responsibility for our patients' well-being, to become a tangible partner with our patients in maintaining their functional independence, and to help our patients survive ischemic cardiovascular events and escape a premature death. Peripheral arterial disease (PAD) threatens this functional independence and clearly predicts a premature mortality, and so we are forced to ask ourselves, "Have we served as an ideal clinical partner?" The need for a devoted partnership of primary care physicians and the PAD patient is most critical when PAD is severe. Severe or "critical" limb ischemia results when atherosclerotic disease progression has not been previously impeded and limb blood flow is so reduced that basic metabolic functions (such as preservation of skin integrity) cannot be met. This scenario is all too common, as current standards of general health care do not include efforts to identify PAD in its earlier stages, and pharmacologic and lifestyle interventions to retard atherosclerosis do not provide complete protection.

Progressive limb arterial atherosclerosis and/or thrombosis may so impede lower extremity blood flow that ischemic pain occurs at rest, skin ulceration may be provoked by minor trauma, and nonhealing wounds may progress to frank gangrene. The great majority of nontraumatic amputations in our country result from severe PAD.

This monograph, the third in the PAD Primary Care Series, was created to offer all primary care practitioners an office-based primer on current standards of care for patients with severe PAD. Although atherosclerosis preventive efforts will undoubtedly be enhanced in the decade ahead, the aging of our communities can be predicted to lead to an increased incidence of patients with critical limb ischemia. Recognition of the ischemic etiology of these symptoms and signs, which are reviewed in this monograph, is required if care is to be delivered. Also noted is the central importance of the vascular laboratory to permit the treating physician to obtain objective data to confirm the diagnosis of PAD to localize causal arterial stenoses, and to formulate an initial therapeutic plan. The rest of the monograph focuses on the development of an individualized treatment approach. Patients with critical limb ischemia may benefit from thrombolytic, surgical, or percutaneous revascularization techniques, or a combination of these techniques. The noninvasive vascular laboratory and both traditional (contrast angiography) and newer imaging (magnetic resonance angiography) modalities can provide physician and patient with their therapeutic options for revascularization.

As sponsors of the PAD Primary Care Series, the Society for Vascular Medicine and Biology and the Society for General Internal Medicine are united in the mission to improve vascular care in this country. Please consider joining or supporting your vascular and general medical professional societies so we can work together to accomplish our public health goals.

Sincerely,

Alan T. Hirsch, MD
President, Society for Vascular Medicine and Biology
On behalf of the Education Committee, Officers, and Trustees
Associate Professor of Medicine
Vascular Medicine Program
Minnesota Vascular Diseases Center
University of Minnesota Medical School
Minneapolis, Minnesota

Introduction

J. Michael Bacharach, MD, MPH
Section Head, Vascular Medicine and Intervention
North Central Heart and Vascular Institute
Sioux Falls, South Dakota

Peripheral arterial disease (PAD) may manifest with varying degrees of severity, reflecting the underlying involvement of systemic arteriosclerotic disease. PAD may be asymptomatic altogether or involve pain only during exercise (intermittent claudication). These degrees of symptomaticity reflect mild-to-moderate disease severity, already covered in detail in previous installments of this Continuing Medical Education series on diagnosis and treatment of PAD.

With progression of PAD, symptoms become more persistent. Severe PAD may progress to critical limb ischemia, where symptoms are unremitting and the patient can no longer function. The degree of ischemia is such that amputation is a major risk. Moreover, considering that severity of PAD may well reflect severity of systemic disease, the patient with critical limb ischemia is also at increased risk of cardio- and cerebrovascular events.

This monograph, Severe PAD: Limb Salvage and Revascularization Failure—the third in the PAD series—discusses the pathophysiology, diagnosis, and therapeutic options in critical limb ischemia. The goal is limb salvage; but where this is no longer possible, the intervention of last resort—amputation—must be given its due, and siting parameters are discussed.

In the lead article, Michael R. Jaff, DO, FACP, FACC, presents a review of the context of chronic critical limb ischemia. He notes the lack of a formal definition, either clinically (because such a definition would be too subjective) or pathophysiologically (because strict hydrodynamic criteria, using objective tests, are relatively unfamiliar at the primary care level). Possibly, a combination of the two diagnostic approaches will prevail. After describing several proposed combination methodologies, the author details the clinical signs and symptoms of critical limb ischemia encountered at presentation (including the special case of the diabetic patient). Finally, he reviews the available noninvasive vascular tests in the diagnostic algorithm. These include ankle-brachial index, toe systolic blood pressure, segmental pressures and pulse-volume recordings, and duplex ultrasonography. Contrast arteriography—the standard imaging modality—is then described and the potential benefits of magnetic resonance imaging are discussed.

Once the diagnosis of critical limb ischemia has been established, approaches to limb salvage therapy must be considered. In the second article, I discuss the variables that underlie progression of PAD from severe to critical ischemia, including degree and extent of arterial occlusion and presence of both systemic and local factors that contribute to progression of disease (eg, comorbidity or modifiable risk factors such as smoking). Again, diabetic patients are given special mention—they have a sevenfold higher rate of lower extremity amputation than those without diabetes.

When a stage of critical limb ischemia is reached, noninvasive approaches such as pharmacotherapy are no longer adequate; arterial reconstruction becomes necessary. However, before proceeding to surgical or endovascular reperfusion, it is necessary to have a clear picture of the circulatory anatomy of the affected limb.

The article then compares surgical (ie, bypass grafting) with endovascular (ie, balloon angioplasty or stenting) revascularization: each approach has its pros and cons, depending on individual circumstances. Lastly, the role of thrombolytic therapy is discussed, both as primary therapy and as adjunctive therapy. Although research is ongoing, findings so far show great promise.

Despite the substantial progress in treatment of severe PAD, amputation remains an important option where revascularization has failed or is deemed unlikely to succeed. In the final article, I discuss this last resort in critical limb ischemia. Perhaps the most important decision is the amputation site. Although a distal site has greater rehabilitation potential, it exposes the patient to increased risk of failure to heal because of inadequate regional perfusion. Conversely, a proximal site has poor rehabilitation potential but there is less likelihood of reoperation.

Reliance on clinical assessment alone may lead to suboptimal choice of amputation site, ending in failure. Thus, additional evaluation by noninvasive techniques may be very helpful. ∎

Severe Peripheral Arterial Disease and Critical Limb Ischemia: Incidence, Pathophysiology, Presentation, Methods of Diagnosis

Michael R. Jaff, DO, FACP, FACC
Director of Vascular Medicine and Vascular Laboratory
Integrated Cardiovascular Therapeutics
Woodbury, New York

Objective: To describe the incidence, historical clues, physical examination findings, and methods of diagnosis in patients with severe peripheral arterial disease and critical limb ischemia.

Patients with lower extremity peripheral arterial disease (PAD) may progress to severe, limb-threatening ischemia. Ischemic rest pain, nonhealing ulcerations, and gangrene are all harbingers of poor outcomes. These patients are at high risk of limb loss. Many patients who require amputation due to severe PAD do not recover their preprocedure level of activity. In addition, PAD severe enough to require amputation carries a significant risk of comorbid cardiovascular and cerebrovascular events such as myocardial infarction and stroke. Prompt detection and evaluation of severe limb ischemia followed by aggressive revascularization are required for limb salvage and preservation of overall health.

Lower extremity peripheral arterial disease (PAD) may be asymptomatic, cause limb pain with exercise (intermittent claudication), or progress to a severe level of ischemia that may result in limb loss. Previous monographs in this series have addressed the prevalence, clinical manifestations, and diagnostic options for mild and moderate PAD. This monograph reviews the risks and clinical scenarios that result from severe PAD, and compares therapeutic alternatives for revascularization. This article discusses the pathophysiology, signs and symptoms, and methods of diagnosis of severe PAD.

In contrast to intermittent claudication, which (by definition) occurs with exercise only, critical limb ischemia (CLI) is a constant and relentless problem. Patients with CLI are unable to function, unable to sleep, and are at increased risk of major limb amputation and cardiovascular and cerebrovascular events.

There are two types of CLI. Acute limb ischemia, characterized by "the 5 P's" of pain, pallor, pulselessness, paresthesia, and paralysis, is beyond the scope of this article. Chronic CLI is the more common form and is reviewed here in detail.

A formal, uniformly accepted definition of CLI does not exist. A clinical definition alone is too subjective and cannot be the sole method of describing CLI. The finding of ischemic rest pain, ischemic ulcerations, or gangrene may be misinterpreted as alternative diagnoses. The use of strict hemodynamic criteria alone may be difficult for all physicians to adopt, especially if familiarity with these objective tests is poor.

Many authors have proposed different defining criteria, but most support the use of a combination of clinical and hemodynamic parameters. However, these combined parameters can be quite cumbersome and confusing. One such combination has been proposed by Carter (1997): patients with ischemic rest pain, ulcers, or gangrene; ankle systolic pressure of ≤50 mm Hg *or* toe systolic pressure ≤30 mm Hg; and low-amplitude toe or foot pulse wave, or transcutaneous Po_2 ≤10 mm Hg in the supine position and <40 mm Hg while sitting, measured on the forefoot with the electrode set at 44°C. The European Working Group on Critical Leg Ischemia (1991) definition and the Rutherford–Becker classification (Rutherford et al, 1997) are described in Tables I and II and serve as more commonly accepted definitions of this syndrome.

INCIDENCE AND PATHOPHYSIOLOGY OF CRITICAL LIMB ISCHEMIA

The exact incidence of chronic CLI is difficult to determine. It is generally accepted that 15% of patients over 50 years of age have symptomatic PAD, as manifested by intermittent claudication. Estimates are that 15% to 20% of patients with intermittent claudication will deteriorate to CLI. Therefore, approximately 1% or 20 million American adults over the age of 50 may eventually develop CLI (Weitz et al, 1996).

CLI is most commonly due to the pathophysiology of PAD, although thromboangiitis obliterans (Buerger's disease), vasculitis of small vessels, ergotamine abuse, and other unusual conditions can result in ischemic disease of the legs and feet. However, CLI develops when arterial stenoses or occlusions cause severe impairment of blood flow to the point where basal requirements for tissue oxygenation cannot be met. This occurs despite development of collateral vessel formation and poststenotic arteriolar vasodilatation.

Factors which lead to progressive limb ischemia

Table I. Criteria for Definition of Critical Leg Ischemia According to the European Working Group on Critical Leg Ischemia

- Persistent ischemic rest pain requiring analgesia for >2 weeks
  and
- Ankle systolic pressure ≤50 mm Hg and/or toe systolic pressure ≤30 mm Hg
  or
- Ulceration or gangrene of the foot or toes
  and
- Ankle systolic pressure ≤50 mm Hg and/or toe systolic pressure ≤30 mm Hg

Reprinted with permission from the European Working Group on Critical Leg Ischemia. Circulation 1991;84(suppl IV):IV-1–IV-26.

Table II. Criteria for Definition of Critical Limb Ischemia According to the Rutherford–Becker Classification

Grade	Category	Clinical Description	Objective Criteria
0	0	Asymptomatic—no hemodynamically significant occlusive disease	Normal treadmill* or reactive hyperemia test
	1	Mild claudication	Completes treadmill exercise; AP after exercise >50 mm Hg but ≥20 mm Hg lower than resting value
I	2	Moderate claudication	Between Categories 1 and 3
	3	Severe claudication	Cannot complete standard treadmill exercise **and** AP after exercise <50 mm Hg
II	4	Ischemic rest pain	Resting AP, 40 mm Hg, flat or barely pulsatile ankle or metatarsal PVR; TP <30 mm Hg
III	5	Minor tissue loss—nonhealing ulcer; focal gangrene with diffuse pedal ischemia	Resting AP <60 mm Hg, ankle or metatarsal PVR flat or barely pulsatile; TP <40 mm Hg
	6	Major tissue loss—extending transmetatarsally; functional foot no longer salvageable	Same as Category 5

AP = ankle pressure; PVR = pulse-volume recording; TP = toe pressure.
* Treadmill protocol: 2 miles per hour, 12% constant grade. Reprinted with permission from Rutherford RB, et al. J Vasc Surg 1997;26:517–38.

include impaired vasomotion, hemorheology, thrombosis and fibrinolysis, and altered platelet function. The proposed mechanisms by which CLI occurs include collapse of precapillary arterioles, vasospasm, microthrombosis, interstitial edema, platelet aggregation, leukocyte activation and adhesion, and local activation of the immune system (European Working Group on Critical Leg Ischemia, 1991).

Diabetes mellitus is well known to cause a more anatomically distal, diffuse, and severe presentation of critical limb ischemia (Palumbo et al, 1991). Alterations in sensation of the feet may occur in patients with advanced PAD (Matsen et al, 1986). However, the combination of peripheral neuropathy and diabetes increases the risk of serious foot lesions which, if not addressed promptly, may lead to gangrene. Patients with diabetes, PAD, and peripheral neuropathy may not sense foreign objects in footwear, alteration in temperature, or even the development of blisters, ingrown toenails, or intertriginous skin breakdown. All of these factors are precursors to skin ulceration, infection, gangrene, and ultimate limb loss.

CLINICAL MANIFESTATIONS

Clinical symptoms and signs are of importance when the diagnosis of CLI is in question. Ischemic rest pain is classically described as an ache, pain, numbness, or squeezing sensation, often in the arch of the foot and toes, that occurs when the leg is elevated. The most uncomfortable time for the patient with CLI is during the evening, while resting. Patients with ischemic rest pain frequently awaken from sleep. Relief of rest pain occurs when the leg is placed in a dependent position. A historical point often confusing to physicians with limited experience in caring for patients with CLI is that of improvement in rest pain with ambulation. Patients often note relief of ischemic rest pain when they begin walking. This is a result of improved arteriolar flow due to gravitational effects.

Ischemic ulcers have a characteristic appearance: they appear distally, at the ends of the toes and over bony prominences; they are dry and devitalized; there is no sign of vascularity; and the base is pale, often gray or black. There may be a densely adherent fibrinous exudate over the ulcer. A hallmark of ischemic ulcers is the intense pain associated with the ulcer. Ischemic ulcers can appear in unusual locations, suggesting an alternative etiology; for example, an ischemic-appearing ulcer on the thigh or calf might suggest etiologies such as those listed in Table III. Findings such as delayed capillary refill time, abnormal foot color, atrophic skin over the foot, and lack of foot hair are generally not helpful in determining the presence and severity of CLI

Table III. Causes of Ischemic Ulcers in Atypical Locations

- Arteriosclerosis obliterans and superimposed trauma
- Systemic vasculitis
- Atheroemboli (blue-toe syndrome)
- Insect bite (classically, brown recluse spider)

(McGee and Boyko, 1998).

Gangrene, or complete lack of viable tissue, is the end stage of CLI. This often appears as a gray or black ulcer base, dry, and very painful. If secondary infection develops, gangrene can become "wet" and develop a malodorous, purulent drainage, along with increased erythema and pain. This latter scenario requires prompt hospitalization and aggressive treatment, including parenteral antimicrobial therapy, debridement of devitalized tissue, and revascularization.

Palpation of peripheral pulses is of great importance in the evaluation of patients with suspected CLI. It is unusual to palpate the dorsalis pedis or posterior tibial arteries in patients with severe limb ischemia. In those patients with lifestyle-limiting intermittent claudication, however, pedal pulses at rest may be palpable in the face of moderate aortoiliac occlusive disease. The bedside diagnostic test of greatest accuracy is the elevation/dependency test, whereby the limb is elevated for 30 to 60 seconds. In an ischemic limb, the foot will become pallorous. With dependency, the foot develops an intense, ruborous, red/purple color. This is strongly suggestive of advanced PAD.

The cornerstone of management of patients with chronic CLI is prompt referral. Delay in diagnosis may lead to underutilization of aggressive revascularization and often leads to increased risk of limb loss and lack of functional mobility. In patients with diabetes mellitus, it is recommended that annual assessment be performed for the presence of symptoms of lifestyle-limiting intermittent claudication or progressive deterioration in pain-free walking distance, along with palpation of leg pulses. If these symptoms are present, if pulses are absent, or if signs of CLI are discovered, prompt referral to a vascular center should be considered (Orchard and Strandness, 1993).

METHODS OF DIAGNOSIS

Noninvasive vascular testing is the next step in the diagnostic algorithm for CLI. The initial test, which can be performed at the bedside of patients, is the ankle-brachial index (ABI) (reviewed by Jeffrey W. Olin in an earlier monograph within this series). A resting ABI <0.4 strongly suggests the likelihood of CLI. In patients with this level of ABI, a toe systolic blood pressure determination should be performed by a qualified vascular laboratory. Many patients, especially those with medial vessel wall calcification, may have an artificially elevated ABI, which is not a valid reflection of the level of PAD. In one series of patients with insulin-dependent diabetes mellitus, 47% of patients demonstrated vessel calcification at the level of the metatarsus (Maser et al, 1991).

A toe systolic blood pressure determination has been suggested to accurately predict the likelihood of wound healing. In one series, patients with foot ulcers, diabetes mellitus, and a toe systolic blood pressure <20 mm Hg demonstrated a spontaneous healing rate of only 29%. In this same series, similar patients with a toe systolic blood pressure of ≥30 mm Hg demonstrated a 92% wound healing rate (Holstein, 1984). In patients with intermittent claudication, diminished toe systolic blood pressure also portends a poor prognosis. In a series of 56 men with stable intermittent claudication, all had toe systolic blood pressures of ≤40 mm Hg and were followed for a mean of 31 months. Thirty-four percent developed ulceration, rest pain, or gangrene. Of those patients who deteriorated, 26% required limb amputation. Twenty-four percent of the patients who had stable intermittent claudication actually demonstrated a rise in toe systolic blood pressures >40 mm Hg. Of no surprise, diabetes predicted a higher probability of clinical deterioration (Bowers et al, 1993).

The addition of segmental pressures and pulse-volume recordings can aid in localization of PAD. Progressive limb ischemia causes characteristic changes in the plethysmographic waveform of the pulse-volume recording, and can predict severity of limb ischemia (Jaff and Dorros, 1998). Arterial duplex ultrasonography is an accurate and reproducible method of determining the exact location and severity of arterial stenoses and occlusions, with high sensitivity and specificity (Whelan et al, 1992).

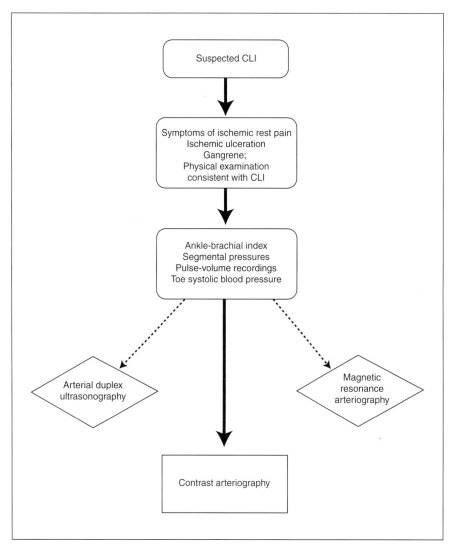

Figure. Algorithm for diagnosis of chronic critical limb ischemia (CLI).

Magnetic resonance arteriography (MRA) has recently been studied as a method of preoperative assessment of patients with lower extremity PAD. Potential advantages are obvious, and include minimally invasive testing (peripheral intravenous cannula) and lack of iodinated contrast. Initial interest in MRA of lower extremity arteries was aimed at defining angiographically occult runoff vessels, identifying 22% of the runoff vessels not visualized by conventional contrast arteriography (Owen et al, 1992). However, several investigators have suggested that lower extremity arterial revascularization can be effectively performed with MRA as the sole preoperative imaging modality (Carpenter et al, 1994). These bypass grafts demonstrate comparable success and durability compared with those in which contrast arteriography was used to detect the target vessel for bypass (Carpenter et al, 1996).

However, the standard preoperative imaging modality is contrast arteriography, often performed from the retrograde femoral or antegrade brachial/axillary approach. Standard contrast arteriography must visualize the abdominal aorta (including the renal arteries) and iliac arteries, infrainguinal vessels (with attention to the status of the profunda femoris artery, an important "natural" collateral in the patient with CLI), and infrapopliteal vessels. An examination is not complete without a foot angiogram. Several different angiographic techniques are available to image smaller, heavily diseased arteries (Kozak et al, 1988).

Unless a true vascular emergency exists, consideration should be given to (at least) noninvasive evaluation of the coronary arteries prior to revascularization. If symptoms of a carotid stenosis are discovered or a carotid bruit is heard, carotid duplex ultrasonography should also be performed.

An algorithm for the diagnosis of chronic CLI is found in the Figure. Chronic CLI represents the end of the spectrum of PAD in which limb loss is likely if prompt attention and effective revascularization are not provided to the patient. Recognition of risk factors, symptoms and signs, as well as an appreciation for the natural history of CLI are crucial to successful outcomes. A rapid, yet thorough and accurate diagnostic evaluation must be performed prior to revascularization. Methods of revascularization will be addressed in forthcoming articles. ■

Key Points

• CLI represents the severe form of lower extremity PAD, which, if unrecognized and untreated, may lead to limb amputation.

• Approximately 20 million Americans suffer from CLI annually.

• Prompt diagnosis is critical to prevent limb loss.

• Ischemic rest pain is the classic symptom, described as an ache or pain in the arch of the foot and/or toes that worsens with elevation and improves with dependency.

• Ischemic ulcerations and gangrene are painful, dry, devitalized lesions commonly found on distal aspects of the feet and toes and over bony prominences. These are harbingers of progressive necrosis.

• Noninvasive testing for ABIs, toe systolic blood pressures, segmental limb pressures, and pulse-volume recordings should be performed in all nonemergent patients with CLI.

• Although color arterial duplex ultrasonography and MRA offer promise as noninvasive preoperative tests for patients with CLI, standard contrast arteriography is the cornerstone for preoperative assessment prior to revascularization.

BIBLIOGRAPHY

Bowers BL, Valentine RJ, Myers SI, et al. The natural history of patients with claudication with toe pressures of 40 mm Hg or less. J Vasc Surg 1993;18: 506–11.

Carpenter JP, Baum RA, Holland GA, Barker CF. Peripheral vascular surgery with magnetic resonance angiography as the sole preoperative imaging modality. J Vasc Surg 1994;20:861–71.

Carpenter JP, Golden MA, Barker CF, et al. The fate of bypass grafts to angiographically occult runoff vessels detected by magnetic resonance angiography. J Vasc Surg 1996;23:483–9.

Carter SA. The challenge and importance of defining critical limb ischemia. Vasc Med 1997;2:126–31.

European Working Group on Critical Leg Ischemia. Second European Consensus Document on Chronic Critical Leg Ischemia. Circulation 1991;84(suppl IV):IV-1–IV-26.

Holstein P. The distal blood pressure predicts healing of amputations on the feet. Acta Orthop Scand 1984;55:227–33.

Jaff MR, Dorros G. The vascular laboratory: a critical

component required for successful management of peripheral arterial occlusive disease. J Endovasc Surg 1998;5:146–58.

Kozak BE, Bedell JE, Rosch J. Small vessel leg angiography for distal vessel bypass grafts. J Vasc Surg 1988;8:711–5.

Maser RE, Wolfson SK, Ellis D, et al. Cardiovascular disease and arterial calcification in insulin-dependent diabetes mellitus: interrelations and risk factor profiles. Pittsburgh Epidemiology of Diabetes Complications Study–V. Arterioscler Thromb Vasc Biol 1991;11:958–65.

Matsen FA, Craig RW, Robertson CL, et al. Factors relating to the sensory acuity of limbs with peripheral vascular insufficiency. Surgery 1986;99:45–60.

McGee SR, Boyko EJ. Physical examination and chronic lower-extremity ischemia. Arch Intern Med 1998;158:1357–64.

Orchard TJ, Strandness DE. Assessment of peripheral vascular disease in diabetes. Report and recommendations of an International Workshop sponsored by the American Diabetes Association and the American Heart Association. Circulation 1993;88:819–28.

Owen RS, Carpenter JP, Baum RA, et al. Magnetic resonance imaging of angiographically occult runoff vessels in peripheral arterial occlusive disease. N Engl J Med 1992;326:1577–81.

Palumbo PJ, O'Fallon M, Osmundson PJ, et al. Progression of peripheral occlusive arterial disease in diabetes mellitus. Arch Intern Med 1991;151:717–21.

Rutherford RB, Baker JD, Ernst C, et al. Recommended standards for reports dealing with lower extremity ischemia. Revised version. J Vasc Surg 1997;26:517–38.

Weitz JI, Byrne J, Clagett GP, et al. Diagnosis and treatment of chronic arterial insufficiency of the lower extremities: a critical review. Circulation 1996;94:3026–49.

Whelan JF, Barry MH, Moir JD. Color flow Doppler ultrasonography: comparison with peripheral arteriography for the investigation of peripheral vascular disease. J Clin Ultrasound 1992;20:369–74.

Severe Occlusive Peripheral Arterial Disease and Critical Limb Ischemia. Part I. Clinical Approach and Therapeutic Options for Revascularization

J. Michael Bacharach, MD, MPH
Section Head, Vascular Medicine and Intervention
North Central Heart and Vascular Institute
Sioux Falls, South Dakota

Objective: To describe the many complex factors that influence progression of severe PAD and choice of therapeutic options.

The progression of occlusive peripheral arterial disease (PAD) from functional arterial insufficiency to severe limb ischemia and ultimately critical limb ischemia is complex and influenced by many variables. These variables include the extent and location of arterial occlusive disease and the presence of systemic and local factors that can contribute to impaired healing or that may promote an accelerated progression of the atherosclerotic process. Therapy, therefore, needs to address not only revascularization but must also identify associated diseases that influence the progression of atherosclerosis. The presence and severity of such associated comorbidities often influence the course of disease and ultimately the reconstruction options. The options that currently exist for arterial reconstruction include both surgical and endovascular techniques. Despite the availability of a range of techniques, the optimal revascularization procedure is not known. Revascularization options need to be individualized and depend on the extent of occlusive disease and associated comorbidities that may influence the risk–benefit profile.

By the time a PAD patient has progressed to critical ischemia there is typically no functional reserve. In this setting, even a small trauma or injury can result in limb loss. Because of the natural history of the disease in patients with critical limb ischemia, the prognosis is, at best, dismal. These patients have high rates of functional disability, limb loss, and premature cardiovascular mortality. Criqui et al (1992) nicely demonstrated the relation between survival and PAD severity: In subjects with severe and symptomatic PAD, only 25% survived 10 years.

FACTORS THAT INFLUENCE RISK OF LIMB LOSS AND PROGRESSION TO CRITICAL LIMB ISCHEMIA

The increased risk of progression of atherosclerotic occlusive disease to limb-threatening ischemia and amputation is multifactorial. The extent and location of disease is an important consideration in treatment. Typically, disease that is more diffuse and distal makes arterial reconstruction much more difficult, often resulting in incomplete revascularization or revascularization failure. Systemic considerations include cardiopulmonary status, overall nutritional status, and cardiovascular risk factors that influence the progression of disease, such as smoking or the presence of diabetes mellitus.

The influence of diabetes on critical limb ischemia and limb loss requires special mention. Diabetic patients have a sevenfold higher rate of lower extremity amputation than those without diabetes (Jonason and Ringquist, 1985). The increased risk of amputation in the diabetic population is multifactorial. Typically, diabetic patients have more diffuse and distal atherosclerotic disease that makes revascularization more difficult. There is increased risk of local trauma related to peripheral sensory neuropathy that may result in tissue damage, or local factors that impair wound healing. Additionally, impaired immunologic response to infection often sets the stage for premature limb loss.

Of the modifiable risk factors, smoking is the most significant independent risk factor for the development of progressive PAD and is associated with either disabling claudication or limb-threatening ischemia (Taylor and Porter, 1995). Additionally, continued smoking influences lower extremity vascular reconstruction resulting in lowered patency (Ameli et al, 1989).

THERAPEUTIC OPTIONS

By the time critical limb ischemia is reached, nonsurgical interventions such as exercise, risk-factor modification, and pharmacologic therapy are inadequate to deal with the problem. (Nevertheless, they remain important management components to help prevent progression of disease and to prevent the cardio- and cerebrovascular complications such as myocardial infarction, stroke, and death that are so frequently associated with PAD.) Progression to critical limb ischemia thus constitutes a definite indication to pursue arterial reconstruction, either surgically or endovascularly.

Since the spectrum of symptoms and severity depends on the extent of occlusive PAD present and the available collateral circulation, delineating the anatomy is an important principle in selecting revascularization options. The "gold standard" for delineating anatomy has been detailed digital subtraction contrast arteriography. This allows for determination of extent and location of the arterial occlusive disease. Newer noninvasive methods, such as magnetic resonance angiography, are evolving and may well supplant routine digital subtraction arteriography in the future.

Once the arterial anatomy is delineated, and if disease is sufficiently localized, the practitioner has a choice between endovascular and surgical revascularization. The choice is dependent on numerous variables including the location and extent of arterial occlusive disease, available collateral circulation, comorbidities, and surgical risk.

SURGICAL REVASCULARIZATION FOR CRITICAL LIMB ISCHEMIA

Currently in the United States, it is estimated that there are over 100,000 bypass operations performed per year and 70,000 foot or lower limb amputations. While there is no one optimal surgical revascularization procedure, there currently exist a variety of techniques that allow for durable reconstruction and limb salvage. Ideal anatomic conditions for successful surgical reconstruction include unobstructed inflow and patent distal runoff. The influence of distal runoff cannot be underestimated. This runoff influences both early and long-term patency.

There exists extensive literature on the surgical treatment of lower extremity ischemia. The success of surgical interventions has been evaluated from the standpoints of operative morbidity and mortality as well as patency of the surgical repair. To adequately assess surgical intervention one needs to consider the surgical site, such as aortoiliac or infrainguinal bypass; type of bypass conduit material, autogenous or prosthetic; and site of distal anastomosis and distal runoff. The specific procedures that have been utilized include anatomic and extra-anatomic bypass, as well as endarterectomy. Despite wide variability in the types of surgical procedures and individual characteristics that can influence success, there are some basic issues regarding safety and efficacy of surgical treatment for limb-threatening ischemia. Several surgical series have documented the ability of surgical revascularization to provide durable salvage of unselected limbs in 85% to 89% of cases (Taylor et al, 1991). Important basic approaches that have allowed surgeons to achieve these results include detailed arteriography to recognize inflow and outflow problems, use of autogenous conduits for infrainguinal bypass, and continued surveillance following reconstruction. McLafferty et al (1995) demonstrated progression of lower extremity atherosclerosis after revascularization and its frequent occurrence. After a mean follow-up interval of 4.8 years, 53% of 151 patients evaluated had progressive lower extremity atherosclerosis on angiography or duplex examination. Reoperation for recurrent lesions was necessary in 10% to 15% of patients during follow-up.

PREVENTING GRAFT FAILURE

Despite initial surgical success, lower extremity vascular grafts eventually fail for a variety of reasons. In high-risk, limb-salvage settings, associated factors such as poor outflow, marginal vein graft, or use of prosthetic material result in high failure rates. The exact role and benefit of adjuvant pharmacotherapy remains unclear. Antiplatelet agents (eg, aspirin, ticlopidine, and clopidogrel) and anticoagulants, such as warfarin, are useful in the setting of prosthetic conduits that may fail due to spontaneous thrombosis. To date, there is no effective way to inhibit vein graft or anastomotic neointimal hyperplasia (Kraiss and Johansen, 1995).

Perhaps the most significant and long-term influence on lower extremity graft survival is atherosclerosis risk-factor reduction. Interventions specifically aimed at arresting the progression of atherosclerosis, such as treatment of hyperlipidemia and hypertension or through smoking cessation, need to be aggressively pursued in patients with lower extremity grafts, both autogenous and prosthetic (Kraiss and Johansen, 1995).

AUTOGENOUS VERSUS PROSTHETIC BYPASS GRAFTING

A full discussion of choice of surgical procedure and type of conduit used is beyond the scope of this article. It is, however, important to recognize that these choices, particularly of the type of conduit, have a significant influence on long-term durability and patency (Table).

It is currently well accepted, based on data from multiple centers, that autogenous greater saphenous vein grafts significantly improve patency over prosthetic grafts. At 5 years, the primary patency rate for autogenous vein grafts to the popliteal artery was 68% compared with the 38% patency rate for PTFE (Teflon) grafts in a study done by Veith and associates (1986). The difference between autogenous and prosthetic graft material was even more dramatic in the infrapopliteal

segment in which the 4-year primary patency rate for autogenous vein grafts was 49% compared with only a 12% patency rate for PTFE grafts (Ascer et al, 1987) (Figure 1).

Critical limb ischemia typically occurs in patients who are elderly and have multiple comorbidities. Concern about submitting a patient to revascularization and the potential rigors of a long hospitalization, intensive care, and perhaps multiple procedures to achieve adequate limb salvage requires assessment of global risk versus limb benefit.

A question that is not infrequently asked is whether primary amputation would be more desirable than submitting a patient to a revascularization procedure. Although amputation remains an important surgical option, attempted revascularization is usually preferable. While there have been no specific studies comparing revascularization with amputation for limb-threatening ischemia, a nonrandomized study by Ouriel and colleagues (1998) demonstrated a greater benefit for revascularization. Operative mortality, hospital stay, and long-term survival were all superior in the revascularization group, and the advantage over the amputation group was greatest in the patient subgroup with the highest predicted operative risk.

ENDOVASCULAR THERAPY FOR CRITICAL LIMB ISCHEMIA

Over the last decade, there has been exponential growth in the development and utilization of endovascular procedures for arterial occlusive disease. Specific techniques include atherectomy, balloon angioplasty, stenting, and laser therapy. Although there have been a few anecdotal and observational studies with regard to atherectomy and laser ablation, the mainstay of endovascular therapy has been percutaneous balloon angioplasty and stenting.

Table. Vascular Surgical Reconstruction Results

Type of Reconstruction	Patency Rate (%) at 5 Years
Aortoiliac (prosthetic)	80–90
Femoropopliteal above knee (autologous vein)	70
Femoropopliteal below knee (autologous vein)	40
Femoropopliteal below knee (prosthetic)	20

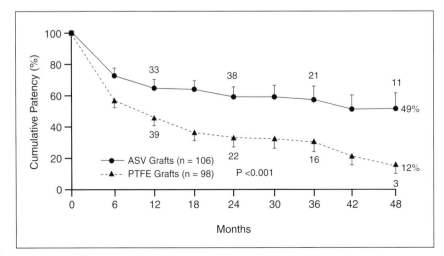

Figure 1. Four-year primary patency rate for autogenous saphenous vein (ASV) grafts versus PTFE (Teflon) grafts in the infrapopliteal segment. From Ascer et al (1987).

Despite the burgeoning use of endovascular therapy, however, there is a paucity of data that provide specifics on optimal patient selection and long-term durability of endovascular techniques (Isner and Rosenfield, 1993). The patency resulting from endovascular techniques is influenced by location and runoff in much the same way as surgical revascularization is influenced by location of the distal anastomosis and runoff. Typically, percutaneous transluminal angioplasty (PTA) and stenting in the aortoiliac segment have higher technical success rates and improved patency compared with infrainguinal endovascular procedures. Figure 2 demonstrates reported patency for iliac PTA Figure 3 demonstrates reported patency for femoropopliteal PTA (Stokes et al, 1990).

Much of the currently available literature is either observational or anecdotal. Data from Johnston et al (1987) regarding PTA of both iliac arteries and femoral popliteal segments is noteworthy for the statistical methods used to analyze the data as well as adherence to strict clinical and hemodynamic criteria. As for surgical revascularization techniques, distal runoff had a profound influence on long-term patency after PTA. Using a multiple-regression model, this study demonstrated that factors predictive of a favorable outcome for balloon angioplasty included stenotic rather than occlusive lesions, good distal runoff, and more proximally situated lesions. Using this analysis, surgery produced better results than balloon angioplasty in patients with diabetes or diffuse vascular disease.

The Toronto study (Johnston et al, 1987) was a prospective trial done prior to the extensive development and utilization of endovascular stents. Data from the preliminary endovascular stent studies have been encouraging. Patency rates (from 3 to 5 years) for iliac occlusive disease treated with angioplasty and stent placement were 92% at 8.7 months with sustained clin-

Figure 2. Cumulative patency rates following iliac angioplasty for arteriosclerosis obliterans. Reprinted from Rutherford and Durham (1992).

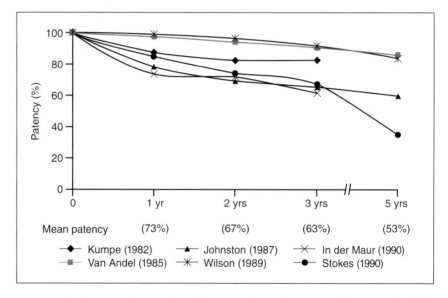

Figure 3. Long-term patency rates in femoropopliteal angioplasty. Modified from Stokes et al (1990).

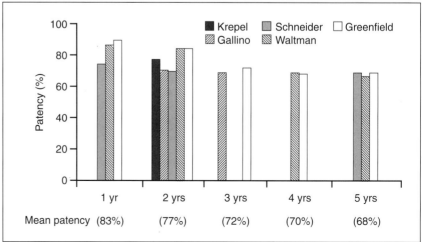

ical benefit at 2 years of 84.1% (Palmaz et al, 1992). Sullivan et al (1997) demonstrated a patency rate for primary iliac artery stenting of 89% at 1 year when measured by ankle-brachial index. When evaluated by thigh-brachial index, patency rates were 98%, 93%, and 84% at 6, 12, and 24 months, respectively. Utilization of endovascular stents in the infrainguinal segment has not been as encouraging. Restenosis or reocclusion rates with stents in the femoral popliteal segment have been as high as 50% on the basis of very limited experience.

Balloon angioplasty of the distal, femoral, popliteal, and tibial segments has been suggested to be safe and less invasive than surgery (Casarella, 1988). Although there is hemodynamic benefit in selected patients, the technique has not shown the long-term durability of autologous vein bypass (Brown et al, 1993). Nevertheless, it represents an important therapeutic option in treating patients with critical limb ischemia. In the femoral popliteal segment, technical success and durability of PTA correlate with lesion morphology and length. A 5-year cumulative patency rate of 75% has been achieved in focal stenoses shorter than 2 cm. A 1-year cumulative patency rate for occlusions longer than 3 cm is significantly lower (Krepel et al, 1985). In general, percutaneous balloon angioplasty of lesions shorter than 5 cm is considered to be more durable than PTA of lesions longer than 10 cm (Capek et al, 1991).

There have been no randomized trials comparing infrapopliteal balloon angioplasty with surgical revascularization. There are, however, prolific data from a large number of case series on infrapopliteal PTA. While there is no specific consensus on long-term durability, there is growing recognition that infrapopliteal PTA is an effective and safe technique (Stokes et al, 1990) (Figure 3). Infrapopliteal PTA has been used successfully for limb salvage; however, long-term durability has not been demonstrated. Anatomic selection appears to be the most important factor. Patients with focal disease and restorable runoff will generally benefit. Patients with an incomplete pedal arch have lower patency and clinical success rates. Overall clinical effectiveness is estimated to be approximately 80% at 2 years in appropriately selected patients (Bakal et al, 1996).

There have been few studies comparing surgery and PTA directly. Hunink et al (1995) compared PTA with bypass surgery using a multistate transitional simulation model. Their conclusions were that angioplasty is the preferred initial treatment in patients with disabling claudication and femoral popliteal stenosis or occlusion and in patients with chronic critical ischemia and stenosis. Alternatively, bypass surgery was the preferred initial treatment in patients with chronic critical ischemia and a femoral popliteal occlusion.

THROMBOLYTIC THERAPY FOR ARTERIAL OCCLUSIVE DISEASE

The ability of thrombolytic agents to dissolve intravascular thrombus has been known for nearly 5 decades. The application of catheter-directed, intra-arterial thrombolysis has evolved and become an important endovascular option in the treatment of patients with critical limb ischemia. Thrombolytic agents are delivered directly into the thrombus via an indwelling arterial catheter. This promotes rapid fibrinolytic dissolution and fewer side effects than a systemically delivered drug. Thrombolytic therapy has been used as both a primary and an adjunctive technique in patients with critical limb ischemia, both in acute and chronic presentations.

A number of recent trials have demonstrated that (1) patient mortality and major amputation are diminished when thrombolytic agents are employed, and (2) thrombolysis can reduce the need for open surgical procedures. In the Rochester trial (Ouriel et al, 1994), thrombolytic therapy was compared with operative revascularization in the initial treatment of acute peripheral arterial ischemia. Although the trial was relatively small, involving only 114 patients, mortality was significantly lower in the thrombolytic therapy group (16% vs 42% at 12 months). There was no difference in the rate of major amputation (approximately 18% at 12 months in each group). Based on this trial, it was concluded that thrombolytic therapy was associated with a reduction in cardiopulmonary complications, which resulted in the mortality benefit. The rate of limb salvage was similar in both treatment groups (Figure 4).

Two larger trials were then performed comparing thrombolytic therapy with operative intervention in a prospective, randomized fashion. The Surgery versus Thrombolysis for Lower Extremity Ischemia (STILE) trial (The STILE Investigators, 1994) compared surgery with thrombolysis for ischemia of the lower extremity, including both acute and chronic ischemic limbs. Both tissue plasminogen activator (t-PA) and urokinase were used and compared with operative intervention. The trial was prematurely stopped because a primary endpoint of adverse effect versus outcome was reached: A significantly greater proportion of patients treated with thrombolysis were observed to suffer ongoing and recurrent ischemia compared with the surgical-treatment group (Figure 5). However, a subsequent post-hoc analysis of a subset of patients with bypass-graft occlusions concluded that thrombolytic therapy was

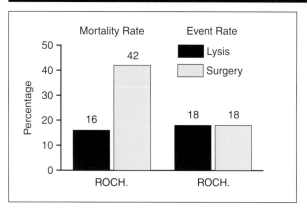

Figure 4. Mortality and amputation rates at 12 months in randomized trials of thrombolysis versus surgery in lower extremity arteriosclerosis obliterans. ROCH. = Rochester trial.

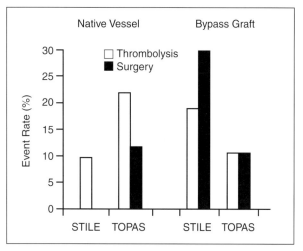

Figure 5. Event rates (major amputation or death) at 1 year in randomized trials of thrombolysis versus surgery in native vessel versus bypass graft in lower extremity arteriosclerosis obliterans. STILE = Surgery versus Thrombolysis for Lower Extremity Ischemia trial; TOPAS = Thrombolysis or Peripheral Arterial Surgery study.

associated with significant benefit over primary operation (Weaver et al, 1996). The thrombolytic therapy-treated group had a lower number of surgical procedures as well as a lower amputation rate at 1 year. From the STILE trial, it was concluded that urokinase and t-PA were equivalent with respect to the outcome measure evaluated. Patients with acute limb ischemia of <14 days' duration had a lower rate of amputation when treated with thrombolytic therapy compared with immediate operation. Patients with bypass-graft occlusions had a lower amputation rate at 1 year compared with patients undergoing primary operation (Figure 5).

The most recent trial was the Thrombolysis or Peripheral Arterial Surgery (TOPAS) study (Ouriel et al,

1996). This was a multicenter trial comparing recombinant urokinase with primary operation in patients with acute arterial ischemia. There were 272 patients in both the urokinase group and the surgical group. There was no difference in the rate of either major amputation or death between the groups within 1 year of follow-up. The trial established equivalence between the 2 treatment arms (Figure 3).

One of the major issues in the use of thrombolytic therapy that was not addressed by any of the surgical-versus-thrombolytic therapy trials was its use as an adjunct to either surgery or endovascular techniques. Although there have been no randomized trials, there are both observational and anecdotal data on the use of thrombolytic therapy in an adjunctive fashion that has allowed surgical or endovascular reconstruction which would not have been possible if done primarily. Specific applications include occluded bypass graft, with no identifiable surgical target vessels, as well as for thrombosed native popliteal aneurysms where no distal runoff is identified that would allow for surgical reconstruction. Following thrombolysis, the aneurysm is resected and distal circulation restored. There remains some controversy as to the use of thrombolysis in acute limb ischemia or when a thromboembolus has occurred that is well localized. This is a situation in which embolectomy may be the optimal treatment.

Intra-arterial thrombolytic therapy has a role in both primary and adjunctive treatment in the patient with critical limb ischemia. Primary care physicians should note that despite great potential benefits, intra-arterial thrombolytic therapy may be limited by requirements for a long duration of infusion necessary to complete treatment. Typically, the duration of an infusion is approximately 24 hours and occasionally longer, and in situations of acute limb-threatening ischemia, there may not be adequate time for thrombolytic therapy to achieve revascularization. Additionally, as the duration of infusion increases there is an increase in morbidity, particularly from bleeding complications.

FUTURE TREATMENT OPTIONS FOR PATIENTS WITH CRITICAL LIMB ISCHEMIA

Surgical and endovascular reconstruction in patients with atherosclerotic occlusive disease has been plagued by both progression of disease and development of restenosis at the reconstruction site. One of the primary causes of restenosis is the development of neointimal hyperplasia. To date, there is no available medication or procedure that suppresses neointimal hyperplasia. However, drug therapy and brachytherapy (localized radiation) are being investigated in an effort to limit or prevent restenosis.

Key Points

• Factors that influence progression of critical limb ischemia and the risk of limb loss include the extent and location of disease; systemic considerations, such as cardiopulmonary status; and cardiovascular risk factors that influence the progression of disease, such as smoking or the presence of diabetes mellitus.

• Diabetic patients have a sevenfold higher rate of lower extremity amputation than patients without diabetes.

• Progression of critical limb ischemia constitutes a definite indication to pursue arterial reconstruction, either surgically or endovascularly.

• Clinical evaluation includes delineating the arterial anatomy.

• Detailed digital subtraction arteriography allows for the determination of the extent and location of arterial occlusive disease. Newer methods, such as magnetic resonance angiography, are evolving and may supplant routine digital subtraction arteriography as the "gold standard."

• Surgical revascularization can provide for durable salvage of unselected limbs in 85% to 90% of cases.

• The most significant influences on surgical graft survival are the use of autogenous vein and presurgical assurance of adequate inflow and outflow.

• Endovascular therapy is an important option in the treatment of patients with critical limb ischemia. The technical success and durability of PTA correlate with lesion morphology and length. Shorter stenotic lesions have better patency than longer arterial occlusions. Distal runoff substantially influences long-term patency.

• Thrombolytic therapy has demonstrated safety and efficacy in the treatment of acute arterial ischemia.

• Future therapies include angiogenesis and pharmacotherapy to inhibit neointimal hyperplasia in the restenotic process.

One of the most exciting areas of research is in techniques for therapeutic angiogenesis. Isner and colleagues (1995) proposed arterial gene therapy using vascular endothelial growth factor (VEGF) to promote angiogenesis. Initially, a rabbit model of hind limb ischemia was used; VEGF demonstrated encouraging results. Subsequent investigations utilized these techniques in humans with administration of VEGF intra-arterially or intramuscularly. Phase I trials in carefully selected patients have been encouraging, and many investigators are cautiously optimistic about the future of these techniques. If fruitful, angiogenesis may allow treatment of patients for whom surgical or endovascular reconstruction is not currently feasible.

SUMMARY

Recognition of critical limb ischemia and the factors that influence successful revascularization are important in determining therapeutic alternatives. Both endovascular (ie, PTA and stents) and surgical techniques can be effective. Care of the patient and optimizing treatment strategies require close collaboration between the primary care physician and vascular specialist. ∎

BIBLIOGRAPHY

Ameli FM, Stein M, Provan JL, Prosser R. The effect of postoperative smoking on femoropopliteal bypass grafts. Ann Vasc Surg 1989;3:20–5.

Ascer E, Collier P, Gupta SK, Veith FJ. Reoperation for PTFE bypass failure: importance of distal outflow site and operative techniques in determining outcome. J Vasc Surg 1987;5:298–310.

Bakal CW, Cynamon J, Sprayreger S. Infrapopliteal percutaneous transluminal angioplasty: what we know. Radiology 1996;200:33–6.

Brown KT, Moore ED, Getrajdman GI, Saddekni S. Infrapopliteal angioplasty long-term follow-up. J Vasc Intervent Radiol 1993;4:139–44.

Capek P, McLean GK, Berkowitz HD. Femoropopliteal angioplasty: factors influencing long-term success. Circulation 1991(suppl I);83:I–70.

Casarella WJ. Percutaneous transluminal angioplasty below the knee: new techniques, excellent results. Radiology 1988;169:271–2.

Criqui MH, Langer RD, Franck A, et al. Mortality over a period of 10 years in patients with peripheral arterial disease. N Engl J Med 1992;326:381–6.

Hunink MG, Wong JB, Donaldson MC, et al. Revascularization of femoropopliteal disease: a decision and cost-effective analysis. JAMA 1995:274:165–71.

Isner JM, Rosenfield K. Redefining the treatment of

peripheral artery disease. Role of percutaneous revascularization. Circulation 1993;88:1534–7.

Isner JM, Walsh K, Symes J, et al. Arterial gene therapy for therapeutic angiogenesis in patients with peripheral artery disease. Circulation 1995;91:2687–92.

Johnston KW, Rae M, Hogg-Johnston SA, et al. Five-year results of a prospective study of percutaneous transluminal angioplasty. Ann Surg 1987;206:403–13.

Jonason T, Ringquist I. Factors of prognostic importance for subsequent rest pain in patients with intermittent claudication. Acta Med Scand 1985; 218:27–33.

Kraiss LW, Johansen K. Pharmacologic intervention to prevent graft failure. Surg Clin North Am 1995; 75:761–72.

Krepel VM, Van Andel GJ, Van Erp WFM, et al. Percutaneous transluminal angioplasty of the femoropopliteal artery: initial and long-term results. Radiology 1985;156:325–8.

McLafferty RB, Moneta GL, Musser PA, et al. Progression of atherosclerosis in arteries distal to lower extremity revascularizations. J Vasc Surg 1995;22: 450–6.

Ouriel K, Flore WM, Geary JE. Limb threatening ischemia in the medically compromised patient: amputation or revascularization. Surgery 1998; 104:667–72.

Ouriel K, Shortell CK, DeWeese JA, et al. A comparison of thrombolytic therapy with operative revascularization in the initial treatment of acute peripheral arterial ischemia. J Vasc Surg 1994;19:1021–30.

Ouriel K, Veith FJ, Sasahara AA, and the TOPAS Investigators. Thrombolysis or Peripheral Arterial Surgery: phase I results. J Vasc Surg 1996;23:64–73.

Palmaz JC, Laborde JC, Rivera FJ, et al. Stenting of the iliac arteries with the Palmaz stent: experience from a multicenter trial cardiovascular intervention. Radiology 1992;15:291–7.

Stokes KR, Strunk HM, Campbell DR, et al. Five-year results of iliac and femoropopliteal angioplasty in diabetic patients. Radiology 1990;174:977–82.

Sullivan TM, Childs MB, Bacharach JM, et al. Percutaneous transluminal angioplasty and primary stenting of the iliac arteries in 288 patients. J Vasc Surg 1997;25:829–39.

Taylor LM, Hamre D, Dalman RL, Porter JM. Limb salvage and amputation for critical ischemia: the role of vascular surgery. Ann Surg 1991;126:1251–8.

Taylor LM, Porter JM. Natural history and nonoperative treatment of chronic lower extremity ischemia. In: Rutherford R, ed. Vascular Surgery. 4th ed. Philadelphia: WB Saunders Co; 1995:758–66.

The STILE Investigators. Results of a prospective randomized trial evaluating surgery vs. thrombolysis for ischemia of the lower extremity. Ann Surg 1994;220:251–68.

Veith FJ, Gupta SK, Ascer E, et al. Six-year prospective multicenter randomized comparison of autologous saphenous vein and expanded polytetrafluoroethylene grafts in infrainguinal internal reconstructions. J Vasc Surg 1986;3:104–14.

Weaver FA, Camerato AJ, Youngblood M, et al. Surgical revascularization versus thrombolysis for nonembolic lower extremity native artery occlusions: results of a prospective randomized trial. J Vasc Surg 1996;24:513–21.

SELECTED READINGS

Becker GJ, Katzen BT, Pave MD. Noncoronary angioplasty. Radiology 1989;170:921.

Citterio F, Castagneto M. Lower limb revascularization in diabetes. Rays Int J Radiol Sci 1997;22:605–11.

Durham JR, Horowitz JD, Wright JG, et al. Percutaneous transluminal angioplasty of tibial arteries for limb salvage in the high-risk diabetic patient. Ann Vasc Surg 1994;8:48–53.

Gloviczki P, Morris SM, Bower TC, et al. Microvascular pedal bypass for salvage of the severely ischemic limb. Mayo Clin Proc 1991;66:243–53.

Henry M, Amor M, Elhevenot G, et al. Palmaz stent placement in iliac and femoropopliteal arteries: primary and secondary patency in 310 patients with 2-4 year follow-up. Radiology 1995;197:167–74.

Johnson BL, Glickman MH, Bandyk DF. Failure of foot salvage in patients with end-stage renal disease after surgical revascularization. J Vasc Surg 1995;22:280–6.

Lassila R, Lepantalo M. Cigarette smoking and the outcome after lower limb surgery. Acta Chir Scand 1988;154:635–40.

Milford MA, Weaver FA, Lundell CJ, Yellin AE. Femoropopliteal percutaneous transluminal angioplasty for limb salvage. J Vasc Surg 1988;8:292.

Ouriel K, Veith FJ, Sasahara AA. Comparison of recombinant urokinase with vascular surgery as initial treatment for acute arterial occlusion of the legs. N Engl J Med 1998;338:1105–11.

Riggs P, Ouriel K. Thrombolysis in the treatment of lower extremity occlusive disease. Surg Clin North Am 1995:75:633–45.

Rosenfield K, Isner JM. Disease of peripheral vessels. In: Topol EJ, ed. Textbook of Cardiovascular Medicine. Philadelphia: Lippincott-Raven Publications; 1998: 2597–621.

Rutherford RB, Durham JR. Percutaneous balloon angioplasty for arteriosclerosis obliterans: long-term result. In: Yao JS, Pearce WH, eds. *Technologies in Vascular*

Medicine. Philadelphia, Pa: WB Saunders Co; 1992.

Rutherford RB, Flanigan DP, Gupta SK, et al. Suggested standards for reports dealing with lower extremity ischemia. J Vasc Surg 1986;4:80–94.

Saab MH, Smith DC, Aka PK, et al. Percutaneous transluminal angioplasty of tibial arteries for limb salvage. Cardiovasc Intervent Radiol 1992;15:211–6.

Schwarten DE. Clinical and anatomical considerations for nonoperative therapy in tibial disease and the results of angioplasty. Circulation 1991;83(suppl L):286–90.

Schwarten DE, Cutcliff WB. Arterial occlusive disease below the knee: treatment with percutaneous transluminal angioplasty performed with low-profile catheters and steerable guidewires. Radiology 1988;169(1):71–4.

Taylor LM, Edwards JM, Porter JM. Present status of reversed vein bypass grafting: five-year results of a modern series. J Vasc Surg 1990;11:193–205.

The Collaborative Rotablator Atherectomy Group (CRAG). Peripheral atherectomy with the rotablator: a multicenter report. J Vasc Surg 1994;19:509–15.

Treiman GS, Treiman RL, Ichikawa BS. Should percutaneous transluminal angioplasty be recommended for treatment of infrageniculate popliteal artery or tibioperoneal trunk stenosis? J Vasc Surg 1995; 22:457–65.

Weitz J, Byrne J, Clagett PG, et al. Diagnosis and treatment of chronic arterial insufficiency of the lower extremities: a critical review. Circulation 1996;94: 3026–49.

Wholey MH, Maynar MA, Wholey MH, et al. Comparison of thrombolytic therapy of lower-extremity acute, subacute, and chronic arterial occlusions. Cathet Cardiovasc Diagn 1998;44:159–69.

Severe Occlusive Peripheral Arterial Disease and Critical Limb Ischemia. Part II. Amputation

J. Michael Bacharach, MD, MPH
Section Head, Vascular Medicine and Intervention
North Central Heart and Vascular Institute
Sioux Falls, South Dakota

Objective: To define criteria for amputation assessment and determination of amputation level for optimal functional outcome.

Despite modern advances in the field of vascular surgical technique and new endovascular interventions, the vascular physician continues to be confronted with the patient requiring amputation because of severe peripheral arterial disease (PAD). Amputation remains an important therapeutic option in patients who experience tissue loss, pain, or extremity dysfunction secondary to vascular insufficiency. The basic goal of amputation is to resect diseased tissue in a manner that effectively enables healing at a site that will result in the best functional outcome and greatest rehabilitation potential. There are both systemic and local factors that play an important role in selecting the level of amputation. Although a detailed analysis of all the possible factors is beyond the scope of this article, there are a number of areas of assessment important to consider.

It is well recognized that amputation success or failure is complex and dependent on numerous factors. One needs to consider a number of systemic factors in clinically assessing the patient. The tenets of wound healing include adequate nutrition, adequate regional perfusion, and the absence of infection or mechanical features that would inhibit healing. While seemingly simplistic, it is nevertheless important to evaluate the patient's overall health. General assessment includes nutritional state, the possibility of systemic infection, control of diabetes, and control of hypertension. Special attention to cardiac function and pulmonary status is also warranted. Optimization of hemodynamics and gas exchange has important implications, both for healing and surgical risk at time of amputation.

Within the context of general assessment, the patient's potential for rehabilitation is an important consideration. If the patient's performance status is severely compromised and rehabilitation potential poor, a proximal amputation where there is no question that it will heal is warranted. If the performance status is adequate, then a more distal amputation often has greater rehabilitation potential. Distal amputation,

however, exposes the patient to increased risk of failure of amputation-site healing. The challenge is to assess the factors that influence successful healing of a distal amputation, and apply this assessment to selected patients.

There are a number of local factors for healing that also need to be considered: the extent of nonviable tissue, presence of local infection, and vascular supply. The presence of infection needs adequate evaluation. Infection can present as necrotic tissue or ulcers with purulent drainage, cellulitis, or osteomyelitis. It is important to remember that infection can be occult. Osteomyelitis can be difficult to diagnose and is a particular problem in the diabetic population. Traditional radiography has high specificity but relatively low sensitivity. The addition of bone scans and 24-hour leukocyte scans can significantly improve detection of osteomyelitis. Newman et al (1991), in a study of diabetic patients, demonstrated the significant limitations of clinical examination and plain radiography. Only 32% of 28 diabetic foot ulcers with established osteomyelitis were suspected clinically. Radiography had a specificity of 92% but a sensitivity of only 28%. The addition of bone scans and 24-hour leukocyte scans improved the sensitivity and specificity to 89% and 69%, respectively. Regional perfusion is perhaps the most important local factor in selecting an amputation site. Objective determination of the adequacy of blood flow at a proposed amputation site is one of the most challenging problems. Clinical determinants of blood flow, while useful, have significant limitations. Features of the physical examination, such as skin temperature, location and quality of pulses, presence or absence of dependent rubor, and wound-edge bleeding, provide insufficient information when amputation levels are closely related to areas with signs and symptoms of ischemia. Too much reliance on these clinical factors can lead to suboptimal selection of the amputation level and result in amputation failure and the need to perform additional surgery.

Full discussion of amputation would not be complete without some mention of the noninvasive assessment of amputation level. Recognition that clinical criteria alone have limitations in predicting amputation wound-site healing has led to numerous efforts to find a complementary technique that would aid in more accurate prediction. Many methods have been proposed and evaluated with varying degrees of success. These noninvasive tests use a variety of instrumentation and depend on different physiologic properties. The tests commonly employ the principles of indirect measurement of arterial perfusion and thus provide a more accurate physiologic assessment of arterial disease. Unfortunately, no one noninvasive test has emerged as a recognized "gold standard." Limitations in sensitivity, specificity, and reproducibility plague many of the methods. Moreover, some of the tests are cumbersome, time consuming, or require complex instrumentation. An additional caveat is to recognize that different laboratories have different capabilities and limitations. Clearly, these differences can and will influence noninvasive testing. No matter how sensitive and specific an individual test is, if the laboratory has technical or personnel limitations, the test will provide suboptimal results.

A full discussion of noninvasive testing methods is beyond the scope of this article. There are, however, a number of basic studies that are worth mentioning.

One of the most common noninvasive techniques is segmental Doppler determination of systolic blood pressures. This provides simple and reproducible means of measuring arterial perfusion. A variety of absolute pressures have been proposed as predictors of healing or failure to heal. While exact values are not known, healing of below-knee amputations is likely if calf pressure is >70 mm Hg and ankle pressure exceeds 30 mm Hg in the nondiabetic patient (Raines et al,

1976). For diabetic patients who often have greater incompressibility of arteries, ankle pressures may be artificially elevated and do not accurately reflect local perfusion. Ankle pressures ≥90 mm Hg in diabetic patients may be required for below-knee amputation. In the case of noncompressible arteries, there are some data to suggest that toe pressures may more accurately reflect perfusion (Ramsey et al, 1983): Toe pressures ≥30 mm Hg suggest that healing is likely. Although the technique of segmental Doppler pressure determination provides acceptable results for below-knee and more proximal amputations, it has little or no predictive value for distal amputations.

Key Points

• Amputation is an important option in the treatment of patients with severe nonrevascularizable ischemia.

• Systemic and local factors play an important role in selecting an appropriate level of amputation.

• The goal of amputation is to provide the best functional outcome and the greatest rehabilitation potential.

• The basic tenets of wound healing include adequate nutrition, adequate regional perfusion, and absence of infection or mechanical features that could inhibit healing.

• General preamputation assessment of a patient includes attention to nutritional state, presence of systemic infection, and adequate control of diabetes and hypertension.

• Special attention to cardiac function and pulmonary status is important.

• The presence of infection needs adequate evaluation. Osteomyelitis can be difficult to diagnose and is a particular problem in the diabetic population. The addition of bone scans and 24-hour leukocyte scans can significantly improve detection of osteomyelitis in diabetic patients.

• Noninvasive assessment of arterial perfusion can be helpful; however, no one test is recognized as the "gold standard."

There are numerous other noninvasive methods that have been used to help predict amputation-site healing. These include measurements of skin temperature, transcutaneous oxygen tension, transcutaneous carbon dioxide tension, and skin perfusion using xenon-133 or fluorescein dye. Although these tests have demonstrated some degree of statistical reliability for amputation healing, no absolute levels have been determined, and from a pragmatic standpoint, most of them are not routinely available outside large academic centers.

Recent approaches considered for improving healing assessment include magnetic resonance imaging (MRI). With the current level of technology, MRI has the ability to perform angiographic evaluation as well as to quantitate flow by tissue volumes. Such techniques are evolving rapidly and should soon be much more widely available.

CONCLUSION

In patients with severe PAD who experience tissue loss, pain, or extremity dysfunction, and who are not amenable to revascularization, amputation remains an important therapeutic option. Evaluation of patients facing amputation is multifaceted and includes assessment of general condition and overall health, in addition to local factors at the proposed site of amputation. Assessment of the adequacy of blood flow at the proposed amputation site is an important challenge. Noninvasive assessment can be invaluable in helping to make this determination; however, to date there is no one perfect test to predict amputation success or failure. ∎

BIBLIOGRAPHY

Newman LG, Waller J, Palestro CJ, et al. Unsuspected osteomyelitis in diabetic foot ulcers. JAMA 1991; 266:1246–51.

Raines JK, Darling RC, Buth J, Brewster DC, Austen WG. Vascular laboratory criteria for the management of peripheral vascular disease of the lower extremities. Surgery 1976;79:21–9.

Ramsey DE, Manka DA, Sumner DS. Toe blood pressure—a valuable adjunct to ankle pressure measurement for assessing peripheral arterial disease. J Cardiovasc Surg 1983;24:43–8.

SUGGESTED READINGS

Ameli FM, Bryne P, Provan JL. Selection of amputation level and prediction of healing using transcutaneous tissue oxygen tension. J Cardiovasc Surg 1989;30:220–4.

Bacharach JM, Rooke TW, Osmundson PJ, Gloviczki P. Predictive value of transcutaneous oxygen pressure and amputation success by use of supine and elevation measurements. J Vasc Surg 1992;15: 558–63.

Byrne RL, Nicholson ML, Woolford TJ, Callurn KG. Factors influencing the healing of distal amputations performed for lower limb ischaemia. Br J Surg 1992;79:73–5.

Dickhaut SC, DeLee JC, Page CP. Nutritional status: importance in predicting wound-healing after amputation. J Bone Joint Surg Am 1984;66:71–5.

Durham JR. Lower extremity amputation levels: indications, methods of determining appropriate levels, technique, prognosis. In: Rutherford RB, ed. Vascular Surgery. Philadelphia: WB Saunders; 1989:1687–712.

Harris JP, McLaughlin AF, Quinn RJ. Skin blood flow measurement with xenon-133 to predict healing of lower extremity amputations. Aust New Zealand J Surg 1986;56:413–5.

Hodgson KJ, Sumner DS. Noninvasive assessment of lower extremity arterial disease. Ann Vasc Surg 1988; 2:174–84.

Kald A, Carlsson R, Nilsson E. Major amputation in a defined population: incidence, mortality, and results of treatment. Br J Surg 1989;76:308–10.

Kram HB, Appel PL, Shoemaker WC. Multisensor transcutaneous oximetric mapping to predict below-knee amputation wound healing: use of critical PO_2. J Vasc Surg 1989;9:796–800.

Kram HB, Appel PL, Shoemaker WC. Prediction of below-knee amputation wound healing using noninvasive laser Doppler velocimetry. Am J Surg 1989; 158:29–31.

Lind J, Kram M, Bodtker S. The influence of smoking on complications after primary amputations of the lower extremity. Clin Orthop Relat Res 1991;267: 211–7.

Malone JM, Anderson GG, Lalka SG, et al. Prospective comparison of noninvasive techniques for amputation level selection. Am J Surg 1987;154:179–84.

Mars M, Mills RP, Robbs IV. The potential benefit of preoperative assessment of amputation wound healing potential in peripheral vascular disease. S Afr Med J 1993;83:16–8.

Oishi CS, Fronek A, Golbranson FL. The role of non-invasive vascular studies in determining levels of amputation. J Bone Joint Surg Am 1988;70:1520–30.

Pedersen NW, Pedersen D. Nutrition as a prognostic indicator in amputations. Acta Orthop Scand 1992; 63:675–8.

Penington G, Warmington S, Hull S, Freijah N. Rehabilitation of lower limb amputees and some implications for surgical management. Aust New Zealand J Surg 1992;62:774–9.

Pinzur MS, Littooy F, Daniels J, et al. Multidisciplinary preoperative assessment and late function in dysvascular amputees. Clin Orthop Relat Res 1992;281: 239–43.

Pinzur MS, Sage R, Stuck R, Ketner L, Osterman H. Transcutaneous oxygen as a predictor of wound healing in amputations of the foot and ankle. Foot Ankle Int 1992;13:271–2.

Ratliff DA, Clyne CA, Chant AD, Webster JH. Prediction of amputation wound healing: the role of transcutaneous PO_2 assessment. Br J Surg 1984;71:219–22.

Silverman DG, Roberts A, Reilly CA, et al. Fluorometric quantification of low-dose fluorescein delivery to predict amputation site healing. Surgery 1987;101: 335–41.

Stoner HB, Taylor L, Marcuson RW. The value of skin temperature measurements in forecasting the healing of a below-knee amputation for end-stage ischaemia of the leg in peripheral vascular disease. Eur J Vasc Endovasc Surg 1989;3:355–61.

Wagner WH, Keagy BA, Koth MM, Burnham SJ, Johnson G Jr. Noninvasive determination of healing of major lower extremity amputation: the continued role of clinical judgement. J Vasc Surg 1988;8: 703–10.

Wyss C, Harrington R, Burgess E. Transcutaneous oxygen tension as a predictor of success after an amputation. J Bone Joint Surg Am 1988;76:203–7.

The American Journal of Medicine®

CONTINUING EDUCATION SERIES

AN OFFICE-BASED APPROACH TO THE DIAGNOSIS AND TREATMENT OF PERIPHERAL ARTERIAL DISEASE

PART IV: Morbidity of PAD: Medical Approaches to Claudication

SERIES EDITOR
ALAN T. HIRSCH, MD

GUEST EDITOR
WILLIAM R. HIATT, MD

Jointly sponsored by
The Excerpta Medica Office of Continuing Medical Education, the Society for Vascular Medicine and Biology, and the Society of General Internal Medicine

SGIM *Society of General Internal Medicine*

Dear Colleague:

This monograph is designed to aid primary care physicians in fulfilling their ethical obligation to diminish pain and suffering. This, of course, includes treatment of claudication, the primary symptom of peripheral arterial disease (PAD).

Physicians who treat PAD have traditionally asked only one question: "How severe does the claudication have to be to merit revascularization?" This question is no longer central to the care of individuals who suffer from claudication. It is no longer appropriate to classify a particular severity of claudication as an arbitrary threshold above which comprehensive treatment is not merited. All claudication is associated with a diminution of quality of life, and we must therefore attempt to obtain "quality-of-life–sensitive" claudication histories from our patients. It may take 10 minutes of office time to hear a patient describe his or her activity restrictions due to claudication. Do we allocate time for such histories in the bustle of a busy office practice? We should, since a large and increasing number of patients suffer claudication for many years without this history being taken or actions effectively initiated to alleviate the symptoms. However, if "managing claudication" during the office visit is constrained by the rigors of "managed care," then it may be feasible to collect this information with objective, standardized questionnaires (discussed in this monograph). Nevertheless, questionnaires cannot replace physician empathy, which is integral to all effective interventions.

Empathy for the claudication patient is central to becoming a "vascular clinician." We have all experienced the intolerable limb "exhaustion" at some time in our youth, when we exceeded our individual functional capacity during vigorous exercise. Empathy means appreciating how we would feel if such discomfort occurred every day, year after year, limiting our walking to a matter of blocks, with little hope of improvement. Indeed, we should have a personal interest in our ability to ameliorate claudication, as epidemiologic facts suggest that many readers of this monograph will one day suffer PAD and claudication.

When patients with moderate claudication are surveyed using a standard quality-of-life questionnaire (MOS SF-36), the morbidity caused by claudication is revealed to be marked and comparable to that evoked by severe heart failure or severe chronic lung disease. No longer can claudication be viewed as a mere inconvenience that "cramps the style" of those affected. In the past we may not have felt confident that there were *effective clinical tools* to successfully intervene to ameliorate these symptoms. Such tools now exist. These range from exercise programs that can improve functional status to new drugs like cilostazol (Pletal®) that are very effective in improving walking ability in claudication patients. The lifestyle and pharmacologic tools of the primary care physician should be as sharp and precisely wielded as the scalpel used by the vascular surgeon who attempts to revascularize the ischemic limb. The Society for Vascular Medicine and Biology and the Society of General Internal Medicine hope this monograph, the fourth in the PAD primary care series, will provide the primary care physician with an up-to-date primer in the use of these tools.

Sincerely,

Alan T. Hirsch, MD
President, Society for Vascular Medicine and Biology
On behalf of the Education Committee, Officers, and Trustees
Associate Professor of Medicine
Vascular Medicine Program
Minnesota Vascular Diseases Center
University of Minnesota Medical School
Minneapolis, Minnesota

Introduction and Overview

William R. Hiatt, MD
Professor of Medicine
Section of Vascular Medicine, Division of Geriatrics
University of Colorado Health Sciences Center
Denver, Colorado

Peripheral arterial disease (PAD) is a manifestation of systemic atherosclerosis that affects a large segment of the US population. The estimated prevalences of PAD and the symptom of claudication are shown in the Table. The principal means of determining prevalence of PAD in a population is the ankle-brachial index. Several epidemiologic studies have used this index as a screening tool and have shown that prevalence of the disease increases dramatically with age (Criqui et al, 1985a; Hiatt et al, 1995). Using US census estimates of the number of Americans in each age category leads to an estimated total prevalence of 8.4 million individuals with PAD.

As with most atherosclerotic diseases, some PAD patients are asymptomatic during the early stages of the disease. However, with progression of arterial occlusions, patients develop the major symptom of PAD, which is intermittent claudication. This is typically defined as cramping or discomfort in the calf muscle that occurs with exercise and is relieved with rest. Depending on the degree of arterial occlusion, these symptoms can occur in the thigh or buttock muscles as well. In epidemiologic surveys, the Rose Claudication Questionnaire has classically been used to define the presence or absence of claudication (Rose and Blackburn, 1968). Although it is a rigorous instrument with which to evaluate this symptom, when compared with clinical assessment, the questionnaire may have relatively low sensitivity albeit high specificity for determining claudication (Criqui et al, 1985b). Despite the limitation, numerous studies have been performed with it throughout the world, thereby providing the estimates of claudication prevalence listed in the Table. Based on US census data, this leads to a total estimate of over 4 million patients with claudication (Fowkes et al, 1991). Thus 40% to 50% of PAD patients have symptomatic intermittent claudication.

PATHOPHYSIOLOGY

The pathophysiology of claudication is primarily determined by reduced arterial blood flow due to atherosclerotic occlusion of major conduit vessels of the lower extremity. An easily measured manifestation of this occlusion process is the reduction in ankle pressure. Metabolic demand of skeletal muscle of the lower extremity is relatively low at rest and therefore there is typically adequate perfusion of skeletal muscle, skin, and other tissues in the leg to maintain normal metabolic rates. With exercise, however, there is a marked increase in skeletal muscle metabolism, which in normal individuals results in a 20- to 40-fold increase in blood flow and oxygen delivery (Lundgren et al, 1988). In contrast, in patients who are unable to appropriately increase blood flow during exercise, a supply-demand mismatch occurs, resulting in skeletal muscle ischemia (Lundgren et al, 1988). This leads to the symptom of intermittent claudication. When the patient stops walking, skeletal muscle metabolic demand returns to a basal rate and after 5 to 10 minutes the ischemic pain abates.

Although the initial insult in the patient with claudication is clearly hemodynamic, the pathophysiology of the symptom cannot be totally explained by reduced

Table. Prevalences of Peripheral Arterial Disease (PAD) and the Symptom of Claudication

Age (y)	Abnormal Ankle-Brachial Index (%)	Estimated US PAD Prevalence	Rose Claudication Questionnaire (%)	Estimated US Claudication Prevalence
40–59	3	2.1 million	2	1.4 million
60–69	8	1.6 million	3.5	0.7 million
≥70	19	4.7 million	8	2.0 million
Total		8.4 million		4.1 million

blood flow alone. Several investigators have observed, for example, that measurements of calf blood flow or ankle blood pressure do not correlate well with treadmill exercise performance (Hiatt et al, 1988; Pernow and Zetterquist, 1968). Thus other factors must also play a significant role in the pathophysiology of claudication. To address these issues, skeletal muscle has been evaluated directly using a muscle biopsy technique. The results of these studies have shown that in patients with claudication, there is marked evidence of skeletal muscle denervation in the leg (Regensteiner et al, 1993a). This has been shown to lead to skeletal muscle weakness and accounts for some of the impaired exercise performance. In addition, a number of metabolic abnormalities have been described in these patients. During the course of a typical day, a patient with claudication may experience several episodes of skeletal muscle ischemia followed by reperfusion. This leads to an increase in oxidant stress and potential for free-radical injury (Belch et al, in press). Thus there are recent reports of mitochondrial DNA injury associated with an alteration in oxidative phosphorylation expression (Bhat et al, 1999). Further evidence of impaired metabolism comes from observations of changes in skeletal muscle carnitine metabolism. Carnitine is an important cofactor that provides a buffer molecule for the acyl-CoA pool. During normal metabolic conditions there is rapid flux and turnover as fatty acids, proteins, and carbohydrates are converted to acyl-CoA intermediates. Accumulation of acylcarnitines was seen uniquely in ischemic skeletal muscle in patients with claudication (Hiatt et al, 1992). Further, patients with the greatest accumulation had the lowest treadmill exercise performance (Hiatt et al, 1992). Thus alterations in skeletal muscle carnitine metabolism provide insight into the pathophysiology of PAD.

In summary, the symptom of claudication is initiated by reduction in skeletal muscle blood flow and oxygen delivery during exercise. However, patients with chronic occlusive disease have alterations in skeletal muscle neurologic and metabolic function leading to further impairments in oxidative metabolism and reduced exercise performance. Evidently, treatment approaches need to account for this complex pathophysiology. A simple reperfusion of the lower extremity with bypass surgery or angioplasty does not in fact normalize exercise performance (Regensteiner et al, 1993b). A number of different pharmacologic approaches may be necessary to address the different pathophysiologic mechanisms. This allows for multiple approaches to the treatment of claudication that go beyond simply trying to modify skeletal muscle blood flow.

CLINICAL SEVERITY OF CLAUDICATION

Patients with claudication typically present to the primary care physician complaining of leg discomfort that occurs with exercise. At first glance, this may appear to be a relatively benign symptom, but several studies have revealed the severity of claudication in daily life. When tested using graded treadmill exercise techniques, patients with claudication have marked impairment in performance. Measurements of peak oxygen uptake reveal that these patients have an approximately 50% reduction in peak exercise capacity compared with healthy age-matched controls (Hiatt et al, 1987). This puts them at a severity level similar to New York Heart Association class III heart failure patients. In addition, the impact of claudication on daily activity in community-based performance has been assessed by several questionnaires. Here again, patients with claudication report that their symptoms severely limit daily ambulatory activity and physical function capability (Regensteiner et al, 1996). These reductions in daily activity are also similar to those of patients with severe heart failure; they thus indicate profound limitation in physical performance. The emotional state and mental health of these patients are relatively normal when compared with healthy age-matched controls (Regensteiner et al, 1996). Thus claudication greatly limits the physical functioning realm of patients' daily activities. Treatment modalities must address this limitation by focusing on improving physical performance, peak exercise performance, and ambulatory activity.

This monograph, the fourth in a series of continuing medical education (CME) publications on the clinical aspects of PAD, addresses several critical issues regarding the diagnosis and management of intermittent claudication. In the introduction, I have focused on the remarkably high prevalence of claudication in the United States, the pathophysiology, and the associated profound impact of daily activities and exercise performance. In the first article, Judith Regensteiner, PhD, discusses means to assess outcomes in patients with claudication to monitor treatment effects. It is absolutely critical that all patients with symptom-limiting claudication have a measure of their impairment determined either by treadmill or by questionnaire. This information further enables the clinician to determine which treatments are successful and should be continued and which are not. In the following article, I review the well-established modalities of medical therapy in treating claudication. These include a formal, supervised exercise program and proven (and emerging) drug therapies. There is also a brief discussion of when interventional therapy is appropriate.

Finally, Anne B. Newman, MD, MPH, describes a practical and cost-effective approach to the integration of data for assessing outcomes and different treatment modalities into daily clinical practice.

The editors would like to thank the Society for Vascular Medicine and Biology and the Society of General Internal Medicine for their role in the development of this publication. We hope this monograph, published under the auspices of *The American Journal of Medicine*®, will provide useful—even critical—information for practicing clinicians as to how they can best manage their patients with claudication. ■

BIBLIOGRAPHY

Belch JJ, Mackay IR, Hill A, et al. Oxidative stress is present in atherosclerotic peripheral arterial disease and further increased by diabetes mellitus. Int Angiol 1995;14:385–8.

Bhat HK, Hiatt WR, Hoppel CL, Brass EP. Skeletal muscle mitochondrial DNA injury in patients with unilateral peripheral arterial disease. Circulation. In press.

Criqui MH, Fronek A, Barrett-Connor E, et al. The prevalence of peripheral arterial disease in a defined population. Circulation 1985a;71:510–5.

Criqui MH, Fronek A, Klauber MR, et al. The sensitivity, specificity, and predictive value of traditional clinical evaluation of peripheral arterial disease: results from noninvasive testing in a defined population. Circulation 1985b;71:516–22.

Fowkes FGR, Housley E, Cawood EHH, et al. Edinburgh artery study: prevalence of asymptomatic and symptomatic peripheral arterial disease in the general population. Int J Epidemiol 1991;20:384–92.

Hiatt WR, Hoag S, Hamman RF. Effect of diagnostic criteria on the prevalence of peripheral arterial disease. The San Luis Valley diabetes study. Circulation 1995;91:1472–9.

Hiatt WR, Nawaz D, Brass EP. Carnitine metabolism during exercise in patients with peripheral vascular disease. J Appl Physiol 1987;62:2383–7.

Hiatt WR, Nawaz D, Regensteiner JG, Hossack KF. The evaluation of exercise performance in patients with peripheral vascular disease. J Cardiopulm Rehabil 1988;12:525–32.

Hiatt WR, Wolfel EE, Regensteiner JG, Brass EP. Skeletal muscle carnitine metabolism in patients with unilateral peripheral arterial disease. J Appl Physiol 1992;73:346–53.

Lundgren F, Bennegard K, Elander A, et al. Substrate exchange in human limb muscle during exercise at reduced blood flow. Am J Physiol 1988;255:H1156–H1164.

Pernow B, Zetterquist S. Metabolic evaluation of the leg blood flow in claudicating patients with arterial obstructions at different levels. Scand J Clin Lab Invest 1968;21:277–87.

Regensteiner JG, Hargarten ME, Rutherford RB, Hiatt WR. Functional benefits of peripheral vascular bypass surgery for patients with intermittent claudication. Angiology 1993b;44:1–10.

Regensteiner JG, Steiner JF, Hiatt WR. Exercise training improves functional status in patients with peripheral arterial disease. J Vasc Surg 1996;23:104–15.

Regensteiner JG, Wolfel EE, Brass EP, et al. Chronic changes in skeletal muscle histology and function in peripheral arterial disease. Circulation 1993a;87:413–21.

Rose GA, Blackburn H. Cardiovascular Survey Methods. Geneva: WHO Monograph Series; 1968. No. 56.

Medical Treatment of Claudication

William R. Hiatt, MD
Professor of Medicine
Section of Vascular Medicine, Division of Geriatrics
University of Colorado Health Sciences Center
Denver, Colorado

Objective: To review the advantages and limitations of therapeutic approaches to claudication, based on available data.

Current treatment strategies for symptomatic peripheral arterial disease (PAD) include risk-factor modification, exercise rehabilitation, claudication drug therapy, and the selective use of angioplasty or bypass surgery (Table). The primary risk factors for PAD that must be aggressively managed are cigarette smoking, diabetes, dyslipidemia, and hypertension. Supervised exercise rehabilitation is an effective and unequivocally safe approach to improving physical function and reducing symptoms. Two drugs have been approved in the United States for use in claudicating patients: pentoxifylline, which is of modest efficacy, and now cilostazol, which appears to offer significant benefit. Peripheral bypass surgery and angioplasty have also shown benefit in some patients, but with greater associated costs and potential risks.

RISK-FACTOR MODIFICATION

Cardiovascular risk-factor modification for PAD was reviewed in the second monograph of this series. In this monograph, the benefits of risk-factor modification on peripheral circulation and claudication are reviewed.

Smoking

Tobacco use is perhaps the single most important risk factor associated with PAD. The estimated risk for developing intermittent claudication in persons over age 45 who are current smokers is up to 16-fold times that of nonsmokers (Hirsch et al, 1997). The 5-year mortality rate for patients who continue to smoke is >60%. In addition, those who continue to smoke have a greater likelihood of disease progression and amputation (Jonason and Bergstrom, 1987). Persons with claudication who quit smoking have markedly decreased rates of myocardial infarction and stroke compared with those who continue smoking (Faulkner et al, 1983; Lassila and Lepantalo, 1988). However, the effects of smoking cessation on claudication severity are modest at best (Jonason and Bergstrom, 1987; Quick

and Cotton, 1982). Thus, patients who quit smoking can expect improved survival and decreased progression of PAD, but only a modest improvement in claudication symptoms and walking distance.

Diabetes

Cardiovascular disease causes approximately 65% of deaths in persons with type 2 diabetes (Andersson and Svardsudd, 1995). Diabetes is an especially important risk factor for the development and progression of PAD (Brand et al, 1989). The role of intensive blood glucose control has been well established in the prevention of microvascular complications of diabetes. Comparatively less is known about intensive blood sugar control in the management of macrovascular complications. Recent publications from the United Kingdom Prospective Diabetes Study (UKPDS) Group have helped clarify this matter. In this study, patients with type 2 diabetes given intensive therapy with sulfonylureas or insulin had fewer diabetes-related endpoints and microvascular complications and tended to have fewer myocardial infarctions than patients given diet therapy (UKPDS, 1998b). Patients given intensive therapy with metformin had fewer diabetes events, diabetes-related deaths, and lower all-cause mortality (UKPDS, 1998a). Unfortunately, neither treatment regimen was associated with a reduction in PAD risk or amputations. In the same study, tight blood pressure control was associated with reductions in diabetes endpoints and strokes, but not in PAD events. Thus, there are now data to support the benefits of aggressive blood sugar and blood pressure control in type 2 diabetes. These therapies will reduce the risk of cardiovascular events in patients with type 2 diabetes, but their ability to modify the risk of PAD in terms of symptom relief and risk of amputations has not been fully evaluated. In contrast, trials of lipid-lowering agents have shown that lowering serum cholesterol in diabetic patients can significantly reduce coronary artery disease (CAD) mortality (Pyorala et al, 1997). Finally, considering the significance of smoking as a risk factor for PAD, smoking cessation may be of special relevance for patients with diabetes.

Dyslipidemia

The dyslipidemias present another important risk factor for PAD. Several large, well-controlled trials have demonstrated the value of lowering the serum cholesterol level in patients with underlying coronary disease or at increased risk for coronary events. Meta-analyses used to evaluate results of the cholesterol-lowering trials have clearly demonstrated that patients with cardiovascular disease should have a target serum low-density lipoprotein cholesterol level of ≤100 mg/dL (Gould et al, 1998; Grundy, 1998). In these trials, for every 10% reduction in serum total cholesterol level, CAD mortality risk was reduced by 15% and total mortality risk by 11% (Gould et al, 1998).

In patients with PAD, few studies have evaluated the benefits of lipid-lowering therapies on claudication risk or symptom relief. However, in the Scandinavian Simvastatin Survival Study, the risk of new or worsening claudication was reduced by 38% compared with placebo (Pedersen et al, 1998). Another theoretical benefit of lipid-lowering therapy is to improve endothelial function, which potentially may translate into improved walking distance in patients with claudication.

Hypertension

Hypertension is associated with the development of atherosclerosis, particularly in the coronary and cerebral circulation (Stokes et al, 1987). In patients with PAD, hypertension increases risk of claudication by 2- to 3-fold (Hiatt et al, 1995). Furthermore, treatment of hypertension is essential for preventing or limiting cardiovascular morbidity and mortality (specifically in

Table. Treatment Approaches for Symptomatic Peripheral Arterial Disease

Risk-factor modification

- Smoking cessation
- Diabetes control
- Dyslipidemia management
- Hypertension control

Supervised treadmill walking exercise rehabilitation

Drug therapy

- Cilostazol
- Pentoxifylline

Invasive therapy

- Peripheral bypass surgery
- Percutaneous transluminal angioplasty

terms of stroke and myocardial infarction). The sixth report of the Joint National Committee on Prevention, Detection, Evaluation, and Treatment of High Blood Pressure provides recommendations for managing hypertension (JNC VI, 1997). These guidelines have been updated by the World Health Organization, International Society of Hypertension (World Health Organization, 1999). In patients with cardiovascular disease, two drugs are often needed to achieve target blood pressure goals. Ideally this should be a systolic blood pressure <130 mm Hg and a diastolic blood pressure <85 mm Hg.

All classes of antihypertensive agents, including β-adrenergic blockers, are acceptable for use in patients with PAD (Hiatt et al, 1985). However, medications that lower systemic blood pressure produce a corresponding decrease in limb perfusion pressure. As a result, large decreases in blood pressure may adversely affect claudication walking distance (Solomon et al, 1991). The primary goal of therapy is successful blood pressure reduction, but if the patient notices worsening claudication with the lowering of blood pressure, additional therapies to treat the claudication may be in order.

EXERCISE THERAPY

Over the past 40 years, walking exercise has been recommended as a nonsurgical treatment for claudication (Foley, 1957). A review of the literature has identified 28 trials of exercise conditioning in the PAD population, of which 12 employed a controlled (sometimes randomized) design (Creasy et al, 1990; Dahllof et al, 1976; Gardner and Poehlman, 1995; Hedberg et al, 1988; Hiatt et al, 1990; Mannarino et al, 1989). In most of these studies, the change in walking ability with treatment was evaluated with a constant-load treadmill protocol. The improvement in pain-free walking time ranged from 44% to 290%, with an average increase of 134%. The peak walking time increased from 25% to 183%, with an average increase of 96%. Thus, the ability to sustain walking exercise for longer duration with less claudication pain was improved by training. Studies that employ a graded treadmill protocol have shown improvements in peak exercise performance and peak oxygen consumption (Hiatt et al, 1990). The improvement in peak oxygen consumption indicates that patients can perform activities requiring higher work intensities, such as climbing stairs, gardening, and dancing (activities that were not possible on entry into the study). These same studies have also shown that at a given submaximal workload, exercise training decreases heart rate (Dahllof et al, 1976; Hiatt et al, 1990), ventilation, and oxygen consumption (Hiatt et al, 1990). These changes may contribute to the ability to sustain walking exercise for longer times before claudication pain limits the activity. In addition, there is virtually no morbidity or mortality from exercise rehabilitation.

A supervised exercise program should last up to 60 minutes per session, with monitoring by a skilled nurse or technician. Patients should be encouraged to walk primarily on a treadmill, because this most closely reproduces walking in the community setting. The initial workload of the treadmill is set to a speed and grade that bring on claudication pain within 3 to 5 minutes. Patients walk at this workload until they achieve claudication of moderate severity. They then rest until the claudication abates and resume exercise. This repeated on-and-off exercise is continued throughout the supervised rehabilitation setting. Patients should be reassessed clinically on a weekly basis as they are able to walk farther and farther at their chosen workload. This ongoing reassessment should lead to increases in speed or grade, or both, allowing patients to successfully exercise at increasingly difficult workloads. The net result will be a training benefit (Hiatt et al, 1994). The standard duration of an exercise rehabilitation program is 3 to 6 months, which should yield a 100% to 200% improvement in peak exercise performance on the treadmill. In addition, there should be significant improvements in walking speed and distance, as verified by the Walking Impairment Questionnaire (WIQ); and improvements in physical function and vitality, as revealed by the Medical Outcomes Study Short Form-36 (MOS SF-36) questionnaire (Regensteiner et al, 1996).

A recent trial compared bypass surgery and exercise rehabilitation in patients with claudication (Lund-gren et al, 1989). The results showed that improvements in treadmill exercise performance were greater with surgery than with rehabilitation at 6 and 12 months. However, the complication and mortality rates were significantly greater in the surgical groups, with no complications directly attributed to the exercise therapy. In another study, patients with claudication were randomized to angioplasty or an exercise program (Creasy et al, 1990). The results indicated little improvement in exercise performance in the angioplasty group, with a 25% complication rate. In contrast, the exercise group had a significant improvement in exercise performance, with no complications. Importantly, neither of these studies addressed changes in quality of life or disability resulting from surgery or angioplasty. However, these studies demonstrated that both surgery and an exercise program are effective in the treatment of claudication, whereas the functional benefits of angioplasty are less well established.

The functional benefits of exercise training have been assessed with a battery of questionnaires, including the WIQ, the MOS SF-36, and the Physical Activity Recall instrument (Regensteiner et al, 1996; Regensteiner et al, 1990). These analyses demonstrated that, in the community, treated subjects could walk a greater distance, at a faster speed, and thus perform activities that were considered difficult-to-impossible before the treatment (eg, return to work, dancing, outdoor activities, and shopping). In addition, improvements in weekly caloric expenditure and physical functioning were observed. Control subjects had no change in their level of disability (from questionnaire evaluations) during the course of the study. Thus, a supervised treadmill walking exercise program improved peak exercise performance, relieved the pain of intermittent claudication, and facilitated the ability to walk greater distances and at faster speeds in the community.

The mechanisms by which exercise training improves exercise performance are not well understood. Initially, it was believed that an exercise program would increase skeletal muscle blood flow, thereby improving muscle function and walking ability (Alpert et al, 1969). However, we and others have shown that changes in blood flow with training are modest and not correlated to changes in exercise performance (Ericsson et al, 1970; Hiatt et al, 1990). Another adaptation with training in PAD patients is an improvement in peripheral muscle metabolism, as evidenced by an increase in the extraction of oxygen across the leg during exercise, despite no change in total blood flow (Zetterquist, 1970). Recent observations have confirmed improvements in skeletal muscle metabolism with exercise training (Hiatt et al, 1996). The importance of these findings is that claudication is not simply a disease of abnormal hemodynamics. Therefore, a variety of treatment strategies can be used to improve exercise performance.

PHARMACOLOGIC THERAPY
Pentoxifylline
Pentoxifylline (Trental®) was the first drug approved for treatment of claudication in the United States. This medication has hemorheologic effects that reportedly explain its benefit. However, in randomized controlled trials, the treatment effects of pentoxifylline are relatively modest and clinical benefit is not well substantiated (Hood et al, 1996).

In one of the first randomized trials, pentoxifylline was shown to improve maximal walking distance by 12% compared with placebo, but these differences were not statistically significant in the primary analysis (Porter et al, 1982). More recently, a 21% treatment benefit of pentoxifylline compared with placebo was demonstrated, but again this difference lacked statistical significance (Lindgarde et al, 1989). Importantly, any changes in treadmill walking distance on this medication have not been related to improvements in quality of life or community-based functional status. Therefore, both patients and physicians have found this drug to be of modest benefit. It may be that a more severely affected population (ankle-brachial index [ABI] <0.80 and symptoms >1 year) may be the most responsive (Lindgarde et al, 1989).

Cilostazol
Cilostazol (Pletal®) was recently approved by the US Food and Drug Administration (FDA) for symptomatic treatment of claudication. This medication has undergone an extensive clinical development program, including 8 randomized controlled trials. Two of these studies have been published and reveal highly statistically significant improvements in exercise performance on the drug for both absolute claudication distance and initial claudication distance (Dawson et al, 1998a; Money et al, 1998). In one study, the difference between placebo and drug was >50% for the absolute claudication distance. In addition to improving treadmill-walking distance, cilostazol was also shown to significantly improve the ABI (Money et al, 1998a). Thus, a partial mechanism of action of this medication may be improved limb perfusion.

In unpublished studies, there appears to be a dose response, with the standard 100-mg BID dosage providing the most efficacy. Thus, patients who experience side effects may benefit from a reduced dosage of 50 mg BID.

A recent double-blind study compared the effects of 100 mg cilostazol twice a day, 400 mg pentoxifylline three times a day, and placebo in patients with claudication. Duration of the study was 24 weeks and involved 698 subjects. Maximal walking distance increased 33.5% with placebo, 30.4% with pentoxifylline, and 53.9% with cilostazol. There were no statistical differences between pentoxifylline and placebo in terms of maximal walking distance. Cilostazol, however, was significantly better in improving walking distance than either placebo or pentoxifylline. Similar results were obtained for pain-free walking distance (Dawson et al, 1998b).

An important consideration in studies of cilostazol was the measurement of functional status using the WIQ and MOS SF-36 questionnaire (Money et al, 1998). Results of the MOS SF-36 questionnaire revealed that the physical component was significantly improved by cilostazol compared with placebo. The subscale scores of physical function, bodily pain, general health, and physical role all improved. On the WIQ, walking speed and claudication pain severity were also improved. Thus, patients experience improved physical performance, walking ability, and functional status on this medication.

Cilostazol is generally well tolerated, with the most predominant side effects including headache, loose stools, and dizziness. However, phosphodiesterase inhibitors, such as cilostazol, should not be administered to patients with heart failure. Previous experience with drugs in this class (eg, milrinone) suggests an increased mortality risk in patients with heart failure.

Clinical heart failure is not common in patients with claudication, but a medical history and physical examination are minimally required before prescribing cilostazol. Because ischemic events (eg, myocardial infarction, stroke) are common in patients with PAD, the physician should reevaluate the benefit/risk ratio of cilostazol at regular (ie, annual) intervals. With this caution in mind, a large proportion of patients with claudication should benefit from this new medication.

Carnitines
Patients with PAD develop metabolic abnormalities in the skeletal muscle of the lower extremity (Hiatt et al, 1992). Carnitine and propionyl-L-carnitine are metabolically active agents that improve ischemic muscle metabolism and exercise performance. Clinical trials performed with L-carnitine and propionyl-L-carnitine have shown consistent improvement in exercise performance, with propionyl-L-carnitine demonstrating greater efficacy of the two (Brevetti et al, 1997; Brevetti et al, 1992). The optimal dosage of propionyl-L-carnitine

appears to be 2 g BID (Brevetti et al, 1995). With this treatment, the improvement in absolute claudication distance compared with placebo is approximately 25% to 30%. Quality of life has also been improved by this medication, and there appear to be no serious side effects (Brevetti et al, 1997). Propionyl-L-carnitine is still under investigation and has not been approved for use in the United States. Further studies will be necessary, but it is anticipated that this drug will be under FDA review in the near future.

Prostaglandins

Prostaglandin (PG) drugs, including iloprost and beraprost, had been primarily evaluated in patients with critical limb ischemia (Trubestein et al, 1989). These agents hold promise for the management of ischemic ulcers and for limb preservation. In one study, patients were treated with pentoxifylline, placebo, or PGE_1 in addition to an exercise program. The combination of exercise plus PGE_1 was significantly more effective than pentoxifylline alone or no medication (Scheffler et al, 1994). Findings of another study showed a >50% improvement in maximal walking distance with PGE_1 compared with placebo, along with improvement in quality of life (Belch et al, 1997). Importantly, these studies used intravenous formulations of the medication. Oral analogues of PGs have not been as well studied. A small trial found modest efficacy with beraprost, but also significant side effects such as headache, flushing, and gastrointestinal intolerance (Lievre et al, 1996). Thus, the utility of PGs in claudication has not yet been fully evaluated.

Naftidrofuryl

Naftidrofuryl (nafronyl oxalate) has been available for treating claudication for several decades. It has several proposed mechanisms of action, including antagonizing 5-hydroxytryptamine receptors, possibly improving hemorheologic factors and skeletal muscle metabolism. Several placebo-controlled trials have shown the drug to be more effective than placebo, but there was also a negative trial (Adhoute et al, 1990; Kriessmann and Neiss, 1988; Trubestein et al, 1984b). This medication is not currently under study in the United States and is not available for clinical use.

Buflomedil

Buflomedil is an antiadrenergic agent that promotes vasodilation and improves hemorheology. Although several small studies have shown benefit, this medication is not under development in the United States (Trubestein et al, 1984a).

Antiplatelet Agents

There is no evidence supporting the use of aspirin to improve claudication symptoms. However, aspirin and other antiplatelet drugs are useful in reducing cardiovascular events in this patient population. Comparatively more data are available on the use of ticlopidine, an adenosine diphosphate antagonist. This medication has potent antiplatelet effects, and in several small randomized trials has demonstrated a modest benefit on claudication symptoms (Balasano et al, 1989; Fagher, 1994). Ticlopidine is not, however, approved for treatment of claudication and is not under development for this indication. Clopidogrel (Plavix®) is a new antiplatelet agent indicated for the secondary prevention of ischemic events in patients with PAD. This drug has not been evaluated for any potential efficacy in improving claudication (CAPRIE Steering Committee, 1996).

Vasodilators

Vasodilators were the first medications studied for treatment of claudication. In theory, these agents should improve skeletal muscle blood flow; but studies have found no evidence of clinical efficacy for this indication (Coffman, 1979).

Growth Factors

Both vascular endothelial growth factor and basic fibroblast growth factor are under development for treatment of critical limb ischemia and claudication (Baumgartner et al, 1998; Isner et al, 1995). These drugs have the novel mechanism of action of stimulating collateral blood vessel formation as well as capillary proliferation in ischemic skeletal muscle. Although still in early clinical development, they hold significant promise for treating the spectrum of vascular disease.

Other Agents

The amino acid L-arginine has been shown to improve nitric oxide formation and endothelial-dependant vasodilation in patients with atherosclerosis. Several studies have been performed with this compound in small groups of patients with claudication. These studies have shown improvements in pain-free and maximal walking distance. Thus, while larger studies are necessary, it is interesting to speculate that manipulations of endothelial function may also provide important new therapeutic avenues for patients with PAD (Maxwell et al, 1999; Murohara et al, 1998; Boger et al, 1998).

Many other classes of drugs have been tried for the treatment of claudication, including nitrates, with some small studies showing modest benefit of nitroglycerin (Walker et al, 1998). Chelation therapy has also been popular, but several well-controlled trials found no clinical benefit with this treatment (Guldager et al, 1992; Lyngdorf et al, 1996). Despite the considerable interest shown in developing new drugs to treat claudication, few of these agents have reached completion of a clinical development program. The only effective medication with FDA approval is cilostazol.

INVASIVE THERAPIES

In patients with critical limb ischemia (ischemic pain at rest, nonhealing ulcers, and gangrene), peripheral bypass surgery is indicated to restore blood flow for tissue healing and limb salvage (Blair et al, 1989; Veith et al, 1990). This was noted in the third monograph of this series. In patients with claudication, however, there are no uniform criteria defining when an invasive procedure is necessary. Currently, bypass surgery or percutaneous transluminal angioplasty is recommended for consideration if claudication symptoms limit occupational, social, or leisure activities, and the patient has failed medical therapy (Donaldson and Mannick, 1980; Jamieson, 1988; Myhre, 1990; Rutherford, 1984). These guidelines have led to widely varying practice standards. Increasingly, many institutions do not offer surgery at all for the treatment of claudication. Most reports indicate that 15% to 30% of peripheral bypass operations are for claudication (Brewster et al, 1989; Kent et al, 1988), and this rate reaches 70% to 80% in a minority of centers (Spence et al, 1981; Wilson et al, 1989). Recently, surveys indicate that <10% of patients treated with infrainguinal arterial reconstructions have claudication, whereas >90% of these procedures are performed for critical limb ischemia (Byrne et al, 1999).

The most widely studied outcome of invasive therapy has been long-term graft patency rate. In patients with aortoiliac disease, the 5-year graft patency rate is 89%, and surgical mortality is 4.4%, with a morbidity of 11.4% (Doubilet and Abrams, 1984). Patency rates for angioplasty are 63% over 5 years for aortoiliac disease, with a mortality of 0.2% and a morbidity of 2.3% (Doubilet and Abrams, 1984). In other series, angioplasty has had higher complication rates (Johnston et al, 1987; Wilson et al, 1989). For femoropopliteal disease, surgery has a 5-year patency rate of 60%, mortality of 2.6%, and morbidity of 6.7%. With angioplasty for femoropopliteal disease, the 5-year patency rate is 40% to 60%, but morbidity and mortality rates are low and similar to those described for aortoiliac angioplasty (Johnston et al, 1987). Importantly, surgical graft patency rates do not necessarily translate into improved function. In the few studies in

which functional evaluation has been incorporated, bypass surgery improved treadmill walking time and muscle function, but patients still had claudication and limited activity (Hedberg et al, 1988; Lundgren et al, 1989; Strandness, 1970).

The functional benefits of angioplasty in the treatment of claudication also have not been well defined (Creasy et al, 1990). Because angioplasty is less invasive and expensive than surgery (Tunis et al, 1991), it may be used in a wider spectrum of patients. However, the proliferation of invasive procedures to treat claudication has led to concern that surgery and angioplasty are overused, resulting in increased costs of medical care as well as exposing patients unnecessarily to the potential morbidity and mortality of the procedures. Recently, several experts have called for a medical approach to the treatment of claudication, with a focus on other therapies such as exercise rehabilitation (Coffman, 1991). Nonoperative treatment of claudication is characterized by documented efficacy, minimal cardiovascular risks, and low costs.

CONCLUSIONS AND RECOMMENDATIONS

All patients with claudication manifest systemic atherosclerosis. Thus, the primary goal of therapy is to reduce the systemic risk by modifying cardiovascular risk factors. An aggressive approach to smoking cessation, diabetes therapy, lipid lowering, and treatment of blood pressure should result in reduced risk of cardiovascular events and cardiovascular mortality. Modification of these risk factors should delay the progression of peripheral atherosclerosis but is not likely to improve claudication symptoms. Antiplatelet therapies are also critical in the treatment of patients with PAD. The major benefit of these agents is reduction in systemic risk rather than improvement in clinical symptoms.

Exercise rehabilitation is a well-established treatment for claudication. This approach requires a supervised program, motivated patients, and a commitment to maintaining therapy for 3 to 6 months. Patients who adhere to such a program can expect significant improvement in treadmill performance, quality of life, and functional status. Exercise also carries no risk and therefore can be universally recommended for patients with claudication. The benefits of exercise training are limited to those individuals who are motivated to maintaining long-term compliance.

Several new and effective pharmacologic treatments are now available. Pentoxifylline and now cilostazol are approved for treatment of claudication, but the clinical benefits of pentoxifylline are modest. Cilostazol is therefore the most effective pharmacologic therapy currently available in the United States, but should only be used in appropriate candidates.

Interventional therapies can also be effective for treating claudication. Peripheral bypass surgery carries a risk of morbidity and mortality, but in selected patients, it can significantly improve claudication symptoms. Peripheral angioplasty has similar potential benefit, but it has been less well studied in terms of relieving claudication symptoms. Both interventional strategies should be reserved for patients who initially fail risk-factor modification and medical therapies. A subgroup of patients who have an isolated occlusion or short stenosis of the iliac artery may also be primary candidates for angioplasty. Overall, patients with claudication can now enjoy a wide range of therapeutic choices including lifestyle modification, exercise conditioning, pharmacotherapy, and selective use of revascularization procedures. ■

Key Points

• Modification of cardiovascular risk factors—especially cigarette smoking and hyperlipidemia—is important for patients with PAD.

• Exercise rehabilitation will improve walking ability, physical function, and vitality in patients with claudication.

• Cilostazol is an effective medication currently available for treatment of claudication.

• Other promising claudication treatments in development include propionyl-L-carnitine, prostaglandins, and specific growth factors.

• Invasive therapies (peripheral bypass surgery and angioplasty) may benefit selected patients who have not responded to medical therapy.

BIBLIOGRAPHY

Adhoute G, Andreassian B, Boccalon H, et al. Treatment of stage II chronic arterial disease of the lower limbs with the serotonergic antagonist naftidrofuryl: results after 6 months of a controlled, multicenter study. J Cardiovasc Pharmacol 1990;16 (suppl 3): S75–S80.

Alpert JS, Larsen OA, Lassen NA. Exercise and intermittent claudication. Blood flow in the calf muscle during walking studied by the xenon-133 clearance method. Circulation 1969;39:353–9.

Andersson DK, Svardsudd K. Long-term glycemic control relates to mortality in type II diabetes. Diabetes Care 1995;18:1534–43.

Balasano F, Coccheri S, Libretti A, et al. Ticlopidine in the treatment of intermittent claudication: a 21 month double-blind trial. J Lab Clin Med 1989;114:84–91.

Baumgartner I, Pieczek A, Manor O, et al. Constitutive expression of phVEGF165 after intramuscular gene transfer promotes collateral vessel development in patients with critical leg ischemia. Circulation 1998;97:1114–23.

Belch JJF, Bell PRF, Creissen D, et al. Randomized, double-blind, placebo-controlled study evaluating the efficacy and safety of AS-013, a prostaglandin E_1 prodrug, in patients with intermittent claudication. Circulation 1997;95:2298–2302.

Blair JM, Gewertz BL, Moosa H, Lu CT, Zarins CK. Percutaneous transluminal angioplasty versus surgery for limb-threatening ischemia. J Vasc Surg 1989;9:698–703.

Boger RH, Bode-Boger SM, Thiele W, et al. Restoring vascular nitric oxide formation by L-arginine improves the symptoms of intermittent claudication in patients with peripheral arterial occlusive disease. J Am Coll Cardiol 1998;32(5):1336–44.

Brand FN, Abbott RD, Kannel WB. Diabetes, intermittent claudication, and risk of cardiovascular events. Diabetes 1989;38:504–9.

Brevetti G, Perna S, Sabba C, et al. Superiority of L-propionyl carnitine vs L-carnitine in improving walking capacity in patients with peripheral vascular disease: an acute, intravenous, double-blind, cross-over study. Eur Heart J 1992;13:251–5.

Brevetti G, Perna S, Sabba C, Martone VD, Condorelli M. Propionyl-L-carnitine in intermittent claudication: double-blind, placebo-controlled, dose titration, multicenter study. J Am Coll Cardiol 1995;26:1411–6.

Brevetti G, Perna S, Sabba C, Martone VD, Di Lorio A, Barletta G. Effect of propionyl-L-carnitine on quality of life in intermittent claudication. Am J Cardiol 1997;79:777–80.

Brewster DC, Cambria RP, Darling RC, et al. Long-term results of combined iliac balloon angioplasty and distal surgical revascularization. Ann Surg 1989;210: 324–31.

Byrne J, Darling RC, Chang BB, et al. Infrainguinal arterial reconstruction for claudication: Is it worth the risk? An analysis of 409 procedures. J Vasc Surg 1999;29:259–69.

CAPRIE Steering Committee. A randomised, blinded, trial of clopidogrel versus aspirin in patients at risk of ischaemic events (CAPRIE). Lancet 1996;348: 1329–39.

Coffman JD. Intermittent claudication—be conservative. N Engl J Med 1991;325:577–8.

Coffman JD. Vasodilator drugs in peripheral vascular disease. N Engl J Med 1979;300:713–7.

Creasy TS, McMillan PJ, Fletcher EWL, Collin J, Morris PJ. Is percutaneous transluminal angioplasty better than exercise for claudication? Preliminary results from a prospective randomized trial. Eur J Vasc Surg 1990;4:135–40.

Dahllof A, Holm J, Schersten T, Sivertsson R. Peripheral arterial insufficiency. Effect of physical training on walking tolerance, calf blood flow, and blood flow resistance. Scand J Rehab Med 1976;8:19–26.

Dawson DL, Cutler BS, Meissner MH, Strandness DEJ. Cilostazol has beneficial effects in treatment of intermittent claudication: results from a multicenter, randomized, prospective, double-blind trial. Circulation 1998a;98:678–86.

Dawson DL, Beebe HG, Davidson WH, Chinoy DA, Herd JA, Hiatt WR, Heckman JD, Bortey EB, Forbes WP. Cilostazol or pentoxifylline for claudication? Circulation 1998b;98:58.

Donaldson MC, Mannick JA. Femoropopliteal bypass grafting for intermittent claudication. Arch Surg 1980;115:724–7.

Doubilet P, Abrams HL. The cost of underutilization. Percutaneous transluminal angioplasty for peripheral vascular disease. N Engl J Med 1984;310:95–102.

Ericsson B, Haeger K, Lindell SE. Effect of physical training on intermittent claudication. Angiology 1970;21:188–92.

Fagher B. Long-term effects of ticlopidine on lower limb blood flow, ankle/brachial index and symptoms in peripheral arteriosclerosis. A double-blind study. The STIMS Group in Lund. Swedish Ticlopidine Multicenter Study. Angiology 1994;45:777–88.

Faulkner KW, House AK, Castleden WM. The effect of cessation of smoking on the accumulative survival rates of patients with symptomatic peripheral vascular disease. Med J Aust 1983;1:217–9.

Foley WT. Treatment of gangrene of the feet and legs by walking. Circulation 1957;15:689–700.

Gardner AW, Poehlman ET. Exercise rehabilitation programs for the treatment of claudication pain. A meta-analysis. JAMA 1995;274:975–80.

Gould AL, Rossouw JE, Santanello NC, Heyse JF, Furberg CD. Cholesterol reduction yields clinical benefit: impact of statin trials. Circulation 1998;97:946–52.

Grundy SM. Statin trials and goals of cholesterol-lowering therapy. Circulation 1998;97:1436–9.

Guldager B, Jelnes R, Jorgensen SJ, et al. EDTA treatment of intermittent claudication—a double-blind, placebo-controlled study. J Int Med 1992; 231:261–7.

Hedberg B, Langstrom M, Angquist KA, Fugl-Meyer AR. Isokinetic plantar flexor performance and fatigability in peripheral arterial insufficiency. Acta Chir Scand 1988;154:363–9.

Hiatt WR, Hoag S, Hamman RF. Effect of diagnostic criteria on the prevalence of peripheral arterial disease. The San Luis Valley diabetes study. Circulation 1995;91:1472–9.

Hiatt WR, Regensteiner JG, Hargarten ME, Wolfel EE, Brass EP. Benefit of exercise conditioning for patients with peripheral arterial disease. Circulation 1990;81:602–9.

Hiatt WR, Regensteiner JG, Wolfel EE, Carry MR, Brass EP. Effect of exercise training on skeletal muscle histology and metabolism in peripheral arterial disease. J Appl Physiol 1996;81:780–8.

Hiatt WR, Stoll S, Nies AS. Effect of β-adrenergic blockers on the peripheral circulation in patients with peripheral vascular disease. Circulation 1985; 72:1226–31.

Hiatt WR, Wolfel EE, Meier RH, Regensteiner JG. Superiority of treadmill walking exercise vs. strength training for patients with peripheral arterial disease. Implications for the mechanism of the training response. Circulation 1994;90:1866–74.

Hiatt WR, Wolfel EE, Regensteiner JG, Brass EP. Skeletal muscle carnitine metabolism in patients with unilateral peripheral arterial disease. J Appl Physiol 1992;73:346–53.

Hirsch AT, Treat-Jacobson D, Lando HA, Hatsukami DK. The role of tobacco cessation, antiplatelet and lipid-lowering therapies in the treatment of peripheral arterial disease. Vasc Med 1997;2:243–51.

Hood SC, Moher D, Barber GG. Management of intermittent claudication with pentoxifylline: meta-analysis of randomized controlled trials. Can Med Assoc J 1996;155:1053–9.

Isner JM, Walsh K, Symes J, et al. Arterial gene therapy for therapeutic angiogenesis in patients with peripheral arterial disease. Circulation 1995;91:2687–92.

Jamieson C. The management of intermittent claudication. Practitioner 1988;232:613–6.

Johnston KW, Rae M, Hogg-Johnston SA, et al. 5-year results of a prospective study of percutaneous transluminal angioplasty. Ann Surg 1987;206:403–13.

Joint National Committee on Prevention, Detection, Evaluation, and Treatment of High Blood Pressure. The sixth report [see comments]. [published erratum appears in Arch Intern Med 1998 Mar 23;158(6):573]. Arch Intern Med 1997;157:2413–46.

Jonason T, Bergstrom R. Cessation of smoking in patients with intermittent claudication. Acta Med Scand 1987;221:253–60.

Kent KC, Donaldson MC, Attinger CE, Couch NP, Mannick JA, Whittemore AD. Femoropopliteal reconstruction for claudication. Arch Surg 1988;123:1196–8.

Kriessmann A, Neiss A. Clinical effectiveness of naftidrofuryl in intermittent claudication. Vasa J Vasc Dis 1988;24(suppl):27–32.

Lassila R, Lepantalo M. Cigarette smoking and the outcome after lower limb arterial surgery. Acta Chir Scand 1988;154:635–40.

Lievre M, Azoulay S, Lion L, Morand S, Girre JP, Boissel JP. A dose-effect study of beraprost sodium in intermittent claudication. J Cardiovasc Pharmacol 1996;27:788–93.

Lindgarde F, Jelnes R, Bjorkman H, et al. Conservative drug treatment in patients with moderately severe chronic occlusive peripheral arterial disease. Scandinavian Study Group. Circulation 1989;80:1549–56.

Lundgren F, Dahllof A, Lundholm K, Schersten T, Volkmann R. Intermittent claudication—surgical reconstruction or physical training? A prospective randomized trial of treatment efficiency. Ann Surg 1989;209:346–55.

Lyngdorf P, Guldager B, Holm J, Jorgensen SJ, Jelnes R. Chelation therapy for intermittent claudication: a double-blind, randomized, controlled trial [letter; comment]. Circulation 1996;93:395–6.

Mannarino E, Pasqualini L, Menna M, Maragoni G, Orlandi U. Effects of physical training on peripheral vascular disease: a controlled study. Angiology 1989;40:5–10.

Maxwell AJ, Anderson B. Improvement in walking distance and quality of life in peripheral arterial disease by a nutritional product designed to enhance nitric oxide activity. J Am Coll Cardiol 1999;33:277a.

Money SR, Herd JA, Isaacsohn JL, et al. Effect of cilostazol on walking distances in patients with intermittent claudication caused by peripheral vascular disease. J Vasc Surg 1998;27:267–74.

Murohara T, Asahara T, Silver M, Bauters C, Masuda H, Kalka C, Kearney M, Chen D, Symes JF, Fishman MC, Huang PL, Isner JM. Nitric oxide synthase modulates angiogenesis in response to tissue ischemia. J Clin Invest 1998;101:2567–78.

Myhre HO. Is femoropopliteal bypass surgery indicated for the treatment of intermittent claudication? Acta Chir Scand 1990;555(suppl):39–42.

Pedersen TR, Kjekshus J, Pyorala K, et al. Effect of simvastatin on ischemic signs and symptoms in the Scandinavian Simvastatin Survival Study (4S). Am J Cardiol 1998;81:333–5.

Porter JM, Cutler BS, Lee BY, et al. Pentoxifylline efficacy in the treatment of intermittent claudication: multi-center controlled double-blind trial with objective assessment of chronic occlusive arterial disease patients. Am Heart J 1982;104:66–72.

Pyorala K, Pedersen TR, Kjekshus J, Faergeman O, Olsson AG, Thorgeirsson G. Cholesterol lowering with simvastatin improves prognosis of diabetic patients with coronary heart disease. A subgroup analysis of the Scandinavian Simvastatin Survival Study (4S). Diabetes Care 1997;20:614–20.

Quick CRG, Cotton LT. The measured effect of stopping smoking on intermittent claudication. Br J Surg 1982;69(suppl):S24–S26.

Regensteiner JG, Steiner JF, Hiatt WR. Exercise training improves functional status in patients with peripheral arterial disease. J Vasc Surg 1996;23:104–15.

Regensteiner JG, Steiner JF, Panzer RJ, Hiatt WR. Evaluation of walking impairment by questionnaire in patients with peripheral arterial disease. J Vasc Med Biol 1990;2:142–52.

Rutherford RB. Evaluation and selection of patients for vascular surgery. In: Rutherford RB, ed. Vascular Surgery, 2nd ed. Philadelphia, Pa: WB Saunders Co; 1984:11–8.

Scheffler P, de la Hamette D, Gross J, Mueller H, Schieffer H. Intensive vascular training in stage IIb of peripheral arterial occlusive disease. The additive effects of intravenous prostaglandin E1 or intravenous pentoxifylline during training. Circulation 1994;90:818–22.

Solomon SA, Ramsay LE, Yeo WW, Parnell L, Morris-Jones W. β blockade and intermittent claudication: placebo controlled trial of atenolol and nifedipine and their combination. BMJ 1991;303:1100–4.

Spence RK, Freiman DB, Gatenby R, et al. Long-term results of transluminal angioplasty of the iliac and femoral arteries. Arch Surg 1981;116:1377–86.

Stokes J, Kannel WB, Wolf PA, Cupples LA, D'Agostino RB. The relative importance of selected risk factors for various manifestations of cardiovascular disease among men and women from 35 to 64 years old: 30 years of follow-up in the Framingham Study. Circulation 1987;75:V65–V73.

Strandness DE. Functional results after revascularization of the profunda femoris artery. Am J Surg 1970;119:240–5.

Trubestein G, Balzer K, Bisler H, et al. Buflomedil in arterial occlusive disease: results of a controlled multicenter study. Angiology 1984a;35:500–5.

Trubestein G, Bohme H, Heidrich H, et al. Naftidrofuryl in chronic arterial disease: results of a controlled multicenter study. Angiology 1984b;35:701–8.

Trubestein G, von Bary S, Breddin K, et al. Intravenous prostaglandin E1 versus pentoxifylline therapy in chronic arterial occlusive disease—a controlled randomised multicenter study. Vasa J Vasc Dis 1989;18(suppl 28):44–9.

Tunis SR, Bass EB, Steinberg EP. The use of angioplasty, bypass surgery, and amputation in the management of peripheral vascular disease. N Engl J Med 1991;325:556–62.

UK Prospective Diabetes Study (UKPDS) Group. Effect of intensive blood-glucose control with metformin on complications in overweight patients with type 2 diabetes (UKPDS 34) [see comments]. [published erratum appears in Lancet 1998 Nov 7;352 (9139): 1557]. Lancet 1998a;352:854–65.

UK Prospective Diabetes Study (UKPDS) Group. Intensive blood-glucose control with sulphonylureas or insulin compared with conventional treatment and risk of complications in patients with type 2 diabetes (UKPDS 33) [see comments]. Lancet 1998b;352: 837–53.

Veith FJ, Gupta SK, Wengerter KR, et al. Changing arteriosclerotic disease patterns and management strate-gies in lower-limb-threatening ischemia. Ann Surg 1990;212:402–12.

Walker SR, Tennant S, MacSweeney ST. A randomized, double-blind, placebo-controlled, crossover study to assess the immediate effect of sublingual glyceryl trinitrate on the ankle brachial pressure index, claudication, and maximum walking distance of patients with intermittent claudication. J Vasc Surg 1998; 28:895–900.

Wilson SE, Wolf GL, Cross AP. Percutaneous transluminal angioplasty versus operation for peripheral arteriosclerosis. J Vasc Surg 1989;9:1–8.

World Health Organization. International Society of Hypertension Guidelines for the Management of Hypertension. Guidelines Subcommittee. J Hypertens 1999;17:151–83.

Zetterquist S. The effect of active training on the nutritive blood flow in exercising ischemic legs. Scand J Clin Lab Invest 1970;25:101–11.

Assessing Ambulation, Functional Status, and Quality of Life in Patients with Claudication

Judith G. Regensteiner, PhD
Associate Professor of Medicine
University of Colorado Health Sciences Center
Section of Vascular Medicine
Denver, Colorado

Objective: To review assessment instruments that can be used in clinical practice in evaluating functional status and quality of life in the patient limited by claudication.

Intermittent claudication resulting from peripheral arterial disease (PAD) causes limitation of ambulatory activities and impairment of functional status and quality of life. Treatment goals include symptom relief and improvement of ambulatory capacity. Clinicians should be prepared to assess the effects of treatment on preservation of function, limitation of symptoms, and improvement in quality of life. A range of useful assessment instruments are available for evaluating the patient with claudication. For example, the ankle-brachial index (ABI) provides a measure of the severity of underlying vascular disease; treadmill exercise testing offers an objective assessment of functional status; the 6-minute walk test is another functional measure that is well suited for clinical practice; and various questionnaires (eg, the Walking Impairment Questionnaire [WIQ] and the Medical Outcomes Study SF-36 [MOS SF-36]) are used to assess physical function and/or emotional and social domains. These instruments are essential for providing clinicians with the information needed to evaluate treatment approaches and make management decisions.

In clinical medicine, the assessment of functional status and quality of life is a relatively new but growing field (McDowell and Newell, 1996). Functional status assessment methodologies have been applied in numerous clinical trials and have become key outcome measures in the management of chronic diseases. As a result, instruments have been developed and validated rigorously to assess functional status and quality of life in patients with claudication (Regensteiner et al, 1996; Regensteiner et al, 1990; Regensteiner et al, 1993; Brazier et al, 1993; EuroQol Group, 1990; Chambers, 1993; Chambers, 1984). Importantly, these instruments can be used to assess results of any of the medical or interventional treatments used to improve walking ability in claudicating patients.

Several types of treatment have been developed for patients with claudication. Exercise rehabilitation has been shown in numerous studies to be effective in improving exercise performance and relieving claudication pain (Hiatt et al, 1990a; Hiatt et al, 1994; Larson and Lassen, 1966; Lepantalo et al, 1984; Dahllof et al, 1974; Patterson et al, 1997). Peripheral bypass surgery and angioplasty in selected patients with appropriate perfusion anatomy have also succeeded in relieving symptoms (Regensteiner et al, 1993; Thompson and Garrett, 1980; Doubilet and Abrams, 1984; Jeans et al, 1986). Finally, new pharmacologic agents are being developed (Hiatt, in press) such as cilostazol, which has been shown to improve both treadmill walking and quality-of-life parameters and was recently cleared for marketing by the US Food and Drug Administration (Tsuchikane et al, 1998; Dawson et al, 1998).

Patients with claudication often have comorbid conditions that may also interfere with quality of life. In fact, such conditions may potentially impair quality of life more than claudication. If the goal is to identify the limitations imposed by claudication and the benefit of interventions for improving walking ability, assessment measures are most easily interpreted in patients whose primary limiting factor is claudication. However, these instruments will also incorporate the limitations caused by comorbid conditions. For example, the development of osteoarthritis in a person with claudication may further impair walking; this will manifest in a worsened questionnaire score.

METHODS USED TO ASSESS FUNCTIONAL STATUS

Appropriate evaluation methods are required in order to determine the benefit of any claudication therapy. These methods should be standardized and quantified so that both the baseline condition of patients and the outcomes of treatment can be clearly identified. The Table summarizes the strengths and limitations of some of the more commonly used methods of functional assessment.

Hemodynamic Assessment

The peripheral circulation is commonly assessed by measuring resting and postexercise systolic blood pressures in the ankle and arm with a Doppler ultrasonic instrument. At rest, the ABI indicates the severity of the underlying vascular disease (Hiatt et al, 1990b). In a large population of controls and diabetics, abnormal ABIs were defined as <0.90 at rest and a 20% decrease after exercise (Hiatt et al, 1990b; Orchard et al, 1993).

Before the ABI is measured, patients should rest for 10 to 15 minutes. Blood pressure measurements in the dorsalis pedis, posterior tibial, and brachial arteries are duplicated to provide greater assurance of accuracy (Hiatt et al, 1988). These tests are easy to perform, well tolerated by patients, require only simple equipment (ie, a hand-held Doppler), and are relatively inexpensive. Measurement of the ABI is important for assessing change in the severity of PAD. In addition, in some studies, ABI has been correlated with measures of functional status (Siemanski and Gardner, 1997), although it is not considered a primary marker of functional limitation.

Treadmill Testing in PAD

Treadmill testing prior to undergoing treatment and after completion of the program is an objective means of assessing change in performance. Importantly, exercise-testing protocols used in PAD patients must be much less strenuous than those employed with healthy individuals; this entails reduced speed and less rapidly increasing grade (Currie et al, 1995). Two types of treadmill protocol—graded and constant-load—have been

validated as objective measures of functional status (Hiatt et al, 1988). The measures most commonly used to evaluate treadmill performance are claudication-free walking time or distance (initial claudication distance, ICD) and maximal, claudication-limited walking time or distance (absolute claudication distance, ACD). The latter measure is used most frequently in clinical trials as the primary end point.

Six-Minute Walk Test

This test was found to yield reproducible results in repeated assessments that did not involve treatment (evidence of reliability); importantly, these results correlated with measures of treadmill walking. The 6-minute walk test has potentially great practical benefit, because it does not require equipment and is easily adapted for use in a clinical setting. It has been validated in one study so far (Montgomery and Gardner, 1998). Further validations would help ensure greater acceptance among practitioners.

Questionnaire Assessments

Ideally, patients with claudication should undergo a treadmill test to provide an objective measure of walking ability. Treadmill testing can also assess the presence of cardiac disease, a common comorbidity in patients with claudication. For comprehensive evaluation of functional status in the PAD population, community-based measures (ie, questionnaires) should be incorporated as well. In fact, questionnaires that have been appropriately validated can serve as the primary measure of functional status when treadmill testing is not an option. As with treadmill testing, criteria must be established to judge the utility of a questionnaire. In brief, a questionnaire should be valid, reliable, and sensitive to change (Feinstein, 1987). Especially in a busy clinical practice, it is important that assessments also be practical, so that the patient and the health care professional can readily work with the instrument.

Two main types of questionnaires have been used in the claudicating patient. Functional status questionnaires evaluate aspects of walking as well as habitual physical activity levels and general ability to carry out normal activities (McDowell and Newell, 1996). Quality-of-life questionnaires evaluate life satisfaction, morale, and happiness (McDowell and Newell, 1996). The term "quality of life" denotes the patient's perceived well-being in physical, emotional, and social terms. Following are capsule evaluations of specific questionnaires used to evaluate walking ability, functional status, and quality of life in the claudicating population.

Table. Assessment of Methods Used to Evaluate Functional Status in Persons with Claudication

Instrument	Strengths	Limitations	Recommendations
Ankle-brachial index (ABI) (Hiatt et al, 1990b; McDermott et al, 1998)	Measure of disease severity In some studies, correlated with measures of functional status	Not strongly (or sometimes at all) correlated with measures of functional status in many studies	Use *primarily* to evaluate disease severity, only as a *secondary* marker of functional status
Treadmill test (Hiatt et al, 1988; Hiatt et al, 1990a)	Objective measure of walking ability Sensitive to treatment effect Reproducible	Relatively expensive Time/availability Does not measure community-based functional status	Use in clinical trials In clinical setting, use only when objective endpoint is needed
Six-minute walk (Montgomery and Gardner, 1998; McDermott et al, 1998)	Objective Somewhat reproducible Easily available Less expensive than treadmill	Limited validation data Not as reproducible as treadmill data Does not measure community-based functional status	Potentially useful as treadmill surrogate after more validation accomplished
Activity devices (Regensteiner et al, 1996; Siemanski et al, 1997)	Reflect daily ambulatory activity level	Limited validation data Subject to user capability	Use as research tool
Questionnaires			
Walking Impairment Questionnaire (WIQ) (Regensteiner et al, 1996, 1990, 1993; McDermott et al, 1998)	Assesses limitations in walking Validated against treadmill walking, 6-minute walk	Administered to patient	Use to assess functional status/quality of life in the clinical setting
Low Level Physical Activity Recall (LOPAR) (Regensteiner et al, 1996)	Habitual physical activity level (work, housework, leisure) Validated against treadmill walking	Administered to patient Requires more training to administer than the other questionnaires suggested	Use as research tool
Medical Outcomes Study SF-36 (MOS SF-36) (Regensteiner et al, 1996)	Measures physical functioning in peripheral arterial disease Self-administered Wide utilization, much comparison data with other disease states and normal controls	Primarily sensitive in aspects of the physical component; may not be sensitive in aspects of the mental component	Use to assess functional status/quality of life in the clinical setting

Functional Status Questionnaires

The WIQ is used to assess the ability of PAD patients to walk defined distances and speeds and to climb stairs (Regensteiner et al, 1996; Regensteiner et al, 1990; Regensteiner et al, 1993; McDermott et al, 1998). The questionnaire also evaluates claudication severity and the presence of other (nonclaudication) symptoms that may limit walking. The WIQ has been used extensively in PAD patients to evaluate changes in community-based walking ability resulting from exercise training or peripheral bypass surgery (Regensteiner et al, 1996;

Regensteiner et al, 1990; Regensteiner et al, 1993). It has also been applied in numerous trials of pharmacologic agents to treat claudication. The WIQ was validated against measures of treadmill walking (ACD and ICD) (Regensteiner et al, 1996; Regensteiner et al, 1990; Regensteiner et al, 1993) and against the 6-minute walk test (McDermott et al, 1998). This questionnaire can be administered by health care personnel in approximately 5 minutes.

The Low Level Physical Activity Recall (LOPAR) questionnaire provides a global measure of physical activity by assessing total energy expenditure at work and during home and leisure-time activities, as recalled by the patient at the end of the week (Regensteiner et al, 1996). The LOPAR was modified from the original Physical Activity Recall questionnaire (Sallis et al, 1985) to enable activity measurement in the very sedentary individual. The LOPAR has been used extensively in PAD patients and in persons with diabetes or impaired glucose tolerance (Regensteiner et al, 1996; Regensteiner et al, 1995). It has been validated against measures of graded treadmill walking (ACD and ICD) (Regensteiner et al, 1996). Health care personnel administer this questionnaire in about 8 minutes.

Combined Functional Status and Quality-of-Life Questionnaires

The MOS SF-36 has been validated and found reliable in large populations of healthy and diseased individuals (Tarlov et al, 1989; Stewart et al, 1989). It is used to measure physical function, physical role, general health perception, bodily pain, mental health, social functioning, emotional role, and vitality. These domains are aggregated in physical and mental component scores. The MOS SF-36 also evaluates perceived change in health status over the past year, thereby combining elements of the functional status questionnaire and the quality-of-life questionnaire. It has been broadly used in chronic disease states (including PAD and cardiac conditions) and in healthy individuals (Regensteiner et al, 1996; Tarlov et al, 1989; Stewart et al, 1989). In the PAD population, the MOS SF-36 has been validated against measures of graded treadmill walking for evaluation of exercise rehabilitation and pharmacologic interventions (Regensteiner et al, 1996; Hiatt, in press). In contrast to the uniformly significant changes typically observed in physical function and overall physical component scores after effective treatments, elements from the mental component are not usually modified by treatments that improve walking ability. This questionnaire is self-administered and takes 5 to 10 minutes to complete.

Although not validated against treadmill walking, the Nottingham Health Profile (NHP) questionnaire has been widely used in European centers to evaluate patients with claudication (Hunt et al, 1985; McDowell et al, 1978). It is similar to the MOS SF-36 in that it evaluates the physical, social, and emotional health domains. Other questionnaires of this combined type include the European Quality of Life Scale (EuroQol) (Brazier et al, 1993; EuroQol Group, 1990) and the McMaster Health Index Questionnaire (MHIQ) (Chambers, 1993; Chambers, 1984). The 5 domains covered by the EuroQol are mobility, self-care, role

function, family and leisure activities, and pain and mood. The MHIQ covers physical, emotional, and social functions.

The questionnaires discussed above are the most widely used and accepted for patients with claudication. They do not, however, represent an exhaustive list of all instruments available for this patient population. Other methods that have had at least initial success in assessing functional status include the use of pedometers and accelerometers (Siemanski et al, 1997).

EFFECTS OF CLAUDICATION ON FUNCTIONAL STATUS AND QUALITY OF LIFE AT BASELINE AND AFTER INTERVENTIONS

Assessments of functional status and quality of life have been reported in claudicating patients who have received exercise rehabilitation, peripheral bypass surgery, angioplasty, and pharmacologic therapy. Data from some of these studies are presented below to show the results and importance of evaluating these characteristics.

Baseline Assessment

At the baseline measurement point of an intervention study, or in the absence of an intervention, it is apparent that claudication causes severe disability. Using the WIQ in studies, we have observed that claudicating patients reported a 50% decrease in walking distance and speed compared to normal age-matched controls. The habitual physical activity score (LOPAR) and physical functioning score (MOS SF-36) were decreased as well (Regensteiner et al, 1996). Several other studies have reported similar findings (Khaira et al, 1996; Pell, 1995; Currie et al, 1995; Ponte and Cattinelli, 1995). Using the MOS SF-36, Pell reported that all scores were lower in patients with claudication compared to population norms (Pell, 1995). Khaira, using the NHP, reported that patients with claudication have greater perceived problems in the areas of energy, pain, emotional reactions, sleep, and physical mobility (Khaira et al, 1996). As a whole, the data show that claudication has adverse effects on functional status and quality of life, in addition to specific ambulatory ability.

Exercise Rehabilitation

All studies of exercise conditioning in persons with PAD have reported an increase in graded treadmill exercise performance and a lessening of claudication pain severity during exercise (Hiatt et al, 1990a; Hiatt et al, 1994; Larsen and Lassen, 1966; Lepantalo et al, 1984; Dahllof et al, 1974; Patterson et al, 1997). The improvement in pain-free walking time ranges from 44% to

300% and in maximal walking time increases from 25% to 442%. The consistency of findings suggests that exercise training programs have a clinically important impact on functional capacity in PAD patients.

Randomized trials carried out to evaluate the efficacy of exercise rehabilitation have utilized questionnaires to assess change in functional status (Regensteiner et al, 1996; Regensteiner et al, 1990). In one study, 29 patients with disabling claudication were randomized to 1 of 2 exercise programs (treadmill training or strength training) or a control group (Regensteiner et al, 1996; Hiatt et al, 1994). After 24 weeks of treadmill training, improvements were observed in the WIQ, LOPAR, and MOS SF-20 scores. In contrast, minimal benefits in functional status measured by treadmill walking or questionnaire resulted from strength training. Control subjects showed no change in treadmill or community-based functional variables (Regensteiner et al, 1996; Hiatt et al, 1994).

Two studies compared the effectiveness of a hospital-based program of exercise rehabilitation to a home-based rehabilitation program (Patterson et al, 1997; Regensteiner et al, 1997). In one study, patients in the home-based program received initial instructions and weekly phone calls to check on their progress, whereas the hospital-based program involved supervised exercise 3 times a week. It was found that only the hospital-based program improved functional status and quality of life, as measured by treadmill walking, the MOS SF-36, and the WIQ (Regensteiner et al, 1997). In the other study, the home-based group received weekly lectures and weekly exercise instructions, whereas the hospital-based group received the same lecture program and supervised exercise (Patterson et al, 1997). MOS data and the treadmill walking score improved in both groups, with greater benefit accruing to those in the hospital-based program. Importantly, in both studies, questionnaire and treadmill responses were concordant.

Peripheral Bypass Surgery

Successful interventional treatment will improve limb perfusion as assessed by the ABI. However, changes in blood flow per se may not correlate well with changes in functional status (Hiatt et al, 1990b). The latter, therefore, must be assessed separately. A study evaluating exercise performance and functional status in patients with claudication who received peripheral bypass surgery revealed that these measures were substantially improved by the surgery (Regensteiner et al, 1993). The benefits included improvements of 100% in treadmill walking time, 200% in ability to walk distances, and 100% in ability to walk at faster speeds

(as measured by the WIQ), along with improvements in claudication symptoms.

Percutaneous Transluminal Angioplasty

A randomized study comparing angioplasty and medical treatment in patients with claudication showed that angioplasty produced greater improvements in treadmill walking and pain score on the NHP questionnaire (Whyman et al, 1996). However, of the 600 patients screened, only 62 were found to have lesions suitable for this intervention. Other studies have employed the EuroQol to evaluate functional status and quality of life in 29 patients with claudication before and after angioplasty (Cook et al, 1996, 1997). Perceived health state, mobility, usual activities, pain, and mood were all found to improve significantly following angioplasty.

Pharmacologic Intervention

A multicenter study examining the effects of cilostazol on walking distances in 239 patients with intermittent claudication found improvements in some measures of functional status (Money et al, 1998). Walking speed improved on the WIQ, as did the specific measure of walking difficulty. Improvement was also observed in the physical component score of the MOS SF-36. These changes were concordant with observed treadmill walking performance. This study provides one example of assessment measures determining the potential functional benefits of drug therapy in claudication patients. Additional drug therapy trials are ongoing, all of which incorporate functional status and quality-of-life evaluations.

Practical Suggestions for the Office-based Clinician

Measurement of the ABI is a simple and important tool for assessment of PAD severity. Treadmill testing provides an objective measure of exercise performance, but may not be possible for all patients in the clinical setting. In a busy office-based practice, administration of the WIQ and MOS SF-36 will yield the most specific (walking ability) and broadest overall (functional status/quality of life) evaluations with only a minimal investment of time. Because the patient self-administers the MOS SF-36, it can be given up on check-in for optimal efficiency. The WIQ can be administered when the patient is seated in an examination room. Before the questionnaires are given, it is important to reassure patients that they are not being "tested" on their knowledge or detailed recall, but rather should answer the questions based on their initial response.

SUMMARY

Intermittent claudication impairs functional status and quality of life. Reducing this disability is therefore an important goal of treatment. To evaluate the efficacy of an intervention designed to improve functional status requires that appropriate outcome measures be used to assess all treatments. Such outcome measures should include questionnaire assessments as well as treadmill testing. Thus, functional status changes resulting from any intervention can be evaluated, and interventions can be compared to one another using consistent methodologies. This information is important to the busy clinician because all treatments have costs, measurable in terms of money, time, comorbidity, effort, pain, and benefit. Appropriate questionnaires may help clinicians in making critical decisions about optimal utilization of treatments. In the case of the patient who is limited in his or her daily activities by claudication, such decisions should be made with functional end points in mind. ■

Key Points

- Functional status (ie, walking ability) and quality of life are the critical parameters for assessment of claudication patients.

- When feasible, treadmill testing offers the optimal objective measure of functional status. The 6-minute walk test has great practical potential for use in clinical settings.

- Appropriate questionnaires, if validated against treadmill testing, can also serve as reliable measures of functional status.

- Combined functional status and quality-of-life questionnaires can be used to evaluate both physical status (walking capability) and emotional and social aspects of patients' lives.

- Standardized assessment measures have been effectively incorporated in clinical trials evaluating exercise rehabilitation, peripheral bypass surgery, angioplasty, and pharmacologic therapy in patients with claudication.

- In a busy office-based practice, use of easily administered questionnaires can rapidly provide information that can help guide treatment decisions.

ACKNOWLEDGMENT

Dr. Regensteiner is supported by a Clinical Research Grant from the American Diabetes Association.

BIBLIOGRAPHY

Brazier J, Hones N, Kind P. Testing the validity of the EuroQol and comparing it with SF-36 Health Survey questionnaire. Qual Life Res 1993;2:169–80.

Chambers LW. The McMaster Health Index Questionnaire. In: Wenger NK, Mattson ME, Furberg CD, Elinson J, eds. Assessment of Quality of Life in Clinical Trials of Cardiovascular Therapies. New York: Le Jacq; 1984:160–4.

Chambers LW. The McMaster Health Index Questionnaire: an update. In: Walker SR, Rosser RM, eds. Quality of Life Assessment: Key Issues in the 1990s. Dordrecht, Netherlands: Kluwer Academic Publishers; 1993:131–49.

Cook TA, Galland RB. Quality of life changes after angioplasty for claudication: medium-term results affected by comorbid conditions. Cardiovasc Surg 1997;5(4):424–6.

Cook TA, O'Regan M, Galland RB. Quality of life following percutaneous transluminal angioplasty for claudication. Eur J Vasc Endovasc Surg 1996;11:191–4.

Currie IC, Wilson YG, Baird RN, Lamont PM. Treatment of intermittent claudication: the impact on quality of life. Eur J Vasc Endovasc Surg 1995;10:356–61.

Dahllof A, Bjorntorp B, Holm J, Schersten T. Metabolic activity of skeletal muscle in patients with peripheral arterial insufficiency. Effect of physical training. Eur J Clin Invest 1974;4:9–15.

Dawson DL, Cutler BS, Meissner MH, Strandness DE Jr. Cilostazol has beneficial effects in treatment of intermittent claudication: results from a multicenter, randomized, prospective, double-blind trial. Circulation 1998;98(7):678–86.

Doubilet P, Abrams HL. The cost of underutilization. Percutaneous transluminal angioplasty for peripheral vascular disease. N Engl J Med 1984;310:95–102.

EuroQol Group. EuroQol: a new facility for the measurement of health-related quality of life. Health Policy 1990;16:199–208.

Feinstein AR. Clinimetrics. New Haven, Conn: Yale University Press; 1987.

Hiatt WR. Current and future drug therapies for claudication. Vasc Med (in press).

Hiatt WR, Marshall JA, Baxter J, et al. Diagnostic methods for peripheral arterial disease in the San Luis Valley Diabetes Study. J Clin Epidemiol 1990a;43:597–606.

Hiatt WR, Nawaz D, Regensteiner JG, Hossack KF. The evaluation of exercise performance in patients with peripheral vascular disease. J Cardiopulm Rehabil 1988;12:525–32.

Hiatt WR, Regensteiner JG, Hargarten ME, et al. Benefit of exercise conditioning for patients with peripheral arterial disease. Circulation 1990b; 81:602–9.

Hiatt WR, Wolfel EE, Meier RH, Regensteiner JG. Superiority of treadmill walking exercise vs. strength training for patients with peripheral arterial disease. Implications for the mechanism of the training response. Circulation 1994;90:1866–74.

Hunt SM, McEwen J, McKenna SP. Measuring health status: a new tool for clinicians and epidemiologists. J R Coll Gen Pract 1985;35:185–8.

Jeans WD, Danton RM, Baird RN, Horrocks M. A comparison of the costs of vascular surgery and balloon dilatation in lower limb ischaemic disease. Br J Radiol 1986;59:453–6.

Khaira HS, Hanger R, Shearman CP. Quality of life in patients with intermittent claudication. Eur J Vasc Endovasc Surg 1996;11(1):65–9.

Larsen OA, Lassen NA. Effect of daily muscular exercise in patients with intermittent claudication. Lancet 1966;2:1093–6.

Lepantalo M, Sundberg S, Gordin A. The effects of physical training and flunarizine on walking capacity in intermittent claudication. Scand J Rehabil Med 1984;16:159–62.

McDermott MM, Kiang L, Guralnik JM, et al. Measurement of walking endurance and walking velocity with questionnaire: validation of the walking impairment questionnaire in men and women with peripheral arterial disease. J Vasc Surg 1998;28:1072–81.

McDowell I, Newell C. Measuring Health. 2nd ed. New York, New York: Oxford University Press; 1996.

McDowell IW, Martini CJM, Waugh W. A method for self-assessment of disability before and after hip replacement operations. Br Med J 1978;8:857–9.

Money SR, Herd JA, Isaacsohn JL, et al. Effect of cilostazol on walking distances in patients with intermittent claudication caused by peripheral vascular disease. J Vasc Surg 1998;27:267–74.

Montgomery PS, Gardner AW. The clinical utility of a six-minute walk test in peripheral arterial occlusive disease patients. J Am Geriatr Soc 1998;46:706–11.

Orchard TJ, Strandness DE, Cavanaugh PR, et al. Assessment of peripheral vascular disease in diabetes. Report and recommendations of an international workshop. Circulation 1993;88:819–28.

Patterson RB, Pinto B, Marcus B, et al. Value of a supervised exercise program for the therapy of arterial claudication. J Vasc Surg 1997;25:312–8.

Pell JP. Impact of intermittent claudication on quality of life. The Scottish Vascular Audit Group. Eur J Vasc Endovasc Surg 1995;9:469–72.

Ponte E, Cattinelli S. Quality of life in a group of patients with intermittent claudication. Angiology 1995;47:247–51.

Regensteiner JG, Hargarten ME, Rutherford RB, Hiatt WR. Functional benefits of peripheral vascular bypass surgery for patients with intermittent claudication. Angiology 1993;44:1–10.

Regensteiner JG, Meyer T, Krupski W, et al. Comparison of home vs hospital based rehabilitation for patients with peripheral arterial disease. Angiology 1997; 48:291–9.

Regensteiner JG, Sippel J, McFarling ET, et al. Effects of non-insulin dependent diabetes on maximal exercise performance. Med Sci Sports Exerc 1995; 27:875–81.

Regensteiner JG, Steiner JF, Hiatt WR. Exercise training improves functional status in patients with peripheral arterial disease (PAD). J Vasc Surg 1996;23:104–15.

Regensteiner JG, Steiner JF, Panzer RJ, Hiatt WR. Evaluation of walking impairment by questionnaire in patients with peripheral arterial disease. J Vasc Med Biol 1990;2:142–52.

Sallis JF, Haskell WL, Wood PD, et al. Physical activity assessment methodology in the five-city project. Am J Epidemiol 1985;121:91–106.

Siemanski DJ, Cowell LL, Montgomery PS, et al. Physical activity monitoring in patients with peripheral arterial occlusive disease. J Cardiopulm Rehabil 1997; 17:43–7.

Siemanski DJ, Gardner AW. The relationship between free-living daily physical activity and the severity of peripheral arterial occlusive disease. Vasc Med 1997;2:286–91.

Stewart AL, Greenfield S, Hays RD, et al. Functional status and well-being of patients with chronic conditions: results from the Medical Outcomes Study. JAMA 1989;262:907–13.

Tarlov AR, Ware JE, Greenfield S, et al. The Medical Outcomes Study. An application of methods for monitoring the results of medical care. JAMA 1989; 262:925–30.

Thompson JE, Garrett WV. Peripheral-arterial surgery. N Engl J Med 1980;302:491–503.

Tsuchikane E, Katoh O, Sumitsuji S, et al. Impact of cilostazol on intimal proliferation after directional coronary atherectomy. Am Heart J 1998; 135(3):495–502.

Whyman MR, Fowkes FG, Kerracher EM, et al. Randomized controlled trial of percutaneous transluminal angioplasty for intermittent claudication. Eur J Vasc Endovasc Surg 1996;12:167–72.

Integrating Evaluation and Treatment of Intermittent Claudication into Clinical Practice

Anne B. Newman, MD, MPH
Associate Professor of Medicine and Epidemiology
University of Pittsburgh
Pittsburgh, Pennsylvania

Objective: To present a broad strategy for primary prevention of PAD, secondary prevention of claudication, and tertiary prevention of limb loss.

The articles in this series of monographs have explored many important facets of the clinical problem of intermittent claudication. This section presents an integrated preventive and treatment strategy for managing patients in an office-based practice. Such a strategy encompasses (1) primary prevention in younger adults; (2) secondary prevention, which in cardiovascular disease (CVD) refers to prevention of recurrent or progressive morbidity; and (3) tertiary prevention, which involves medical therapies to limit disability. Key insights that have emerged from recent studies should help broaden our view of what constitutes significant peripheral arterial disease (PAD).

AGE AS A RISK FACTOR FOR PAD

PAD has always been a common condition of the elderly. Several large population studies in the United States (Newman et al, 1993), Great Britain (Fowkes et al, 1991), and the Netherlands (Meijer et al, 1998) have all shown the strong association between PAD and aging. Although extensive atherosclerosis increases the risk for early mortality, the burden of atherosclerosis appears to accumulate in individuals who survive. Older adults who have PAD also have extensive systemic atherosclerosis, even when neither clinical cardiovascular disease (CVD) nor intermittent claudication has been diagnosed.

Figure 1 illustrates the relationship between a low ankle-brachial index (ABI), age, and CVD history in men and women enrolled in the Cardiovascular Health Study (Newman et al, 1993). The prevalence of an ABI <0.9 was higher in those study participants who had a history of CVD but was also substantial in those without clinical CVD. A low ABI was observed in fewer than 10% of women and in about 15% of men between the ages of 65 and 69 years, but the frequency of this finding increased to about 40% in men and women over 80 years of age.

SYMPTOMS OF PAD

Several studies have shown that few patients with a low ABI report classic intermittent claudication, thus indicating that many individuals with PAD may be asymptomatic or have atypical claudication that does not meet classic Rose criteria. More recent studies of symptoms and outcomes suggest that such patients may experience nonspecific symptoms that are not recognized as PAD. For example, women with PAD detected by the finding of a low ABI have more reported difficulty with mobility tasks, lower leg strength, and lower physical activity (Vogt et al, 1994). Patients with PAD also perform more poorly on tests of gait (Montgomery and Gardner, 1998), exhibiting smaller steps and slower cadence (Scherer et al, 1998). These studies and others (McDermott et al, 1999) suggest that many individuals with PAD are not truly asymptomatic but instead have nonspecific impairments, such as neuropathy and leg weakness, that may be mistakenly attributed to another condition or to aging itself.

Loss of mobility is a major health problem among older people, with at least 10% of community-based adults over 65 years of age limited in their ability to walk. Further work is under way to determine the preva-

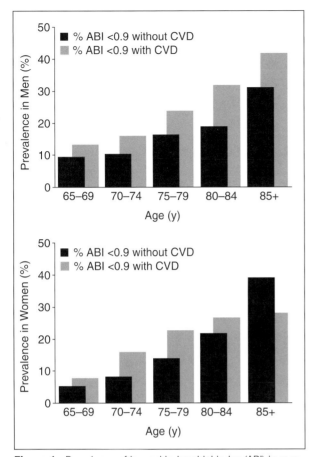

Figure 1. Prevalence of low ankle-brachial index (ABI) in men and women of different age-groups with and without cardiovascular disease (CVD). (Adapted from Newman AB, et al, 1993, and reprinted with permission.)

lence of these symptoms or impairments in the general population. Prevention and treatment of PAD are likely to improve lower extremity function in older people (Regensteiner et al, 1996).

PAD: A SYSTEMIC DISEASE

There is ample evidence from both clinical and population studies that PAD is a manifestation of advanced systemic atherosclerosis. Individuals with PAD face the same risk of CVD mortality as do patients who have already had an acute myocardial infarction (AMI) or stroke (Newman et al, 1999). Therefore, it is paramount that those with PAD be managed in a similar way to other persons with CVD with regard to secondary prevention. Aggressive lipid-lowering and antiplatelet agents have been shown to reduce morbidity from heart disease (Sacks et al, 1996; Shepherd et al, 1995; Scandinavian Simvastatin Survival Study Group, 1994; Downs et al, 1998), and presumably will be shown in future studies to decrease the risk of worsening PAD.

Guidelines for integrating knowledge about PAD into an overall strategy of secondary prevention of CVD are discussed later in detail.

NEW TREATMENTS FOR PAD

There are many promising agents that are effective in the treatment of claudication. Claudication symptoms can now be successfully ameliorated with cilostazol. Other drugs, such as antiplatelet therapy, novel vasodilators, prostaglandin analogues, metabolic agents, and angiogenic-stimulating factors are under study, but none has yet shown a functional improvement that exceeds the proven effects of a supervised exercise program.

In practice, the treatment of PAD must often be coordinated with numerous other treatments. Since PAD patients are at high risk for other CVD events, most should already be prescribed an aspirin for CVD prevention. If the patient cannot tolerate aspirin, another antiplatelet agent such as clopidogrel should be prescribed.

Surgery and angioplasty are established treatments and have specific indications. Bypass surgery is mainly used for limb salvage, while angioplasty is used when claudication limits daily activities or when medical therapy fails. New, minimally invasive percutaneous vascular procedures that can be performed by a vascular interventionist are of great interest as they expose the patient to lower operative risk. However, there may be wide geographic variation in the availability and efficacy of such techniques as percutaneous stenting or laser atherectomy (Pockus, 1995). Referral to a center that offers these newer procedures should be considered for patients who are at highest operative risk and fail conventional treatment.

PRIMARY CARE

Physicians are more likely to look for early PAD in an individual patient if there is a clear opportunity to improve health outcomes with specific treatments. As discussed in the 2 earlier chapters in this monograph, treatment of PAD patients has been increasingly evaluated in clinical trials with carefully measured, important functional outcomes. Referral for invasive revascularization procedures should be reserved for those patients with claudication pain that is unresponsive to medical therapy and limits activity, exhibits poor wound healing, or where limb loss is threatened. Since only a minority of these patients will require surgical intervention, the primary care physician should always maintain responsibility for global medical management. Many of these patients have multiple medical problems and the primary care or vascular medicine physician is in the best position to provide integrated care. The specific treatments for the pain and limitations imposed by PAD should be incorporated into a comprehensive management plan for all the patient's medical problems.

In the primary care setting, there is an opportunity for primary, secondary, or tertiary prevention at each individual patient encounter. Figure 2 illustrates an algorithm for a preventive approach to PAD in clinical practice.

PRIMARY PREVENTION

In younger adults, a primary prevention approach should focus on the prevention of the development of atherosclerosis and all related adverse consequences of CVD. A recent analysis of Framingham data has shown that the lifetime risk of CVD is 1 in 2 for men and 1 in 3 for women (Lloyd-Jones et al, 1999). It is well

known that the lesions of atherosclerosis begin early in life, even in childhood. Although the future threat of claudication or amputation is much less than for stroke or MI (Weitz et al, 1996), it is still an important additional reason to urge patients to modify their CVD risk factors. The risk factors for coronary heart disease and PAD are essentially the same. Practicing prevention and using algorithms designed for CVD should also reduce the incidence of PAD (Expert Panel, 1993). Smoking, hyperlipidemia, and diabetes are particularly strong risk factors for PAD and should be managed aggressively.

SECONDARY PREVENTION

Secondary prevention is appropriate in patients with confirmed intermittent claudication, even if this is the only symptom of systemic atherosclerosis. Preventive treatment should be targeted toward slowing the

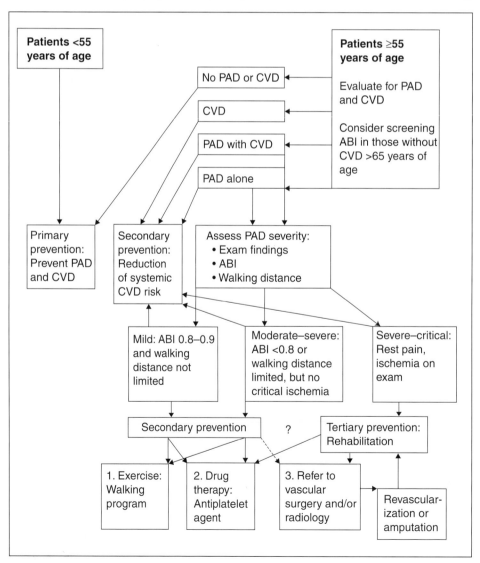

Figure 2. A preventive approach to management of patients with peripheral arterial disease (PAD). CVD = cardiovascular disease; ABI = ankle-brachial index.

progression of disease to disability or death by stabilizing or improving the circulation. The algorithm in Figure 2 illustrates the importance of diagnosing PAD in the context of the total picture of CVD. This algorithm is designed to remind us that all older patients with either PAD or other CVD, or both, should receive the same scrutiny for preventive treatment as do survivors of MI or stroke. This includes smoking cessation, exercise, lipid lowering, blood pressure control, and glucose and weight control. The management of PAD per se will vary with the severity of the obstruction and impairment.

Treatment of Intermittent Claudication

Once PAD has been diagnosed, the choice of a secondary versus tertiary treatment approach will depend on the severity of disease. Secondary preventive treatment in the patient with PAD includes the prevention of limiting leg pain or impairments such as weakness and neuropathy without typical claudication. While the vast majority of patients will not progress to amputation, this extreme outcome is so disabling that it is of the utmost importance to avert. Diabetes and PAD are the major causes of amputation in developed countries. Admittedly, no clinical trial has yet been performed regarding the prevention of limb loss and there is likewise no evidence that screening for PAD will prevent complications. Nonetheless, knowledge of the severity of arterial obstruction permits closer monitoring. In addition, patients should be educated to report worsening ischemic pain, infection, or ulceration.

Observational data from Denmark on the use of surgery or angioplasty for limiting leg pain have shown a decrease in the rate of amputation in parallel with the increase in the number of vascular reconstructions (Ebskov et al, 1994). These findings provide indirect evidence that invasive therapy can reduce this most dreaded outcome of PAD. However, there is little evidence that early intervention will reduce amputation. One study comparing percutaneous revascularization with exercise showed that although both modalities were effective, exercise yielded a substantially greater benefit (Hiatt et al, 1990). Thus, this study demonstrated that large-vessel revascularization is not necessary to achieve functional improvement. For this reason, medical therapy should be used as the first line of treatment in preventing progression of PAD.

In patients with intermittent claudication, both symptoms and functioning can be improved through exercise and medical treatment with antiplatelet agents. Details of specific supervised exercise programs and medications are discussed in Dr. William R. Hiatt's article in this monograph. It is not known whether treatment of atherosclerosis per se will improve symptoms and functioning in the legs, although this is quite possible. While it has not been demonstrated that medical treatment will decrease the risk of amputation, data demonstrating that lipid-lowering therapy and aspirin reduce the risk of MI and stroke is assumed to extend to the prevention of amputation as well.

Reduction of Systemic Risk

There is clear evidence that antiplatelet treatment reduces other CVD events in this high-risk population with PAD (Janzon et al, 1990). In addition, there is ample evidence that aspirin, which has both antiplatelet and anti-inflammatory effects, is important in the secondary prevention of MI and stroke. Thus, all patients with PAD are candidates for antiplatelet therapy.

There is strong surrogate evidence to suggest that lipid-lowering treatment yields benefits in all vascular beds affected by atherosclerosis (Shepherd et al, 1995; Downs et al, 1998). A meta-analysis of lipid-lowering trials in patients after myocardial infarct, which looked at stroke as a secondary outcome, demonstrated a reduction in the incidence of stroke when all trials were considered together, although not enough events had occurred in any single trial to show a benefit (Crouse et al, 1998). Individuals with PAD must be classified along with survivors of MI and stroke as candidates for secondary prevention of CVD. The presence of PAD is a clinical manifestation of CVD and therefore should be recognized as a reason to reduce serum low-density lipoprotein cholesterol (LDL-C) level to <100 mg/dL. In addition, all patients should be advised to stop smoking and to exercise. Blood pressure, blood glucose levels, and body weight should be monitored and kept under control.

It has been argued that any older patient who has no clinical signs of CVD should be screened for subclinical PAD. If PAD is present, the patient should be placed on antiplatelet therapy. If the serum LDL-C level remains >100 mg/dL after dietary modification, the patient should receive a lipid-lowering agent as well. Subclinical PAD may be diagnosed by physical examination, but this approach is insensitive, especially in patients with milder degrees of obstruction. At least one third of patients over the age of 65 will have a clinical diagnosis of CVD. About 10% of those individuals without CVD will have a low ABI and face a similarly high risk of CVD events. Many CVD prevention programs include screening with ABI measurements, electrocardiography, and sometimes carotid duplex scanning to determine whether there is evidence of subclinical atherosclerosis. If atherosclerosis is present, these patients are treated with aggressive lipid-lowering therapy as part of a secondary preventive strategy. Thus, subclinical markers of disease can identify additional patients who can be reclassified as candidates for secondary prevention. Relative to the high cost of lipid-lowering drugs, the costs of a Doppler scan and the time required to perform ABI measurements are quite small. A nurse can be trained in the office setting to measure blood pressure in the ankles and arms with a Doppler scanner. Although technical and professional costs are reimbursed by Medicare when this procedure is performed in a vascular laboratory, the test cannot be billed as an office procedure. However, because testing would demonstrate only minimal degrees of atherosclerosis in many older adults with high cholesterol levels (Weverling-Rijnsburger et al, 1997), the use of such measures might actually rule out the need for costly drug therapy (Manolio et al, 1992). Primary care physicians should purchase a small Doppler scanner for office use when PAD is suspected as a contributing factor to pain and other symptoms in older adults, or when the presence of a low ABI would determine whether or not to proceed with expensive, lifelong lipid-lowering therapy (Figure 3).

TERTIARY PREVENTION

Tertiary prevention includes limb salvage therapy with surgery or percutaneous angioplasty in patients with critical ischemia, as well as rehabilitation of patients with advanced disability, including amputees. Exercise programs yield improvement even in patients with severe advanced PAD that is thought to be end-stage disease. If amputation is required, strenuous efforts should be made to avoid loss of the contralateral leg,

since the energy costs of double amputation are so extreme as to preclude ambulation in many patients (Cutson and Bongiorni, 1996).

The primary care physician plays an important role in optimizing rehabilitation of the patient who has lost a limb or is unable to walk because of PAD. Angina and

Key Points

• The prevalence of PAD increases with age.

• PAD is a disabling manifestation of systemic atherosclerosis, but can be prevented and treated.

• Medications and revascularization improve symptoms, but are relatively costly and have not been shown to be better than supervised exercise. Together, exercise, medications, and revascularization can improve claudication symptoms.

• The primary care physician should coordinate the care of the patient with PAD, managing all manifestations of atherosclerosis.

• Primary prevention of CVD should also prevent PAD.

• Secondary prevention consists of aggressive modification of risk factors for recurrent CVD; an exercise program is the mainstay of treatment for claudication.

• Tertiary prevention measures include limb salvage therapy (angioplasty or lower extremity bypass) and rehabilitation of amputees.

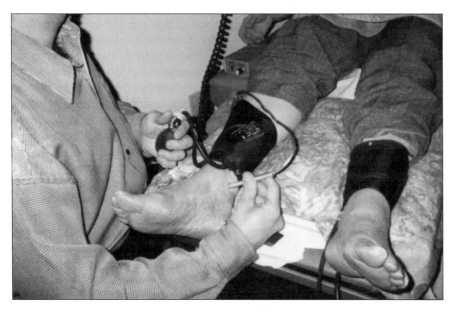

Figure 3. Method of recording ankle systolic pressure.

other medical complications of immobility, including deep venous thrombosis and infection, can become major management issues during rehabilitation. Attentive medical care can prevent many of these complications and contribute substantially to the optimal functioning of the patient with PAD. ■

BIBLIOGRAPHY

Crouse JR III, Byington RP, Furberg CD. HMG-CoA reductase inhibitor therapy and stroke risk reduction: an analysis of clinical trials data. Atherosclerosis 1998;138:11–24.

Cutson TM, Bongiorni DR. Rehabilitation of the older lower limb amputee: a brief review. J Am Geriatr Soc 1996;44:1388–93.

Downs JR, Clearfield M, Weis S, et al, for the AFCAPS/TexCAPS Research Group. Primary prevention of acute coronary events with lovastatin in men and women with average cholesterol levels. Results of AFCAPS/TexCAPS. JAMA 1998;279:1615–22.

Ebskov LB, Schroeder TV, Holstein PE. Epidemiology of leg amputation, the influence of vascular surgery. Br J Surg 1994;81:1600–3.

Expert Panel on the Detection, Evaluation, and Treatment of High Blood Cholesterol in Adults. Summary of the Second Report of the NCEP Expert Panel on Detection, Evaluation and Treatment of High Blood Cholesterol in Adults. JAMA 1993;269(23):3015–23.

Fowkes FGR, Housley E, Cawood EHH, et al. Edinburgh artery study: prevalence of asymptomatic and symptomatic peripheral arterial disease in the general population. Int J Epidemiol 1991;20:384–92.

Hiatt WR, Regensteiner JG, Hargarten ME, et al. Benefit of exercise conditioning for patients with peripheral arterial disease. Circulation 1990;81:602–9.

Janzon L, Berqvist D, Boberg J, et al. Prevention of myocardial infarction and stroke in patients with intermittent claudication: effects of ticlopidine. Results from the Swedish Ticlopidine Multicenter study. J Intern Med 1990;227(5):301–8.

Lloyd-Jones DM, Larson MG, Beiser A, Levy D. Lifetime risk of developing coronary artery disease. Lancet 1999;353:89–92.

Manolio TA, Furberg CD, Wahl PW, et al. Eligibility for cholesterol referral in community-dwelling older adults. Ann Intern Med 1992;116:641–9.

McDermott MM, Mehta S, Greenland P. Exertional leg symptoms other than intermittent claudication are common in peripheral arterial disease. Arch Intern Med 1999;159:387–92.

Meijer WT, Hoes AW, Rutgers D, et al. Peripheral arterial disease in the elderly, the Rotterdam Study. Arterioscler Thromb Vasc Biol 1998;18:185–92.

Montgomery PS, Gardner AW. The clinical utility of a six-minute walk test in peripheral arterial occlusive disease patients. J Am Geriatr Soc 1998;46:706–11.

Newman AB, Shemanski L, Manolio TA, et al, for the Cardiovascular Health Study Collaborative Research Group. Ankle-arm index as a predictor of cardiovascular disease and mortality in the Cardiovascular Health Study. Arterioscler Thromb Vasc Biol 1999;19:538–45.

Newman AB, Siscovick DS, Manolio TA, et al. Ankle-arm index as a marker of atherosclerosis in the Cardiovascular Health Study. Circulation 1993;88:837–45.

Pockus DB. Revascularization in peripheral vascular disease: stents, atherectomies, lasers and thrombolytics. AACN Clinical Issues 1995;6:536–46.

Regensteiner JG, Steiner JF, Hiatt WR. Exercise training improves functional status in patients with peripheral arterial disease. J Vasc Surg 1996;23:104–15.

Sacks FM, Pfeffer MA, Moye LA, et al, for the Cholesterol and Recurrent Events Trial Investigators (CARE). The effect of pravastatin on coronary events after myocardial infarction in patients with average cholesterol levels. N Engl J Med 1996;335:1001–9.

Scandinavian Simvastatin Survival Study Group. Randomised trial of cholesterol lowering in 4444 patients with coronary heart disease: the Scandinavian Simvastatin Survival Study (4S). Lancet 1994; 344:1383–9.

Scherer SA, Bainbridge JS, Hiatt WR, Regensteiner JG. Gait characteristics in patients with claudication. Arch Phys Med Rehabil 1998;79:529–31.

Shepherd J, Cobbe SM, Ford I, et al, for the West of Scotland Coronary Prevention Study Group (WOSCOPS). Prevention of coronary heart disease with pravastatin in men with hypercholesterolemia. N Engl J Med 1995;333:1301–7.

Vogt M, Cauley JA, Kuller LH, Nevitt MC. Functional status and mobility among elderly women with lower extremity arterial disease. J Am Geriatr Soc 1994;42:923–9.

Weitz JI, Byrne J, Clagett P, et al. Diagnosis and treatment of chronic arterial insufficiency of the lower extremities: a critical review. Circulation 1996; 94:3026–49.

Weverling-Rijnsburger AWE, Blauw GJ, Lagaay AM, et al. Total cholesterol and risk of mortality in the oldest old. Lancet 1997;350:1119–23.

The American Journal of Medicine®

CONTINUING EDUCATION SERIES

AN OFFICE-BASED APPROACH TO THE DIAGNOSIS AND TREATMENT OF PERIPHERAL ARTERIAL DISEASE

PART V: Management of Peripheral Arterial Disease: Moderate Claudication

SERIES EDITOR
ALAN T. HIRSCH, MD
GUEST EDITOR
EMILE R. MOHLER III, MD

Jointly sponsored by
The Excerpta Medica Office of Continuing Medical Education and the Society for Vascular Medicine and Biology

Introduction and Overview

Alan T. Hirsch, MD
Director, Vascular Medicine Program
Minnesota Vascular Diseases Center
University of Minnesota Medical School
Minneapolis, Minnesota

Emile R. Mohler III, MD
Director, Vascular Medicine Program
University of Pennsylvania School of Medicine
Philadelphia, Pennsylvania

Patients with claudication can benefit from therapies designed not only to ensure longer life, but to improve the quality of life as well. A robust scientific database can guide therapeutic choices. The relative risks and benefits of a potential lifestyle change, a prescription, a percutaneous procedure, or a surgical bypass technique for claudicants are generally well defined. Nevertheless, it can often be a challenging task for primary care physicians to coordinate the care of their peripheral arterial disease (PAD) patients who frequently have symptomatic atherosclerotic disease in multiple vascular territories. This monograph is designed to make that job easier.

Words carry deep meanings and sometimes will generate different expectations, especially given the suffering usually encountered by patients with claudication. Patients can and do respond with exquisite sensitivity to the words used to describe their therapeutic choices. For example, if an option is called:

• *Interventional*—does this imply that: "This will simply make you better"? or "This is a much more serious condition"? or

• *Lifestyle change*—does this imply that: "You must abandon how you've lived for the past 30+ years"? or "You must do all the work by yourself"? or

• *Surgical bypass*—does this imply that: "You will be in the hospital and you will be cured by a specific skilled provider"? or "You're helpless to do anything yourself about your condition"?

• *Drug therapies*—does this imply that: "You will take pills that will immediately make you feel better and live longer"? or "Will there be a problem getting your insurance company to pay for them"?

Physicians need to be aware of the connotations and subtle implications of the language they use. Describing the short- and long-term risks and short- and long-term benefits requires sensitivity. In truth, all therapies that ameliorate the symptoms of claudication are intrinsically "interventional," and primary care physicians have adequate tools at hand to intervene positively in the care of their patients. Speaking to a patient with empathy about their claudication can be "interventional" if fear is alleviated and options are offered.

This monograph offers you a series of case management discussions so that your decisions regarding medical, percutaneous, or surgical therapies can be placed into a broad perspective of choice. In the first article, Emile R. Mohler III, MD, describes the documented benefits of a dual approach to improving claudication symptoms that employs both exercise and pharmacologic therapies to benefit the patient in the most truly "minimally invasive" form possible. For nearly all patients with PAD and claudication, such an approach will usually suffice to ameliorate symptoms to satisfy the lifestyle needs of the patient.

In the second article, Haraldur Bjarnason, MD, describes the benefits of a percutaneous, endovascular approach for individuals with claudication due to aortoiliac artery occlusive disease. Iliac artery angioplasty, with or without stent placement, serves as an excellent example of cost-effective revascularization that can rapidly produce symptom relief with excellent durability. Whereas other anatomic presentations of PAD can also benefit from a percutaneous approach, only anatomic aortoiliac disease has the dual benefit of both strong trial data and clinical experience, allowing primary care physicians to be truly confident of offering carefully selected patients real long-term clinical benefit.

In the third article, Michael R. Lepore, MD, and Samuel R. Money, MD, discuss the potential benefits that can accrue to patients in whom surgical bypass is required to alleviate severe symptoms, especially for those patients in whom either exercise or drug therapies fail, or in whom a percutaneous approach is not technically feasible. These authors caution physicians and patients that surgical bypass can only alleviate the limb symptoms, while systemic atherosclerosis may progress and lead to perioperative or long-term cardiac or cerebrovascular ischemic events. Thankfully, continuing excellence in anesthetic and surgical techniques produces improved outcomes at a decreased risk. No matter which intervention is used for each patient, control of atherosclerosis risk factors is paramount.

Selection of the right therapeutic intervention for patients with PAD can sometimes be difficult. We hope that this monograph improves your understanding of the various treatment options for your patients with PAD symptoms. All patients with claudication can benefit from therapies designed to prolong life and improve its quality. The Society for Vascular Medicine and Biology hopes that this monograph published under the auspices of *The American Journal of Medicine*® will provide primary care physicians with increasing confidence in their central role as coordinators of care, who, along with the vascular specialist, provide optimum treatment for patients with PAD. ∎

Evaluation and Treatment of Patients with Moderate Claudication

Emile R. Mohler III, MD
Director, Vascular Medicine Program
University of Pennsylvania School of Medicine
Philadelphia, Pennsylvania

Objective: To explain, with the assistance of a clinical vignette, an integrated, noninvasive approach for evaluation and treatment of patients with moderate claudication.

Patients with peripheral arterial disease (PAD) suffering from moderate claudication have a relatively low risk of lower limb amputation. However, these patients frequently do not know they are at high risk for myocardial infarction (MI) and stroke, and usually seek medical attention to improve walking capacity. The office evaluation of patients with moderate claudication begins with a detailed history and physical examination that may include measurement of the ankle-brachial index (ABI). The treatment plan should include risk-factor modification and antiplatelet therapy. Most patients with moderate claudication can improve pain-free walking distance (PFWD) with exercise and pharmacologic therapy, without the need for revascularization. Patients may be disappointed that there is no quick fix but usually want to try exercise and pharmacologic therapy to improve both walking distance and longevity after a detailed explanation of clinical options.

CLINICAL VIGNETTE

A 73-year-old man visits the office with the complaint of calf-pain when walking. This discomfort now occurs when he walks only 2 blocks, compared with the 5 blocks that he was able to walk 3 years previously. His leg symptom is described as a "cramping sensation" that disappears within 5 minutes after discontinuation of walking. The discomfort recurs when the patient resumes walking. He does not have this discomfort at rest, or alleviation of the symptoms with changes in posture, such as leaning forward. There is no cramping pain in the leg at night and no history of foot ulceration. The patient does not present a history of coronary artery disease and specifically does not have any symptoms to suggest angina or congestive heart failure (CHF). He was given a prescription for pentoxifylline (Trental®) 3 months prior, but there was no significant relief using this medication, prompting this visit. Other current medications include ginseng, shark cartilage, garlic, and naproxen sodium (Aleve®).

Clinical Presentation and Patient Goals

This patient has classic symptoms of claudication that begin after a predictable walking distance and promptly resolve after discontinuation of exercise (Mohler, 1999). He does not have any symptoms of rest pain to suggest critical limb ischemia (CLI). At first glance, it may seem that his risk factors for atherosclerosis are minimal as he presented with no history of diabetes, hyperlipidemia, or hypertension. However, the patient had a history of 35 pack-years of tobacco use, and although he quit cigarette smoking approximately 40 years ago, this history serves as an important predisposing risk to development of PAD (Jonason and Bergstrom, 1987). Additionally, the patient's father had died at 69 years of age from MI, serving as another familial precedent for the development of atherosclerosis. He is a retired construction worker and had certainly looked forward to remaining active in his retirement. Desiring to travel, play golf, and exercise to stay fit in his senior years, he is devoted to improving his current lifestyle.

The Physical Examination

The physical examination revealed a blood pressure of 160/90 mm Hg bilaterally, with a heart rate of 78 bpm. The patient is 6'2" and weighs 211 lb. Examination of the head, eyes, ears, nose, and throat revealed an arcus corneae, but no thyromegaly. The neck was supple and there were no carotid bruits. The cardiovascular examination was without evidence of murmur, but an S_4 gallop was present. There were no abdominal bruits heard, and no mass was present. The femoral pulses were 2/4+ bilaterally and without femoral bruits. The popliteal pulses were not appreciated bilaterally. The dorsalis pedis and posterior tibial pulses also were not palpable. There was no lower extremity edema or ulceration; however, there was evidence for delayed capillary refill, pallor with leg elevation, and dependent rubor. The patient's ABI was calculated in the office and revealed a right dorsalis pedis-to-brachial artery index of 0.57; right ankle posterior tibial-to-brachial artery index of 0.51; left ankle dorsalis pedis-to-brachial artery index of 0.51; and a left ankle posterior tibial-to-brachial artery index of 0.51. The ABI is useful in stratifying patients' severity of disease: an ABI >0.75 is considered mild disease; 0.5 to 0.74, moderate disease; <0.5, severe disease; and <0.25 indicates poor wound healing. An ABI >1.2 may reflect medial calcification (especially in a diabetic patient) and should prompt further evaluation in the vascular laboratory, with pulse-volume recordings (PVRs) measuring blood volume and not arterial pressure.

Laboratory Testing

Specific laboratory tests should include a lipid profile. The laboratory results of this patient revealed the following: triglycerides, 126 mg/dL; total cholesterol, 239 mg/dL; high-density lipoprotein cholesterol, 43 mg/dL; and low-density lipoprotein cholesterol (LDL-C), 171 mg/dL. Emerging risk factors such as lipoprotein(a) [Lp(a)] and homocysteine should also be considered, especially if LDL-C is not significantly elevated. Lp(a) was elevated at 230 mg/dL (normal, <20 mg/dL). A single fasting homocysteine level was obtained and was elevated at 20 μmol/L (normal, ≤12 μmol/L). Serum creatinine was elevated at 1.7 mg/dL, and liver enzymes were within normal limits. The complete blood count and other routine chemistries were unremarkable.

Clinical Utility of the Noninvasive Laboratory

The patient was then referred to the vascular laboratory to determine the level of disease and thus underwent a lower extremity arterial evaluation that measured resting segmental pulse volumes and systolic pressures (Figure 1). Thigh pressures and PVR amplitudes were within normal limits, bilaterally. Calf pressures were significantly reduced bilaterally, in the left more than the right leg. Also, the calf-level PVR amplitudes were reduced bilaterally, with the left PVR amplitude more broadened than the right. There was also a >20-mm Hg decrease in the ankle pressures compared to the calves'. These findings were strongly suggestive of distal bilateral superficial femoral artery and/or popliteal arterial occlusive disease (AOD), as well as bilateral infrapopliteal AOD. The ABIs were consistent with moderate disease, bilaterally. An ABI <0.9 is 95% sensitive for detecting PAD on angiography. Some vascular laboratories also use duplex Doppler ultrasonography to image the arterial system. An angiogram is usually reserved for patients under consideration for lower extremity revascularization.

Creation of an Individualized Treatment Plan

As commonly occurs, this patient presented with a history of walking impairment that had slowly worsened for nearly 3 years. Such patients usually seek medical attention simply to identify methods that might improve their lifestyle-limiting walking symptoms. Although all clinicians will seek to satisfy this request to decrease their ambulatory limitation, our responsibility as physicians is broader. Thus, the initial discussion with the patient regarded his cardiovascular risk for MI and stroke (Figure 2). Like most patients who present with claudication, this patient was surprised to learn that "untreated" claudication has a 5-year mortality from cardiovascular ischemic events that approaches 30% (Criqui et al, 1985). The patient was told of the importance of decreasing his atherosclerosis risk-factor burden, not only to prevent progression of the AOD in his lower extremities but also to prevent future MI and stroke. As per the National Cholesterol Education Program (NCEP) guidelines, the patient was administered a statin drug with the aim of lowering LDL-C below 100 mg/dL. Folic acid at 1 mg/d was also prescribed to lower the homocysteine level. Elevated homocysteine levels were recently found to be associated with increased mortality and progression of coronary artery disease in patients with PAD (Taylor et al, 1999). Most patients require a prescription to obtain this high dosage of vitamin. An increased level of Lp(a) is also associated with PAD (Cantin et al, 1995). Although niacin may mildly reduce Lp(a) levels, there is no effective pharmacologic agent for this condition.

In addition to lipid lowering, a cornerstone of therapy to prevent ischemic events for patients with claudication is antiplatelet drugs (Antiplatelet Trialists' Collaboration I, 1994; Balsano, 1989; Giansante et al, 1990; Mohler, 1999). In the Physicians' Health Study,

325 mg of aspirin every other day did not reduce claudication, although it did decrease the need for surgery of the peripheral artery (Goldhaber et al, 1992). Aspirin was also shown to reduce the incidence of lower extremity graft occlusion (Antiplatelet Trialists' Collaboration II, 1994; Hess et al, 1985). Another class of antiplatelet agent, adenosine diphosphate (ADP) receptor blockers, is also effective in reducing cardiovascular and cerebrovascular events. One such agent, ticlopidine (Ticlid®), was found in a randomized controlled study to reduce the composite end point of sudden death, MI, and stroke (Blanchard et al, 1994). The Swedish Ticlopidine Multicenter Study (Fagher, 1994) reported no improvement in walking distance; however, a meta-analysis of 5 studies found walking capacity to be improved during treatment with ticlopidine (Palareti et al, 1988). Another study of ticlopidine conducted in France found improved graft patency in patients with a lower extremity venous bypass graft (Becquemin, 1997). Although effective in preventing ischemic events, ticlopidine was reported to cause neutropenia and, more rarely, thrombotic thrombocytopenic purpura; thus, blood monitoring is required for patients using this medication. A newly approved ADP receptor blocker, clopidogrel (Plavix®), was found to be more effective than aspirin in reducing cardiovascular and cerebrovascular ischemic events in the CAPRIE (Clopidogrel versus Aspirin in Patients at Risk of Ischemic Events) study (CAPRIE Steering Committee, 1996). There was no significant neutropenia compared to aspirin in this study, and thus laboratory monitoring was not necessary.

The patient received counseling on the long-term medical versus revascularization approaches for treatment of claudication. He was informed that supervised exercise training could increase PFWD from 100% to 200% after 6 months of therapy and was enrolled in a cardiovascular rehabilitation program. The optimal exercise program is supervised, with at least 3 sessions per week lasting >30 minutes. Patients should be encour-

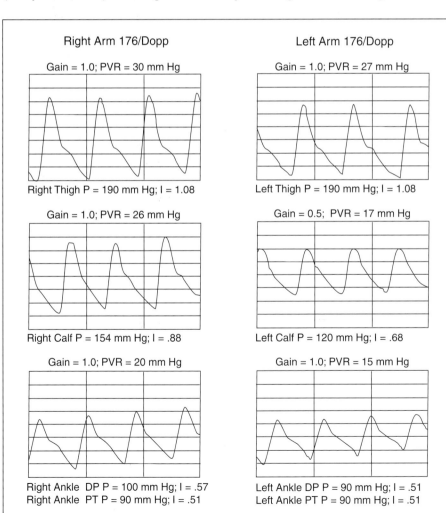

Figure 1. Resting segmental pulse-volume recordings and systolic pressures done in the vascular laboratory. Dopp = Doppler ultrasonography; PVR = pulse volume recording; P = pressure; I = index; DP = dorsalis pedis; PT = posterior tibial.

Right Arm 176/Dopp

Gain = 1.0; PVR = 30 mm Hg

Right Thigh P = 190 mm Hg; I = 1.08

Gain = 1.0; PVR = 26 mm Hg

Right Calf P = 154 mm Hg; I = .88

Gain = 1.0; PVR = 20 mm Hg

Right Ankle DP P = 100 mm Hg; I = .57
Right Ankle PT P = 90 mm Hg; I = .51

Left Arm 176/Dopp

Gain = 1.0; PVR = 27 mm Hg

Left Thigh P = 190 mm Hg; I = 1.08

Gain = 0.5; PVR = 17 mm Hg

Left Calf P = 120 mm Hg; I = .68

Gain = 1.0; PVR = 15 mm Hg

Left Ankle DP P = 90 mm Hg; I = .51
Left Ankle PT P = 90 mm Hg; I = .51

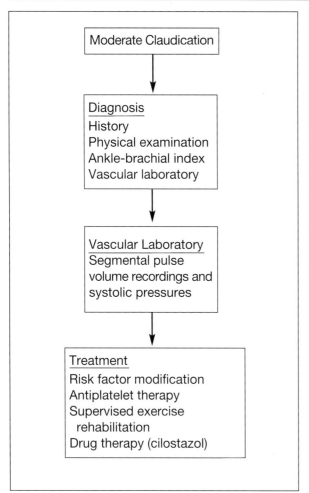

Figure 2. Algorithm for diagnosis and treatment of moderate claudication.

Table. Initial Treatment of Moderate Claudication from Peripheral Arterial Disease

- Risk-factor reduction
  - Smoking cessation
  - Lower low-density lipoprotein cholesterol to <100 mg/dL
  - Strict control of hypertension
  - Strict control of diabetes mellitus
- Antiplatelet therapy
- Exercise rehabilitation
- Drug therapy (cilostazol, Pletal®)

aged to walk to the point of moderate discomfort, and best results are achieved after 6 months of regular exercise. In addition, the patient was informed of cilostazol (Pletal®), a newly available medication that could improve claudication symptoms. The presumed mechanisms of action of this drug include vasodilation and inhibition of platelet activation through phosphodiesterase inhibition. The standard dosage is 100 mg BID ingested on an empty stomach. A reduced dosage to 50 mg BID should be considered when cilostazol is coadministered with drugs such as ketoconazole, erythromycin, diltiazem, or omeprazole. This medication is contraindicated in patients with CHF of any severity. Patients being considered for its use should be carefully screened for signs and symptoms of CHF. In one study of 81 patients with moderately severe claudication treated for 12 weeks, cilostazol increased initial claudication distance and maximum claudication distance walked by 35% and 41%, respectfully. In a second study,

a 16-week randomized trial of 239 patients found that cilostazol increased the maximum distance walked by 41% compared with 15% with placebo (Dawson et al, 1998). Other pharmacologic agents such as long-acting prostaglandins (Dormandy and Belcher, 1997) and metabolic enhancers such as carnitine (Brevetti et al, 1995) are currently under investigation but not yet approved for use in the United States. Therapeutic angiogenesis using various growth factors is under investigation as a means to improve lower extremity blood flow but is not yet available for clinical use (Baumgartner et al, 1998).

Patients with claudication commonly seek complementary and alternative medicine (CAM) to improve walking distance. Gingko biloba tree extracts are popular botanical supplements in the United States and Europe. The main active ingredients, flavonoids and terpenoids, appear to have vasodilatory action and also inhibit platelet-activating factor (PAF). A review of 8 clinical studies indicates that gingko biloba is superior to pentoxifylline and placebo for improving PFWD (75% to 110%) and maximum walking distance (53% to 119%) (Ernst, 1996). Patients taking gingko biloba should be cautioned on potential increased risk of bleeding, especially when also taking coumadin or antiplatelet drugs, due to antagonism of PAF. More clinical studies are needed before gingko biloba can be routinely recommended to patients with claudication.

Another CAM therapy is chelation therapy. A review of 4 published randomized controlled trials found that use of chelation therapy did not benefit walking distance in patients with PAD (Ernst, 1997) and therefore should not be recommended to patients with claudication. The patient in this clinical vignette was taking ginseng, shark cartilage, and garlic, none of which improved PFWD.

CONCLUSIONS AND RECOMMENDATIONS
In summary, patients with PAD should be counseled on their increased risk of MI and stroke. All atherosclerosis

risk factors should be treated and antiplatelet therapy given to lower the risk of a cardiovascular event (Table). An improvement in PFWD can be accomplished with noninvasive medical therapy. Although new pharmacologic therapy is emerging, supervised exercise is the most effective means to reduce walking impairment. Revascularization is reserved for patients with severe lifestyle-limiting symptoms or in the case of CLI. ■

Key Points

• Patients with moderate claudication are easily diagnosed in the office setting by measuring the ABI.

• The vascular laboratory is useful in determining the level and extent of PAD.

• Cardiovascular risk factors should be identified and aggressively treated in patients with PAD.

• Antiplatelet agents should be prescribed, unless contraindicated, in all patients with PAD.

• Symptoms of moderate claudication usually improve with supervised exercise and pharmacologic therapy.

• Surgical or radiographic-based intervention is reserved for patients with significant inhibition of lifestyle or symptoms of CLI.

BIBLIOGRAPHY

Antiplatelet Trialists' Collaboration. Collaborative overview of randomised trials of antiplatelet therapy–I: Prevention of death, myocardial infarction, and stroke by prolonged antiplatelet therapy in various categories of patients. BMJ 1994;308: 81–106.

Antiplatelet Trialists' Collaboration. Collaborative overview of randomised trials of antiplatelet therapy–II: Maintenance of vascular graft or arterial patency by antiplatelet therapy. BMJ 1994;308: 159–68.

Balsano F, Coccheri S, Libretti A, et al. Ticlopidine in the treatment of intermittent claudication: a 21-month double-blind trial. J Lab Clin Med 1989; 114:84–91.

Baumgartner I, Pieczek A, Manor O, et al. Constitutive expression of phVEGF165 after intramuscular gene transfer promotes collateral vessel development in patients with critical limb ischemia. Circulation 1998;97:1114–23.

Becquemin JP. Effect of ticlopidine on the long-term patency of saphenous-vein bypass grafts in the legs. Etude de la Ticlopidine après Pontage Femoro-Poplité and the Association Universitaire de Recherche en Chirurgie. N Engl J Med 1997;337: 1726–31.

Blanchard J, Carreras LO, Kindermans M. Results of EMATAP: a double-blind placebo-controlled multi-centre trial of ticlopidine in patients with peripheral arterial disease. Nouvelle Revue Française d'Héma-tologie 1994;35:523–8.

Brevetti G, Perna S, Sabba C, et al. Propionyl-L-carnitine in intermittent claudication: double-blind, placebo-controlled, dose titration, multicenter study. J Am Coll Cardiol 1995;26:1411–6.

Cantin B, Moorjani S, Dagenais GR, Lupien PJ. Lipoprotein(a) distribution in a French Canadian population and its relation to intermittent claudication (the Quebec Cardiovascular Study). Am J Cardiol 1995; 75:1224–8.

CAPRIE Steering Committee. A randomised, blinded trial of Clopidogrel versus Aspirin in Patients at Risk of Ischaemic Events (CAPRIE). Lancet 1996;348: 1329–39.

Criqui MH, Fronek A, Barrett-Connor E, et al. The prevalence of peripheral arterial disease in a defined population. Circulation 1985;71:510–5.

Dawson DL, Cutler BS, Meissner MH, Strandness DEJ. Cilostazol has beneficial effects in treatment of intermittent claudication: results from a multi-center, randomized, prospective, double-blind trial. Circulation 1998;98:678–86.

Dormandy JA, Belcher G. Clinical use of prostacyclins. In: Rubanyi GM, Dzau VJ, eds. The Endothelium in Clinical Practice. New York, NY: Marcel Dekker, Inc; 1997:71–94.

Ernst E. Chelation therapy for peripheral arterial occlusive disease, a systematic review. Circulation 1997;96:1031–3.

Ernst E. Gingko biloba in the treatment of intermittent claudication. A systematic review based on controlled studies in the literature. Fortschr Med 1996;114:85–7.

Fagher B. Long-term effects of ticlopidine on lower limb blood flow, ankle/brachial index and symptoms in peripheral arteriosclerosis. A double-blind study. The STIMS Group in Lund. Swedish Ticlopidine Multicenter Study. Angiology 1994;45:777–88.

Giansante C, Calabrese S, Fisicaro M, et al. Treatment

of intermittent claudication with antiplatelet agents. J Int Med Res 1990;18:400–7.

Goldhaber SZ, Manson JE, Stampfer MJ, et al. Low-dose aspirin and subsequent peripheral arterial surgery in the Physicians' Health Study. Lancet 1992;340:143–5.

Hess H, Mietaschk A, Deichsel G. Drug-induced inhibition of platelet function delays progression of peripheral occlusive arterial disease. A prospective double-blind arteriographically controlled trial. Lancet 1985;1:415–9.

Jonason T, Bergstrom R. Cessation of smoking in patients with intermittent claudication. Effects on the risk of peripheral vascular complications, myocardial infarction and mortality. Acta Med Scand 1987;221:253–60.

Mohler ER. Peripheral arterial disease. Current Treatment Options in Cardiovascular Medicine 1999; 1:27–34.

Palareti G, Poggi M, Torricelli P, et al. Long-term effects of ticlopidine on fibrinogen and hemorheology in patients with peripheral arterial disease. Thromb Res 1988;52:621–9.

Taylor LM, Moneta GL, Sexton GJ, et al. Prospective blinded study of the relationship between plasma homocysteine and progression of symptomatic peripheral arterial disease. J Vasc Surg 1999;29: 8–19.

Moderate Claudication: The Role of Percutaneous Angioplasty and Stents in Provision of Cost-Effective Care for Symptomatic PAD

Haraldur Bjarnason, MD
Assistant Professor, Department of Radiology
University of Minnesota Medical School
Minneapolis, Minnesota

Objective: To offer a clinical perspective on the role of percutaneous angioplasty and stent placement for the treatment of iliac artery disease.

Atherosclerotic disease of the iliac arteries and distal abdominal aorta is reasonably common in the elderly population, and is more frequently found in hypertensive patients or patients who smoke. In these individuals, proximal limb arterial disease may present with a wide range of symptoms; some patients are asymptomatic, while others present with classic claudication.

The syndrome of distal aortic or iliac artery disease (IAD) may often present as a classic set of symptoms that can be easily recognized by all clinicians. This syndrome is characterized by discomfort or fatigue in the buttock, hip, and/or thigh muscles with initial exercise, and more distal calf claudication with progressive exercise. Frequently, these symptoms develop over a prolonged period of time, and the magnitude of claudication may be variably mild, moderate, or severe depending on the amount of collateral arterial vessels that have developed around the iliac stenosis or occlusion. When distal aortic or common IAD is associated with decreased pudendal artery blood flow, erectile dysfunction may also be present. The clinical presentation is referred to as Leriche's syndrome. Such a presentation of buttock or gluteal claudication with impotence is very suggestive of obstruction or severe narrowing of the distal abdominal aorta or both common iliac arteries, with decreased pressure to the internal iliac arteries and thereby to the penile arteries. A more uncommon clinical presentation of proximal leg aortoiliac occlusive disease (AOD) occurs in women 30 to 60 years of age with a history of

smoking and/or severe hyperlipidemia. This syndrome is often referred to as the small aortic syndrome and is characterized by relatively aggressive atherosclerotic occlusive disease that arises within a small, native distal abdominal aorta and iliac arteries and/or that leads to a severely stenotic residual distal aortic lumen (Cronenwett et al, 1980). In addition to suffering classic thigh claudication, these patients may develop an acute worsening of their claudicatory symptoms, which may occur when sudden thrombosis is superimposed upon the severely stenotic distal aortic or iliac vessels.

On clinical examination, these patients usually present with decreased pulses in 1 or both common femoral arteries, with or without a prominent femoral bruit; more distal popliteal and ankle pulses may be absent. The office-based, ankle-brachial index (ABI) measurement may be normal or moderately decreased, as pelvic collaterals may be robust, supporting the ankle blood pressure at near-normal levels at rest, despite the presence of severe IAD. For such patients, clinical suspicion (eg, typical claudication symptoms) should prompt the primary care physician (PCP) to document the presence of high-grade IAD by referring

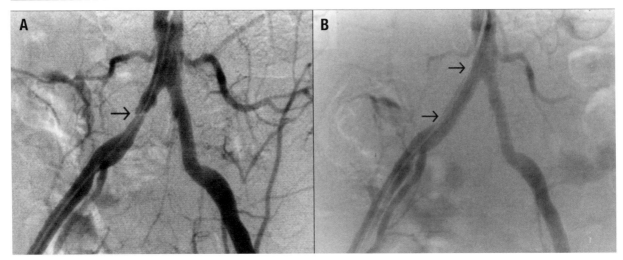

Figure 1. (A) A 45-year-old diabetic patient who smokes with right lower extremity claudication. Doppler ultrasound revealed high-grade stenosis in the right common iliac artery. An angiogram was performed which revealed a severe (95%–99%) short stenosis of the common iliac artery (arrow) with a narrow segment proximal and distal. There was a 100-mm Hg pressure difference from above to below the stenosis. **(B)** It was elected to place a stent primarily. Primary angioplasty would also have been reasonable. A Palmaz® stent was placed (2 arrows) on an 8-mm balloon. Angiographic results were good, and there was no pressure difference across the stenosis after stent placement. The patient was discharged 2 hours after the procedure.

the patient for more definitive diagnostic testing in the noninvasive vascular laboratory. A Doppler exercise stress test can unmask IAD, as the "normal" ABI value at rest (ie, 0.9–1.2) will fall in a diagnostic manner within the first 3 minutes of recovery from exercise. Noninvasive vascular laboratory duplex imaging or Doppler flow studies will usually detect IAD, but if these studies are restricted to the infrainguinal region, focal stenoses may not be discerned unless the pelvic vessels are also interrogated. Segmental pressure studies will demonstrate a pressure differential between the arm and thigh sites. Doppler ultrasound techniques, when interrogation is performed in the proximal leg, can reproducibly demonstrate the increased velocity at the site of stenosis in the iliac arteries. As noted previously, such noninvasive studies can be challenging because of the depth of these arterial sites and the occasional presence of overlying gas-filled bowel loops, which may obscure ideal visualization. Angiography has thus been regarded as the gold standard to provide a diagnostic anatomic evaluation in these patients. More recently, magnetic resonance angiography (MRA) has become more widely available, and effective anatomic evaluations can now be obtained by MRA with contrast medium.

The treatment options for patients with pelvic atherosclerotic disease have changed significantly in the past 20 years. Traditional treatment was usually either conservative (eg, exercise and control of risk factors) or surgical, but newer endovascular treatments with percutaneous transluminal angioplasty (PTA) or stent placement have almost entirely replaced the surgical option (Fig. 1). This article outlines the role of endoluminal treatment for moderate claudication caused by iliac arterial atherosclerosis.

TREATMENT OPTIONS

The optimal treatment for patients with aortoiliac or isolated iliac arterial obstructive disease depends on the character and severity of the limiting ambulatory symptoms. Patients with relatively mild symptoms can benefit greatly from an exercise program and obtain adequate improvement so that their symptoms do not limit daily activity (see fourth monograph in this series, or Colledge, 1997). The Society for Vascular Surgery (SVS) and the Society of Cardiovascular and Interventional Radiology (SCVIR) have adapted a classification system, modified from that initially developed by Rutherford et al, for acute and chronic ischemia (Rutherford et al, 1986; Rutherford and Becker, 1991). This system is useful to help categorize patients for various treatment options.

The decision to treat patients with either endovascular or surgical modalities depends largely on patients' general health. Endovascular therapy is generally believed to be less invasive with lower morbidity, permitting revascularization to be offered to more patients than might traditionally have been treated by surgical therapies (Fig. 2). PCPs should note that percutaneous revascularization is quite safe, but the rare severe

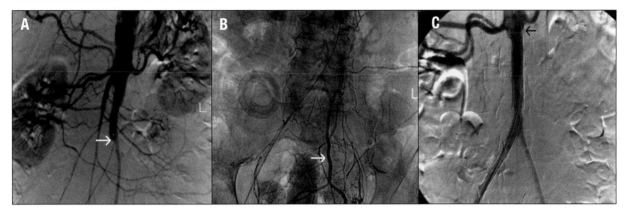

Figure 2. (A) A 57-year-old man with paraplegia and a long history of smoking. He had developed severe leg ischemia and faced amputation at the hip level. An angiogram performed at an outside institution revealed a normal aorta to the level of the renal arteries, but the vessel tapers off to the inferior mesenteric artery (IMA) (arrow) where it becomes occluded. The common femoral arteries were then reconstituted from the IMA. **(B)** The lower portion of the pelvis with the IMA (arrow). **(C)** By means of ultrasound, a puncture was made into the common femoral arteries and catheters advanced through the occluded iliac arteries and distal aorta. Thrombolytic infusion was then given over 48 hours and Wallstent® placed from the level of the renal arteries (arrow) to the common femoral arteries on each side. Amputation was performed at a much lower level, improving the care for the patient who was otherwise in good condition.

complications that can arise during such treatment may lead to an open surgical procedure. The morbidity of these operative procedures may be higher than that of elective operative procedures.

ENDOVASCULAR TREATMENT

Background. In 1964, Dotter and Judkins described the first percutaneous angioplasty. This creative approach was their first using a coaxial polyethylene catheter system for dilation of the popliteal artery. This system was used successfully for several years but was cumbersome and required a large puncture in the artery. In 1974, Grüntzig and Hopff described the first use of balloon-expandable catheters for dilation of arterial stenoses. This procedure led to revolutionary changes in the fields of interventional radiology and cardiology, enabling low-profile catheters to be placed across the narrow vessel and the balloon to be inflated and deflated, requiring only a small puncture in the artery. This procedure contrasts with those using polyethylene dilators which required creation of an arterial hole equal in size to the diameter of the dilated artery.

Since then, there has been great progress in endovascular treatment for peripheral arterial disease. PTA has developed rapidly and has become the primary treatment replacing surgery for certain types of iliac and aortic disease. In the past 10 years, endoluminal stents have become an expected treatment option for coronary artery disease and are an important part of the endoluminal armamentarium for iliac artery treatment. These stents are metal cylinders which are expanded inside the lumen of the vessel against the vessel wall. The stents are placed either via balloon catheter (balloon-expandable stents) or they are self-expandable, deployed inside the vessel. Initially, metal stents were used only when angioplasty either failed due to vessel recoil or if the procedure caused a significant intimal dissection, resulting in a free flap of the intima which then could be "tacked down" with a stent. Experts have debated whether stents have a better long-term outcome in the treatment of IAD than angioplasty alone. There have been only a few published studies comparing the 2 methods, but there appears to be a general consensus that the 2 are complementary (Tetteroo et al, 1998).

ANGIOPLASTY

Basic Principles. Modern angioplasty balloons are built onto the end of a catheter made of polyethylene or similar material. The catheters can be inserted over a guidewire, and the outer diameter of the catheter itself is usually 5 to 6 Fr. The balloons come in different lengths and diameters, from as small as 2 mm to more than 20 mm. For iliac artery angioplasty, the usual diameters used are 6 to 10 mm and occasionally 12 mm, depending on the location and vessel size. The usual length of the balloon is 4 cm, but different lengths are available. The balloons are constructed so that they can expand up to the nominated diameter and cannot exceed that diameter. Most balloons are wrapped around the shaft of the catheter, and when expanded, will unwrap and form a cylinder. When deflated, they will rewrap around the balloon shaft.

The same balloon can be used for more than 1 angioplasty procedure in the same patient. The balloons are inflated with an inflator device. The normal pressure used is 8 to 10 atm, but most balloons will take up to 17 to 20 atm of pressure.

Techniques. For iliac and distal aortic angioplasty, access to the arterial system is gained either through one or both common femoral arteries. The puncture is pointed retrograde toward the patient's head, and introducer sheaths are inserted to allow for repeated access into the vessel. Heparin (normally 4,000 to 5,000 U as a bolus) is usually administered to the patient prior to crossing the lesion.

Initially, a soft guidewire is advanced across the lesion with the help of a steering catheter. Soft wires are used to avoid damage to the vessel, dissection under the plaque, or embolization. As soon as the guidewire and catheter have been advanced above the area, an angiogram is performed. When the stenotic or occluded segment has been identified, an appropriately sized balloon is selected. The size is 1 to 2 mm larger than the diameter of the nearest normal segment next above the stenosis. The balloon is then slowly inflated across the stenosis until the waist that will form at the stenosis has been fully expanded. This is usually achieved with 3 to 4 atm of pressure. The balloon is left inflated for 15 to 30 seconds. It is then deflated to allow flow through the area, and as many as 2 dilatations are often performed. The balloon is then removed, leaving the wire across the area. An angiography catheter is brought in above the area treated.

Pressure measurements are taken before and after angioplasty both above and below the treated area. A 15- to 20-mm Hg pressure difference between measurements is regarded as significant. In general, satisfactory results are obtained if the gradient is 5 mm Hg or lower.

Indications. The typical iliac artery stenosis that would be treated with angioplasty is a short, isolated eccentric stenosis found in the major leg arteries, such as the common iliac artery (*Guidelines for Percutaneous Transluminal Angioplasty*, 1990; Wilson et al, 1989; Johnston et al, 1982).

External iliac artery stenoses tend to respond less favorably to angioplasty than do stenoses of the common iliac artery. Long stenoses and ulcerated stenoses are less favorably improved with angioplasty. Total arterial occlusions do not respond as well to angioplasty as do focal short stenoses (Johnston, 1992).

Results. Case studies and meta-analyses of case studies for the outcome of angioplasty in aortoiliac disease have been published. The results of several case studies for angioplasty outcomes are listed in the Table. The technical success rate is between 78.6% and 98.6% after angioplasty. Becker and colleagues (1989) performed a detailed review of the published experience available for an accumulated total of 2697 iliac artery angioplasties. The 2-year patency rate was 81%, and the 5-year patency rate was 72% (Becker et al, 1989). Johnston (1992) analyzed 984 patients, evaluating the degree of stenosis and the runoff flow. They found an overall patency rate of 65% and 53% at 2 and 5 years of follow-up, respectively (Johnston 1992). Wilson and colleagues (1989) compared surgical treatment for aortoiliac disease with angioplasty and found no difference in terms of patency at 3 years (Wilson et al, 1989).

One of the main shortcomings of balloon angioplasty is elastic recoil that leads to restenosis immediately or shortly after the procedure, formation of intimal flaps, and intimal hyperplasia, which develops later. Metal stents have significantly improved the outcome after angioplasty by allowing for treatment of those limitations.

STENTS

Basic Principles. Metal stents are expandable metal cylinders that are deployed within a vessel to scaffold the vessel wall. These stents can be divided into 2 principal types: balloon-expandable and self-expandable stents. The balloon-expandable stents are made of moldable metal and are placed onto a balloon catheter. The stents are then carried on the balloon catheter across the stenosis and expanded by inflating the balloon. The diameter of the stent is determined by the size of the balloon catheter. Self-expandable stents have their own nominated diameter which is predetermined by the manufacturer. They are carried into the vessel on a delivery system and then released to expand to the nominated diameter within the vessel. These also can be dilated after deployment, but often the dilatation is performed prior to stent placement. The basic difference between these 2 types of stents is that the balloon-expandable stents can be deformed or crushed by external forces and will not regain their shape without redilatation. The self-expandable stents will, on the other hand, regain their previous form despite external deformity. The Palmaz® (Johnson & Johnson, Warren, New Jersey) stent is the best known of the balloon-expandable type, and the Wallstent® (Boston Scientific, Minneapolis, Minnesota) is the best known representative of the self-expandable stents.

Table. Reported Patency Results of Angioplasty in Aortoiliac Disease

Reference	Initial Success	Primary Patency			
		1 Year	**2 Years**	**4 Years**	**5 Years**
PTA studies					
Gupta, et al*	78.6	79	76	76	76
Tegtmeyer, et al[†]	93.0	96	90	87	85
Stokes, et al[‡]	94.3	85	74	67	34
Jeans, et al[§]	88.3	67	62	58	57
Jorgensen, et al[§]	93.1	79	72	65	63
Johnston[§]	98.6	77	67	58	54
Johnston[§]	81.9	60	53	NA	NA
Stent studies					
Long, et al[§]	98.0	84	69	41	NA
Vorwerk, et al[§]	98.0	87	83	78	54
Wolf, et al[§]	100.0	94	NA	NA	NA
Vorwerk, et al[§]	97.0	95	88	82	72
Strecker, et al*	100.0	95	95	NA	NA
Henry, et al[§]	99.0	94	91	86	NA
Martin, et al[§]	97.0	81	71	NA	NA
Murphy, et al[§]	91.0	78	53	NA	NA

Data are percentages. NA = Not available. Primary and secondary patency were both reported in some articles, but primary patency was tabulated here.

*Initial failures excluded from long-term results.

[†]Data in 10 patients lost to follow-up were excluded from the reported life-table analysis. We revised the life-table results including these as censored observations.

[‡]Reported patency excludes 4 technical failures and 4 immediate clinical failures.

[§]Initial failures included in the long-term results.

Modified from Bosch et al, 1997.

Techniques. Balloon-expandable stents are mounted onto a regular balloon catheter, as described previously. The balloon and stent are then advanced across the stenotic area in the same manner as described for balloon angioplasty. The balloon is slowly inflated in the same manner as for angioplasty. When full expansion has been achieved, the balloon is deployed and the stent inserted; the balloon can then be removed. The stents also can be redilated to larger diameters if needed.

The self-expandable stents are usually deployed across a stenotic area after dilatation has been performed. They also can be placed across a stenosis and followed by dilatation. The balloon-expandable stents usually permit more precise positioning than the self-expandable stents. They also often have more expandable force than self-expandable stents.

Indications. The indications for endovascular stents have been debated. Primary stenting (ie, stenting without prior angioplasty) has been advocated by many experts. The approved indication is failed angioplasty, either because of recoil or intimal dissection. For this indication, balloon-expandable stents have proved very beneficial (Bosch et al, 1998).

Results. A relatively large randomized study comparing primary stenting to primary PTA for IAD failed to demonstrate substantial differences between the 2 techniques (Tetteroo et al, 1998). On the other hand, selective stent placement in cases of failed PTA was found to be a cost-effective treatment compared with primary stent placement or PTA alone (Bosch et al, 1998). The technical success rate for stent placement is very high—between 91% and 100% (Table). The long-term outcomes are also good, with a patency rate of 53% to 95% at 2 years and high patency rates even at 5 years (Bosch and Hunink, 1997). The complication rates are also lower for stent placement than for angioplasty (Tetteroo et al, 1998). Another randomized

Key Points

• Iliac artery occlusive disease most commonly presents with buttock, thigh, or hip claudication.

• Noninvasive vascular laboratory testing will suggest the presence of iliac or aortic disease in most cases, but may not pinpoint the location if nonimaging methods are used.

• Conventional angiography is the gold standard for anatomic evaluation of IAD. Magnetic resonance angiography is a new noninvasive technique which also provides good anatomic definition of the iliac arteries.

• In many cases, endovascular methods (eg, PTA or stent placement) have replaced surgical methods in the treatment of IAD.

• The role of primary stenting is still debated.

study has shown a substantial difference in patency rates at 5-year follow-up for patients treated with primary stent placement versus those with angioplasty. The 5-year patency rates were 70% in the PTA group compared with 93% in the primary stent group (Richter et al, 1991).

CONCLUSIONS

The treatment of IAD has changed dramatically over the past 10 to 20 years. The changes can be related to the development of angioplasty as described by Dotter and Judkins (1964) and Grüntzig and Hopff (1974). Until the late 1980s, treatment for AOD was surgical. In the past 10 years, surgery for IAD has become nearly obsolete and has been replaced by endovascular methods. There are few studies comparing the surgical method to the endovascular method, but the results of angioplasty and stent placement are similar to those of studies previously reported in the surgical literature. The morbidity and mortality reported in these studies are substantially less using endovascular methods compared with surgical methods.

Treatment of AOD is usually performed on an outpatient basis. These patients typically do not require anticoagulation, except during the procedure itself. More complicated cases may require overnight admission to the hospital and prolonged anticoagulation.

The future of endovascular treatment must still be written, but in selected cases, aortic aneurysms and iliac artery aneurysms are currently treated with metal stents covered with Gore-tex® or other materials. In the future, all iliac and aortic disease may be treated through endovascular methods. ■

BIBLIOGRAPHY

Becker GJ, Katzen BT, Dake MD. Noncoronary angioplasty. Radiology 1989;170:921.

Bosch JL, Hunink MGM. Meta-analysis of the results of percutaneous transluminal angioplasty and stent placement for aortoiliac occlusive disease. Radiology 1997;204:87–96.

Bosch JL, Tetteroo E, Mali WPTM, Hunink MGM, for the Dutch Iliac Stent Trial Study Group. Iliac arterial occlusive disease: cost-effectiveness analysis of stent placement versus percutaneous transluminal angioplasty. Radiology 1998;208:641–8.

Colledge J. Lower-limb arterial disease. Lancet 1997;350:1459–64.

Cronenwett J, Davis J, Gooch J, et al. Aortoiliac occlusive disease in women. Surgery 1980;88:775.

Dotter CT, Judkins MP. Transluminal treatment of arteriosclerotic obstruction: description of a new technique and a preliminary report of its application. Circulation 1964;30:654.

Grüntzig A, Hopff H. Percutaneous recanalization after chronic arterial occlusion with a new dilator-catheter (modification of the Dotter technique) (author's transl). Dtsch Med Wochenschr 1974;99:2502–10, 2511.

Guidelines for Percutaneous Transluminal Angioplasty. Standards of Practice Committee of the Society of Cardiovascular and Interventional Radiology. Radiology 1990;177:619.

Gupta AK, Ravimandalam K, Rao VRK, et al. Total occlusion of iliac arteries: results of balloon angioplasty. Cardiovasc Intervent Radiol 1993;16:165–77.

Henry M, Amor M, Ethevenot G, et al. Palmaz stent placement in iliac and femoropopliteal arteries: primary and secondary patency in 310 patients with 2-4 year follow-up. Radiology 1995;197:167–74.

Jeans WD, Armstrong S, Cole SEA, Horrocks M, Baird RN. Fate of patients undergoing transluminal angioplasty for lower-limb ischemia. Radiology 1990;177:559–64.

Johnston KW. Factors that influence the outcome of aortoiliac and femoropopliteal percutaneous transluminal angioplasty. Surg Clin North Am 1992;72:843.

Johnston KW. Iliac arteries: reanalysis of results of balloon angioplasty. Radiology 1993;186:207–12.

Johnston KW, Colapinto RF, Baird RJ. Transluminal dilation – an alternative? Arch Surg 1982;117:1604.

Jorgensen B, Skovgaard N, Norgard J, Karle A, Holstein

P. Percutaneous transluminal angioplasty in 226 iliac artery stenoses: role of the superficial femoral artery for clinical success. Vasa J Vasc Dis 1992;21:382–6.

Long AL, Sapoval MR, Beyssen BM, et al. Strecker stent implantation in iliac arteries: patency and predictive factors for long-term success. Radiology 1995;194:739–44.

Martin EC, Katzen BT, Benenati JF, et al. Multicenter trial of the Wallstent in the iliac and femoral arteries. J Vasc Intervent Radiol 1995; 6:843–9.

Murphy TP, Webb MS, Lambiase RE, et al. Percutaneous revascularization of complex iliac artery stenoses and occlusions with use of Wallstents: three-year experience. J Vasc Intervent Radiol 1996;7:21–7.

Richter GM, Roeren TH, Noedge G, et al. Superior clinical results of iliac stent placement versus percutaneous transluminal angioplasty: four-year success rates of a randomized study [Abstract]. Radiology 1991;181(suppl):161.

Rutherford RB, Becker GJ. Standards for evaluation and reporting the results of surgical and percutaneous therapy for peripheral arterial disease. Radiology 1991;181:277.

Rutherford RB, Flanigan DP, Gupta SK, et al. Suggested standards for reports dealing with lower extremity ischemia. J Vasc Surg 1986;4:80.

Stokes KR, Strunk HM, Campbell DR, et al. Five-year results of iliac and femoropopliteal angioplasty in diabetic patients. Radiology 1990;174:977–82.

Strecker EPK, Hagen B, Liermann D, et al. Iliac and femoropopliteal vascular occlusive disease treated with flexible tantalum stents. Cardiovasc Intervent Radiol 1993;16:158–64.

Tegtmeyer CJ, Hartwell GD, Selby JB, et al. Results and complications of angioplasty in aortoiliac disease. Circulation 1991;83(suppl):153–60.

Tetteroo E, van der Graaf Y, Bosch JL, et al, for the Dutch Iliac Stent Trial Study Group. Randomised comparison of primary stent placement versus primary angioplasty followed by selective stent placement in patients with iliac-artery occlusive disease. Lancet 1998;351:1153–8.

Vorwerk D, Günther RW, Schürmann K, Wendt G. Aortic and iliac stenoses: follow-up results of stent placement after insufficient balloon angioplasty in 118 cases. Radiology 1996;198:45–8.

Vorwerk D, Günther RW, Schürmann K, Wendt G, Peters I. Primary stent placement for chronic iliac artery occlusions: follow-up results in 103 patients. Radiology 1995;194:745–9.

Wilson SE, Wolf GL, Cross AP. Percutaneous transluminal angioplasty versus operation for peripheral arteriosclerosis. J Vasc Surg 1989;9:1.

Wolf YG, Schatz RA, Knowles HJ, et al. Initial experience with the Palmaz stent for aortoiliac stenoses. Ann Vasc Surg 1993;7:254–61.

Surgical Treatment of Intermittent Claudication

Michael R. Lepore, MD
Vascular Surgery Fellow
Ochsner Clinic
New Orleans, Louisiana

Samuel R. Money, MD
Chief, Division of Vascular Surgery
Ochsner Clinic
New Orleans, Louisiana

Objective: To review the indications for and current concepts of vascular surgery as they relate to the treatment of intermittent claudication.

Surgical treatment of intermittent claudication (IC) has long been a topic of controversy in the field of vascular surgery. The subject has spawned considerable ongoing debate, such as the potential risk of surgery to life and limb, the relative efficacy of endovascular versus surgical repair, and the choice of conduit (synthetic vs autologous vein graft [AVG]) for infrainguinal bypass. Assessment of claudication and its medical treatment have recently been covered quite extensively in this journal (Hirsch and Hiatt, 1999). Once all conservative (nonoperative) treatment modalities such as atherosclerosis risk modification, exercise programs, and pharmacotherapy for IC have been exhausted, a decision in favor of surgical intervention requires an understanding of the disease and its treatment outcomes.

The Framingham Study and its ongoing program of epidemiologic follow-up helped to establish that IC represents a powerful marker of global cardiovascular risk. This is due to the systemic nature of atherosclerosis as coronary and cerebral arterial disease contribute to the associated morbidity and mortality in this group of patients (Kannel et al, 1970). In fact, it has been reported that the 5-year risk of limb loss is 3% to 20% (Kannel et al, 1970; Kent et al, 1988; Rosenthal et al, 1990). When analyzing the subset of patients with claudication alone (no critical ischemia), the 5-year amputation rate has been reported to be 3% (Alinaji et al, 1978). Thus, the risk of limb loss appears to be lower in patients with claudication alone when examining the spectrum of all patients with peripheral arterial disease. The 5-year mortality rate for patients with claudication is 29%; 60% of deaths are from coronary artery disease, 15% from cerebrovascular disease, and the remainder from nonatherosclerotic causes (Criqui et al, 1992; Szilagyi et al, 1986). This balance of risk to limb versus life is central to all vascular surgical procedural decisions.

Analyzing the vascular surgery workforce issues, Stanley et al (1996) reported a phenomenon of which we are all too aware: an ongoing increase in the elderly population. This will continue at a fairly steady rate with rapid changes expected by the year 2010. The oldest of the 75 million baby boomers will reach age 65 during that year. The next 20 years (2010 to 2030) will see a 70% increase in those over 65 years of age (Table I). This translates to a higher incidence of IC and its accompanying surgical implications.

Initial attempts at modifying behavior and its inherent atherosclerosis risk factors (eg, smoking cessation, diet modifications, etc) have been shown to exert an overall impact on symptoms as well as progression of disease and thus should always be instituted (Kannel and McGee, 1985). Additionally, various exercise programs are known to be effective and need to be implemented in combination with proven pharmacologic agents such as pentoxifylline and cilostazol (Hiatt et al, 1990b; Gardner and Poehlman, 1995; Money et al, 1998; Dawson et al, 1998). When all of these medical therapeutic measures have been used,

Table I. Population Projections in the United States, in Millions (Percentage of Total)

Year	Total Population	≥55 Years of age	≥65 Years of age
1992, survey year	255.0	52.1 (20.4)	31.2 (12.2)
1995	263.4	54.9 (20.8)	33.6 (12.8)
2000	276.4	59.0 (21.3)	35.3 (12.8)
2005	288.3	65.8 (22.8)	37.0 (12.8)
2010	300.4	74.7 (24.9)	40.1 (13.3)
2020	325.9	96.1 (29.5)	53.8 (16.5)
2030	350.0	107.6 (30.7)	70.2 (20.1)

Modified from the middle series projections of the US Census Bureau, wherein the most probable fertility rates, life-expectancy, and net immigration data are used to predict population numbers. Reprinted with permission from Stanley JC, et al. J Vasc Surg 1996;23:172–81.

Table II. Using the Ankle-Brachial Index (ABI) to Assess the Severity of Arterial Obstruction

Severity	ABI
Normal	>0.90
Mild	0.70–0.89
Moderate	0.50–0.69
Severe	<0.50

Reprinted with permission from Hiatt WR, et al. *Circulation* 1990b;81:602–9.

but the patient remains dissatisfied with his or her current functional status, then surgical options need to be considered.

PATIENT SELECTION

The clinical significance of IC is dictated by each patient's lifestyle. The pain and discomfort experienced by an active laborer during everyday activities may not be an issue to a sedentary desk worker. Highly motivated patients who have been active until recently or whose job is in jeopardy may be good candidates as well, having failed conservative attempts at improvement. Alternatively, high surgical risk patients with severe comorbid disease will likely succumb to their comorbidities before complications related to advanced lower extremity ischemia ever become an issue.

PATIENT EVALUATION

After a commitment has been made to consider surgical revascularization for any individual patient, basic principles should be followed: (1) arteriography should *not* be obtained unless either endovascular or surgical bypass is planned; (2) arteriography must be performed in a manner that achieves a complete examination, extending from the infrarenal aorta to the pedal arches, with adequate visualization of runoff vessels; (3) arterial disease is often worse than it appears because angiography provides only a 2-dimensional view of a 3-dimensional disease process (Hertzer, 1977).

Once again, given the typical accompanying comorbidities in this group of patients, adequate workup of the cardiovascular, cerebrovascular, and pulmonary systems must be considered. The aggressiveness of

this workup will be dictated by a patient's medical history as well as specifics of the planned operational approach and anesthetic exposure he or she will experience in the planned procedure.

TREATMENT

Planning appropriate surgical treatment necessitates an understanding of the severity of disease. This is aided by a good vascular laboratory, where the patient has likely been followed during attempts at conservative management. The laboratory will give clues to the affected arterial level of disease based on the segmental pressures and ankle-brachial index (ABI). The ABI is calculated by dividing the Doppler-derived systolic pressure in each ankle by the higher of the 2 Doppler-derived systolic pressures in the arms. The number obtained will dictate severity of disease (Table II) (Gray and Sullivan, 1997). However, some patients may have medial calcinosis leading to falsely elevated pressures. In these cases, toe pressure indices or pulse-volume recordings may prove to be important. Arteriography, as discussed previously, definitively identifies the level(s) of arterial involvement in the disease process. The more involved levels of disease typically equate to increased severity.

The vascular surgery principle to be followed at all times revolves around the initial treatment of proximal disease. This translates to the treatment of aortoiliac, then femoropopliteal, followed by tibioperoneal arterial disease. Treatment of distal disease first (ie, femoropopliteal bypass in the presence of significant ipsilateral iliac stenosis) will likely result in graft failure if adequate inflow is not present.

AORTOILIAC DISEASE

Considering treatment of aortoiliac disease, the 2 potential options for invasive intervention are percutaneous transluminal angioplasty, with or without stenting (PTAS or PTA), or aortofemoral bypass (AFB). PTAS or PTA is most ideal for unilateral short-segment (<5 cm) stenosis. Success rates are reported to range

Table III. Angioplasty Versus Surgery

Angioplasty	Bypass Surgery

Aortoiliac angioplasty (with stenting)*
    75% to 90% patency at 3 to 5 years
	Aortoiliac or aortobifemoral
	    5-year patency: 80% to 90%
	    10-year patency: 75% to 80%

Superficial femoral angioplasty (with/without stenting)
    40% to 50% patency at 2 years
	Femoropopliteal bypass (above-knee)
	    5-year patency
	        Synthetic: 55% to 62%
	        AVG: 60% to 75%

Popliteal/tibial angioplasty
    10% to 40% initial patency
	Femoropopliteal bypass (below-knee)
	    5-year patency
	        Synthetic: 35% to 40%
	        AVG: 60% to 70%

Long-term patency unclear[†]	Femorotibial bypass
	    5-year patency
	        Synthetic: 10% to 15%
	        AVG: 50% to 60%

*Optimal lesion is a single lesion <5 cm.

[†] Unproven success rates.

AVG = autologous vein graft.

from 75% to 90% at 3 to 5 years, comparable to those for aortofemoral reconstruction (Sullivan et al, 1997). On the other hand, diffuse bilateral disease and/or long-segment stenosis or occlusion should be treated by an AFB and not a PTAS. Five-year patency rates of bypass are reported to be from 80% to 90% (Szilagyi et al, 1986; Abbott and Kwolek, 1995). Because we are comparing a percutaneous to an aortic procedure with its inherent risks, patient selection is crucial to clinical success.

INFRAINGUINAL DISEASE

When considering treatment of disease below the inguinal ligament, there are several factors to consider. The various modalities for each level of disease, from proximal to distal, are outlined below. PTA of short-segment, superficial, femoral artery stenosis has reported early success rates equivalent to bypass, but long-term results are inconsistent at best (Capek et al, 1991). It is generally accepted that stents should only be used selectively, as longer lesions frequently stenose or occlude resulting in increased technical difficulties for future surgical bypass procedures (Gray and Olin, 1997). The use of stents below the inguinal ligament is questionable, except as an experimental or "final strategy" for limb salvage when surgical reconstruction is not an option. Therefore, stenting should not be considered in the treatment of IC until more

information is available.

Consideration of femoral-to-above-knee popliteal bypass raises the controversial question of what type of material to use, synthetic conduit or AVG. Choosing the type of prosthetic does not appear to have much impact on graft patency, as proved in a large multi-center, randomized, prospective study (Abbott et al, 1997) comparing Dacron® to polytetrafluoroethylene (PTFE). Primary patency rates were reported to be 62% and 57% at 5 years, respectively. The investigators did report that the use of prosthetic material should be restricted to older nonsmokers with favorable anatomy (ie, good distal runoff vessels).

Veith et al (1986) found initial patency rates of synthetic conduit or AVG to the above-knee popliteal artery to be equivalent at 2 years. They did identify a drop-off in PTFE patency at 4 years that was not statistically significant. The other argument that has been proposed for using synthetic material in the above-knee popliteal position is based on the premise, "save the vein for later." This does not appear to be a valid argument, however, as the frequency of secondary below-knee repair following failure of the above-knee popliteal graft in a 20-year experience was shown to be 7% (Berlakovich et al, 1994). These studies clearly indicate that when given the option, the best results can be obtained if AVG is used as the bypass conduit.

PTA for below-knee disease remains unproven.

Key Points

• Patient selection is probably the single most important part of the decision-making process when it comes to surgical treatment of IC. It will dictate both success and overall morbidity and mortality.

• Always consider the patient's other comorbidities (ie, coronary and cerebrovascular atheroscleroses) when selecting the surgical treatment for IC.

• Arteriography should *only* be obtained when endovascular or surgical reconstruction is planned; it has its own inherent risks.

• Arteriography should be complete from the infrarenal aorta to the pedal arches, with good visualization of runoff vessels.

• Autologous vein graft is the conduit of choice, especially in the treatment of IC.

The largest published series offers respectable early patency rates but has follow-up on only one third of its patients (Schwarten, 1991). Bypass should be the primary mode of treatment for below-knee IC, if it is to be performed at all. There is a significant difference between the primary patency rates of AVGs and PTFE below the knee (49% vs 12%, respectively), making AVG the primary conduit of choice (Veith et al, 1986). The Veterans Administration Cooperative Study (1988) showed no difference in the use of reversed saphenous vein or in situ saphenous vein for distal bypass procedures in the treatment of below-knee disease. Synthetic materials should only be used for limb salvage and *never* considered for treatment of IC.

Surgical treatment of the patient with IC has been discouraged for fear of graft failure, limb loss, and perioperative complications that may fare worse than the natural history of the disease. However, a recently published study (Byrne et al, 1999) of 409 patients revealed cumulative patient survival rates of 93% and 80% at 4 and 6 years, respectively. This seems acceptable considering that the Framingham Study (Kannel et al, 1970) found the 5-year mortality of the claudicant to be about 25%. Nonetheless, it is important to have an overall knowledge of various modalities of treatment and outcomes when considering any interventions in the patient with IC (Table III). The primary care physician provides an indispensable perspective on each patient's potential benefit and risk when surgical revascularization is considered. ∎

BIBLIOGRAPHY

Abbott W, Kwolek C. Aortofemoral bypass for atherosclerotic disease. In: Current Therapy in Vascular Surgery. 3rd ed. St. Louis, Mo: Mosby; 1995:355–9.

Abbott WM, Green RM, Matsumoto T, et al. Prosthetic above-knee femoropopliteal bypass grafting: results of a multicenter randomized prospective trial. J Vasc Surg 1997;25:19–28.

Alinaji, Barter CF, Berkowitz HD, et al. Femoropopliteal vein grafts for claudication: analysis of 100 consecutive cases. Ann Surg 1978;188:79–82.

Berlakovich GA, Herbst F, Mittlbock M, et al. The choice of material for above knee femoropopliteal bypass: a 20 year experience. Arch Surg 1994;129:297–302.

Byrne J, Darling C III, Change B, et al. Infrainguinal arterial reconstruction for claudication: is it worth the risk? An analysis of 409 procedures. J Vasc Surg 1999;29:259–69.

Capek P, McLean GK, Berkowitz HD. Femoropopliteal angioplasty: factors influencing long-term success. Circulation 1991:83(suppl I):I70–I80.

Criqui MH, Langer RD, Fronek A, et al. Mortality over a period of 10 years in patients with peripheral arterial disease. N Engl J Med 1992;326:381–6.

Dawson DL, Cutler BS, Meissner MH, et al. Cilostazol has beneficial effects in treatment of intermittent claudication: results from a multicenter, randomized, prospective, double-blind trial. Circulation 1998;98:678–86.

Gardner AW, Poehlman ET. Exercise rehabilitation programs for the treatment of claudication pain: a meta-analysis. JAMA 1995;274:975–80.

Gray BH, Olin JW. Limitations of percutaneous transluminal angioplasty with stenting for femoropopliteal arterial occlusive disease. Semin Vasc Surg 1997;220:251–68.

Gray BH, Sullivan TM. Vascular claudication: how to individualize treatment. Cleve Clin J Med 1997;64(8):429–36.

Hertzer N. Surgical management of intermittent claudication. Am Fam Phys 1977;16(3):108–16.

Hiatt WR, Regensteiner JF, Hargarten ME, et al. Benefit of exercise conditioning for patients with peripheral arterial disease. Circulation 1990b;81:602–9.

Hirsch AT, Hiatt WR. An office-based approach to the diagnosis and treatment of peripheral arterial disease. Part IV: Morbidity of PAD: medical approaches to claudication. CME Series. AM J Med 1999.

Kannel WB, McGee DL. Update on some epidemiologic features of intermittent claudication: the Framingham study. J Am Geriatr Soc 1985;33:13–8.

Kannel WB, Skinner JJ, Schwartz MJ, et al. Intermittent

claudication: incidence in the Framingham study. Circulation 1970;41:875–83.

Kent CC, Donaldson MC, Attinger CE, et al. Femoropopliteal reconstruction for claudication: the risk to life and limb. Arch Surg 1988;123:1196–8.

Money SR, Herd AJ, Isaacsohn JL, et al. Effect of cilostazol on walking distances in patients with intermittent claudication caused by peripheral vascular disease. J Vasc Surg 1998;27:267–75.

Rosenthal D, Evans D, Mckinsey J, et al. Prosthetic above knee femoropopliteal bypass for intermittent claudication. J Cardiovasc Surg 1990;31:462–8.

Schwarten DE. Clinical and anatomical considerations for nonoperative therapy in tibial disease and results of angioplasty. Circulation 1991;83(suppl I):I86–I90.

Stanley JC, Barnes RW, Ernst CB, et al. Vascular Surgery in the United States: Workforce Issues Report of the Society for Vascular Surgery and the International Society for Cardiovascular Surgery, North American Chapter, Committee on Workforce Issues. J Vasc Surg 1996;23:172–81.

Sullivan TN, Childs MB, Bacharach JM, et al. Percutaneous transluminal angioplasty and primary stenting of the iliac arteries in 288 patients. J Vasc Surg 1997;25:829–38.

Szilagyi DE, Elliot JP, Smith RF, et al. A thirty year survey of the reconstructive surgical treatment of aortoiliac occlusive disease. J Vasc Surg 1986;3:421–36.

Veith FJ, Gupta SK, Ascer E, et al. Six-year prospective multi-center randomized comparison of autologous saphenous vein and expanded polytetrafluoroethylene grafts in infrainguinal arterial reconstructions. J Vasc Surg 1986;3:104–14.

Veterans Administration Study Group 141. Comparative evaluation of reversed and in situ vein bypass grafts in distal popliteal and tibial-peroneal revascularization. Arch Surg 1988;123:434–8.

The American Journal of Medicine®

CONTINUING EDUCATION SERIES

AN OFFICE-BASED APPROACH TO THE DIAGNOSIS AND TREATMENT OF PERIPHERAL ARTERIAL DISEASE

PART VI: A Primer to the Vascular Laboratory for the Primary Care Physician

SERIES EDITOR
ALAN T. HIRSCH, MD
GUEST EDITOR
MICHAEL R. JAFF, DO, FACP, FACC

Jointly sponsored by
The Excerpta Medica Office of Continuing Medical Education and the Society for Vascular Medicine and Biology

Introduction and Overview

Alan T. Hirsch, MD
Director, Vascular Medicine Program
Minnesota Vascular Diseases Center
University of Minnesota Medical School
Minneapolis, Minnesota

Michael R. Jaff, DO, FACP, FACC
Medical Director, Center for Vascular Care
Co-Director, Vascular Diagnostic Laboratory
Washington Hospital Center
Washington, DC

This Continuing Education Series on the primary care of peripheral arterial disease (PAD), published under the auspices of *The American Journal of Medicine*®, has provided a comprehensive overview of the natural history, pathophysiology, and available treatment options. It is a premise of this series and of the Society for Vascular Medicine and Biology that the primary care physician is ideally positioned to assume a major proportion of the responsibility for the management of patients with all forms of vascular disease, especially PAD. A critical aspect of this management is an appreciation for current methods of diagnosis. The classical office-based history and clinical examination were once considered sufficient for patients with PAD. This may have been true when there were few therapeutic options, in an era when pessimism prevailed over the provision of effective medical interventions. However, on completion of the medical history, physical examination, and performance of the ankle-brachial index, the noninvasive vascular diagnostic laboratory serves as a logical and effective "next step" in the diagnostic pathway.

Although it may at first seem that the tests performed in the vascular laboratory are complex and require dedicated vascular specialty training for their interpretation, we believe that most primary care physicians can easily become proficient in appreciating the benefits, limitations, and accuracy of these tests. The relationship of the primary care physician to vascular technology is essentially no different from other diagnostic evaluations. Just as there is benefit in understanding the relative utilities of a plain chest radiograph, chest computed tomography (CT) scan, or "physiologic" pulmonary function studies, so too the primary care physician is well positioned to understand and use pulse volume recordings, duplex ultrasound, or Doppler waveform techniques. With this knowledge, appropriate therapeutic decisions can be made and the primary care physician can truly remain "primary" in helping the patient choose therapeutic options and determine if a vascular specialty referral is needed.

This sixth monograph is thus dedicated to improving the understanding by the primary care physician of the vascular diagnostic laboratory in facilitating an accurate diagnosis in PAD.

In the article by G. Allen Holloway, Jr, MD, the therapeutic role of the vascular diagnostic laboratory for the primary care physician is summarized by reviewing specific clinical scenarios in vascular medicine, and how the tests available in the diagnostic laboratory can be used appropriately.

Dr. Jaff then reviews the role of direct visualization of the lower extremity arterial circulation with arterial duplex ultrasonography techniques. Duplex ultrasonography utilizes the physics of sound waves to assess the velocity of blood flow. The faster the velocity recorded in sequential arterial segments, the higher the degree of stenosis. Arterial duplex ultrasonography is useful in localizing areas of atherosclerotic stenoses and occlusions. It is also very helpful in evaluating patients after suspected iatrogenic vascular injury (ie, catheter-induced pseudoaneurysms or arteriovenous fistulae).

Thom Rooke, MD, writes about the role of physiologic tests in the diagnosis of PAD. These are most appropriately the first vascular laboratory tests performed in patients with PAD. They help confirm the diagnosis of intermittent claudication, and will assess the true functional limitations of patients with PAD. In addition, these tests are very helpful in establishing levels of improvement in limb perfusion after initiation of treatments, whether the treatment relies on a medical, surgical, or endovascular technique.

Please note that, currently, the patient who "complains the most" is often the one patient referred for limb bypass surgery. Inasmuch as patients "interpret" pain and functional limitations idiosyncratically, would it not be more appropriate to objectively evaluate the claudication functional limitation before such a potentially morbid procedure, with its incipient cardiovascular risk, is prescribed? Would a patient who complains of dyspnea be referred for lung surgery without prior performance of pulmonary function studies?

Finally, Rolf R. Paulson, MD, FACP, provides important data on the diagnosis of arterial aneurysms.

Abdominal aortic aneurysms arise in an age-dependent manner and are detected with increasing frequency as the population ages. If unidentified, there is a significant risk of rupture and death. Although less well-recognized in office practice, aneurysms of the popliteal artery remain an important cause of critical limb ischemia, primarily due to distal embolization of thrombotic material, and acute thrombosis of the aneurysm. Dr. Paulson provides a logical diagnostic approach to these potentially lethal disorders and discusses clinically useful diagnostic tests including duplex ultrasonography, helical CT scanning, magnetic resonance arteriography, and arteriography.

We sincerely hope that this comprehensive approach to the diagnosis of PAD will lead to better therapeutic decision-making. To accomplish this, the vascular laboratory will need to be recognized and used as a method of documenting the PAD diagnosis and the adequacy of therapy over a patient's lifetime. ■

Indications for Referral to the Vascular Laboratory

G. Allen Holloway, Jr, MD
Director, Vascular Laboratory
Director, Medical Research
Department of Surgery
Maricopa Medical Center
Phoenix, Arizona

Objective: To provide guidelines on how to use the vascular laboratory to assist the primary care physician in establishing the diagnosis of PAD and in following the results of treatment.

The vascular laboratory provides valuable resources for the collection of noninvasive, quantitative physiologic and anatomic information about the vascular status of patients under the supervision of a primary care physician. The several basic types of noninvasive vascular tests are briefly described in this paper along with the value of the information derived from each test. The clinical indications that suggest that patients would benefit from referral to the noninvasive vascular laboratory are then discussed and a testing algorithm for use in patients with peripheral arterial disease (PAD) is proposed. Finally, the integration of this vascular laboratory information into the long-term primary care of the patient, including how this information might prompt vascular specialty referral, is reviewed.

The vascular laboratory is a resource to provide noninvasive quantitative and semi-quantitative (anatomic) information about the vascular status of a patient for the primary care physician, especially diagnostic information about atherosclerotic lower extremity disease or PAD. Although there are currently no "uniform vascular laboratories," standards for accreditation have been developed by the Intersocietal Commission for the Accreditation of Vascular Laboratories (http://www.icavl.org/) and over 1200 laboratories have received accreditation in one or more of the areas of arterial, venous, carotid, and abdominal (visceral vascular) testing (Thiele, 1993). Despite the potential diversity of noninvasive vascular laboratory approaches to the assessment of vascular disorders, most laboratories employ tests of the arterial system that are quite universal (Nicolaides, 1993). Procedures are available to evaluate both anatomic and physiologic properties of the peripheral arteries (Kempczinski, 1982; Zierler and Strandness, 1992).

TYPES OF TESTS

Available studies are usually subdivided into anatomic and physiologic testing modalities. In most cases, physiologic testing is first performed to assess the presence or absence of disease and, if disease is present, to determine its severity. Arterial pressures are measured in the extremities using a Doppler ultrasound system to detect flow, because distinct Korotkoff sounds are not heard in either the lower extremity or distal upper extremity using standard stethoscopes and cuffs. The Doppler instrument provides a reproducible measurement of systolic blood pressure that cannot be achieved by use of an office stethoscope. By comparing the peripheral arterial pressure (usually in the ankle) with the reference central pressure (typically a Doppler-derived blood pressure measurement in the brachial artery), an index of the pressure difference between the 2 sites can be obtained. This ankle-brachial index (ABI) is an indication of obstruction present between the 2 sites (Baker and Dix, 1981; Carter and Lezack, 1971; Nicolaides, 1993). In cases in which the arteries are incompressible (eg, in patients with diabetes mellitus, resulting in falsely elevated pressures), pressure measurements may also be made in the digits (Bone and Pomajzl, 1981). Arterial flow waveforms may be obtained using the same Doppler system. This is valuable in patients with noncompressible arteries and provides a semiquantitative measure of the degree of obstruction (Zierler and Strandness, 1992).

Arterial pressures may also be measured at different levels on the extremity, for example, high thigh, low thigh, high calf. A fall in pressure between 2 levels—with 20 mmHg commonly being considered significant—indicates the presence of an obstruction at that level. This "segmental pressure" test can provide a cost-effective assessment that can differentiate focal from diffuse, and proximal from distal PAD.

Anatomic abnormalities can also be precisely visualized using ultrasound techniques. Vascular structures, as well as other adjacent anatomic structures, can be visualized using duplex imaging, which can show the normal vasculature as well as intrinsic and extrinsic abnormalities. Atherosclerotic changes are visualized within the arteries to demonstrate both luminal narrowing and to provide ultrasonic characterization of the plaque itself. Commercially available Doppler ultrasound systems reveal blood velocities and are now combined with a B-mode system; this dual approach that combines both imaging and blood flow velocity analysis is known as a "duplex" ultrasonography system (Kohler, 1993). Blood flow velocities and anatomic images can be viewed simultaneously, allowing correlation between anatomic and physiologic data (Zierler, 1997).

Measurement of volume changes in a limb, called *plethysmography*, can be correlated semiquantitatively with blood flow to that extremity using several different types of sensors (Kempczinski, 1982). Pulse volume recordings are used in some laboratories to accomplish this and may provide a similar type of information to that obtained from Doppler arterial waveforms. A final technique used in some vascular laboratories is transcutaneous oximetry. Here, the partial pressure of oxygen, measured at the skin surface, is used as an indirect measure of capillary perfusion and its adequacy for healing (Padberg, 1996; Rooke, 1992).

An arteriogram should usually not be considered as an initial diagnostic study and should not be ordered as such. Because of the potential complications and morbidity of this invasive procedure, arteriography should generally be used only when a specific revascularization intervention is being considered and a more precise anatomic arterial "roadmap" is required to better define the potential revascularization approach.

INDICATIONS FOR TESTING

The diagnosis of PAD can be established from patient histories in the great majority of patients who present with symptoms; in most of these patients, the noninvasive techniques of the vascular laboratory can

Table I. Arterial Diseases that Merit Evaluation in the Vascular Laboratory

Limb pain
- Claudication
  - Baseline assessment of PAD severity
  - Follow-up assessment
    - Natural history evaluation to stage disease progression
    - Post-revascularization, to assess restenosis risk
- Ischemic rest pain, to assess prospects for revascularization
- Acute arterial occlusion – sudden onset of severe ischemic pain
  - Thrombosis, in situ
  - Embolism, cardiac or arterial source

Nonhealing wounds
- Arterial
- Venous
- Other

Vasospasm
- Primary
- Secondary

Potential vascular trauma
- Vascular injury after general trauma
- Iatrogenic (eg, pseudoaneurysms and arterial dissections)
- Proximity of injury to vascular structures

Perioperative arterial evaluation
- Saphenous vein mapping prior to surgical bypass grafting
- Postoperative graft surveillance

Aneurysms
- Abdominal aortic
- Peripheral arterial (eg, popliteal)

Thoracic outlet syndrome
- Arterial
- Venous
- Neurogenic

provide adequate guidance toward subsequent therapy (Criqui et al, 1985a; Olin, 1998). However, quantitative or semiquantitative determination of disease severity will serve both to confirm the diagnosis and, in severe cases, to help clarify whether some form of interventional therapy is needed. It can also allow the physician to follow the progress of the disease and therapy (Criqui et al, 1985b). Table I provides a list of some of the most common conditions that should suggest referral to the vascular laboratory. Table II suggests

Table II. What Tests Are Indicated for PAD?

Asymptomatic	Claudication		Critical Limb Ischemia
	Mild	*Moderate*	
ABIs with waveforms	ABIs with waveforms	Segmental pressures	Segmental pressures
		or	Duplex ultrasound
		PVR	Transcutaneous oximetry
		or	Arteriography
		Duplex ultrasound	

Algorithm suggested by the author for referral to the vascular laboratory. Tests are recommended by the severity of peripheral arterial disease (PAD). Each vascular laboratory will have its own algorithm for application of these tests in each clinical vignette.
ABI = ankle-brachial index; PVR = pulse volume recordings.

specific tests that can be used to determine different severity levels of PAD.

Exercise-induced limb pain (claudication) is the most common symptom of PAD. In patients experiencing claudication, an ABI may be performed in the office or by referral to a laboratory, along with determinations of either arterial flow or pressure waveforms, to define the anatomic level of disease. Such studies also provide data that allow the primary physician to follow the progression of PAD, if any, because these quantitative tests provide a much greater measure of sensitivity than can be obtained from the vascular history alone. It should be noted, however, that sequential arterial flow or pressure waveform studies might not be consistently reimbursed. Presently, payers suggest that ABIs should be part of the routine physical examination performed by a primary care physician.

Exercise Doppler studies, in which ankle blood pressure is assessed both before and after exercise, can be helpful in patients in whom the diagnosis of vascular claudication is uncertain and in which atypical symptoms might instead be caused by musculoskeletal or neurologic abnormalities (ie, pseudoclaudication). In a patient with a history of leg pain that appears to be claudication and who develops the typical pain with exercise, but who has no concomitant exercise-induced decrease in ankle arterial pressures, the diagnosis of vascular claudication is essentially ruled out and another cause, for example, pseudoclaudication secondary to spinal stenosis or arthritis, should be investigated (Bartholomew, 1999). In these cases, the value of the vascular laboratory is its ability to effectively exclude the PAD diagnosis. Exercise studies can also be used to evaluate progression of disease and effectiveness of treatment, but it is up to the practitioner to decide whether the expense is warranted for the additional information obtained. The clinician must

decide the relative value of the subjective description of the severity of claudication versus the value of knowing objectively the absolute claudication functional limitation. There are cases when the data from the clinical history alone can be misleading. For example, a patient may present with loud complaints suggestive of severe claudication or rest pain, but may, in fact, have only mild arterial obstruction and not merit revascularization. Alternatively, a more stoic patient who appears to be nearly "asymptomatic" may, with provocative exercise testing, demonstrate more profound exercise impairment. The role of exercise testing is covered more extensively in the fourth monograph of this series.

Claudication occurring at less than 50 feet of walking distance should be, from the perspective of our clinical practice, an absolute criterion for referral to a vascular laboratory to document the severity of PAD and as a prelude to consideration of therapeutic interventions. This is also true for patients with more severe presentations of PAD that cause rest pain, gangrene, and ischemic ulcers. These latter conditions fit within the diagnosis of critical limb ischemia; if left untreated, there is a high probability of limb loss (Harris et al, 1995). Physiologic studies will assess the severity of the problem, and duplex examination of the lower extremity arterial system can demonstrate both the anatomic location of the stenoses or occlusions and the physiologic severity of lesions present within the system. In some cases, revascularization might be undertaken using these data alone without an arteriogram (Cossman et al, 1989).

The acute onset of lower extremity pain, especially in the context of a clinical examination that demonstrates decreased or absent pulses, should automatically trigger an effort by the treating physician to determine whether severe ischemia is present and at what level. The tools of the vascular laboratory are central to this immediate effort to document acute ischemia secondary to acute arterial occlusion, because such sudden and severe ischemia represents a vascular emergency that requires immediate vascular surgical consultation. Physiologic studies are usually performed first, leading to noninvasive and invasive anatomic studies as indicated (O'Donnell, 1993).

Patients with symptoms suggestive of vasospastic disease in either the upper or lower extremity should also be referred to the vascular laboratory. Measurements of digital blood pressures can be obtained, both before and during the presence of symptoms. Vasospastic symptoms can be stimulated in the vascular laboratory by cold provocation, and pressure measurements in the digits help to provide assessment of the severity of the disease process (Bartelink et al, 1993; Nielsen, 1978; Brennan et al, 1993). Symptoms can be caused by either primary vasospastic disease or be provoked as a secondary phenomenon in patients who suffer an upstream fixed arterial stenosis or occlusion (eg, a patient with atherosclerosis in the more proximal subclavian artery or more distal palmar arch). Treatment should be based on physiologic and often anatomic information. Ultrasound resolution of specific arteries in the distal extremities may not be adequate to define the anatomy of such small vessels, and therefore contrast angiography may be required.

Physiologic evaluation of patients with nonhealing lower extremity ulcers should be considered mandatory to either confirm or rule out an ischemic component. Blunt or sharp extremity trauma with decreased or absent pulses will also usually warrant a referral to the vascular laboratory for physiologic and possibly anatomic evaluation and, in many cases, may eliminate the necessity for invasive angiographic procedures (Bynoe et al, 1991; Johansen et al, 1991; Schwartz et al, 1993).

It is also important for patients suspected or known to have abdominal aortic or peripheral aneurysms to undergo physiologic vascular evaluation. Aortic as well as peripheral aneurysms frequently contain a significant clot, and aortic aneurysms may be heavily atherosclerotic. Because internal plaques and thrombosis can cause luminal narrowing and ischemia, and because they can serve as the source of peripheral emboli, these aneurysmal structures can lead to limb loss through either acute occlusion or rupture. Anatomic studies will usually be performed concomitantly to define the characteristics of the aneurysm. Pseudoaneurysms are occasionally seen following surgical or interventional procedures at suture lines or sites of puncture, and can usually be diagnosed easily and sometimes treated using color duplex ultrasound by direct compression of the pseudoaneurysm with the ultrasonic probe or direct injection of thrombin (Coley et al, 1995; Dean et al, 1996).

Baseline physiologic and possibly anatomic studies should be obtained soon after vascular intervention procedures and endovascular therapy have been performed. The success of these interventions can then be monitored by repeat physiologic and, if indicated, anatomic studies at regular intervals. If studies reveal decreased function of the graft or intervention, additional procedures can be considered before severe worsening or occlusion occurs (Gahtan et al, 1995; Kinney et al, 1991; Papanicolaou et al, 1995).

INDICATIONS FOR VASCULAR SPECIALTY CONSULTATION

When is it appropriate for a primary care clinician to request a consultation by a vascular specialist? Such consultations are usually made when the clinical presentation suggests that a vascular disease may be responsible for a serious threat to life or limb, and the history, physical examination, and physiologic or anatomic vascular studies confirm the presence of a severe arterial abnormality. Studies that reveal critical limb ischemia—as usually indicated by gangrene, ischemic ulceration, or rest pain—is an absolute indication for vascular specialty consultation in an attempt to prevent limb loss. This is particularly important in patients with acute-onset ischemia presenting with the 5 Ps (pain, pallor, pulselessness, paresthesias, and paralysis) for whom there is only a limited time in which limb salvage can be accomplished. In this case, immediate vascular surgical consultation should be sought. A similar approach should be employed when evaluation of a graft or intervention suggests impending failure, so that corrective surgical or percutaneous intervention might be undertaken before the graft failure occurs. Nonhealing ulcers of any etiologies that are suspected of having a significant ischemic component should also be referred for consideration for revascularization because corrective procedures often lead to improved, if not total, ulcer healing. Arterial or peripheral aneurysms should always be referred for vascular evaluation, even if they are not symptomatic or associated with decreased function on physiologic vascular examination. The possibility of rupture and its severe consequences must be evaluated, and the potential for embolization and consequent limb threat are always present. Patients with vascular trauma should also be considered for consultation, and any indication of vascular injury related to either blunt or sharp traumatic injury should be referred to a vascular surgeon, interventional radiologist, or vascular medicine specialist. ■

Key Points

● The vascular laboratory is useful in assessing the severity of PAD discovered through patient history and a physical examination.

● Both physiologic and anatomic studies can provide information for either instituting treatment or following the progress of therapeutic interventions.

● Patients with critical limb ischemia should be evaluated promptly in the vascular laboratory and referred to a vascular specialist for treatment.

● Abdominal aortic and peripheral arterial aneurysms often rupture or thrombose, and both physiologic and anatomic studies are indicated to assess the degree of magnitude of risk and to determine the anatomic configuration.

● Nonhealing lower extremity ulcers are often associated with an inadequate arterial blood supply; therefore, patients with suspected ischemic ulcers should undergo physiologic studies to evaluate the severity of any underlying arterial disease and to elucidate the potential benefit of revascularization.

● Trauma with potential or actual vascular injury can be evaluated in the vascular laboratory, but should always be referred promptly to a vascular specialist.

BIBLIOGRAPHY

Baker JD, Dix DE. Variability of Doppler ankle pressure with arterial occlusive disease: an evaluation with ankle index and brachial-ankle pressure gradient. Surgery 1981;89:134–7.

Bartelink ML, Wollersheim H, Leesmans E, et al. A standardized finger cooling test for Raynaud's phenomenon: diagnostic value and sex differences. Eur Heart J 1993;14:614–22.

Bartholomew JR. Large artery occlusive disease. Rheum Dis Clin North Am 1999;25:669–86.

Bone GE, Pomajzl MJ. Toe blood pressure by photoplethysmography: an index of healing in forefoot amputation. Surgery 1981;89:569–74.

Brennan P, Silman A, Black C, et al. Validity and reliability of three methods used in the diagnosis of Raynaud's phenomenon: the UK Scleroderma Study Group. Br J Rheumatol 1993;32:357–61.

Bynoe RP, Miles WS, Bell RM, et al. Noninvasive diagnosis of vascular trauma by duplex ultrasonography. J Vasc Surg 1991;14:346–52.

Carter SA, Lezack JD. Digital systolic pressures in the lower limbs in arterial disease. Circulation 1971;43:905–14.

Coley BD, Roberts AC, Fellmeth BD, et al. Postangiographic femoral artery pseudoaneurysms: further experience with US-guided compression repair. Radiology 1995;194:307–11.

Cossman DV, Ellison JE, Wagner WH, et al. Comparison of contrast arteriography to arterial mapping with color-flow duplex imaging in the lower extremities. J Vasc Surg 1989;10:522–8.

Criqui MH, Coughlin SS, Fronek A. Noninvasively diagnosed peripheral arterial disease as a predictor of mortality: results from a prospective study. Circulation 1985b;72:768–73.

Criqui MH, Fronek A, Klauber MR, et al. The sensitivity, specificity, and predictive value of traditional clinical evaluation of peripheral arterial disease: results from noninvasive testing in a defined population. Circulation 1985a;71:516–22.

Dean SM, Olin JW, Piedmonte M, et al. Ultrasound-guided compression closure of postcatheterization pseudoaneurysms during concurrent anticoagulation: a review of seventy-seven patients. J Vasc Surg 1996;23:28–34.

Gahtan V, Payne LP, Roper LD, et al. Duplex criteria for predicting progression of vein graft lesions: which stenoses can be followed. J Vasc Technol 1995;19:211–5.

Harris PA, Da Silva AF, Holdsworth J, et al. Critical limb ischaemia: management and outcome. Report of a national survey. Eur J Vasc Endovasc Surg 1995;10:108–13.

Johansen K, Lynch K, Paun M, et al. Non-invasive vascular tests reliably exclude occult arterial trauma in injured extremities. J Trauma Stress 1991;31:515–22.

Kempczinski RF. Segmental volume plethysmography in the diagnosis of lower extremity arterial occlusive disease. J Cardiovasc Surg 1982;23:125–9.

Kinney EV, Bandyk DF, Mewissen MW, et al. Monitoring functional patency of percutaneous transluminal angioplasty. Arch Surg 1991;126:743–7.

Kohler TR. Duplex scanning for the evaluation of lower limb arterial disease. In: Bernstein EF, ed. Noninvasive Diagnostic Techniques in Vascular Disease, Fourth Edition. St Louis: Mosby; 1993:520–6.

Nicolaides AN. Basic and practical aspects of peripheral arterial testing. In: Bernstein EF, ed. Vascular Diagnosis. 4th ed. St Louis: Mosby; 1993:481–5.

Nielsen SL. Raynaud's phenomena and finger systolic pressure during cooling. Scand J Clin Lab Invest 1978;38:765–70.

O'Donnell TF Jr. Arterial diagnosis and management of acute thrombosis of the lower extremity. Can J Surg 1993;36:349–53.

Olin JW. Clinical Evaluation and Office-Based Detection of Peripheral Arterial Disease. In: Hirsch AT, ed. An Office-Based Approach to the Diagnosis and Treatment of Peripheral Arterial Disease, Part I: The Epidemiology and Practical Detection of PAD. Belle Mead, NJ: Excerpta Medica; 1998;10–7.

Padberg FT. Transcutaneous oxygen (TcPO$_2$) estimates probability of healing in the ischemic extremity. J Surg Res 1996;60:365–9.

Papanicolaou G, Zierler RE, Beach KW, et al. Hemodynamic parameters of failing infrainguinal bypass grafts. Am J Surg 1995;169:238–44.

Rooke TW. The use of transcutaneous oximetry in the non-invasive vascular laboratory. Int Angiol 1992;11:36–40.

Schwartz MR, Weaver FA, Yellin AE, et al. The utility of the color flow Doppler examination in penetrating extremity arterial trauma. Am Surg 1993;59:375–8.

Thiele BL. Accreditation of vascular laboratories. In: Bernstein EF, ed. Vascular Diagnosis. 4th ed. St Louis: Mosby; 1993:36–8.

Zierler RE, Strandness DE Jr. Nonimaging physiologic tests for assessment of extremity arterial disease. In: Zwiebel WJ, ed. Introduction to Vascular Ultrasonography. 3rd ed. Philadelphia, Pa: WB Saunders Co; 1992:201–21.

Zierler RE, Zierler BK. Duplex sonography of lower extremity arteries. Semin Ultrasound CT MRI 1997;18:39–56.

Duplex Ultrasonography in the Diagnosis of Peripheral Arterial Disease

Michael R. Jaff, DO, FACP, FACC
Medical Director, Center for Vascular Care
Co-Director, Vascular Diagnostic Laboratory
Washington Hospital Center
Washington, DC

Objective: To understand the basics of arterial ultrasound technology and the advantages of ultrasound in the diagnosis of PAD and to define a diagnostic algorithm for patients with PAD.

The most important aspects of the diagnosis of peripheral arterial disease (PAD) are a complete history and thorough physical examination. These will lead to an appropriate diagnosis in more than 90% of patients. Patients with mild intermittent claudication (IC) who are able to function fully may only need a clinical evaluation in combination with an ankle-brachial index (ABI). This information alone will allow for risk stratification and the development of a treatment algorithm, including risk-factor modification, exercise therapy, and possibly pharmacologic intervention. In patients in whom IC interferes with their activities or vocation or in those suffering from critical limb ischemia, more information is needed to determine the optimal treatment program. Arterial duplex ultrasonography is a highly accurate, painless, safe, and reproducible noninvasive method of determining the precise location of arterial stenoses, occlusions, and sites of vascular trauma (eg, pseudoaneurysm). This information will allow the physician to determine whether there is a role for endovascular therapy (percutaneous transluminal angioplasty [PTA]), surgical revascularization, or aggressive medical therapy.

WHAT IS ARTERIAL ULTRASOUND, AND HOW IS IT PERFORMED?

Ultrasound is widely used in virtually every field of medicine. Although the physics of ultrasound are quite complex, the fundamental concepts are simple and ingenious.

Ultrasound is the use of sound waves whose frequencies are above those heard by humans (typically >20,000 cycles per second [Hz]). Commercially available ultrasound units generate frequencies of 2 to 10 million cycles per second (MHz). When an electronic voltage is transmitted to an oscillator within an ultrasound probe, or transducer, a crystal vibrates and emits an ultrasound beam with a defined frequency in the range of 2 to 10 MHz. The ultrasound beam hits various targets in its path (ie, soft tissue, bone, flowing blood) and is reflected back to the crystal (Stewart and Grubb, 1992).

Ultrasound units available today use B-mode ("brightness") technology to provide a real-time, gray-scale image. This gives the operator a "live" image of the artery in question that is updated several times per second. Ultrasound equipment uses several different transducers, which emit varying ultrasound frequencies. High-frequency probes (ie, 10 MHz) provide excellent image resolution, but the beam attenuates rapidly and cannot penetrate very deeply. These types of probes are used to visualize such superficial structures as extracranial carotid arteries and venous varicosities. Low-frequency probes (ie, 2 MHz) penetrate to visualize deeper structures while sacrificing image resolution. These probes are used for deep abdominal imaging, such as the renal arteries, abdominal aorta, and mesenteric arteries and veins.

The term *duplex ultrasound* refers to B-mode, real-time imaging and focused analysis of the velocity of flowing blood in arteries and veins using Doppler. Christian Doppler described the physics of ultrasound by identifying the Doppler shift (Nelson and Pretorius, 1988). Using the variables of velocity of flowing blood, velocity of sound in tissue, the difference between the frequency of transmitted and reflected sound, and the cosine of the angle of the ultrasound beam to the direction of flowing blood, the velocity of blood in vessels can be measured. This is the basis for all vascular ultrasonography and allows modern ultrasonographers to quantitate degrees of stenosis based on the velocity of blood in various segments of vessels.

Many vascular beds have been studied using duplex ultrasonography. Each arterial system that undergoes duplex interrogation generates ranges of flow velocities that determine degrees of stenosis within the artery. These velocity ranges provide categories of stenosis severity that can then be reported.

In peripheral arterial duplex ultrasound testing, imaging of the iliac, common femoral, superficial femoral, deep femoral, popliteal, and tibial arteries is performed using a 5.0- to 7.5-MHz transducer. The vessels are studied in the longitudinal plane, and Doppler velocities are obtained using a 60-degree Doppler angle (Figure 1). Vessels are classified into 1 of 5 categories: normal, 1% to 19% stenosis, 20% to 49% stenosis, 50% to 99% stenosis, and occlusion. The categories are determined by alterations in the Doppler waveform as well as increasing peak systolic velocities (Table). For a stenosis to be classified as 50% to 99%, for example, the peak systolic velocity must increase by

100% compared with the normal segment of artery proximal to the stenosis (Kohler et al, 1987). Color is added to the image to facilitate rapid identification of the arterial segment in question and to identify areas of turbulent or no arterial flow, suggesting occlusion.

WHAT ARE THE ADVANTAGES OF DUPLEX ULTRASOUND TESTING IN PAD?

The ABI is the ideal test for establishing the diagnosis of PAD. It is the easiest, most widely reproducible, and most accurate method of determining the degree of diminished arterial circulation in a limb. Using a standard sphygmomanometer and a handheld continuous-wave Doppler probe, blood pressure in the dorsalis pedis or posterior tibial artery is compared with brachial pressure and a ratio is obtained. Given that systolic pressure normally increases in the peripheral arteries (predominantly as a result of increased stiffness of these vessels), a normal ABI is ≥0.9. An ABI <0.5 suggests significant arterial occlusive disease.

The addition of exercise testing, as noted in Dr. Rooke's article in this issue, provides both hemodynamic and functional information. Exercise testing confirms the diagnosis of IC, documents the functional severity of claudication, and can be used to display improvements in initial and absolute claudicating distances after therapy. However, in patients with moderate to severe IC or critical limb ischemia (ischemic rest pain, nonhealing ulcers, gangrene), the ABI does not localize the arterial stenoses or occlusions. Clearly, more information is required.

Arterial duplex ultrasonography provides an in-depth "road map" of the arteries of the lower extremities. With the identification of stenoses and occlusions, appropriate therapy can be considered. For example, if a patient with limiting IC and an ABI of 0.8 at rest in one limb is found on duplex ultrasonography to have a severe stenosis of the common iliac artery, PTA may be

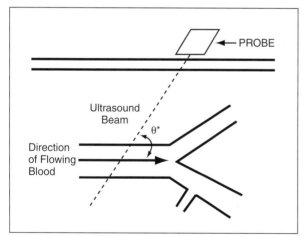

Figure 1. Diagrammatic representation of the angle of the ultrasound beam to the direction of flowing blood. It is the cosine of this angle that is used in the Doppler equation to generate velocity measurements. If the cosine of this angle is ≤60 degrees, published criteria determining the severity of stenosis may be used.
* This angle must be ≤60 degrees in order to use validated, published Doppler criteria to grade stenoses.

Table. Interpretation of Arterial Duplex Ultrasonography

If PSV does *not* increase	<20% Stenosis
If PSV increases by >30% compared with proximal normal segment	20%–49% Stenosis
If PSV increases by 100% compared with proximal normal segment	50%–99% Stenosis
If no flow is identified in the artery	Occlusion

PSV = peak systolic velocity.

optimal therapy. This information would not have been appreciated on the basis of ABI, segmental pressures, and pulse volume recordings alone. Arterial duplex ultrasonography has been used to guide the interventionist in locating a lesion potentially amenable to endovascular therapy (Elsman et al, 1996). This technology has also been used after endovascular therapy to determine the technical success (Silke et al, 1997) and durability of the procedure (Mewissen et al, 1992).

A patient with severe functional limitation resulting from IC may have a long superficial femoral artery occlusion and occlusion of 2 infrapopliteal arteries, both clearly identified on duplex ultrasonography. This patient would not be a candidate for endovascular therapy and would be better served by either aggressive pharmacologic management or surgical revascularization. In one series of 36 patients with critical limb ischemia, 83% of the procedures required were accurately predicted on the basis of duplex scanning alone (Ligush et al, 1998).

The sensitivity of duplex ultrasonography to detect occlusions and stenoses has been reported to be 95% and 92%, respectively, with specificities of 99% and 97%, respectively (Whelan et al, 1992). Limitations have included the identification of 2 stenoses in tandem (Allard et al, 1994), imaging of the infrapopliteal arteries (Larch et al, 1997), and difficulty imaging the inflow common and external iliac arteries (Lewis et al, 1994). On a more practical basis, duplex scanning requires expensive equipment and prolongs examination times compared with physiologic testing.

The accuracy of arterial duplex ultrasonography is so high that many physicians have opted to use it as the sole imaging modality in patients who require surgical revascularization. In an early series of 29 patients who underwent both duplex scanning and arteriography, 6 vascular surgeons devised treatment plans in a blinded fashion to the imaging test. The intraobserver variability was excellent, with agreement in 76% of cases (Kohler et al, 1990). More recently, 41 patients requiring infrainguinal bypass grafts underwent preoperative arterial duplex ultrasonography followed by arteriography and surgery. A vascular surgeon blinded to the procedure performed predicted the operation required as well as the location of the anastomotic sites (Wain et al, 1999). In patients who required femoropopliteal bypass, there was agreement on the type of procedure and the anastomotic locations in 90% of cases. However, in patients who required infrapopliteal bypass, the agreement was only 24% (Wain et al, 1999).

As mentioned, another advantage of arterial duplex ultrasonography is in patients who have been treated previously with surgical or endovascular revascular-

ization. Stenoses will develop in 21% to 30% of patients who have undergone surgical bypass graft revascularization, particularly with the saphenous vein. These stenoses lead to graft thrombosis. Once the graft becomes thrombosed, secondary patency rates are dismal. If the stenosis is detected and repaired before graft thrombosis develops, an estimated 80% of grafts will be salvaged (Bandyk, 1987). A well-organized graft surveillance program is crucial in preserving patency of the bypass graft.

In one series of 170 saphenous vein bypass grafts, 110 stenoses were detected over a 39-month period. In those grafts that underwent surgical revision after detection of a stenosis, 4-year patency was 88%, whereas 4-year patency was 57% in the grafts that did not undergo revision despite stenosis detection (Mattos et al, 1993). Recent data in 106 failing arterial bypass grafts demonstrated that 73 (69%) could be repaired on the basis of duplex scanning alone (Calligaro et al, 1998). The use of

---

Key Points

● Although the ABI provides important information about the presence and overall severity of PAD, even with the addition of segmental limb pressures and pulse volume recordings, it does not provide detailed anatomic data on the locations of arterial stenoses and/or occlusions.

● Arterial duplex ultrasonography of the lower extremities is accurate in defining the anatomic data required to plan treatment strategies (medical, endovascular, surgical), with a sensitivity and specificity over 90%.

● Arterial duplex ultrasonography is helpful in following the adequacy of surgical bypass graft revascularization, detecting areas of stenosis before graft thrombosis, and preserving graft patency.

● Limitations of arterial duplex ultrasonography include the need for expensive diagnostic equipment, prolonged examination times, and difficulty identifying tandem stenoses or tibial artery disease distal to proximal disease.

● Duplex scanning after endovascular therapy is generally performed only in patients who have recurrent symptoms, loss of a previously palpable pulse, or an objective decrease in ABI.

an intensive surveillance program has been less beneficial in prosthetic grafts (Lalak et al, 1994).

The procedure for graft surveillance is similar to that used in native vessel arterial duplex ultrasonography. The inflow artery to the bypass graft is initially imaged using a 5.0- to 7.5-MHz transducer and a Doppler angle of 60 degrees. Subsequently, the proximal anastomosis; proximal, mid-, and distal graft; distal anastomosis; and outflow artery are interrogated. Peak systolic and end-diastolic velocities are obtained at each segment and compared with the segment of graft or native artery proximal to the area being studied. If the ratio of the peak systolic velocity within a stenotic segment relative to the normal segment proximal to the stenosis is >2, this suggests a 50% to 75% diameter reduction. The addition of end-diastolic velocities >100 cm/sec suggests >75% stenosis (Bandyk, 1990).

Vein bypass grafts should be studied within 7 days of construction, and then in 1 month, followed by 3-month intervals for the first year. If the graft remains normal after 1 year, follow-up surveillance should be done every 6 months thereafter. Ankle pressures and waveforms should be performed at the time of each surveillance study. The development of a stenosis during a surveillance examination should prompt consideration of arteriography, using either contrast arteriography or magnetic resonance technology (Jaff et al, 1998).

Early experience suggests that the data obtained with arterial duplex ultrasonography soon after balloon angioplasty may overestimate residual stenosis and may be a limitation of this technology following endovascular therapy (Sacks et al, 1990). In addition, no study has demonstrated improved limb salvage rates with a surveillance program after endovascular therapy. Many physicians use arterial duplex ultrasonography after endovascular therapy only in the face of new or recurrent symptoms, the loss of a previously palpable pulse, or an objective decline in the ABI.

A DIAGNOSTIC ALGORITHM FOR PAD

Patients who are suspected of having PAD of the lower extremities will often benefit from detailed duplex ultrasonography to determine the location and severity of their stenoses and/or occlusions. Duplex ultrasonography provides this detail in a safe, noninvasive, highly accurate way. In combination with the ABI both at rest and with exercise, all of the information required to plan a treatment program is available (Figure 2). ■

BIBLIOGRAPHY

Allard L, Cloutier G, Durand LG, et al. Limitations of ultrasonic duplex scanning diagnosing lower limb arterial stenoses in the presence of adjacent segment disease. J Vasc Surg 1994;19:650–7.

Bandyk DF. Ultrasonic duplex scanning in the evaluation of arterial grafts and dilatations. Echocardiography 1987;4:251–64.

Bandyk DF. Postoperative surveillance of infrainguinal bypass. Surg Clin North Am 1990;70:71–85.

Calligaro KD, Syrek JR, Dougherty MJ, et al. Selective use of duplex ultrasound to replace preoperative arteriography for failing arterial vein grafts. J Vasc Surg 1998;27:89–95.

Elsman BHP, Legemate DA, van der Heyden FWAM, et al. The use of color-coded duplex scanning in the selection of patients with lower extremity arterial disease for percutaneous transluminal angioplasty: a prospective study. Cardiovasc Intervent Radiol 1996;19:313–6.

Jaff MR, Breger R, Deshur W, Pipia J. Detection of an arterial bypass graft threatening lesion by use of duplex ultrasonography and magnetic resonance angiography in an asymptomatic patient. Vasc Surg 1998;32:109–14.

Kohler TR, Nance DR, Cramer MM, et al. Duplex scanning for diagnosis of aortoiliac and femoropopliteal disease: a prospective study. Circulation 1987;76:1074–80.

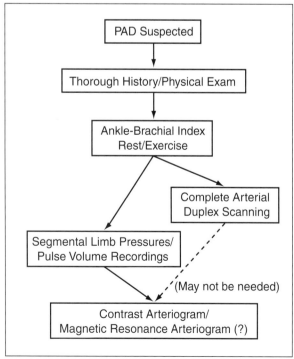

Figure 2. Diagnostic algorithm for peripheral arterial disease (PAD).

Kohler TR, Andros G, Porter JM, et al. Can duplex scanning replace arteriography for lower extremity arterial disease? Ann Vasc Surg 1990;4:280–7.

Lalak NJ, Hanel KC, Hunt J, Morgan A. Duplex scan surveillance of infrainguinal prosthetic bypass grafts. J Vasc Surg 1994;20:637–41.

Larch E, Minar E, Ahmadi R, et al. Value of color duplex sonography for evaluation of tibioperoneal arteries in patients with femoropopliteal obstruction: a prospective comparison with anterograde intra-arterial digital subtraction angiography. J Vasc Surg 1997;25:629–36.

Lewis WA, Bray AE, Harrison CL, et al. A comparison of common femoral waveform analysis with aortoiliac duplex scanning in assessment of aortoiliac disease. J Vasc Technol 1994;18:337–44.

Ligush J, Reavis SW, Preisser JS, Hansen KJ. Duplex ultrasound scanning defines operative strategies for patients with limb-threatening ischemia. J Vasc Surg 1998;28:482–91.

Mattos MA, van Bemmelen PS, Hodgson KJ, et al. Does correction of stenoses identified with color duplex scanning improve infrainguinal graft patency? J Vasc Surg 1993;17:54–66.

Mewissen MW, Kinney EV, Bandyk DF, et al. The role of duplex scanning versus angiography in predicting outcome after balloon angioplasty in the femoropopliteal artery. J Vasc Surg 1992;15:860–6.

Nelson TR, Pretorius DH. The Doppler signal: where does it come from and what does it mean? Am J Roentgenol 1988;151:439–47.

Sacks D, Robinson ML, Marinelli DL, Perlmutter GS. Evaluation of the peripheral arteries with duplex US after angioplasty. Radiology 1990;176:39–44.

Silke CM, Grouden MC, Nicholls S, et al. Noninvasive follow-up of peripheral angioplasty: a prospective study. J Vasc Technol 1997;21:23–5.

Stewart JH, Grubb M. Understanding vascular ultrasonography. Mayo Clin Proc 1992;67:1186–96.

Wain RA, Berdejo GL, Delvalle WN, et al. Can duplex scan arterial mapping replace contrast arteriography as the test of choice before infrainguinal revascularization? J Vasc Surg 1999;29:100–9.

Whelan JF, Barry JH, Moir JD. Color flow Doppler ultrasonography: comparison with peripheral arteriography for the investigation of peripheral vascular disease. J Clin Ultrasound 1992;20:369–74.

Role of Exercise Testing and Waveform Analysis for Patients with PAD

Thom W. Rooke, MD
Mayo Clinic
Rochester, Minnesota

Objective: To understand how and why hemodynamic and functional (exercise) tests are important in the assessment of patients with peripheral arterial disease.

Hemodynamic and exercise testing of the lower extremities can be beneficial in the diagnosis and evaluation of patients with peripheral arterial disease (PAD). Hemodynamic tests measure arterial pressure, blood flow velocity, and arterial pulsatility. When combined with some form of stress (eg, dynamic exercise), these hemodynamic assessments enable physicians to assess the objective functional impact of PAD on the patient. In contrast to duplex scanning, which uses expensive ultrasound imaging equipment, exercise tests require relatively inexpensive devices such as continuous-wave Doppler (CWD) devices, pneumatic pressure cuffs, and motorized treadmill, which are simple to operate and yield data that are easy to interpret. Exercise testing is also valuable for detecting associated cardiovascular problems, such as coronary artery disease (CAD) and hypertension. Doppler waveform analysis and exercise treadmill testing are two examples of physiologic tests that relate the impact of PAD on blood flow or limb function, in contrast to imaging tests that provide relatively greater information about arterial structure (eg, location of stenoses). Arterial imaging is examined in more detail in the articles by Jaff and Paulson, which appear in this issue.

WHY PERFORM PHYSIOLOGIC VASCULAR TESTING?

Specific physiologic tests of the peripheral arteries, including exercise testing and waveform analysis, are useful in a variety of clinical circumstances, including documentation of the PAD diagnosis and the functional severity of the limb arterial disease, to mark progression of the natural history of PAD in the patient, and to monitor the patient's response to therapy.

Diagnosis of PAD: Role of the History, Physical Examination, and Vascular Laboratory

A presumptive diagnosis of PAD can usually be made via a directed patient history (eg, claudication) and/or vascular physical examination (eg, absent pulses, ischemic skin changes). However, in some circumstances the diagnosis may not be clear despite the clinician's best effort to obtain a thorough history and despite performance of a complete physical examination. It may be difficult, for example, to distinguish between the symptoms of vasculogenic claudication (caused by arterial stenosis or occlusion) and pseudo-claudication (caused by nerve root impingement of spinal stenosis) because the history and physical examination can be similar in both conditions. Even the most experienced examiner may fail to detect mild degrees of arterial occlusive disease in patients with true vasculogenic claudication. Specific testing to confirm arterial involvement will therefore aid in the diagnosis.

Documentation of the PAD Diagnosis

It is becoming increasingly important to document the presence or absence of arterial occlusive disease for medicolegal purposes, for the satisfaction of third-party payers, and to stage the disease prior to determining the appropriate therapeutic intervention.

Determination of PAD Severity

In situations in which the diagnosis of PAD has already

been made, it may still be necessary to assess and document the severity of the problem. As noted in prior monographs in this series, mild cases of PAD may require only diligent normalization of atherosclerosis risk factors by the primary care physician, whereas more severe limitations of limb blood flow should prompt major efforts to protect the ischemic foot from accidental injury. It is not sufficient to simply say, "this patient has PAD" without assessing and documenting the severity of disease in the medical record and discussing the clinical consequences with the patient.

Progression of the Natural History of PAD

Serial vascular laboratory testing may provide valuable information about the progression (or regression) of disease over time, which may in turn determine the need for, and timing of, treatment. Data demonstrating stability of the disease can serve as an appropriate reward for the patient who has successfully controlled atherosclerosis risk factors, and can provide a salient warning to those who demonstrate rapidly progressive PAD but who have not been as diligent in modifying their lifestyle.

Monitoring the Response to PAD Therapies

Vascular testing provides objective information about the effectiveness of a particular therapy (eg, exercise and lifestyle modifications, claudication pharmacotherapies, bypass surgery, or limb angioplasty).

WHAT TYPE OF INFORMATION DOES VASCULAR TESTING PROVIDE?

Anatomy

The structure of an artery can be evaluated using such imaging techniques as magnetic resonance angiography (MRA) (Owen 1998; Winchester et al, 1998), computed tomography (CT) (Raptopoulos et al, 1996; Rieker et al, 1997; Rieker et al, 1996), and ultrasound (Aly et al, 1998; Wain et al, 1999). Certain noninvasive imaging tests, such as MRA and CT scanning, may be relatively facile and safe but are not traditionally available in most vascular laboratories. Diagnostic duplex ultrasound is the noninvasive laboratory modality most commonly used to image blood vessels.

Hemodynamics

Certain tests assess the severity of a particular arterial lesion (or series of lesions) by determining their effect on arterial pressure, total blood flow, blood flow velocity, or other hemodynamic variables. The ankle-brachial index (ABI) is an important means for assessing change in the severity of PAD.

Functional Assessment

"Functional tests" assess the overall impact of PAD on the ambulatory function of a patient; this determination is important for clinicians because the anatomic and/or hemodynamic severity of occlusive disease is usually quite poorly correlated with the clinical severity of the disease. In some situations, anatomically or hemodynamically severe disease may have minimal functional impact. For example, a patient with a low ABI may be entirely asymptomatic due to the presence of adequate collateral blood flow, and will not require revascularization. Conversely, seemingly mild PAD may produce severe symptoms in certain individuals. For example, a patient with a proximal iliac stenosis may have a normal ABI at rest, but severe exertional limitations. The role of functional exercise testing was reviewed in more detail in Part IV of this series.

ROLE OF EXERCISE TESTING FOR THE PATIENT WITH CLAUDICATION

A functional vascular laboratory test is usually a standard hemodynamic test coupled with some form of stress. The lower-extremity arterial system may be stressed in many ways, including limb elevation, reactive hyperemia, ambient warming, and chemical challenges. However, exercise is generally considered to be the test with the greatest clinical utility, which prompted the inclusion of exercise testing as an important measurable outcome for laboratories accredited by the Intersocietal Commission on the Accreditation of Vascular Laboratories (ICAVL).

Hemodynamic Endpoints

Potentially useful information can be obtained by measuring virtually any clinical parameter that might be affected by exercise. Measurements that have been studied in the past include transcutaneous oxygen (Liu et al, 1996), skin temperature, laser Doppler blood flow, and plethysmographic blood flow changes. For the most part, however, these tests are difficult to use, poorly suited for exercise testing, or otherwise of limited clinical value.

Most vascular laboratories assess ankle and arm arterial pressure at rest and during exercise. Some also study arterial flow velocity and/or arterial pulsatility. These values are relatively easy to measure and provide generally useful information about PAD.

PRESSURE MEASUREMENT

Segmental arterial pressures are measured by placing blood pressure cuffs of appropriate width around the legs at various levels (ankle, calf, thigh); these cuffs are serially inflated above systolic blood pressure to determine the arterial closing pressure (ie, systolic blood pressure) for each segment of the limb. Arterial pressure can be determined by interrogating the artery distal to the cuff with a CWD. When cuff pressure exceeds arterial (systolic) pressure, blood flow ceases. A reference systolic blood pressure measurement is obtained from the arm to provide a comparison with the segmental limb pressures. The most important segmental measurement is the one obtained at the ankle; when this measurement is divided by the arm pressure, the resulting value is called the ABI.

Arterial blood pressure and ABI can be measured in most limbs using a CWD device and pneumatic pressure cuffs. In patients whose arteries are calcified and noncompressible, however, segmental pressures may not be obtainable. Toe pressure, measured using small cuffs that fit around the toes, can usually be determined even when the larger vessels in the leg are calcified. Unfortunately, the reproducibility of toe-pressure measurements is not as good as that for larger vessels (Osmundson et al, 1985).

VELOCITY MEASUREMENT

A common approach to measuring blood velocity is CWD. This equipment is relatively inexpensive, easy to obtain and operate, and should be part of every noninvasive vascular laboratory. In addition to serving as a blood-motion detector, CWD can be used to determine the arterial blood velocity waveform. In normal large arteries the velocity waveform is triphasic (Figure 1A); blood moves forward rapidly during systole and stops—or even reverses—during early diastole (due to the elastic recoil of the vessels). Blood flows in a forward direction again during late diastole. When a hemodynamically significant lesion is present proximal to the point of Doppler interrogation, the triphasic or biphasic characteristics of the signal are lost. The signal becomes monophasic (Figure 1B) because flow occurs in a forward direction only.

CWD assessment is extremely useful, especially in patients who have noncompressible vessels or when pressure measurements are otherwise unobtainable. Quantitative assessment of the continuous-wave

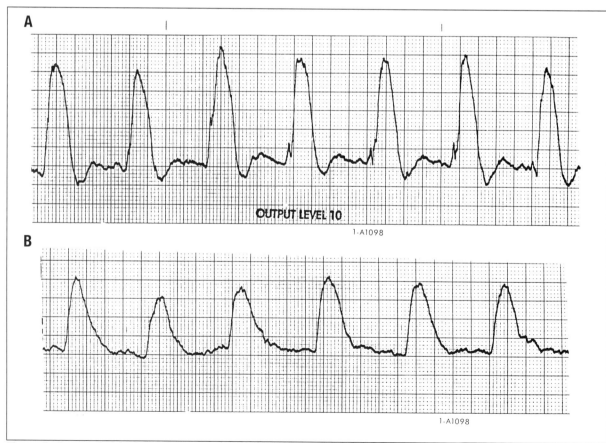

Figure 1. **A**, normal triphasic arterial Doppler signal obtained from the common femoral artery. **B**, monophasic common femoral artery Doppler signal obtained distal to a high-grade iliac artery stenosis.

velocity signal, using contour analyses or mathematic assessments of the acceleration or deceleration times, may provide additional information about occlusive disease (Fronek, 1993), but this type of analysis has been of limited clinical value in most settings.

PULSATILITY MEASUREMENT

The pulse volume recording (PVR) provides information about limb pulsatility (Raines, 1993). This test also uses a series of pneumatic cuffs that encircle the limb at various levels and are inflated to a low, preset value (typically 40 to 60 mm Hg). Blood entering the arteries during cardiac systole causes the limb to enlarge transiently; the increase in limb volume compresses air within the cuff and changes cuff pressure slightly. By recording these cyclic changes in cuff pressure, a "pulsatile" waveform is generated.

The PVR can be analyzed in terms of the amplitude of the tracing or the contour of the curve. Amplitude is affected by vascular patency; as arterial obstruction occurs, amplitude falls. However, such factors as cardiac output, congestive heart failure, and aortic valve disease (stenosis or regurgitation) also affect the measurements. As a result, PVRs may not always accurately reflect vascular patency. PVR reproducibility is also a problem; minor changes in cardiac output or peripheral vascular resistance can greatly affect the amplitude of a tracing.

We use PVRs in our practice primarily to look for abrupt changes in pulsatility along the length of the limb. A decrease in amplitude between segments suggests the presence of hemodynamically significant occlusive disease.

As with CWD, PVRs can also be analyzed quantitatively, and pulse contour may provide useful information in certain settings. However, the clinical utility of this approach is debatable.

PAD EXERCISE TESTING

Different laboratories perform exercise testing in different ways, but the basic principles tend to be the same (Creager, 1997). First, an initial baseline assessment is performed at rest. With the patient lying comfortably, segmental pressure measurements, CWD values, PVRs, or other flow measurements are made. After the initial measurements are complete, the patient exercises, usually following a standard protocol (eg, a Bruce, Naughton, or Gardner-Skinner protocol). Immediately following exercise, some or all of the baseline measurements are repeated. Depending on the patient's rate of hemodynamic recovery, these measurements can be repeated at regular intervals (eg, 1, 3, 5, and 10 minutes) until the values return to baseline.

In our laboratory, lower-extremity arterial exercise testing begins with a lower-extremity hemodynamic study consisting of bilateral segmental artery pressures (with special emphasis on the ABI). We also obtain CWD tracings at the femoral, popliteal, and tibial levels. Multilevel PVRs are likewise measured; the patient is subsequently exercised according to our standard protocol. Following exercise, the patient returns immediately to the examination table and selected measurements are repeated (ie, ABIs and the common femoral CWD assessment). During the immediate postexercise period, values such as flow and pressure tend to change rapidly (ie, the patient does not maintain a "postexercise steady state"); time constraints therefore dictate that only a limited number of tests can be performed during the postexercise period, such as for 10-15 minutes after the conclusion of exercise.

TYPE OF EXERCISE

Almost any type of lower-extremity exercise can be used to produce "stress." Tiptoe maneuvers (McPhail et al, 1998), pedaling a stationary bike, leg lifts, stair climbing (Gardner et al, 1993), and other forms of exercise have been studied. There is a general consensus, however, that walking is the best form for a number of reasons (Regensteiner et al, 1997). The rationale for walking (to stress the legs) is that walking is the activity that usually precipitates claudication under everyday circumstances.

Walking Distances

How far does a patient with PAD need to walk on a treadmill during exercise treadmill testing? There are 2 major approaches to exercise testing. The first involves a "fixed" walking distance. In most laboratories, the patient walks at 2 mph (or 1 mph if he or she cannot maintain the 2-mph pace) up a 10% to 12% grade for a maximum of 5 minutes. This protocol, if completed, takes the patient a maximum of 282 yards and produces, in most patients, a 5-metabolic equivalent (MET) workload.

Recent work suggests that graded exercise protocols may be more accurate and reproducible than fixed protocols (Chaudhry et al, 1997; Hiatt et al, 1994; Hiatt et al, 1995). Graded protocols are similar to those used for cardiac stress testing in patients with CAD. From a clinical research perspective, controversy continues regarding the best protocol for "trials-based" vascular testing. However, for office-based testing any objective and reproducible protocol will provide excellent, clinically relevant information. "Fixed workload" protocols are easier to perform and may be as reproducible as graded protocols. However, it is likely that graded protocols yield more information, particularly with regard to maximum walking distance, than do fixed protocols.

Exercise Testing Standards

Do standards for PAD exercise testing exist? The ICAVL is a national organization that accredits noninvasive vascular laboratories. The ICAVL has established minimal standards for noninvasive testing of the arterial system, including lower-extremity exercise testing. However, controversies remain regarding exercise testing. For example, is continuous electrocardio-

---

Table 1. Interpretation of Exercise Vascular Laboratory Studies (fixed protocol) in Lower Extremities (2 mph, 10% grade, 5-minute maximum) at the Mayo Clinic.

Minimal disease
- No claudication on treadmill
- Mild abnormalities on some, but not necessarily all, of the tests at rest (eg, Doppler examination, ABIs, or PVRs)
- Normal studies at rest but abnormal ABIs after exercise*

Mild disease
- Symptomatic on the treadmill but able to complete a standard test with ease (2 mph, 10% grade, 5 minute maximum)
- ABIs usually >0.8 at rest and >0.5 after exercise*

Moderate disease
- Limiting claudication, unable to complete standard 5-minute treadmill test†
- ABI usually <0.8 at rest and <0.5 after exercise*

Post-exercise
- ABI recovery time usually ≤10 minutes

Severe disease
- Claudication beginning within the first 90 seconds and terminating exercise before 3 minutes†
- Blood pressure indices usually <0.5 at rest and <0.15 after exercise*
- ABI usually <0.5 at rest
- Transmetatarsal PVRs markedly reduced

Post-exercise
- ABI recovery time often >10 minutes

ABI = ankle-brachial index; PVR = pulse volume recording.
*When any systolic blood pressure in the lower extremity is unusually and unexpectedly high (eg, >300 mm Hg), all of the systolic blood-pressure values in the lower extremity become suspect and caution is needed in interpreting them. This usually happens in diabetic or elderly persons with rigid sclerotic arteries. In such cases, the PVR and Doppler arterial signals provide a more accurate assessment of the severity of the occlusive arterial disease.
†Always consider the reason for terminating the treadmill exercise test (eg, claudication, chest pain, patient's request, abnormal electrocardiogram, protocol fulfilled).

---

graphic (ECG) monitoring necessary? Who should directly supervise these studies? Does a physician need to be in attendance? Can a nurse supervise them? Is it appropriate for a trained technician/technologist to perform the studies without additional supervision? These and other issues remain unresolved at this time. Although these issues will be the focus of increasing discussion for many years, we propose that a laboratory choose one or two exercise protocols with which they are comfortable, that they use a motorized treadmill, and that they employ ECG monitoring if available. The exact qualifications for testing supervision will vary with the training and experience at each laboratory, but the personnel must be comfortable with assessing both cardiac and limb ischemic symptoms. Likewise, resources to assess and treat any cardiovascular emergency must be available. These are common sense standards that should be applied to any patient with CAD undergoing stress testing.

Interpreting the Exercise Study

The interpretation of an arterial exercise study is usually based on more than one measurement (Table 1). The drop in ABI produced by exercise is determined after the first postexercise minute; ABI is generally followed at regular intervals until it returns to baseline. Both the decline in ABI and the time for its return to baseline provide quantitative information about disease severity. Table 2 shows the results of exercise testing in a patient with intermittent claudication.

The CWD assessment is repeated in the immediate postexercise period (within the first minute). Because of time constraints, it is usually not possible to obtain a Doppler waveform measurement from each segmental level. In our laboratory, we limit ourselves to a reassessment of the common femoral waveform following exercise. The rationale behind this is that conversion of a waveform from a normal triphasic signal to an abnormal monophasic signal indicates that significant occlusive disease is present in the aortoiliac segment. This localization is extremely valuable because aortoiliac disease has radically different therapeutic and prognostic implications than does femoropopliteal or tibial disease.

The maximal walking distance also provides useful information about disease severity. In many claudication studies, walking distance is considered the primary endpoint because it best predicts the functional impact of a patient's claudication. In individuals with moderate-to-severe claudication, the maximum walking distance (or, in some laboratories, the distance to onset of claudication) can usually be determined using the fixed protocol. In patients with mild claudication, the

Table 2. Results of Exercise Testing in a Patient With PAD. The Patient Exercised for 2.55 Minutes on a Motorized Treadmill (2 mph, progressive grade). The Patient Experienced Pain in the Right Buttock and Groin at 0.5 min.

Protocol Time	Arm	Right DP	Right PT	Left DP	Left PT	Right ABI	Left ABI
Rest	125/80	105	112	128	139	0.90	1.11
Imm. Post.	150/90	60	70	160	140	0.47	1.07
1" Post.	140/90	70		150		0.47	1.00
5" Post.	130/90	75		140		0.50	0.93
10" Post.	130/90	110		140		0.73	0.93

PAD = peripheral arterial disease; DP = dorsalis pedis artery; PT = posterior tibial; ABI = ankle-brachial index.

more strenuous graded protocol may be necessary to determine maximal walking distance or distance to claudication.

Ancillary Benefits of Exercise Testing

Both blood pressure and cardiac status can be evaluated during exercise testing. Blood pressure, especially in patients with known hypertension thought to be controlled with medication, may become volatile with low-level exercise. Many patients who appear to be normotensive at rest will have a marked increase in pressure during or after mild exercise of the type associated with PAD testing. These patients may need closer blood pressure observation and additional medications.

It is also possible to use the peripheral arterial exercise test as a mini–cardiac stress test, especially if ECG monitoring is performed in conjunction with exercise. As noted earlier, a typical patient undergoes a 5-MET workload if he or she completes the fixed protocol. If the patient can do this without symptoms or ECG changes suggestive of ischemia, then it may be reasonable to clear that patient for general anesthesia and/or vascular reconstructive surgery without any additional cardiac testing. Conversely, if the patient is identified as having either symptoms or a positive stress ECG during low-level exercise, the patient is at high likelihood of having significant coronary disease, and an additional specific cardiac workup is necessary. We routinely use lower-extremity exercise testing to help screen and stratify our patients before revascularization therapeutic procedures. ∎

Key Points

- Lower-extremity exercise testing can diagnose, document, or otherwise quantify arterial occlusive disease.

- Lower-extremity exercise testing requires inexpensive equipment (eg, CWD, pneumatic occlusion cuffs, treadmill) and is relatively simple to perform and interpret.

- Many types of lower-extremity exercise can be used to assess PAD (eg, toe raises, stationary bicycling, leg lifts), but walking is generally considered best because it typically precipitates leg symptoms.

- The normal lower-extremity arterial CWD waveform is usually triphasic; a monophasic signal indicates the presence of a hemodynamically significant lesion proximal to the site of interrogation. Doppler studies performed immediately after exercise can be used to detect or localize otherwise occult atherosclerotic lesions.

- Treadmill exercise testing is useful for assessing PAD and can be used to screen for CAD and/or hypertension.

BIBLIOGRAPHY

Aly S, Sommerville K, Adiseshiah M, et al. Comparison of duplex imaging and arteriography in the evaluation of lower limb arteries. Br J Surg 1998;85: 1099–1102.

Chaudhry H, Holland A, Dormandy J. Comparison of graded versus constant treadmill test protocols for quantifying intermittent claudication. Vasc Med 1997;2:93–7.

Creager MA. Clinical assessment of the patient with claudication: the role of the vascular laboratory. Vasc Med 1997;2:231–7.

Fronek A. Quantitative velocity measurements in arterial disease of the lower extremity. In: Bernstein EF, ed. Vascular Diagnosis. 4th ed. St Louis: Mosby; 1993:513–9.

Gardner AW, Skinner JS, Vaughan NR, et al. Comparison of treadmill walking and stair climbing over a range of exercise intensities in peripheral vascular occlusive disease. Angiology 1993;44:353–60.

Hiatt WR, Hirsch AT, Regensteiner JG, Brass EP. Clinical trials for claudication: assessment of exercise performance, functional status, and clinical end points. Vascular Clinical Trialists. Circulation 1995;92:614–21.

Hiatt WR, Wolfel EE, Meier RH, Regensteiner JG. Superiority of treadmill walking exercise versus strength training for patients with peripheral arterial disease: implications for the mechanism of the training response. Circulation 1994;90:1866–74.

Liu Y, Steinacker JM, Opitz-Gress A, et al. Comparison of whole-body thallium imaging with transcutaneous PO_2 in studying regional blood supply in patients with peripheral arterial occlusive disease. Angiology 1996;47:879–86.

McPhail IR, Spittell PC, Weston SA, Bailey KR. Active pedal plantar flexion in patients with intermittent claudication: comparison with treadmill exercise. J Am Coll Cardiol 1998;31:341A.

Osmundson PJ, O'Fallon WM, Clements IP, et al. Reproducibility of noninvasive tests of peripheral occlusive arterial disease. J Vasc Surg 1985;2:678–83.

Owen RS. MR angiography of the peripheral vessels. Magn Reson Imaging Clin North Am 1998;6:385–95.

Raines JK. The pulse volume recorder in peripheral arterial disease. In: Bernstein EF, ed. Vascular Diagnosis. 4th ed. St Louis: Mosby; 1993:534–43.

Raptopoulos V, Rosen MP, Kent KC, et al. Sequential helical CT angiography of aortoiliac disease. Am J Roentgenol 1996;166:1347–54.

Regensteiner JG, Gardner A, Hiatt WR. Exercise testing and exercise rehabilitation for patients with peripheral arterial disease: status in 1997. Vasc Med 1997;2:147–55.

Rieker O, Duber C, Neufang A, et al. CT angiography versus intraarterial digital subtraction angiography for assessment of aortoiliac occlusive disease. Am J Roentgenol 1997;169:1133–8.

Rieker O, Duber C, Schmiedt W, et al. Prospective comparison of CT angiography of the legs with intraarterial digital subtraction angiography. Am J Roentgenol 1996;166:269–76.

Wain RA, Berdejo GL, Delvalle WN, et al. Can duplex scan arterial mapping replace contrast arteriography as the test of choice before infrainguinal revascularization? J Vasc Surg 1999;29:100–07; discussion 107–9.

Winchester PA, Lee HM, Khilnani NM. Comparison of two-dimensional MR digital subtraction angiography of the lower extremity with x-ray angiography. J Vasc Intervent Radiol 1998;9:891–9; discussion 900.

Abdominal Aortic Aneurysm Detection and Management: Role of the Primary Care Physician

Rolf R. Paulson, MD, FACP
Clinical Professor of Medicine
University of North Dakota School of Medicine
Altru Clinic
Grand Forks, North Dakota

Objective: To examine the importance of AAA detection and management in a primary care setting, with currently available diagnostic imaging methods, as well as a review of patient selection and preparation for surgical repair.

Aneurysmal disease of the arteries presents a significant health risk to a growing number of the adult American population. Unidentified abdominal aortic aneurysms (AAAs) cause death due to aneurysm rupture. Popliteal artery aneurysms pose a significant risk of critical limb ischemia and limb loss. The key issues in the primary care setting are for each practitioner to consider the possibility of aneurysmal disease during office visits and to gain familiarity with the value of noninvasive vascular imaging procedures in establishing these critical diagnoses. In addition to establishing the diagnosis of an arterial aneurysm, there are often important associated atherosclerotic conditions that will also require diligent medical management by the primary practitioner. This brief review will not cover intracranial aneurysms.

GENERAL CONSIDERATIONS

Atherosclerosis has traditionally been considered the primary cause of AAA formation in elderly patients. However, this is an oversimplification. Both AAA and other common manifestations of atherosclerosis have an overlapping age-dependent prevalence. This coprevalence has important implications that can facilitate the office-based detection of an AAA and aid in its long-term management. Smoking and hypertension are the atherosclerotic risk factors that are most closely associated with the development of both aortic aneurysmal disease as well as other manifestations of peripheral arterial disease (PAD) (Lederle et al, 1997a). Interestingly, the presence of diabetes is inversely correlated with the development of AAA and may serve as a clue that more common arterial manifestations of atherosclerotic PAD and aneurysmal disease are different conditions (Lederle, 1997). The male-to-female prevalence ratio of AAA is 4:1. There is also a strong familial incidence of AAA, with a 12-fold increased rate of occurrence in siblings (Johansen and Koepsell, 1986). Patients may present with multiple aneurysms in different anatomic locations.

AAA also occurs in conjunction with other systemic arterial diseases, such as temporal arteritis, Ehlers-Danlos syndrome, and Marfan's syndrome (Santos-Ocampo and Hoffman, 1999). There is known to be an increased risk of AAA in patients with known hernias or bronchiectasis, which might be explained by the fact that all 3 illnesses exhibit disorders in collagen structure. Microscopic and biochemical data show destruction of the medial portion of the arterial wall with loss of elastin in all AAA patients.

The mortality of abdominal aneurysms is due to rupture and is age dependent. AAA ruptures rarely result in death in patients <55 years of age. Nonetheless, this syndrome causes as many as 16,220 deaths per year in the United States (National Center for Health Statistics, 1996). When repaired electively (before rupture), mortality is ~2% in low-risk individuals. Postrupture mortality in the hospital is reportedly >50%, although some believe mortality is >90% because many patients with ruptured AAAs do not survive transportation to a health care facility (Johansen, 1995). AAA can be defined as a 50% increase in the diameter of the aorta or as an aortic diameter ≥3.0 cm (normal aortic diameter, 2.0 cm)

(Lederle et al, 1997). Rupture rarely occurs in aortas <4.0 cm in diameter, but the rupture rate rises exponentially at a diameter of >5.5 cm (Figure).

DIAGNOSIS OF AAA

AAAs are usually detected in 1 of 3 common clinical scenarios: (1) In patients who present to the primary care office or emergency room with suspicious clinical signs or symptoms; (2) as an incidental "serendipitous" finding during imaging for other reasons; or (3) as the result of the intentional screening of high-risk individuals.

SYMPTOMATIC PATIENTS WITH AN AAA

The signs and symptoms associated with the presence of an AAA are nonspecific, and consequently clinical practice can result in either overdiagnosis or underdiagnosis. Many causes of abdominal and back pain can exist in patients with or without an AAA and the potential presence of an abdominal aneurysm is rarely part of the initial diagnostic differential diagnosis. Fewer than half the patients with ruptured AAAs present with the classic triad of sudden abdominal or lower back pain, hypotension, and a pulsatile abdominal mass (Perler, 1997). Physical examination may be limited in some high-risk patients by obesity or "guarding." Lederle et al (1994) reported with distressing results a series of patients who had presented to internists with a ruptured AAA. Sixty-one percent of the internists initially missed the diagnosis and frequent misdiagnoses included urinary tract obstruction or infection, spinal disease, and diverticulitis. A miscellaneous symptomatic presentation that can suggest the presence of an AAA is the cholesterol embolus syndrome (also called "blue toe syndrome"[BTS]). Livedo reticularis or multiple blue toes (more common after an angiographic arterial procedure) with good pedal pulses should prompt performance of an abdominal ultrasound study or computed tomography (CT) scan in search of an AAA (Baxter et al, 1990).

In suspected rupture, any imaging must be performed urgently and in close cooperation with a consulting vascular or general surgeon. Diagnostic testing must be accurate and prompt, as delays can interfere with the provision of definitive and potentially life-saving therapy. At times, a simple flat plate abdominal film or cross-table lateral radiograph will show a calcified aorta with widening and provide the diagnosis. Alternatively, urgent ultrasonography can demonstrate the aneurysm. CT or magnetic resonance angiography (MRA) are other excellent alternatives, but the physician or highly qualified health care professional (eg, critical care or emergency room nurse) should also accompany patients with

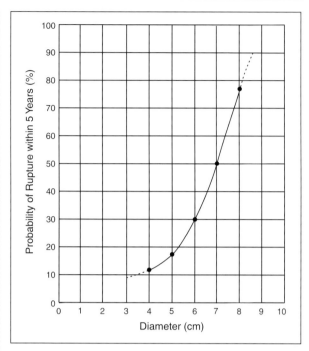

Figure. Aneurysm size is the most important factor contributing to rupture. The probability of rupture increases exponentially in aneurysms >5 cm.

suspected rupture to the scanner, as subsequent rapid transport to the operating room immediately afterward may be necessary.

AAA DISCOVERED BY ROUTINE EXAMINATION OR AS AN INCIDENTAL FINDING

Because most AAAs are asymptomatic, they might be found on routine physical examination or in the process of a workup for some other problem. Rose and Ernst (1995) reported that 75% of AAAs are asymptomatic when first diagnosed.

Palpation directed at locating an AAA is better than routine abdominal palpation. The sensitivity of finding an aneurysm with palpation (via pooled data) ranged from 29% for AAAs 3.0 to 3.9 cm to 50% for AAAs 4.0 to 4.9 cm to 76% for AAAs ≥5.0 cm. Abdominal palpation should be done with the patient supine, knees flexed, and abdomen relaxed. The physician should focus on the area cephalad to the umbilicus. The key measurement is the width of the aorta measured between the index fingers (Lederle and Simel, 1999).

Using the Olmstead County database, Beede et al (1990) reviewed the converse situation of AAA overdiagnosis. Of 116 local residents referred after physical examination for ultrasound regarding suspected AAAs, aneurysms were found in only 17 (positive predictive value, 14.7%).

Table I. Patient Profile for AAA Screening

Age >50 yr, with a history of smoking, hypertension, and coronary artery or peripheral arterial disease

OR

Sibling with AAA

OR

Presence of another arterial aneurysm (eg, popliteal or iliac)

AAA = abdominal aortic aneurysm.
(Data from Lederle, Johnson, Wilson, et al, 1997, Johansen and Koepsell, 1986, Ramesh et al, 1993.)

Table II. Presurgical Cardiac Workup

No coronary artery disease by history, physical examination, or resting ECG—no further workup.

If ≥3 risk factors are present (age >50 yr, diabetes mellitus, angina pectoris, abnormal Q waves on ECG, ventricular ectopy), perform coronary angiography and proceed according to the results. If 1 or 2 risk factors are present, perform dipyridamole-thallium scanning and act according to the result.

ECG = electrocardiogram.
(Reprinted with permission from Eagle et al, 1989.)

How should the primary care physician interpret these data? On the one hand, the office-based abdominal examination is always best performed with a conscious, directed effort. For the elderly patient, patients with a family history of aneurysmal disease, or those with other clinical stigmata of systemic atherosclerosis (history of coronary artery, cerebrovascular, or PAD), a directed physical examination can detect many AAAs and lead to life-saving intervention. As for other potential intra-abdominal diagnoses that can lead to a life-threatening catastrophe if undiagnosed, there will always be patients in whom a referral for diagnostic imaging will be negative.

Whether AAA is found as an incidental finding on physical exams or as part of the workup for another problem, the implications are the same. One needs to evaluate the lesion (in this case AAA) and the patient, and develop a treatment plan as outlined below.

SCREENING PROGRAMS TO DETECT AAA

The third method to diagnose AAA is to perform deliberate population-based screening. Lederle et al (1988) have made a convincing case for screening in high-risk individuals 60 to 75 years of age who have coronary disease or hypertension (see Table I). In a group of 201 people with these risk factors, they found undetected aneurysms in 9% (Lederle et al, 1988). These aneurysms were 3.6 cm to 5.9 cm in diameter. Half the aneurysms were palpable on physical examination (but only when a special effort was made to detect these aneurysms), and the other half were only detectable by ultrasound. The ability of a screening program to provide such high rates of AAA detection, linked to the excellent long-term results obtained with elective vascular surgical repair, would suggest that such AAA screening should be utilized more frequently. However, screening programs to detect AAA have not been well accepted by various task forces and therefore

are not widely performed (Frame et al, 1993). Barriers to the establishment of such programs would include the relative cost of abdominal ultrasound procedures and current payer bias against all vascular "screening." Many vascular medicine professionals feel that this position deserves reevaluation.

IMAGING

In urgent situations in which rupture or contained rupture is suspected, time is critically important. Plain radiographic studies may demonstrate aortic calcification and thus demonstrate the aneurysm in ≤75% of cases. B-mode ultrasonography is readily available and can usually define the presence of an aneurysm. Bowel gas may interfere with the examination, however, and a skilled technologist is needed. CT studies can also define the presence of an aneurysm and give more precise information about surrounding structures. With CT, however, the patient must move out of the emergency room setting. CT may be needed to define the anatomy in the situation of contained rupture. In the emergency setting, the choice of CT versus ultrasonography will depend on local preferences and logistics.

Ultrasound techniques are usually considered to be the method of choice for screening or following AAA size and expansion rate. There is a significant economic benefit from use of ultrasonography over CT or magnetic resonance imaging (MRI), as adequate sensitivity and accuracy can be maintained when this study is performed by a skilled technician. The patient does need to present for examination in the fasting state to eliminate bowel gas, which will obscure the images. MRA and MRI might occasionally be the avenue for serendipitous discovery of an otherwise unsuspected AAA. Because these imaging techniques are slow, they have little to offer the emergency patient. They may have a role (along with angiography and intraluminal ultrasound) in presurgical staging but that is beyond the scope of this article.

Table III. Indications for Surgery in Patients with AAA

AAA >5.0 cm in diameter
>1.0 cm/yr growth
Symptomatic AAA of any size

AAA = abdominal aortic aneurysm. Reprinted with permission from Beckman JA, O'Gara PT. Adv Intern Med 1999;44:267–91

MANAGEMENT OF THE PATIENT WITH AN AAA

Following diagnosis of an AAA, the next step to consider is repair. There is general consensus on the benefit of surgical intervention for AAAs >5.0 cm in diameter. Surgical repair of smaller AAAs from 4.0 to 5.0 cm in diameter is controversial. Nevitt et al (1989) used community-based data from 1951 to 1984 to study 176 patients with intact AAAs at the time of the initial ultrasound study. In the 130 patients with AAAs <5.0 cm, the risk of rupture was 0%; in the 46 patients with AAAs ≥5.0 cm, the risk of rupture was 25% over 5 years. These authors recommended a follow-up imaging study 3 to 6 months after the initial diagnosis, with subsequent ultrasound examinations every 6 to 12 months for small (<5 cm) aneurysms which remain stable in size.

Nevitt et al (1989) did not feel that rate of growth was as an important predictor of risk as was the initial size of the aneurysm at discovery. What to do about aneurysms <5.0 cm in diameter is a source of controversy (Nevitt et al, 1989; Katz et al, 1992).

PREOPERATIVE MEDICAL EVALUATION OF PATIENTS WITH AAA

An important medical issue is the preoperative medical (especially cardiac) evaluation of patients with AAA. Hertzer et al (1984) reported on 289 consecutive patients with AAA who underwent presurgical coronary angiography. Sixty-five percent of the patients had severe coronary artery disease (CAD) (5% severe inoperable, 31% severe correctable, and 29% advanced but compensated); 29% had mild to moderate CAD; and 6% had normal coronary arteries.

More recently, Eagle et al (1989) showed that patients with AAAs could be stratified as to cardiac risk by clinical evaluation (see Tables II, III, and IV). Patients with no evidence of CAD by history, physical examination, or resting electrocardiogram (ECG) had a low postoperative risk and good prognosis. Further cardiac testing is not recommended in these patients. Five clinical risk factors for cardiac problems were evaluated: age >70 years, diabetes mellitus, angina pectoris, abnormal Q waves on ECG, and the presence of ventricular ectopy. In the absence of these factors, risk was low. If ≥3 of these risk factors were present, the

Table IV. Incorrect Diagnosis in 14 of 23 Patients with AAA

Diagnosis	Number of Patients
Urinary tract obstruction or infection	6
Spinal disease	5
Diverticulitis	4
Colon cancer	3
Appendicitis	2
Constipation	1
Renal stone	1
Pulmonary embolus	1

AAA = abdominal aortic aneurysm. Reprinted with permission from Lederle FA, et al. Am J Med 1994;96:163–7.

postoperative cardiac event rate (myocardial infarction or death) was nearly 50%. Coronary angiography with possible revascularization is recommended for these patients before AAA repair. In patients with 1 or 2 of these risk factors, dipyridamole-thallium scanning is recommended. A negative test provides a good prognosis and indicates surgery. A "redistribution" result should lead to coronary angiography with revascularization where appropriate.

There remain patients with severe heart disease in whom perioperative mortality will be high. An exciting new development is the endovascular stent-graft, in which the aneurysm can be repaired percutaneously with minimal open surgery. The hope is that this technique will further decrease the morbidity and mortality of AAA repair. This would be especially welcome in high-risk patients. The technique is investigational now, however, and is only being performed at certain centers (Seelig et al, 1999).

POTENTIAL COMPLICATIONS OF OPERATIVE AAA REPAIR

Potential complications of operative AAA repair are infrequent, and can be divided into early (immediate postoperative) and late. The greatest early risks include perioperative myocardial infarction and renal failure. Pelvic ischemia due to the loss of the hypogastric circulation can cause vasculogenic impotence, necrosis of the perineum, ischemia of the left colon and rectum, or paraplegia. BTS can also occur as a consequence of aneurysm repair.

Late complications of AAA repair may include graft infection, as the graft is a foreign body. Rarely, an aortoenteric fistula may develop in patients with aortic grafts if erosion into the duodenum or bowel occurs, and this may present as brisk gastrointestinal bleeding. Pseudoaneurysms may occur at the proximal or distal ends of the graft prosthesis.

Key Points

- The clinical presentation of a ruptured AAA can easily be mistaken for other conditions. The key for primary care physicians is to be aware of this entity.

- AAA occurs in predictable populations: patients who smoke, are hypertensive, and those with CAD and/or PAD. Aneurysms may occur in multiple arterial beds and occur with a familial predisposition. Knowledge of each of these clinical factors provides an increased opportunity for detection before rupture.

- Elective surgery (before rupture) has low mortality, whereas emergency (postrupture) surgery carries a high mortality.

- Patients should be evaluated for CAD before undergoing elective AAA surgery.

- Indications for surgical referral for AAA include diameter >5.0 cm, rapid growth (>0.5-1.0 cm/yr), or suspicious abdominal or lumbar symptoms.

- Ultrasound is usually the imaging modality of choice both in emergency situations and for screening; however, both CT and MRA studies are excellent, where they are available.

POPLITEAL ANEURYSMS

Popliteal aneurysms may be similar pathologically to AAA, but their clinical presentation and natural history deserve a distinct review. Although the primary risk of AAA is sudden rupture, popliteal aneurysms may more commonly present with sudden distal limb ischemia, as a result of thrombosis within the aneurysm or thromboembolism from the aneurysm. Patients may present with new-onset claudication, or an acutely threatened ischemic limb, or with BTS. If a popliteal aneurysm is found, a directed physical examination and ultrasound examination seeking a contralateral popliteal aneurysm, or an AAA, should be performed. There is no medical treatment of popliteal aneurysms. The ideal surgical therapy of popliteal aneurysms will depend on the clinical presentation. Intra-arterial thrombolysis may offer an immediate therapeutic prospect for acute limb salvage, but aneurysm repair with vein interposition following resection will almost inevitably be required.

The key issue for primary care practices is to consider the possibility of a popliteal aneurysm in the differential diagnosis of any patient who presents with acute limb ischemia (Ramesh et al, 1993).

PSEUDOANEURYSMS

Unlike true aneurysms, pseudoaneurysms are not formed by a stretching of the vascular wall, but rather by a loss of arterial wall continuity. This permits blood to flow outside the arterial wall until it is constrained by the surrounding soft tissue and muscle. This can occur at the juncture of a prosthetic aortic graft and the native aorta or after any prior arterial bypass procedure. Pseudoaneurysms may also be created as an iatrogenic consequence of percutaneous interventional vascular procedures, in which ultrasound can be used in both diagnosis and treatment. The diagnosis and treatment of pseudoaneurysms is reviewed in more detail in the article by Dr. Jaff in this monograph. ∎

BIBLIOGRAPHY

Baxter BT, McGee GS, Flinn WR, et al. Distal embolization as a presenting symptom of aortic aneurysms. Am J Surg 1990;160:197–201.

Beckman JA, O'Gara PT. Diseases of the aorta. Adv Intern Med 1999;44:267–91.

Beede SD, Ballard DJ, James M, et al. Positive predictive value of clinical suspicion of abdominal aortic aneurysm: implications for efficient use of abdominal ultrasonography. Arch Intern Med 1990;150:549–51.

Eagle KA, Coley CM, Newell JB, et al. Combining clinical and thallium data optimizes preoperative assessment of cardiac risk before major vascular surgery. Ann Intern Med 1989;110:859–66.

Frame PS, Fryback DG, Patterson C. Screening for abdominal aortic aneurysm ages 60 to 80 years: a cost-effective analysis. Ann Intern Med 1993;119:411–6.

Hertzer NR, Beven EG, Young JR, et al. Coronary artery disease in peripheral vascular patients: a classification of 1000 coronary angiograms and results of surgical treatment. Ann Surg 1984:199:223–33.

Johansen K. Ruptured abdominal aortic aneurysm. How should recent outcome studies impact current practices? Semin Vasc Surg 1995;82:163–7.

Johansen K, Koepsell T. Familial tendency for abdominal aortic aneurysms. JAMA 1986;256:1934–6.

Katz DA, Littenberg B, Cronenwett JL. Management of small abdominal aortic aneurysms. JAMA 1992;268:2678–86.

Lederle FA, Johnson GR, Wilson SE, et al. Prevalence and associations of abdominal aortic aneurysm detected through screening. Aneurysm Detection and Management (ADAM) Veterans Affairs Cooperative Study Group. Ann Intern Med 1997; 126:441–9.

Lederle FA, and the ADAM VA Cooperative Study Investigators. The relationship of age, gender, race, and body size to infrarenal aortic diameter. J Vasc Surg 1997;26:595–601.

Lederle FA, Parenti CM, Chute EP. Ruptured abdominal aortic aneurysm: the internist as diagnostician. Am J Med 1994;96:163–7.

Lederle FA, Simel DL. Does this patient have abdominal aortic aneurysm? JAMA 1999;281:77–82.

Lederle FA, Walker JM, Reinke DM. Selective screening for abdominal aortic aneurysms with physical exam and ultrasound. Arch Intern Med 1988;148:1753–6.

National Center for Health Statistics. Vital statistics of the United States, 1992, Vol 11, Mortality, Part A. Washington: Public Health Service. 1996.

Nevitt MP, Ballard DJ, Hallett JW. Prognosis of abdominal aortic aneurysms: a population-based study. N Engl J Med 1989;321:1009–14.

Perler BA. The management of patients with ruptured abdominal aortic aneurysms. Adv Surg 1997;30: 21–38.

Ramesh S, Michaels JA, Galland RB. Popliteal aneurysm: morphology and management. Br J Surg 1993;80:1531–3.

Rose WW, Ernst CB. Abdominal aortic aneurysm. Compr Ther 1995;21:339–43.

Santos-Ocampo AS, Hoffman GS. Aneurysms and hypermobility in a 45-year-old woman. Cleveland Clin J Med 1999;66:426–33.

Seelig MH, Oldenburg WA, Hakaim AG, et al. Endovascular repair of abdominal aortic aneurysms: Where do we stand? Mayo Clin Proc 1999;74:999–1010.

The American Journal of Medicine®

CONTINUING EDUCATION SERIES

AN OFFICE-BASED APPROACH TO THE DIAGNOSIS AND TREATMENT OF PERIPHERAL ARTERIAL DISEASE

PART VII: Women and PAD

SERIES EDITOR
ALAN T. HIRSCH, MD
GUEST CO-EDITORS
MARIE D. GERHARD-HERMAN, MD, MMSc
JUDITH G. REGENSTEINER, PhD

Jointly sponsored by
The Excerpta Medica Office of Continuing Medical Education and the Society for Vascular Medicine and Biology

Introduction and Overview

Marie D. Gerhard-Herman, MD, MMSc
Medical Director
Vascular Diagnostic Laboratory
Brigham and Women's Hospital
Assistant Professor of Medicine
Harvard Medical School
Boston, Massachusetts

Alan T. Hirsch, MD
Director, Vascular Medicine Program
Minnesota Vascular Diseases Center
University of Minnesota Medical School
Minneapolis, Minnesota

Judith G. Regensteiner, PhD
Associate Professor of Medicine
Director, Clinical Treadmill Laboratory
University of Colorado Health Sciences Center
Section of Vascular Medicine
Denver, Colorado

This Continuing Education Series on the primary care of peripheral arterial disease (PAD) has provided a comprehensive overview of the natural history, pathophysiology, and available treatment options. It is a premise of this series and of the Society for Vascular Medicine and Biology that the primary care physician is ideally positioned to assume a major proportion of the responsibility for the management of patients with all forms of vascular disease, especially PAD. A critical aspect of this management is a consideration of gender-based differences in the biology of atherosclerosis, in diagnosis of PAD, and the impact of gender on treatment. Importantly, the pink ribbon crossed and worn on people's lapels is synonymous with women's health in America, yet the single largest killer of women, cardiovascular disease, goes largely unrecognized.

This seventh monograph is thus dedicated to improving the understanding by the primary care physician of the role of gender in not only facilitating an accurate diagnosis in PAD, but in assisting with development of appropriate treatments.

In the first article, Molly T. Vogt, PhD, examines the epidemiology of PAD, paying particular attention to the burden this disease imposes on elderly women. Dr. Vogt notes that although as many as 1 in 4 elderly women in the United States is affected by PAD, up to 90% of those affected may be asymptomatic and do not report classic claudication symptoms during walking. These women maintain a high risk of experiencing cardiovascular ischemic events, and therefore would benefit from risk reduction treatments. Unfortunately, their "benign" symptom status challenges the primary care clinician to be more aggressive in fostering appropriate PAD detection.

Dr. Vogt also demonstrates that, despite a perception that PAD is a benign disease, even the mildest manifestations of PAD are associated with impaired mobility and neuromuscular function, reduced quality of life, and increased cardiovascular morbidity and mortality. Moreover, given increased smoking habits among young and middle-aged women, it is very likely that the burden of disease associated with PAD in women will increase dramatically as the baby boom generation matures.

In the article by Marie D. Gerhard-Herman, MD, MMSc, and Catherine M. Wittgen, MD, the impact of gender on the prevalence, treatment, and outcome of PAD is thoroughly examined. Drs. Gerhard-Herman and Wittgen point out that the prevalence of PAD in female patients is greater than previously projected. Moreover, although recent public attention has successfully focused on breast cancer awareness and generated long-needed public health advances, particularly in regard to community-based disease screening and detection, the effects of atherosclerotic disease in women go largely unrecognized, even though mortality is more than 10 times greater than from breast cancer.

Drs. Gerhard-Herman and Wittgen point out that few clinical trials have included women or have specifically addressed the issue of gender in PAD populations and the potential impact of gender on the outcome of PAD. Furthermore, although aneurysmal disease appears to develop less frequently in female patients, and women do not appear to have more comorbid conditions than men, there is a documented "gender gap" regarding the referral of women for potentially life-saving surgical interventions. Specifically, newer technologies are still needed to decrease the profile of these percutaneous delivery systems for endovascular stents and stent-grafts so that they might be better applied to patients with smaller body size and smaller conduit arteries, including women.

In the final article, David E. Bush, MD, reviews the findings of the Heart and Estrogen/Progestin Replacement Study (HERS), the first prospective, randomized, clinical trial designed to determine if treatment with a combined estrogen/progestin preparation might reduce the risk of coronary ischemic events in post-menopausal women with established atherosclerotic coronary artery disease (CAD).

Dr. Bush writes that although many observational studies have shown lower rates of cardiovascular events in women treated with postmenopausal hormone replacement therapy compared with those who were not treated, postmenopausal women with established CAD who took estrogen and/or progestin did *not* have a lower rate of cardiovascular events. Dr. Bush offers several possible explanations why HERS results were not concordant with those of prior observational and epidemiologic studies.

We sincerely hope that this comprehensive approach to the diagnosis and treatment of women with PAD will lead to better therapeutic decision-making for all patients. To accomplish this, primary care doctors and vascular specialists will need to recognize areas in which gender plays a role in the pathogenesis of PAD, and how prevalent societal perceptions of gender-based risk influence treatment. ■

Peripheral Arterial Disease: The Epidemiology and Burden of Disease in Elderly Women

Molly T. Vogt, PhD
Associate Professor of Orthopedic Surgery and Epidemiology
University of Pittsburgh
Pittsburgh, Pennsylvania

Objective: To review the epidemiology of PAD with emphasis on the burden this disease imposes on elderly women.

Peripheral arterial disease (PAD) is currently estimated to affect 20% to 25% of elderly women in the United States, although this condition is not often recognized because as many as 90% of these women are asymptomatic and do not report cramping ischemic pain after exertional stress. Although PAD has been considered a relatively benign condition, even a mild form of this disease is associated with impaired mobility and neuromuscular function, reduced quality of life, and increased cardiovascular morbidity and mortality. PAD is stable in most patients and can be managed by risk-factor reduction, exercise, and drugs, with surgery indicated in <5% of patients. To date there is no evidence that hormone replacement therapy affects the progression of PAD. Currently, the rate and type of surgical interventions vary by gender and race in the United States. Given the estimated growth in the number of elderly in the next 30 years and the smoking habits of young and middle-aged women, it is very likely that the burden of disease associated with PAD will increase dramatically.

INTRODUCTION

Atherosclerosis is a progressive disease that begins in childhood or adolescence and is asymptomatic for many years. Clinical symptoms begin to emerge after age 45 in men and age 55 in women, but the disease may remain undetected even among the elderly. For instance, in the Cardiovascular Health Study almost one third of the women >65 years of age were found to have occult disease in ≥1 vascular bed (Psaty et al, 1992). During the postmenopausal years, the incidence of cardiovascular disease (CVD) begins to increase slowly and by the age of 65 years, the rate of CVD in women approaches that of men (Bush, 1991). Protection against CVD before menopause is thought to be due to the beneficial effects of endogenous estrogens, primarily estradiol-17β, on the cardiovascular system. Both animal and clinical research studies suggest that estrogen acts directly on the arterial walls and modulates vascular reactivity.

The formation of atherosclerotic plaques in the larger arteries of the lower extremities may significantly reduce the blood flow. This, in turn, may cause intermittent claudication or ischemic leg pain distal to the site of arterial narrowing during exercise or while walking. In the majority of patients the claudication is stable. But in 4% to 30% of claudicants, the occlusive process continues and ischemic pain occurs even at rest. Ultimately tissue ulceration and gangrene may result (McDermott, 1999; Vogt et al, 1992). Although the symptomatic stages of PAD have been well characterized, very little is known regarding the factors that influence the progression of disease in either men or women.

DETECTION OF PAD

Estimates of the prevalence of PAD vary widely depending on the criteria employed for defining and diagnosing the disease and population characteristics.

In the physician's office and in many epidemiologic studies, 3 methods are used to diagnose PAD: the Rose Claudication Questionnaire, which assesses the presence or absence of IC; palpation of pulses in the pedal or tibial arteries; and measurement of the ankle-brachial index (ABI) at rest. Since as many as 90% of elderly women with PAD do not have the classic symptoms of claudication and pulses are congenitally absent in ≤12% of the population, the Rose questionnaire, with or without the concomitant palpation of pulses, is a relatively insensitive measure for detecting PAD (Feigelson et al, 1994).

The ABI is a simple, objective, noninvasive measure of the adequacy of blood flow through the distal vessels to the lower extremities (Prineas et al, 1982). The index is defined as the ratio of systolic blood pressures in the posterior tibial artery and the right brachial artery after 5 minutes of rest in the supine position. The pulses are detected with a Doppler device, and a standard mercury manometer can be used to measure blood pressure. When compared with angiography, the gold standard for diagnosis of PAD, measures of the ABI at rest have a sensitivity and specificity of ≥96%. Among diabetic patients the sensitivity may be considerably lower. When arterial walls are rigid due to calcification, the blood pressure measured at the ankle is high and therefore the ABI is also artifactually high.

In the study of ~1500 elderly women enrolled in the Study of Osteoporotic Fractures in the Pittsburgh area, the average ABI in the population was 1.09 (Vogt et al, 1993a). Angiographic studies have indicated that arterial disease is present when the ABI is ≤0.94. However, most research studies have used an index of 0.9 or 0.8 as the cut point for defining the disease. It is clear that the lower the ABI, the more severe the stenotic lesion, and when the ABI is <0.5, multiple large areas of occlusion are usually present.

PREVALENCE OF PAD

It is estimated that PAD occurs in ~8.4 million people in the United States. In women, PAD is rarely found before 60 years of age, but thereafter the prevalence increases rapidly with age. In men, clinical symptoms begin to emerge at a somewhat earlier age (45 years), and the disease is more prevalent before 65 years of age, but the male:female ratio decreases as age increases. By 80 years of age, the prevalence has risen to ~40% in both men and women (Newman et al, 1993).

PAD is asymptomatic in the majority of elderly individuals. Studies suggest that 6% to 30% of elderly patients have claudication symptoms. When claudicants referred for a vascular laboratory for blood flow

Table I. Prevalence of PAD (ABI ≤0.9) in Elderly Women

Patient Demographics	Percent
Nonsmokers	4–6
Smokers	16–25
Systolic hypertensive	25
History of CHD	17
Diabetic	8–34
Diabetic and hypertensive	37
Native American	6
African American	20

PAD = peripheral arterial disease; ABI = ankle-brachial index; CHD = coronary heart disease. Data compiled from Manolio et al, 1995; Newman et al, 1991; Newman et al, 1993; Vogt et al, 1993a.

studies are followed prospectively, ~25% are reported to have progressive worsening of symptoms, with 1% to 10% requiring arterial revascularization and 3% to 5% requiring amputation. In population-based studies however, only 5% to 10% of PAD patients experience symptom progression (Hooi et al, 1999). No difference in the rate of disease progression has been reported between men and women.

Women who smoke or who have a history of hypertension, coronary heart disease, or diabetes have a prevalence of disease that is several-fold greater. The overall prevalence of PAD among African-American women is about twice that of white women, even after adjustment for differences in comorbid conditions and lifestyle factors (Table I).

The risk factors for PAD are very similar to those for coronary artery disease, but smoking is a particularly strong predictor of atherosclerotic disease in the lower extremities (Fowkes, 1989). About 30% of all cases of PAD (defined as an ABI ≤0.9) in women can be attributed to smoking. The other major factors that have been associated with the development and progression of PAD are increasing age, hypertension, diabetes, hyperlipidemia, and a variety of rheologic and thrombotic factors (Table II). Although PAD occurs primarily in postmenopausal women, there is currently no evidence to suggest that decreased estrogen levels are directly related to the development of atherosclerosis in the arteries of the lower extremity.

GENETIC RISK OF PAD

Genetic factors that influence ABI values have not been studied in women. However, in men it has been

Table II. Factors that Influence PAD Development, Progression, and Mortality

Risk Factors	Development	Progression	Mortality
Age	++	0	++
Smoking	++++	++++	++++
Diabetes/impaired glucose tolerance	++++	?	++
Hypertension	+++	?	++
Hyperlipidemia	+	+	0
Rheologic factors	++	?	0
Thrombotic factors	+++	++	0
ABI	−	+++	++++

PAD = peripheral arterial disease; ABI = ankle-brachial index; + = weak or conflicting evidence of influence; ++ = moderate influence; +++ = strong influence; ++++ = very strong influence; 0 = no effect; ? = unknown. Data compiled from Hooi et al, 1999; McDermott, 1999.

demonstrated that genetics may play an important role (Carmelli et al, 2000). It has been known for some time that several risk factors associated with a low ABI (smoking, hypertension, diabetes) are genetically influenced. More recently, using data from white male twin pairs enrolled in the National Heart, Lung, and Blood Institute Twin Study, it was shown that 48% of the variability in observed ABI values could be attributed to genetic effects; the remaining 52% were attributed to nonshared environmental factors (Carmelli et al, 2000). Among the men matched for age, genetics, and shared family environment during childhood, it appeared that individual health practices, particularly smoking and a sedentary lifestyle, were key factors in the development of low ABI values.

PROGRESSION OF PAD

As noted, PAD does not appear to progress significantly in the majority of patients. The major predictors of progression in people with symptomatic PAD are cigarette smoking and initial disease severity (ie, the lower the ABI at the time of PAD diagnosis, the greater the likelihood of progression). There is currently considerable debate about whether the history of diabetes is a risk factor for disease progression based on ABI, but it is clear that diabetic patients are 7 times more likely to need amputations (McDermott, 1999).

The presence of atherosclerotic plaques in the major vessels of the lower extremities is indicative of increased likelihood of major atherosclerotic disease in other vascular beds. Several epidemiologic and clinical studies have demonstrated that PAD diagnosis in an individual is strongly predictive of decreased life expectancy (primarily due to cardiovascular disease) and an increased likelihood of cardiovascular morbidity (Hooi et al, 1999; Criqui et al, 1992; Newman et al, 1999; Vogt et al, 1993b).

EVALUATION OF DISABILITY

Symptomatic PAD is characterized by pain during walking or exercise, which may progress to ischemic pain at rest, ulcers, and gangrene. The number and size of muscle fibers in the affected limb decrease (Farinon et al, 1984) and bone mineral density at the hip may also decrease (Vogt et al, 1997). The resulting lower extremity weakness may in turn cause postural instability and an increased risk of falling (Guralnik et al, 1995). Even among nondiabetic patients, neurologic changes occur early in the disease process. Sensory loss may occur first, followed by motor loss (Koopman et al, 1996; Laghi Pasini et al, 1996). The severity of PAD correlates quite closely with the extent of nerve changes. Muscle denervation, combined with decreased sensory input and increased pain, results in a decline in muscle function, impaired ability to walk, and loss of functional independence.

Women with asymptomatic PAD living in the community report that they are less likely to walk for exercise or exercise vigorously and more likely to experience difficulty in walking 2 to 3 blocks than women of similar age who have normal ABIs (Figure) (Vogt et al, 1994). Similarly, it has been shown that walking ability (measured as distance walked in a 6-minute period) is highly correlated with ABI in claudicants. ABI was the key predictor of walking ability in this patient population (McDermott et al, 1999).

Several studies investigating the health status of patients with PAD have used the Medical Outcomes Short Form-36 (SF-36) but results were not presented separately for men and women. Researchers at Northwestern University (Feinglass et al, 1996) found that ABI was significantly associated with measures of physical function. However, a relatively large 0.3 decrease in ABI corresponded to a small (5.6 points) decrease in physical function score. In The Netherlands, claudicants had

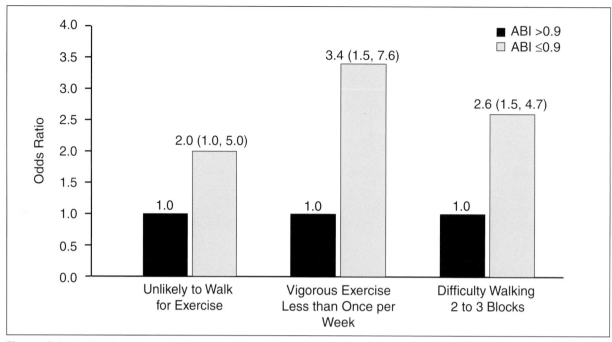

Figure. Relationship of peripheral arterial disease to measures of mobility among community-living women aged ≥65 years. ABI = ankle-brachial index. Data derived from Vogt et al, 1994.

physical function, role physical, and body pain scores on the SF-36 that were 30 to 40 points lower than age- and sex-matched controls from the general population (Bosch and Hunink, 1996). This represents a decrement of ~2 standard deviations in these measures. All other SF-36 scores (social function and emotional health) were also lower among the claudicants. [To date, the influence of asymptomatic PAD on quality of life has not been studied.]

IMPLICATIONS

Current evidence suggests that the burden of disease that lower extremity atherosclerosis imposes on elderly women will increase dramatically during the next 30 years. This increase will be driven primarily by the changing demographics of smoking behavior among women. Chronic cigarette smoking is the major risk factor for PAD with a population-attributable risk of 28% for smoking in women (Vogt et al, 1993a). Currently, ~13% of elderly women in this country smoke cigarettes, but across all age-groups almost one quarter of women are smokers. As middle-aged and younger smokers move into the postmenopausal years, the percentage of older women who smoke will increase substantially. These demographic data, as well as the projected increase in the number of elderly in this country, suggest that the impact of PAD on elderly women and on the US health care system will be a growing problem in the coming years. ∎

Key Points

● PAD occurs in 5% to 35% of postmenopausal women and is usually asymptomatic.

● PAD can best be detected in the physician's office by measurement of the ABI (ratio of systolic blood pressure in the posterior tibial artery to the brachial pressure). ABI is a measure of blood flow to the distal region of the lower extremity.

● The major risk factors for development of PAD and for disease progression are smoking, increasing age, hypertension, and diabetes.

● Whether symptomatic or asymptomatic, women with PAD have decreased life expectancy, increased likelihood of cardiovascular events, mobility limitations, and overall decreased quality of life.

● Demographic data on the smoking trends among women, as well as projected increases in the number of elderly in this country, suggest that the impact of PAD on the elderly population and the US health care system will increase dramatically during the next 30 years.

BIBLIOGRAPHY

Bosch JL, Hunink MGM. The relationship between descriptive and valuational quality-of-life measures in patients with intermittent claudication. Med Decis Mak 1996;16:217–25.

Bush TL. Epidemiology of cardiovascular disease in women. In: Redmond GP, ed. Lipids and Women's Health. New York: Springer-Verlag; 1991:6–20.

Carmelli D, Fabsitz RR, Swan GE, et al. Contribution of genetic and environmental influences to ankle-brachial blood pressure index in the NHLBI Twin Study. Am J Epidemiol 2000;151:452–8.

Criqui MH, Langer RD, Fronek A, et al. Mortality over a period of 10 years in patients with peripheral arterial disease. N Engl J Med 1992;326:381–6.

Farinon AM, Marbini A, Gemignani F, et al. Skeletal muscle and peripheral nerve changes caused by chronic arterial insufficiency. Clin Neuropathol 1984;3:240–52.

Feigelson HS, Criqui MH, Fronek A, et al. Screening for peripheral arterial disease: the sensitivity, specificity, and predictive value of noninvasive tests in a defined population. Am J Epidemiol 1994;140:526–34.

Feinglass J, McCarthy WJ, Slavensky R, et al. Effect of lower extremity blood pressure on physical functioning in patients who have intermittent claudication. J Vasc Surg 1996;24:503–12.

Fowkes FGR. Aetiology of peripheral atherosclerosis: smoking seems especially important. Br Med J 1989;298:405–6.

Guralnik J, Ferrucci L, Simonsick E, et al. Lower-extremity function in persons over the age of 70 years as a predictor of subsequent disability. N Engl J Med 1995;332:556–61.

Hooi JD, Stoffers HE, Knottnerus JA, van Ree JW. The prognosis of non-critical limb ischaemia: a systematic review of population-based evidence. Br J Gen Pract 1999;49:49–55.

Koopman JP, de Vries AC, de Weerd AW. Neuromuscular disorders in patients with intermittent claudication. Eur J Surg 1996;162:443–6.

Laghi Pasini FL, Pastorelli M, Beermann U, et al. Peripheral neuropathy associated with ischemic vascular disease of the lower limbs. Angiology 1996;47:569–77.

Manolio TA, Burke GL, Psaty BM, et al. Black-white differences in subclinical cardiovascular disease among older adults: the Cardiovascular Health Study. J Clin Epidemiol 1995;48:1141–52.

McDermott MM. Ankle brachial index as a predictor of outcomes in peripheral arterial disease. J Lab Clin Med 1999;133:33–40.

McDermott MM, Mehta S, Liu K, et al. Leg symptoms, the ankle-brachial index, and walking ability in patients with peripheral arterial disease. J Gen Intern Med 1999;14:173–81.

Newman AB, Shemanski L, Manolio TA, et al. Ankle-arm index as a predictor of cardiovascular disease and mortality in the Cardiovascular Health Study. Arterioscler Thromb Vasc Biol 1999;19:538–45.

Newman AB, Siscovick DS, Manolio TA, et al. Ankle-arm index as a marker of atherosclerosis in the Cardiovascular Health Study. Circulation 1993;88:837–45.

Newman AB, Sutton-Tyrrell K, Rutan GH, et al. Lower extremity arterial disease in elderly subjects with systolic hypertension. J Clin Epidemiol 1991;44:15–20.

Prineas RJ, Harland WR, Janzon L, Kannel W. Recommendations for use of non-invasive methods to detect atherosclerotic peripheral arterial disease in population studies. Circulation 1982;65:1561A–6A.

Psaty BM, Furberg CD, Kuller LH, et al. Isolated systolic hypertension and subclinical cardiovascular disease in the elderly. Initial findings from the Cardiovascular Health Study. JAMA 1992;268:1287–91.

Vogt MT, Cauley JA, Kuller LH, Hulley SB. Prevalence and correlates of lower extremity arterial disease in elderly women. Am J Epidemiol 1993a;137:559–68.

Vogt MT, Cauley JA, Kuller LH, Nevitt MC. Bone mineral density and blood flow to the lower extremities: the Study of Osteoporotic Fractures. J Bone Miner Res 1997;12:283–9.

Vogt MT, Cauley JA, Kuller LH, Nevitt MC. Functional status and mobility among elderly women with lower extremity arterial disease: the Study of Osteoporotic Fractures. J Am Geriatr Soc 1994;42:923–9.

Vogt MT, Cauley JA, Newman AB, et al. Decreased ankle/arm blood pressure index and mortality in elderly women. JAMA 1993b;270:465–9.

Vogt MT, Wolfson SK, Kuller LH. Lower extremity arterial disease and the aging process: a review. J Clin Epidemiol 1992;45:529–42.

Treatment and Outcomes of Peripheral Atherosclerosis in Women

Marie D. Gerhard-Herman, MD, MMSc
Medical Director
Vascular Diagnostic Laboratory
Brigham and Women's Hospital
Assistant Professor of Medicine
Harvard Medical School
Boston, Massachusetts

Catherine M. Wittgen, MD
Assistant Professor of Surgery
St. Louis University Hospital
St. Louis, Missouri

Objective: To understand the impact of gender on the prevalence, treatment, and outcome of PAD.

A single pink ribbon folded upon itself has become the cultural icon for women's health. This one image has raised awareness of a population at risk for the development of breast cancer, while the No. 1 killer of women goes largely unrecognized. In 1997, >40,000 women succumbed to breast cancer; however, during the same period, atherosclerosis was responsible for nearly 500,000 deaths (Mosca et al, 1997). Because many women and their health care providers underestimate the risk of atherosclerosis, it has been designated the "silent stalker" by the American Heart Association.

INFLUENCE OF GENDER ON INCIDENCE AND PREVALENCE OF PERIPHERAL ARTERIAL DISEASE

The phrase "you've come a long way, baby"— which was used in a cigarette advertising campaign—may now be an ironic commentary on the high prevalence of peripheral arterial disease (PAD) in women. By the year 2040, it is projected that >15% of the population will be women older than the age of 65 (Vogt et al, 1992). As these demographic changes occur, the previously observed patterns of PAD will also change. In the Framingham Study, the biennial incidence rate of intermittent claudication (IC) measured over a 20-year follow-up period was 3.5/1000 for women and 7.1/1000 for men (Kannel and McGee, 1985). Reported estimates of the prevalence of claudication range from 1.2% to 14.1% in women, compared with 2.2% to 14.4% in men, with an increasing incidence with age for both sexes (Schroll and Munck, 1981; Hale et al, 1988; Agner, 1981; Hughson et al, 1978).

Using objective measures of PAD such as the ankle-brachial index (ABI), 3% of women <60 years old and 20% >75 years of age had PAD (Criqui et al, 1985). The Edinburgh Artery Study found that 24.6% of the population 55 to 74 years of age had PAD as determined by an ABI <0.9. Men and women were affected almost equally (Fowkes et al, 1991). In the most recently published observational study, 35% of all women >65 years old were found to have an ABI <0.9 (McDermott et al, 2000). In addition, one third of women with abnormal ABIs reported claudication symptoms. Clearly, the population at risk for PAD will no longer be predominantly male.

Morbidity and Mortality

PAD is the distal manifestation of a systemic illness. Atherosclerotic changes occur in all blood vessels, and the cardiac manifestations of this disease are largely responsible for patient mortality. There is growing evidence that the outcome is worse for women following myocardial infarction (MI) and coronary artery bypass graft (Marrugat et al, 1998). The influence of gender on the morbidity and mortality from interventions for PAD is not well documented. Mortality from these procedures appears largely to be determined by the type of procedure performed and the comorbid risk factors of individual patients. In general, the finding of peripheral atherosclerosis identifies individuals at higher risk of cardiovascular mortality.

Cerebrovascular Disease

In a 10-year population study of the incidence of ischemic stroke, the incidence of transient ischemic attacks was found to be equal between both sexes (Lemesle et al, 1999). In another study, the type and location of cerebral arterial disease was studied by risk-factor analysis (Kim and Choi-Kwon, 1999). Diabetes mellitus was an independent risk factor for large vessel infarction in both sexes, and central obesity in women was associated with a higher incidence of basilar infarction. The influence of sex on the distribution of vascular disease was also noted in a longitudinal study of patients admitted to a community hospital, where men were found to be more likely than women to have intracranial disease (Wityk et al, 1996).

Abdominal Aortic Aneurysm

The one manifestation of vascular disease where women still appear to be a clear minority is aneurysmal disease. Several studies have documented that the overall incidence for abdominal aortic aneurysm (AAA) appears to be rising as the population ages. From 1971 through 1980, the overall incidence in the Olmstead County population was estimated to be 36.5 per 100,000 person-years (Melton et al, 1984). In an epidemiologic necropsy study from 1950 to 1984, the detection rate in men was 81 of 4155 of all autopsies performed for any reason (0.019%) and was 28 of 3142 (0.009%) in women (McFarlane, 1991).

Several attempts have been made to target specific populations at risk for the development of aneurysmal disease in an attempt to decrease patient mortality from unsuspected rupture and emergency surgery. In an ultrasound screening program for the first-degree relatives of patients with AAA, 25% of men were found to have unsuspected aneurysmal disease while only 6.9% of women were affected (Webster et al, 1991). A disparity between the sexes was also noted in a large screening study of hypertensive patients where aneurysms were detected in 4% of men but only 0.9% of women (Williams et al, 1996). Consequently, routine screening of hypertensive women was not recommended.

Presentation of Peripheral Atherosclerosis

At least 70% of individuals with peripheral atherosclerosis diagnosed by noninvasive testing will be asymptomatic (Figure). The symptoms of peripheral atherosclerosis can range from claudication, described

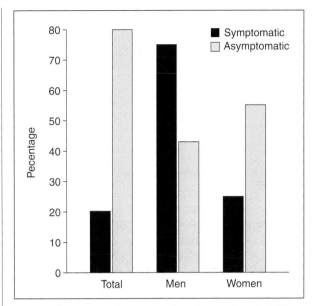

Figure. Percentage of symptomatic and asymptomatic PAD patients by gender.

as discomfort in the muscles of the legs with activity that disappears with rest, to critical limb ischemia. Recent literature suggests that asymptomatic cases are more prevalent in women (Stoffers et al, 1996). In addition, women with critical limb ischemia may be more likely to progress to limb loss. This raises the question of how women recognize and interpret symptoms of PAD.

Impact of Risk Factors

Diabetes mellitus and cigarette smoking are the strongest risk factors for the development of atherosclerosis (Kannel and McGee, 1985). In addition, hyperlipidemia and hypertension are clear risk factors for PAD. Menopause, or the cessation of ovarian function, is associated with increased rates of PAD. Noninvasive testing (eg, ABI) has demonstrated that severe PAD is associated with fasting glucose elevation in men but not in women. Despite this, diabetes mellitus appears to be a greater risk factor for symptomatic PAD in women. Glucose intolerance is associated with a 4-fold increase in risk in women for the development of atherosclerotic disease and only a 2.4-fold increase in risk in men. Even more disturbing is the observation that frank glycosuria increases the risk of PAD in women 8-fold. Together these findings suggest that diabetes may have a more profound impact on the symptomatic progression of peripheral atherosclerosis in women.

The impact of cigarette smoking on the incidence and progression of PAD in women cannot be overstated. As with diabetes, cigarette smoking has a profound impact on the progression of atherosclerosis,

Table. Estrogen Effects in Postmenopausal Women

Beneficial	Detrimental
• LDL, HDL, Lp(a)	• Triglycerides
• Osteoporosis	• Thromboemboli
• Menopausal symptoms	• Endometrial cancer
• Cardiovascular benefit not certain	• Breast cancer
	• Gallbladder disease

LDL = low-density lipoprotein; HDL = high-density lipoprotein; Lp(a) = lipoprotein(a).

the duration of symptomatic disease, and the extent of arterial stenoses. When women quit smoking, they have an improved prognosis as measured by stroke-free survival, decreased incidence of myocardial events, and limb salvage when compared with those who continue to smoke.

Over the past decades more women have become addicted to nicotine and, currently, the fastest growing population of cigarette smokers is teenage girls. As these women age, they will not only be more likely to develop PAD, they will present at an earlier age and with a different distribution of disease when compared with other nonsmoking women. Those who do smoke become symptomatic from PAD an average of 10 years earlier and appear to have more aortoiliac occlusive disease. In one series of patients presenting for aortoiliac revascularization, 93% were women. The most severe example of this accelerated PAD, the hypoplastic aortoiliac syndrome, has been described as "an entity peculiar to women" (Jernigan et al, 1983). This syndrome is characterized by disabling claudication occurring in women in their 30s and 40s, and angiography confirms marked narrowing of the distal aorta and severe stenosis of the iliac bifurcation.

Elevated total cholesterol has been associated with the subsequent development of PAD more often in women than in men (Vitale et al, 1990). The lipid abnormalities associated with highest risk are elevated triglycerides and low high-density lipoprotein cholesterol. Hypertension, specifically elevated systolic blood pressure (SBP), is another strong predictor of lower extremity arterial disease. While an elevated diastolic blood pressure (DBP) may warrant medical therapy for blood pressure control, it appears to be less predictive of future development of PAD than SBP. Other markers that may identify individuals at increased risk include an elevation in C-reactive protein. This marker was associated with subsequent development of claudication in men in the Physicians Health Study and cardiovascular events in women (Ridker et al, 2000).

The role of menopause, or cessation of ovarian function, in the development and progression of peripheral atherosclerosis is poorly understood. In the Heart and Estrogen/progestin Replacement Study (HERS), there was a trend toward less peripheral arterial procedures in the women in the active treatment arm, but no difference in cardiovascular events between the active and placebo treatments (Hulley et al, 1998). This study is reviewed extensively in the accompanying article by Dr. Bush (Table).

MEDICAL TREATMENT
Risk-Factor Reduction
Smoking cessation is associated with a significant decrease in the risk of cardiovascular events, but only a modest change in the symptoms of claudication and greater pain-free walking distance (PFWD) in women. Smoking cessation does, however, halt the PAD progression. Aggressive blood sugar control in the treatment of diabetes has also had similar results. In the United Kingdom Prospective Diabetes Study (UKPDS), men and women receiving intensive therapy had fewer MIs than those on diet therapy. Nonetheless, there was no change in limb loss or risk of PAD with intensive therapy (UKPDS Group, 1998). Clearly, the relationship of intensive blood glucose control to PAD symptoms is poorly understood.

In the trials of lipid lowering in coronary artery disease, it is clear that for every 10% reduction in total serum cholesterol there is a 15% decrease in cardiovascular risk. There are, however, few studies evaluating the impact of lipid-lowering therapy on claudication or the risk for PAD (Gould et al, 1998). In the Scandinavian Simvastatin Survival Study (4S), one of the few to assess the impact of this treatment, the risk of IC was decreased 40% in the active treatment group when compared with placebo.

Patients with hypertension are treated to reduce SBP to <130 mm Hg and DBP to <85 mm Hg to decrease cardiovascular risk (JNC-VI, 1997). Antihypertensive medications are not gender specific and can be used in the majority of women to provide adequate blood pressure control. Unfortunately, large decreases in SBP may cause large decreases in limb pressure and shorten PFWD (Solomon et al, 1991). In contrast, supervised exercise training and the resulting improved physical condition may reduce blood pressure and decrease claudication symptoms.

Pharmacologic Therapy
Cilostazol therapy results in significant improvement in PFWD and in ABI measurements (Dawson et al, 1998). Most importantly, the randomized controlled trials of

this medication have included 20% to 30% women. The inclusion of significant numbers of women in these trials has enabled clinicians to make appropriate recommendations without extrapolating data from exclusively male protocols. One note of caution is that phosphodiesterase inhibitors such as cilostazol should not be administered to any patient (including women) with heart failure, since increased mortality has been observed with other agents in this class.

Propionyl-L-carnitine, a drug which improves muscle metabolism, has been observed to improve PFWD and mean walking distance in men and is being evaluated for claudication in the United States (Brevetti et al, 1995). Significant numbers of women have not been included in these trials to date. Prostaglandins are also being studied in patients with claudication and with critical limb ischemia; results have been inconclusive. The intravenous preparations hold promise for these indications, but treatment is complicated by headache, flushing, myalgia, and gastrointestinal cramping.

Antiplatelet agents do not improve PFWD, but they have been observed to have a profound effect on cardiovascular events in men with claudication. The trials that demonstrated the secondary prevention of vascular disease by prolonged antiplatelet treatment were reviewed by the Antiplatelet Trialists' Collaboration (1988). Unfortunately, the majority of these trials excluded women, and the impact of these agents on cardiovascular events and the secondary prevention of PAD in women is still unknown. One study that included women is the randomized, blinded trial of Clopidogrel versus Aspirin in Patients at Risk of Ischemic Events (CAPRIE Steering Committee, 1996). In this study, the long-term administration of clopidogrel to patients with atherosclerotic vascular disease was slightly more effective than aspirin in reducing the combined cardiovascular endpoint. This suggests that both agents will decrease cardiovascular mortality in women with peripheral atherosclerosis.

THE IMPACT OF GENDER ON REVASCULARIZATION FOR PAD

The same issues which have plagued the understanding of medical treatment are also evident in the data on vascular reconstruction in female patients. Of all the series reported on carotid endarterectomy during the 1980s, none emphasized the impact of female gender on operative results. The number of women affected by this disease is unknown and may have limited past studies. Historical data document that fewer carotid endarterectomies have been performed on women (27% to 42%) despite the fact that the mean age was nearly identical to that of men

(Schneider et al, 1997). In the original North American Symptomatic Carotid Endarterectomy Trial (NASCET), approximately one third of all patients studied were female, but subgroup analysis was not performed to determine if the general conclusions from the study applied to women as well (NASCET Collaborators, 1991). The European Carotid Surgery Trial (ECST) collaborators did comment that when corrected for all other risk factors, multiple regression analysis found an association between female gender and operative risk (Rothwell et al, 1997). This was supported by some studies which indicated that the perioperative neurologic event rate was actually higher in women (Schneider et al, 1997; Rothwell et al, 1997). These results should be interpreted cautiously, however, since recent large series of carotid endarterectomy have demonstrated no impact of female gender on neurologic outcome (Maxwell et al, 1997; Hertzer et al, 1997, Sternbach and Perler, 2000; Ballotta et al, 2000).

Women do not appear to have greater prevalence of comorbid conditions than their male counterparts in these studies, and the proposed mechanism for the previously observed poor neurologic outcome has been hypothesized to be the smaller size of the female internal carotid artery (Schneider et al, 1997). This finding is supported by the higher restenosis rate which is also observed in female patients after primary arterial closure, and the recently observed better neurologic outcomes may reflect a more aggressive practice of routinely closing smaller internal carotid arteries with a patch angioplasty. Despite the paucity of long-term survival studies after carotid surgery, one series (Schneider et al, 1997) did demonstrate that the crude 5-year survival rate was actually better for women (95% versus 85%), while another documented equivalent life-table cumulative survival rates at 1, 3, 5, and 7 years (Ballotta et al, 2000).

Based on a 20-year review of the literature, there are no studies comparing the morbidity in men and women following elective surgery for AAA. This may be partially explained because of the low prevalence of this disease in women and the fact that women are not routinely included in screening studies. While the appropriateness of mandatory screening in women is debatable given the low prevalence of the disease, there is, more importantly, a marked discrepancy in the interventions offered to women who have an AAA. In a 10-year review of >40,000 patients, men were 1.8 times more likely to have abdominal aortic surgery when an aneurysm was present and 1.4 times more likely to have emergent surgery when an aneurysm ruptured (Katz et al, 1997).

This gender bias may be a reflection of the preoperative assessment of risk factors. Greater cardiac comorbidity has been found in female patients in one series (Pleumeekers et al, 1995), while another documented nearly identical cardiac risk factors in all patients with AAA regardless of gender (Starr et al, 1996). A retrospective review recently documented that <10% of women survive emergency surgery for ruptured AAAs compared with approximately 24% of men (Semmens et al, 2000). Regardless of the emergent nature of the procedure, women have 1.4 times greater mortality from any aortic surgery (Katz et al, 1997). Given the current knowledge of the impact of comorbidities, the etiology of this increased mortality is unclear.

This same discrepancy exists in survival data as well. Crude survival studies have found 5-year survival after AAA surgery to be approximately 72% for both men and women. Relative survival, correcting for age, gender, and other causes of mortality, found only an 88% survival for women and a 95% survival for men (Norman et al, 2000).

The impact of gender on arterial size is again a source of major controversy in aneurysmal disease as well. Despite the fact that women have smaller aortas than men, the definition of aortic aneurysm has never been changed to accommodate this difference. Every recommendation that women have been given regarding the timing of an intervention in relation to aortic diameter and rate of growth may subsequently be wrong. This was demonstrated in the United Kingdom Small Aneurysm Trial (Brown et al, 1999) where it was discovered that female aortas were 3 times more likely to rupture, and the average size at rupture was a full centimeter less than that observed in male patients (5 cm vs 6 cm).

Approximately one third of all distal revascularization procedures and amputations are performed on female patients. With other PAD manifestations, women undergoing these procedures have similar risk factors but are consistently 3 to 5 years older than their male counterparts. In a meta-analysis of the 16 population-based studies on limb ischemia, men were more likely to develop claudication symptoms and disease progression than women. The asymptomatic nature of noncritical limb ischemia in female patients did not reflect a benign disease process, however. Asymptomatic patients appeared to have the same increased risk for cardiovascular morbidity and mortality when compared to patients with IC (Hooi et al, 1999).

In all the literature published on the outcome of lower extremity revascularization and risk-factor analysis for graft failure, few have clearly addressed the issue of gender. Two studies of graft patency have identified female gender as an independent predictor of graft failure (Enzler et al, 1996; Magnant et al, 1993) while the remaining 2 were limited by a lack of multivariate statis-

tical methods and could only document a nonsignificant trend to decreased graft patency in female patients (Harris et al, 1993; Tunis et al, 1993).

Again, arterial size appeared to have a significant impact on the success of these reconstructions. In a randomized, multicenter, controlled trial comparing prosthetic above-knee femoropopliteal bypass grafting, the choice of smaller graft diameter was associated with a decrease in 5-year patency from 69.1% to 37.9% regardless of the type of synthetic graft chosen (Green et al, 2000). These data were not analyzed by gender, but the authors did comment that the previously reported adverse effect of gender on graft patency may be related to the increased use of smaller diameter grafts in female patients.

FUTURE RESEARCH

Based on the literature as outlined in this review, the current data raise more questions than they answer. Studies involving greater numbers of female patients would allow clinicians to make better evidence-based recommendations for risk-factor modification and intervention. The single most obvious issue that is unique to women is the role of hormone replacement therapy. Control of hypertension, hyperlipidemia, and diabetes mellitus seems to be inherently correct in arresting the progression of peripheral vascular disease. To what level any of these should be corrected in a female patient is also unknown.

Questions remain regarding quality-of-life assessments and research on whether the outcomes of commonly performed vascular reconstructions in women would also answer some of the most disturbing questions confronting surgeons today. Should women receive carotid endarterectomy for the same degree of stenosis as men? Does the absence of neurologic symptoms obviate the need for surgical intervention? Are the recommendations for AAA repair based on risk factors and size of the aneurysm appropriate for both genders? Is the patency of distal bypass grafts more adversely affected by small arterial size in women, and is operative intervention effective treatment?

As newer technologies become available (and even preferred by both patients and clinicians), the technical limitations imposed by the smaller size of most women become confounding factors. Currently, most women pose a challenge to the large-caliber delivery systems required for aortic stent graft placement. Surgeons are adapting this technology for small arteries with adjunctive procedures including retroperitoneal dissections to isolate the larger iliac vessels for successful deployment. One wonders, however, if these additional procedures defeat the minimally

Key Points

● The prevalence of vascular disease in female patients is greater than previously projected.

● Few trials have included women or have specifically addressed the issue of gender and how it impacts the outcome of PAD.

● Risk-factor modifications, including smoking cessation, control of hypertension, hyperlipidemia, and diabetes mellitus, are key to successful management.

● Aneurysmal disease as currently defined appears to develop less frequently in female patients.

● Newer technologies need to address the profile of the delivery systems for endovascular stents and grafts to increase the applicability to certain patients, such as women with small arteries.

invasive purpose of these grafts and eliminate the ease of recovery that patients have come to expect with this technology. Given the few women who develop these aneurysms, it may never be known if endovascular stents and grafts perform as well in smaller female arteries. In addition, the role of antiplatelet therapy in these patients may also remain unanswered.

CONCLUSIONS

The incidence of PAD is increasing as the population ages. More women will comprise this subgroup of older patients affected by vascular disease. While additional studies are needed on the impact of female gender on the outcome and treatment of PAD, some recommendations remain of paramount importance. Risk-factor modifications, including smoking cessation, control of hypertension, hyperlipidemia, and diabetes mellitus, remain the most important interventions clinicians perform. While estrogen loss contributes to the development of atherosclerosis, there is no clear role for replacement of sex hormones in peripheral atherosclerosis. Surgical reconstruction and endovascular technology can prevent neurologic events, achieve limb salvage in situations of occlusive disease, and prevent life-threatening rupture in the case of aneurysmal disease in both men and women. Whether the surgical approach or the timing of these procedures in the course of the disease need to be modified specifically for female patients remains to be further elucidated. ∎

BIBLIOGRAPHY

Agner E. Natural history of angina pectoris, possible previous myocardial infarction and intermittent claudication during the eighth decade. Acta Med Scand 1981;210:271–6.

Antiplatelet Trialists' Collaboration. Secondary prevention of vascular disease by prolonged antiplatelet treatment. Br Med J 1988;296:320–31.

Ballotta E, Renon L, Da Giau G, et al. Carotid endarterectomy in women: early and long-term results. Surgery 2000;127:264–71.

Brevetti G, Perna S, Sabba C, et al. Propionyl-L-carnitine in intermittent claudication: double-blind, placebo-controlled, dose titration, multicenter study. J Am Coll Cardiol 1995;26:1411–6.

Brown L, Powell J, United Kingdom Small Aneurysm Trial Participants. Risk factors for aneurysm rupture in patients kept under ultrasound surveillance. Ann Surg 1999;230:289–97.

CAPRIE Steering Committee. A randomised, blinded, controlled trial of Clopidogrel versus Aspirin in Patients at Risk of Ischaemic Events (CAPRIE). Lancet 1996;348:1329–39.

Criqui M, Fronek A, Barrett-Connor E, et al. The prevalence of peripheral arterial disease in a defined population. Circulation 1985;71:510–5.

Dawson DL, Cutler BS, Meissner MH, Strandness DE. Cilostazol has beneficial effects in treatment of intermittent claudication: results from a multicenter, randomized, prospective double-blind trial. Circulation 1998;98:678–86.

Enzler M, Ruoss M, Seifert B, Berger M. The influence of gender on the outcome of arterial procedures in the lower extremity. Eur J Vasc Endovasc Surg 1996;11:446–52.

Fowkes FGR, Housley E, Cawood EH, et al. Edinburgh Artery Study: prevalence of asymptomatic and symptomatic peripheral arterial disease in the general population. Int J Epidemiol 1991;20:384–92.

Gould AL, Rossouw JE, Santanello NC, et al. Cholesterol reduction yields clinical benefit: impact of statin trials. Circulation 1998;97:946–52.

Green RM, Abbott WM, Matsumoto T, et al. Prosthetic above-knee femoropopliteal bypass grafting: five-year results of a randomized trial. J Vasc Surg 2000;31:417–25.

The Sixth Report of the Joint National Committee on Prevention, Detection, Evaluation, and Treatment of High Blood Pressure. Arch Intern Med 1997; 157:2413–46.

Hale WE, Marks RG, May FE, et al. Epidemiology of intermittent claudication: evaluation of risk factors. Age Ageing 1988;17:57–60.

Harris E, Taylor L, Moneta G, Porter J. Outcome of infrainguinal arterial reconstruction in women. J Vasc Surg 1993;18:627–36.

Hertzer N, O'Hara P, Mascha E, et al. Early outcome assessment for 2228 consecutive carotid endarterectomy procedures: the Cleveland Clinic experience from 1989 to 1995. J Vasc Surg 1997;26:1–10.

Hooi JD, Stoffers HE, Knottnerus JA, van Ree JW. The prognosis of non-critical ischaemia: a systematic review of population-based evidence. Br J Gen Pract 1999;49:49–55.

Hughson WG, Mann JI, Garrod A. Intermittent claudication: prevalence and risk factors. Br Med J 1978;1:1379–81.

Hulley S, Grady D, Bush T, et al. Randomized trial of estrogen plus progestin for secondary prevention of coronary heart disease in postmenopausal women. Heart and Estrogen/progestin Replacement Study (HERS) Research Group. JAMA 1998;280:605–13.

Jernigan WR, Fallat ME, Hatfield DR. Hypoplastic aortoiliac syndrome: an entity peculiar to women. Surgery 1983;94:752–7.

Kannel WB, McGee DL. Update on some epidemiologic features of the Framingham Study. J Am Geriatr Soc 1985;33:13–8.

Katz DJ, Stanley JC, Zelenock GB. Gender differences in abdominal aortic aneurysm prevalence, treatment, and outcome. J Vasc Surg 1997;25:561–8.

Kim JS, Choi-Kwon S. Risk factors for stroke in different levels of cerebral arterial disease. Eur Neurol 1999;42:150–6.

Lemesle M, Milan C, Faivre J, et al. Incidence of trends of ischemic stroke and transient ischemic attacks in a well-defined French population from 1985 through 1994. Stroke 1999;30:371–7.

Magnant J, Cronenwett J, Walsh D, et al. The surgical treatment of infrainguinal arterial occlusive disease in women. J Vasc Surg 1993;17:67–78.

Marrugat J, Sala J, Masia R, et al. Mortality differences between men and women following first myocardial infarction. JAMA 1998;280:1405–9.

Maxwell J, Rutledge R, Covington D, et al. A statewide, hospital-based analysis of frequency and outcomes in carotid endarterectomy. Am J Surg 1997;174:655–61.

McDermott MM, Fried L, Simonsick E, et al. Asymptomatic peripheral arterial disease is independently associated with impaired lower extremity functioning: the women's health and aging study. Circulation 2000;101:1007–12.

McFarlane MJ. The epidemiologic necropsy for abdominal aortic aneurysm. JAMA 1991;265:2085–8.

Melton LJ, Bickerstaff LK, Hollier LH, et al. Changing incidence of abdominal aortic aneurysms: a population-based study. Am J Epidemiol 1984;120:379–86.

Mosca L, Manson J, Sutherland S, et al. AHA scientific statement on cardiovascular disease in women. Circulation 1997;96:2468–82.

Norman PE, Semmens JB, Lawrence-Brown M, Holman CD. The influence of gender on outcome following peripheral vascular surgery: a review. Cardiovasc Surg 2000; 8:111–5.

North American Symptomatic Carotid Endarterectomy Trial Collaborators. Beneficial effect of carotid endarterectomy in symptomatic patients with high-grade carotid stenosis. N Engl J Med 1991;325:445–53.

Pleumeekers H, Hoes A, van der Does E, et al. Aneurysms of the abdominal aorta in older adults. Am J Epidemiol 1995;142:1291–9.

Ridker PM, Hennekens CH, Buring JE, Rifai N. C-reactive protein and other markers of inflammation in the prediction of cardiovascular disease in women. N Engl J Med 2000;342:836–43.

Rothwell P, Slattery J, Warlow C. Clinical and angiographic predictors of stroke and death from carotid endarterectomy: a systematic review. Br Med J 1997;315:1571–7.

Schneider J, Droste J, Golan J. Carotid endarterectomy in women versus men: patient characteristics and outcomes. J Vasc Surg 1997;25:890–8.

Schroll M, Munck O. Estimation of peripheral arteriosclerotic disease by ankle blood pressure measurements in a population study of 60-year-old men and women. J Chronic Dis 1981;34:261–9.

Semmens J, Norman P, Lawrence-Brown M, Holman C. The influence of gender on the outcome of ruptured abdominal aortic aneurysm. Br J Surg 2000; 87:191–4.

Solomon SA, Ramsey LE, Yeo WW, et al. Beta blockade and intermittent claudication: a placebo controlled trial of atenolol, nifedipine and their combination. Br Med J 1991;6810:1100–04.

Starr JE, Hertzer NR, Mascha EJ, et al. Influence of gender on cardiac risk and survival in patients with infrarenal aortic aneurysms. J Vasc Surg 1996; 23:870–80.

Sternbach Y, Perler BA. The influence of female gender on the outcome of carotid endarterectomy: a challenge to the ACAS findings. Surgery 2000; 127:272–5.

Stoffers HE, Rinkens PE, Kester AD, et al. The prevalence of asymptomatic and unrecognized peripheral arterial occlusive disease. Int J Epidemiol 1996; 25:282–90.

Tunis S, Bass E, Klag M, Steinberg E. Variation in the utilization of procedures for treatment of peripheral arterial disease. Arch Intern Med 1993;153:991–8.

United Kingdom Prospective Diabetes Study (UKPDS) Group. Effect of intensive blood-glucose control with metformin on complications in overweight patients with type 2 diabetes. Lancet 1998;352:854–5.

Vitale E, Zuliani G, Baroni L, et al. Lipoprotein abnormalities in patients with extra-coronary arteriosclerosis. Atherosclerosis 1990;81:95–102.

Vogt MT, Wolfson SK, Kuller LH. Lower extremity arterial disease and the aging process: a review. J Clin Epidemiol 1992;45:529–42.

Webster MW, Ferrell RE, St. Jean PL, et al. Ultrasound screening of first-degree relatives of patients with an abdominal aortic aneurysm. J Vasc Surg 1991;13:9–13.

Williams IM, Hughes OD, Townsend E, et al. Prevalence of abdominal aortic aneurysm in a hypertensive population. Ann R Coll Surg Engl 1996;78:501–4.

Wityk RJ, Lehman D, Klag M, et al. Race and sex differences in the distribution of cerebral atherosclerosis. Stroke 1996;27:1974–80.

Overview of HERS

David E. Bush, MD
Assistant Professor of Medicine
Director, Cardiac Catheterization Laboratory
Johns Hopkins Bayview Medical Center
Baltimore, Maryland

Objective: To review HERS, its major findings, and significance for use of HRT in women with advanced atherosclerotic disease.

Many observational studies have shown lower rates of cardiovascular events in women treated with postmenopausal hormone replacement therapy (HRT) compared with those who were not treated. The Heart and Estrogen/Progestin Replacement Study (HERS) was the first published, randomized, clinical trial designed to determine if treatment with estrogen/progestin reduced the risk of coronary events in postmenopausal women with established atherosclerotic coronary artery disease (CAD). Despite an 11% reduction in low-density lipoprotein cholesterol (LDL-C) and a 10% higher high-density lipoprotein cholesterol (HDL-C) in the active treatment group, there were no differences between active treatment and placebo in cardiovascular events (including nonfatal myocardial infarction [MI], coronary heart disease [CHD] death, unstable angina [UA], coronary revascularization, congestive heart failure [CHF], symptomatic peripheral arterial disease [PAD], stroke, and transient ischemic attack [TIA]). However, a difference in the pattern of risk was noted over the 4 years of the study. In the first year, a 50% higher risk of events was noted in the hormone-treated group relative to placebo. That risk decreased over time, and in the last 3 to 4 years, the risk was 25% lower in the hormone-treated group compared with placebo. No explanation for this finding has been put forth. The results of HERS do not support the general use of estrogen/progestin for the secondary prevention of coronary disease in women. Other studies are required to determine whether HRT has a role in the primary prevention of atherosclerosis and whether different formulations of hormones will show similar or different risk patterns.

BACKGROUND

HERS was the first randomized study of HRT in postmenopausal women for the secondary prevention of coronary events and other atherosclerotic vascular events (Hulley et al, 1998). Prior to HERS, a number of observational studies suggested women with a history of hormone use, either estrogen alone or estrogen/progestin combinations, had decreased rates of cardiovascular events compared with women who did not use HRT (Brett and Madans, 1995; Bush et al, 1987; Henderson et al, 1991; Sullivan et al, 1990). Meta-analyses of these observational trials found 35% to 40% lower rates of cardiac events among women with a history of hormone use compared with those without (Grady et al,

1992; Stampfer and Colditz, 1991). In particular, studies involving women with established CAD suggested a significant effect in the secondary prevention of atherosclerotic cardiovascular events (Sullivan et al, 1990; Stampfer and Colditz, 1991).

Other lines of evidence suggested HRT would have a beneficial effect on cardiovascular events. Estrogen, and estrogen and progestin, have been shown to prevent LDL-C accumulation in coronary arteries in nonhuman primate experimental studies. Oral estrogen therapy is associated with a decrease in LDL-C and an increase in HDL-C (Miller et al, 1991; PEPI Investigators, 1995). High levels of LDL-C are associated with an increased cardiovascular risk and low levels of HDL-C may be a more potent risk factor in women than in men. Thus, the favorable effects on plasma lipids associated with estrogen would be predicted to reduce the rate of adverse cardiovascular events in women. Animal studies have also suggested that the beneficial vascular effects of estrogen may be attenuated by the addition of progestin (Adams et al, 1997). However, observational studies in women generally found similar risk profiles among women taking estrogen alone, and estrogen and progestin, when compared with nonusers of HRT (Nabulsi et al, 1993; Psaty et al, 1994).

POSSIBLE MECHANISMS

The mechanism by which estrogen may be associated with decreased cardiovascular risk is a subject of debate and putative mechanisms are not confined to effects on plasma lipids (de Lignieres, 1993). Only 25% to 50% of the 50% to 80% risk reduction seen in studies examining women with established CAD would be predicted by the lipid effects of hormone therapy alone (Bush et al, 1983; Miller, 1994). This degree of risk reduction suggests that estrogen might lower risk of CAD events by nonlipid-mediated mechanisms. Estrogen has antioxidant properties and beneficial effects on arterial vasoreactivity, which would be predicted to decrease the risk for cardiovascular events (Banka, 1996; Bush et al, 1998). Elevations in fibrinogen and factor VII have been associated with cardiovascular disease. Women taking estrogen or estrogen and progestin in the Atherosclerosis Risk in Communities Study (ARIC) had lower levels of fibrinogen compared with nonusers (Nabulsi et al, 1993). This study also found that factor VII levels were no different among women taking estrogen with progestin but were higher among women taking estrogen alone than non-HRT users. Several investigators have shown that post-menopausal estrogen replacement therapy is associated with a reduction in plasminogen activator inhibitor-1 levels consistent with enhanced fibrinolysis (Koh et al, 1997). Several recent publications have focused on the association between biomarkers for inflammation and CAD. The data from the Women's Health Study indicate that elevated levels of highly sensitive C-reactive protein (CRP) identify individuals at high risk for cardiovascular events over 3 years of follow-up (Ridker et al, 1998). Cross-sectional study data demonstrate that CRP levels are increased in women on HRT compared with those not receiving HRT and a randomized study has shown that estrogen 0.625 mg daily increased CRP by 84% after 6 months (Ridker et al, 1999; Walsh et al, 2000).

The data compiled from observational studies and studies of surrogate markers of cardiovascular risk

(effects on lipids, fibrinogen, and vasomotor function) have, on balance, suggested beneficial effects of hormone replacement. Despite the significant differences in cardiovascular risk found in observational studies, these studies could not fully account for other possible differences between HRT participants and nonparticipants. Some studies have suggested that women who use HRT generally have higher levels of physical activity, lower body mass index, and are better educated (Barrett-Connor, 1991; Grodstein et al, 1996). Thus, it is possible that such biases could account for some of the apparent benefits of HRT. However, these biases could only be controlled by a randomized clinical trial.

HERS

HERS was a randomized, double-blind, placebo-controlled trial of estrogen/progestin in post-menopausal women <80 years old with intact uteri designed to determine whether HRT would result in low rates of cardiovascular events in women with established CAD. Established CAD was defined as an MI, coronary artery bypass graft (CABG), percutaneous coronary revascularization, or a >50% stenosis on coronary angiography. The study enrolled 2763 women who were randomized to receive either daily conjugated equine estrogen 0.625 mg with medroxyprogesterone acetate 2.5 mg or placebo. The primary outcome events were nonfatal MI or CHD death. Secondary cardiovascular outcomes included coronary revascularization procedures (CABG or percutaneous transluminal coronary angioplasty), hospitalization for UA, CHF, stroke, TIA, resuscitated cardiac arrest, and PAD.

After a mean of 4.1 years of follow-up, the principal finding in HERS was that there were no differences in the rate of primary or secondary cardiovascular events between hormone-treated and placebo groups. There were 179 primary events in the HRT group and 172 events in the placebo group (relative hazard 0.99; 95% CI, 0.81 to 1.22) (Hulley et al, 1998; Hulley et al, 1999). The event rate of specified secondary endpoints including UA, coronary revascularization, CHF, peripheral vascular revascularization, stroke, and TIA did not differ between the hormone treatment and placebo groups. No significant differences in the rate of cancer or bone fractures were noted between the groups either, although gallbladder disease was more frequent in the HRT group.

The annual incidence of peripheral arterial events was 2.9% (Hsia et al, 2000). Two hundred thirteen women experienced peripheral arterial events, which were distributed as follows: 46.0% extremity, 38.3% carotid, 7.1% aortic, 6.8% mesenteric/renal, and 1.9%

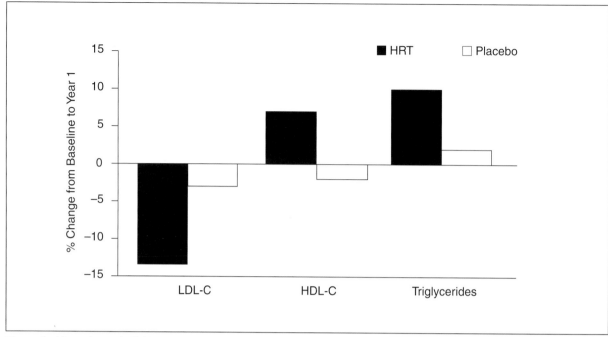

Figure 1. Mean change in lipid profile between baseline and 1 year. JAMA 1998;280:605–13.

cerebral. There were 99 women who had peripheral arterial events in the HRT group and 114 in the placebo group (relative hazard 0.87; 95% CI, 0.66 to 1.14, P = ns). Unlike the pattern seen for primary CHD events, no early increase in the risk of peripheral vascular events was present with active treatment.

HRT compliance was low: 82% in the hormone group by the end of 1 year, and 75% by the end of the third year; 91% and 81% for years 1 and 3 respectively in the placebo group. Despite compliance issues, HRT was associated with favorable trends in lipid profiles. After 1 year, the HRT group had a 14% decline in LDL-C whereas the placebo group had only a 3% decline (P <0.001). Similar divergence was seen in the response of HDL-C with the HRT-treated group showing an 8% increase, whereas the placebo group had a 2% decrease from baseline (P <0.001). Over the same period, triglycerides increased by 10% in the HRT group and by 2% in the placebo group (Figure 1).

RECONCILING HERS WITH OBSERVATIONAL STUDIES

How can the null results of HERS be reconciled with the results of the observational studies and the favorable effect HRT had on lipid profiles within HERS? Several possible explanations have been offered for the lack of benefit of HRT in HERS compared with the significant risk reduction suggested by most observational studies. One possibility is that selection bias in

observational studies overestimated the beneficial effects of HRT. This overestimate could have been due to significant behavioral differences between the 2 groups. Though this undoubtedly could be a factor, it seems unlikely to be the sole explanation given the mechanistic and lipid studies, which have also suggested a cardiovascular benefit for HRT.

Several other factors distinguish the women who participated in HERS from those studied in most observational trials. HERS participants tended to be older and therefore may have had more advanced atherosclerotic disease. It has also been suggested that the progestin used in HERS could have attenuated some of the cardiovascular benefit of estrogen. While animal studies have suggested such a mechanism, observational studies in women have generally found similar degrees of risk reduction associated with estrogen/progestin combinations as with estrogen alone.

Another hypothesis that has been advanced for the discordant results between HERS and observational studies of HRT is that the response to HRT may have been biphasic with an early increase in risk and a later decrease in risk (Herrington, 1999). This pattern of response is supported by the distribution of primary cardiovascular outcome events over the course of the trial. During the first 4 months of the trial, the highest relative hazard of 2.3 was observed for the HRT group, and was 1.5 by the second 4 months. For the entire first year for the HRT group, the relative hazard was 1.52, but

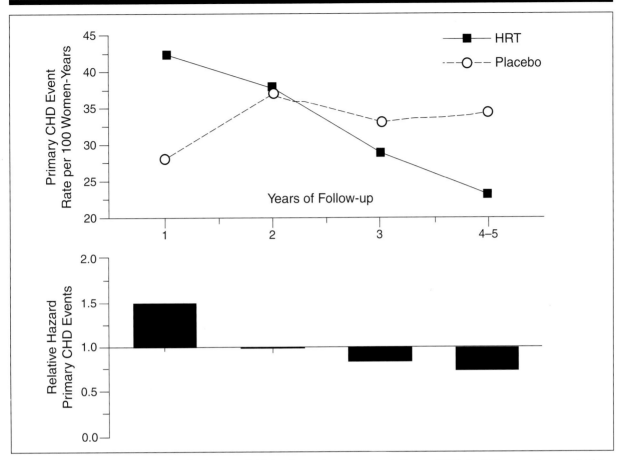

Figure 2. Rate of primary events (nonfatal myocardial infarction and coronary heart disease [CHD] death) by year since randomization. Primary event rate in the hormone treatment group was highest in the first year and lowest in the last years of follow-up. The relative hazard rate for each year is plotted in the lower panel. The relative hazard for those randomized to hormone replacement therapy (HRT) was higher than placebo in the first year but lower than placebo in the last years of follow-up. The P value for the relative hazard time trend is 0.03.

by the second year of treatment it was equal to placebo. In years 3 and 4, HRT had a lower relative hazard rate compared with placebo (0.85 in year 3 and 0.75 for years 4 and 5). The P value for the time trend was 0.03 and appeared largely due to lower rates of nonfatal MI in the HRT group over time (Figure 2).

The HRT group did have higher rates of venous thrombotic events than placebo: there were 25 deep venous thromboses and 11 cases of pulmonary embolism compared with 8 and 4, respectively in the placebo group (P = 0.002). In women taking oral contraceptives, individuals with the mutation of factor V Leiden have much higher rates of venous thrombotic events. It is possible that other genetic variations of the coagulation system or platelet receptors are associated with a high risk of cardiovascular events for women taking HRT. If a small population of women were at substantially higher risk than the rest of the participants

and this high-risk subset had a higher attrition rate from the study, an overall pattern of early harm and later benefit could be observed.

Another explanation of an apparent pattern of early risk and later benefit would be alterations in risk for the entire HRT group over time. The rate of venous thrombotic events did not show a significant time trend over the course of HERS. If HRT had a prothrombotic effect that was also responsible for the primary CHD events, then that risk, too, may have been constant. In contrast, the beneficial effects of HRT on atherosclerosis via plasma lipids—by raising HDL-C and reducing LDL-C—would not be expected to be immediately apparent. If HRT users experienced an immediate increase in risk due to an HRT effect on thrombosis or by destabilizing susceptible plaques that were only later offset by retarding atherosclerosis, a pattern of increased risk followed by decreased risk could result.

Key Points

● Postmenopausal women with established CAD who took estrogen/progestin did not have a lower rate of cardiovascular events compared with placebo.

● Compared with placebo, estrogen/progestin treatment resulted in a net 11% reduction in LDL-C and a 10% increase in HDL-C after 1 year.

● Compared with placebo, there were high rates of thromboembolic events among women taking estrogen/progestin.

● There were no differences in the rates of cancer of the breast, endometrium, or other organs between the estrogen/progestin and placebo groups.

● Several possible explanations have been offered for the fact that HERS results were not concordant with those of observational studies. The most intriguing possibility could be that the risk of cardiovascular events was increased in the first year due to increased thrombosis or HRT-induced adverse events, but the risk was attenuated and ultimately reduced in the later years of the trial, as the beneficial effects of HRT on lipids or other factors had time to take effect.

HERS IN PERSPECTIVE

Caution must be exercised in attributing significance to time pattern of CHD events in HERS. This analysis was not prespecified in the study design and could be a result of chance, although there are biologically plausible hypotheses that could explain this pattern. A final interpretation of this finding will have to await the results of additional studies. Most HERS participants have also agreed to be included in a 2-year extension of their assigned treatment. This may help clarify whether the apparent trend of early risk and later benefit will be sustained.

Other randomized trials evaluating cardiovascular outcomes in women receiving postmenopausal hormone therapy are currently in progress. Several are using coronary angiographic surrogate endpoints including the Women's Angiographic Vitamin and Estrogen (WAVE) trial, Estrogen Replacement and Atherosclerosis (ERA) trial, and Women's Estrogen/Progestin and Lipid Lowering Hormone

Atherosclerosis Regression Trial (WELL-HART) that will be completed within the next 2 years. The Estrogen and Graft Atherosclerosis Research (EAGAR) trial is a randomized angiographic trial of HRT in women with bypass grafts. The Women's Health Initiative Randomized Trial will study the effects of both estrogen/progestin in women with an intact uterus, as well as the effects of unopposed estrogen in women who have had a hysterectomy. The study has a target enrollment of 27,500 women with a planned follow-up of 9 years. A report scheduled in 2005 will provide information on the effect of HRT in primary and secondary prevention of CAD. These randomized trials will add considerably to determining the role of HRT in the management of women with atherosclerosis.

HERS data do not support the use of HRT for the secondary prevention of CHD events. However, HERS results contrast with a large body of observational study data. HERS is the first of a number of randomized, clinical trials assessing HRT for secondary prevention of cardiac atherosclerotic events. It is not known whether these findings are applicable to the primary prevention of CHD events and peripheral atherosclerosis. It is also not known whether different HRT regimens such as unopposed estrogen, estrogens other than conjugated equine estrogens, or estrogen with a different formulation of progestin will have similar results. Interventions that have proven efficacy in the secondary prevention of CHD events include aspirin, beta-blockers, lipid-lowering agents, and smoking cessation. On the basis of the available data, these agents should remain the primary modes of treatment for the secondary prevention of CHD. ■

BIBLIOGRAPHY

Adams MR, Register TC, Golden DL, et al. Medroxyprogesterone acetate antagonizes inhibitory effects of conjugated equine estrogens on coronary artery atherosclerosis. Arterioscler Thromb Vasc Biol 1997;17:217–21.

Banka CL. High density lipoprotein and lipoprotein oxidation. Curr Opin Lipidology 1996;7:139–42.

Barrett-Connor E. Postmenopausal estrogen and prevention bias. Ann Intern Med 1991;115:455–6.

Brett KM, Madans JH. Long-term survival after coronary heart disease. Comparisons between men and women in a national sample. Ann Epidemiol 1995;5:25–32.

Bush DE, Jones CE, Bass KM, et al. Estrogen replacement reverses endothelial dysfunction in postmenopausal women. Am J Med 1998;104:552–8.

Bush TL, Barrett-Connor E, Cowan LD, et al. Cardiovascular mortality and noncontraceptive use of estrogen in women: results from the Lipid Research Clinics Program Follow-Up Study. Circulation 1987;75:1102–9.

Bush TL, Cowan LD, Barrett-Connor E, et al. Estrogen use and all-cause mortality. Preliminary results from the Lipid Research Clinics Program Follow-Up Study. JAMA 1983;249:903–6.

de Lignieres B. The case for a nonplasma lipoprotein etiology of reduced vascular risk in estrogen replacement therapy. Curr Opin Obstet Gynecol 1993;5:389–95.

Grady D, Rubin SM, Petitti DB, et al. Hormone therapy to prevent disease and prolong life in post-menopausal women. Ann Intern Med 1992;117:1016–37.

Grodstein F, Stampfer MJ, Manson JE, et al. Post-menopausal estrogen and progestin use and the risk of cardiovascular disease. N Engl J Med 1996;335:453–61.

Henderson BE, Paganini-Hill A, Ross RK. Decreased mortality in users of estrogen replacement therapy. Arch Intern Med 1991;151:75–8.

Herrington DM. The HERS trial results: paradigms lost? Heart and Estrogen/Progestin Replacement Study. Ann Intern Med 1999;131:463–66.

Hsia J, Simon J, Lin F, et al. Effect of estrogen and progestin on clinical peripheral arterial disease in women with coronary heart disease. J Am Coll Cardiol 2000;35:324A.

Hulley S, Grady D, Bush T, et al. Randomized trial of estrogen plus progestin for secondary prevention of coronary heart disease in postmenopausal women. Heart and Estrogen/Progestin Replacement Study (HERS) Research Group. JAMA 1998;280:605–13.

Hulley S, Grady D, Vittinghoff E, et al. Hormone replacement therapy for secondary prevention of coronary artery disease. JAMA 1999;281:796–7.

Koh KK, Mincemoyer R, Bui MN, et al. Effects of hormone-replacement therapy on fibrinolysis in postmenopausal women. N Engl J Med 1997;336:683–90.

Miller VT. Lipids, lipoproteins, women and cardiovascular disease. Atherosclerosis 1994;108(Suppl):S73–S82.

Miller VT, Muesing RA, LaRosa JC, et al. Effects of conjugated equine estrogen with and without three different progestogens on lipoproteins, high-density lipoprotein subfractions, and apolipoprotein A-I. Obstet Gynecol 1991;77:235–40.

Nabulsi AA, Folsom AR, White A, et al. Association of hormone-replacement therapy with various cardiovascular risk factors in postmenopausal women. The Atherosclerosis Risk in Communities Study Investigators. N Engl J Med 1993;328:1069–75.

PEPI Investigators. Effects of estrogen or estrogen/progestin regimens on heart disease risk factors in postmenopausal women. The Postmenopausal Estrogen/Progestin Interventions (PEPI) Trial. The Writing Group for the PEPI Trial. JAMA 1995;273:199–208.

Psaty BM, Heckbert SR, Atkins D, et al. The risk of myocardial infarction associated with the combined use of estrogens and progestins in postmenopausal women. Arch Intern Med 1994;154:1333–9.

Ridker PM, Buring JE, Shih J, et al. Prospective study of C-reactive protein and the risk of future cardiovascular events among apparently healthy women. Circulation 1998;98:731–3.

Ridker PM, Hennekens CH, Rifai N, et al. Hormone replacement therapy and increased plasma concentration of C-reactive protein. Circulation 1999;100:713–16.

Stampfer MJ, Colditz GA. Estrogen replacement therapy and coronary heart disease: a quantitative assessment of the epidemiologic evidence. Prev Med 1991;20:47–63.

Sullivan JM, Vander ZR, Hughes JP, et al. Estrogen replacement and coronary artery disease. Effect on survival in postmenopausal women. Arch Intern Med 1990;150:2557–62.

Walsh BW, Paul S, Wild RA, et al. The effects of hormone replacement therapy and raloxifene on C-reactive protein and homocysteine in healthy post-menopausal women: a randomized, controlled trial. J Clin Endocrinol Metab 2000;85:214–18.

The American Journal of Medicine®

CONTINUING EDUCATION SERIES

AN OFFICE-BASED APPROACH TO THE DIAGNOSIS AND TREATMENT OF PERIPHERAL ARTERIAL DISEASE

PART VIII: PAD and Risk-Factor Management

SERIES EDITOR
ALAN T. HIRSCH, MD
GUEST EDITOR
JONATHAN L. HALPERIN, MD

Jointly sponsored by
The Excerpta Medica Office of Continuing Medical Education and the Society for Vascular Medicine and Biology

Introduction and Overview

Jonathan L. Halperin, MD
Robert and Harriet Heilbrunn Professor of Medicine
* (Cardiology)*
Mount Sinai School of Medicine
Director, Cardiology Clinical Services
The Zena and Michael A. Wiener Cardiovascular
* Institute*
Mount Sinai Medical Center
New York, New York

Alan T. Hirsch, MD
Director, Vascular Medicine Program
Minnesota Vascular Diseases Center
University of Minnesota Medical School
Minneapolis, Minnesota

This Continuing Education Series is based on the premise, shared by the Society for Vascular Medicine and Biology, that clinicians can recognize and manage patients with peripheral arterial disease (PAD), especially when supported by dissemination of accurate information about the disease and its comorbidities. Previous monographs in this series have provided a comprehensive overview of the pathophysiology, natural history, diagnostic evaluation, and comprehensive management, as well as an exploration of the possible gender-based differences of PAD. Beyond concern for the affected extremity, however, there remains a pressing need for more widespread delivery of effective strategies to prevent the progression and complications of systemic atherosclerosis to improve the prognosis for both life and limb. These considerations have led to the creation of this monograph, which is devoted to a review of atherosclerotic risk factors and office-based risk-factor modification in patients with PAD.

The single most important risk factor predisposing patients to PAD is tobacco smoking. Sheri L. Halverson, MPH, has collaborated with series editor Alan T. Hirsch, MD, to provide the practitioner with a practical approach to tackling this difficult problem. Smoking accelerates the progression of PAD, adversely affects the results of limb revascularization procedures, and increases rates of amputation, myocardial infarction (MI), and stroke in patients with PAD, dramatically reducing survival. The authors present strong evidence that shows how smoking cessation improves prognosis and outline an effective strategy for intervention in smokers with PAD that can easily be implemented in the office setting. Drs. Halverson and Hirsch reinforce what is increasingly becoming known among physicians who treat tobacco addiction: namely, that the most successful interventions are those that involve repeated contacts by various members of a health care team,

especially when those interventions can be specifically linked with a critical event, that is, the diagnosis of PAD. They discuss the available adjunctive medications to facilitate smoking cessation and the issues of professional reimbursement that can be used to advantage in bringing smoking cessation programs into the mainstream of medical care. Perhaps most importantly, this article brings into focus an increasingly important role for primary care physicians as advocates for a proven life-saving strategy.

Francis J. Kazmier, MD, FACP, FACC, then takes on the frustrating problem of diabetes, the second most important risk factor contributing to PAD. Dr. Kazmier notes that almost 80% of patients with diabetes mellitus die of some form of heart or blood vessel disease. The emergence within the past few years of solid evidence indicating the direct benefit of vigorous metabolic control to the cardiovascular outcome of diabetic patients brings a new mandate to the care of patients with this chronic disease. Dr. Kazmier points out that we have learned a great deal about which management approaches are best suited to patients with PAD.

John P. Cooke, MD, PhD, and Roberta K. Oka, RN, DNSc, address the problem of dyslipidemia. Although 90% of PAD patients have dyslipidemia, because PAD is undiagnosed in a majority of cases, many patients who would benefit from lipid-lowering therapy are not receiving it. The risk of PAD increases approximately 10% for every 10-mg/dL increase in total cholesterol concentration, and nearly all PAD patients are candidates for some form of lipid-reduction therapy. Reducing low-density lipoprotein cholesterol with a 3-hydroxy-3-methylglutaryl coenzyme A reductase-inhibitor drug of the statin class is one of the most effective ways to lower mortality in patients with atherosclerosis. In refractory cases, a stepped-care approach is advocated, in which niacin or a bile-acid binding resin such as cholestyramine is added when statin therapy alone is insufficient.

Finally, Killian Robinson, MD, summarizes the role of other risk factors, such as elevated levels of lipoprotein(a), triglycerides, low levels of high-density lipoprotein cholesterol, and hyperhomocysteinemia, many of which play an even more important role in the progression of atherosclerosis in limb arteries than in the coronary or cerebral vessels. Dr. Robinson notes that the role of chronic inflammation as an etiologic factor in the development of atherosclerosis is still unfolding, but this holds the promise that an even broader therapeutic assault on systemic vascular disease may be possible in the near future.

We hope this comprehensive approach to the management of atherosclerotic risk factors in patients with PAD will lead to effective therapeutic interventions aimed beyond the problems of regional circulation to reduce the risk of MI and stroke as well as improve and lengthen the lives of PAD patients. To accomplish this, the physician must see each modifiable risk factor as an opportunity for intervention that may pay lasting dividends over a patient's lifetime. ∎

Tobacco and Peripheral Arterial Disease: Pathogenesis of PAD and the Management of Tobacco Addiction

Sheri L. Halverson, MPH
Tobacco Research Coordinator
Vascular Medicine Program
Minnesota Vascular Diseases Center
University of Minnesota Medical School
Minneapolis, Minnesota

Alan T. Hirsch, MD
Director, Vascular Medicine Program
Minnesota Vascular Diseases Center
University of Minnesota Medical School
Minneapolis, Minnesota

Objective: To review the scientific evidence associating tobacco use with development and progression of PAD and to outline effective strategies for an office-based intervention for smokers with PAD.

Tobacco use is the single most important cause of peripheral arterial disease (PAD). Multiple investigations have documented that tobacco: (1) is the strongest risk factor for the development of PAD, (2) increases the rate of progression of PAD, (3) reduces the success of limb revascularization procedures, (4) markedly increases amputation rates, (5) increases rates of myocardial infarction (MI) and stroke in patients with PAD, and (6) profoundly decreases patient survival. Therefore, it is imperative that all health care professionals provide therapeutic efforts to reduce tobacco use and promote long-term abstinence in patients with PAD.

SMOKING AND ATHEROGENESIS

Tobacco use is known to damage the vascular endothelium, promote intravascular coagulation, and accelerate the progression of atherosclerosis (Hirsch et al, 1997; McGill, 1990; Hutchinson, 1998). Despite all that has been learned about tobacco's adverse effects on blood vessels, the relative contribution of the many adverse substances in tobacco smoke on blood vessels remains obscure. Cigarette smoke contains as many as 4000 constituents that could act individually or synergistically to promote atherogenesis; therefore, it is likely that multiple mechanisms elicit vascular damage.

Tobacco increases the adherence of circulating monocytes to the vascular endothelium (especially CD11b on circulating monocytes and intercellular adhesion molecule-1 and endothelial-leukocyte adhesion molecule-1 on endohelial cells), fosters migration of these adherent monocytes into the subendothelial spaces, and increases the development of foam cells (Kalra et al, 1994). Cigarette smoking also inhibits reverse cholesterol transport via inhibition of lecithin-cholesterol acyltransferase, and this may adversely influence the metabolism of cholesterol associated with low-density lipoprotein (LDL) levels (Chen and Loo, 1995). Since cigarette smokers have higher LDL and lower high-density lipoprotein (HDL) cholesterol levels than nonsmokers, and the susceptibility of LDL to oxidation is greater in smokers, this inhibition of reverse cholesterol transport may be particularly important. In animals exposed to tobacco smoke, the area of damaged atherosclerotic endothelium is increased in a dose-dependent manner.

Tobacco smoke is an oxidant stress and impedes the activity of endothelial-derived nitric oxide synthase; both effects promote atherogenesis. Once atherosclerotic plaques form and impede the natural antithrombotic functions of the endothelium, smoking continues to play a key prothrombotic role. Smoking augments platelet-dependent thrombosis via increases in adeno-

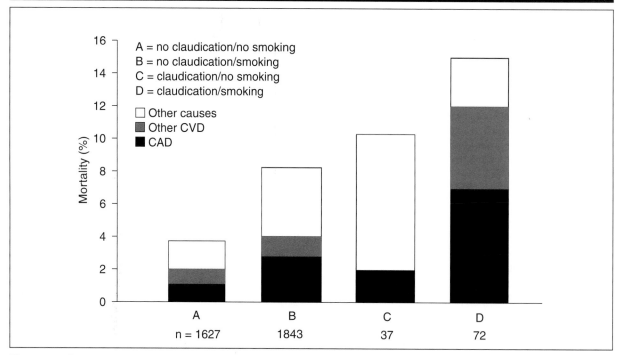

Figure 1. Influence of smoking on 5-year mortality in men with intermittent claudication.
CVD = cardiovascular disease; CAD = coronary artery disease. Adapted from Reunanen et al, 1982.

sine diphosphate–dependent platelet aggregation, increases thromboxane synthesis, thus shortening platelet survival times, and suppresses platelet sensitivity to the anti-aggregation effects of endogenous prostaglandin I_2 (Burghuber et al, 1986). Furthermore, endogenous production of the endothelial prostacyclins, with their vasodilator and antithrombotic effects, is diminished in response to exposure to tobacco smoke (Reinders et al, 1986).

Finally, independent of atherosclerosis, cigarette smoking causes an increase in carbon monoxide that in turn reduces oxygen delivery to tissues. Smoking also causes immediate vasoconstriction of both epicardial and intramyocardial coronary resistance vessels and acetylcholine-induced vasoconstriction in coronary and forearm resistance vessels. These findings have now also been reported in individuals exposed to environmental tobacco smoke (Hutchinson, 1998).

SMOKING AND PAD PREVALENCE
The prevalence of PAD is directly associated with smoking and, conversely, the prevalence of PAD has been shown to decrease with a decline in the prevalence of smoking. The Reykjavik Study (Ingolfsson et al, 1994) was a landmark epidemiologic investigation that prospectively observed Icelandic males for 18 years. Smoking and serum cholesterol were identified as the only significant risk factors, besides age, that predicted

the incidence of intermittent claudication (IC). Smoking increased the risk of IC 8- to 10-fold. More importantly, the prevalence and incidence of IC fell sharply after 1970, as lifestyle-derived exposure to atherosclerotic risk factors improved. The relationship between tobacco use and claudication was also noted in the Framingham Study (Freund et al, 1993). In this American cohort of 5209 individuals, ranging from 30 to 62 years of age at enrollment and followed for 34 years, there was a direct correlation between cigarette smoking and the incidence of IC. A similar relationship was noted between tobacco use and the incidence of stroke and transient ischemic attacks and the total population-based burden of cardiovascular disease.

THE REWARDS OF SMOKING CESSATION
Patients with PAD who continue to smoke face the highest risk of death (as high as 40% to 50% within 5 years). The primary cause of death is MI and stroke, both of which are accelerated by continued tobacco use (Figure 1) (Faulkner et al, 1983; Reunanen et al, 1982). Fortunately, this risk diminishes with smoking cessation. In addition to the beneficial effects of quitting smoking on survival, PAD patients who successfully quit smoking show a slowed rate of PAD progression. Rest pain occurred in 18% of those with claudication who continued to smoke, compared with none in those who quit using tobacco (Figure 2) (Jonason and

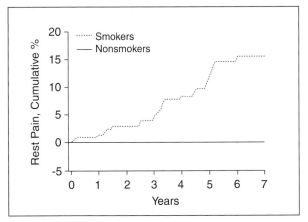

Figure 2. Peripheral arterial disease is more likely to progress from stable claudication to ischemic rest pain in individuals who smoke. Rest pain occurred in 18% of those with claudication who continued to smoke >7 years, compared with none in those who quit using tobacco. Reprinted with permission from Jonason and Bergström, 1987.

Bergström, 1987). Furthermore, individuals with PAD who quit smoking have an improved patency rate of limb bypass grafts and angioplasty sites (Ameli et al, 1989) and decreased amputation rates (Lassila and Lepäntalo, 1988).

The relationship between smoking cessation and the severity of claudication symptoms is less well established. Quick and Cotton (1982) evaluated 61 subjects over a period of 10 months to determine the relationship of smoking status on claudication and the clinical severity of PAD. Subjects who stopped smoking early in the study (n = 15) experienced improved walking distances and ankle pressures, while subjects who continued to smoke (n = 41) did not experience improvements in walking distances or ankle pressures (P <0.001). Gardner (1996) evaluated the exercise capacity of 138 PAD patients with stable claudication. One hundred patients were nonsmokers for an average of 7 years prior to enrollment and 38 patients were current smokers (using an average of 1.5 packs per day for 42 pack-years). Gardner observed that current smokers experienced claudication more quickly when walking and discomfort took longer to subside on resting compared with nonsmokers (P <0.05). Thus, for the individual with PAD, smoking cessation increases the chances of improved ankle pressure and walking distance (Quick and Cotton, 1982), and over time may reduce claudication pain severity and duration (Gardner, 1996).

Despite these findings, data demonstrating that smoking cessation results in improved claudication

symptoms are limited, and the impact appears to be relatively minor. Other claudication interventions (pharmacotherapies, exercise, and revascularization) all appear to offer greater promise for those patients who seek improvement in pain-free walking.

THERAPEUTIC APPROACHES

Contrary to conventional thinking, not all PAD patients resist efforts to reduce tobacco use. Published data confirm that many PAD patients successfully quit smoking and only 30% to 40% of individuals with stable claudication are current smokers, although most have a history of tobacco use (Jonason and Bergström, 1987; Hirsch et al, 1997). However, of individuals with PAD who present for surgical or percutaneous revascularization due to severe PAD, 80% to 90% are current smokers (Hirsch et al, 1997) and spontaneous smoking cessation rates are only ~3% per year in the US adult population (Centers for Disease Control and Prevention, 1993). Therefore, it is imperative that clinicians provide smoking-cessation services for each and every patient with PAD who smokes. These services include the provision of educational materials, behavioral counseling, appropriately aggressive use of pharmacologic treatment(s), and follow-up. Central to the patient's long-term success in reducing tobacco use is access to services for treatment of their, "Tobacco Use Disorder" (*International Classification of Diseases, Ninth Revision, Clinical Modification* [ICD-9-CM] 305.1). A trained health care provider can help each individual smoker with PAD understand that each day of continued tobacco use can be linked to progression of both coronary artery disease and PAD, including its associated pain and disability. Since all PAD patients can benefit immediately from smoking cessation, treatment for tobacco use disorder should not be reserved only for those with the most severe disease.

HOW TO CHOOSE A THERAPEUTIC APPROACH

A number of smoking-cessation strategies have been studied over the last 2 decades. Based on these studies, current approaches focus on a combination of behavioral strategies and pharmacologic interventions, including both nicotine replacement therapies (NRTs) and use of non-nicotine medications (Fiore et al, 1996). The most cost-effective and efficacious therapeutic approaches rely on a combination of techniques (Figure 3) (Cromwell et al, 1997). However, as with many therapies, compliance is important for success and therefore patient preference for a particular approach (pharmacologic intervention, group vs individual counseling, etc) should be considered when choosing the approach(es).

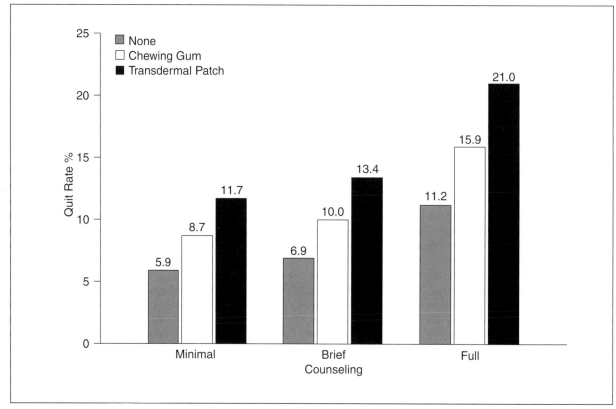

Figure 3. Additive effects of counseling and nicotine replacement therapy on short-term smoking cessation rates. "Background" tobacco quit rate is 5%; data shown include this background rate plus the incremental "marginal quit rate" documented from addition of these behavioral and pharmacologic interventions. Figure is designed based on data from Cromwell et al, 1997.

NICOTINE REPLACEMENT THERAPIES

Nicotine replacement products are available that have been shown to increase long-term cessation rates in randomized, controlled trials. Two products, nicotine patch and nicotine gum, are available over the counter and 2 others, nicotine nasal spray and nicotine oral inhaler, are only available by prescription. All products offer similar long-term abstinence rates (Fiore et al, 2000).

Nicotine patch therapy in patients with medical illnesses, such as smokers with cardiovascular disease, has been shown to be safe (Joseph et al, 1996). In a multicenter trial of 584 patients with cardiac disease, with approximately one third of these patients having documented PAD or cerebrovascular disease, Joseph et al demonstrated comparable tolerance (similar adverse event rates) in the groups treated with nicotine patches or placebo. This is not surprising, as NRT does not cause elevations in plasma nicotine levels comparable to smoking. Thus, in those patients who use NRT, the exposure to nicotine is significantly less than in those who continue to smoke and, theoreti-

cally, there should be fewer vascular effects of nicotine and no exposure to the other harmful compounds that are coadministered in smoke. Safety of other nicotine replacement products in a medically ill population has not yet been evaluated.

NON-NICOTINE PHARMACOTHERAPIES FOR TOBACCO CESSATION

Bupropion hydrochloride (Zyban®, Wellbutrin®) is a non-nicotine product that has been approved as a pharmacologic adjunct for smoking cessation. Hurt and colleagues have demonstrated a 12-month abstinence rate of 23% with 150-mg bid sustained-release bupropion (Hurt et al, 1997). The potential effectiveness of antidepressant medications in smoking cessation has attracted considerable interest in recent years, since several symptoms of nicotine withdrawal mimic symptoms of depression (Covey et al, 1990). The dopaminergic activities of bupropion may contribute to its efficacy for smoking cessation in patients without current symptoms of depression (Hurt et al, 1997).

Smoking and Peripheral Arterial Disease

As an individual with vascular disease, you deserve access to key information that can improve your vascular health and that may save your life. You probably already are aware that tobacco use, in all of its forms, is damaging to your general health. We would like to share with you the following facts about tobacco and peripheral arterial disease (PAD) to help you to decide if you are willing to quit smoking.

- **Tobacco causes PAD** by increasing the formation of leg artery blockages, constricting blood vessels, and causing the blood to clot (with every puff).

- Tobacco is clearly the **most important cause of PAD**. Even a half pack of cigarettes per day may increase the risk of developing PAD by 30% to 50%.

- **Tobacco use causes heart attacks, strokes, and/or death** in as many as 5% to 15% of PAD patients per year. This means that as many as 50% of individuals with PAD who smoke **may develop one of these severe events within 5 years** after diagnosis.

- Tobacco causes PAD to progress much more rapidly, so that ≥**1 in 5 patients** with claudication who smokes will develop leg pain at rest requiring a limb operation, such as artery bypass surgery, angioplasty, or amputation.

- Vascular surgery or angioplasty to repair blood vessels is **much less likely to be successful in patients who smoke**.

- **Amputation** is much more likely to occur in patients who smoke.

- Quitting smoking is associated with a **reduced risk of heart attack, stroke, and death rates** in patients with PAD.

- If you are thinking about quitting smoking, you should do so **as soon as possible.**

Unfortunately, few patients with PAD are told these important facts about tobacco use and PAD. We are committed to helping you stop smoking.

© Regents of the University of Minnesota. Developed by the Vascular Medicine Program, Minnesota Vascular Diseases Center, University of Minnesota.

This is for informational use only and is not a substitute for professional medical care. If you have health concerns, contact your physician.

Figure 4. Tobacco use and peripheral arterial disease. A patient education summary.

WHAT IS A PRACTICAL OFFICE-BASED APPROACH FOR TOBACCO CESSATION IN PATIENTS WITH PAD?

The Agency for Healthcare Research and Quality (AHRQ, formerly the Agency for Health Care Policy and Research) has outlined a clinical practice guideline for smoking cessation (Fiore et al, 2000). This guideline is based on the 5 As (**Ask, Advise, Assess, Assist, Arrange**) and is supported by evidence of efficacy in improving cessation rates. Using the 5 As, we have described a simple office intervention for use with the smoker with PAD.

ASK: As part of the vital signs, identify all tobacco users at every visit. Simple identification of smokers can increase rates of cessation from ~3% to >6% (Fiore et al, 1996).
- Blood Pressure: _____ Pulse: _____ Resp: _____
- Weight: _____ Height: _____ Temp: _____

- Tobacco use: ☐ CURRENT   ☐ FORMER   ☐ NEVER
- Cigarettes per day: _____

ADVISE: Provide a clear, strong, and personal message to all smokers to stop smoking. Relate this message to the patient's condition(s). This simple advice can improve cessation rates >10% (Fiore et al, 2000; Fiore et al, 1996). A clear message relating tobacco use to PAD is preferred (Figure 4).

ASSESS: Determine each smoker's willingness to stop smoking in the next 30 days.
- Ask every smoker, "Are you planning to stop smoking in the next 30 days?"
If **no**: Provide handouts, encourage continued consideration of smoking cessation, and offer future support for quit attempts.
If **yes**: Continue to the **Assist** stage.

Key Points

● Tobacco use is the single most important cause of PAD.

● Smoking cessation improves survival and reduces the rate of progression of PAD.

● A simple office-based intervention for smokers with PAD is effective and can be easily implemented.

● Ideally, office-based smoking-cessation services should be multidisciplinary.

● Medications available for smoking cessation include NRT (patch, gum, nasal spray, oral inhaler) and non-nicotine medication (bupropion).

● Medications for smoking cessation are covered by most insurers, including Medicaid in some states.

ASSIST: Help the patient stop smoking by developing a stop-smoking plan that provides behavioral counseling and appropriate medications for cessation (NRT and/or bupropion). When possible, patients planning on smoking cessation within the next 2 to 4 weeks should be referred to an educator for additional assistance. In addition to saving the time of physicians, referral of the motivated patient to tobacco-cessation nurses, pharmacists, or other tobacco health educators provides a multidisciplinary approach to smoking cessation and dramatically improves cessation rates. Advice from a single health care provider (ie, physician, nurse, pharmacist) is associated with a 12% cessation rate, but advice from multiple providers is associated with a >25% cessation rate (Fiore et al, 1996).

Behavioral counseling for smoking cessation should include a review of both past attempts and the underpinnings of successes and failures. Together, the health care provider and patient can determine which smoking-cessation strategies have worked for the patient and which have not. Habitual behaviors and high-risk social situations that might influence attempts to remain abstinent (eg, use of coffee or alcoholic beverages, driving, etc) should be identified. Specific techniques, such as deep breathing and exercise, should be discussed and practiced for use in some of these high-risk situations. Many patients will harbor specific fears related to smoking cessation, such as weight gain, and these fears should be addressed during counseling. In addition, a stop-smoking plan should include: (1) advising the patient to get rid of all cigarettes and ashtrays on or before the quit date to reduce access to cigarettes and environmental cues to smoke, and (2) identifying family and friends who are available to be called on for support during the cessation process.

Finally, there is a clear dose-response relationship between the amount of time spent counseling for smoking cessation and subsequent smoking-cessation rates. Three to 10 minutes of counseling are associated with a cessation rate of ~12% and a ≥10-minute session is associated with a cessation rate of >18%. However, interventions as short as 3 minutes can result in significantly improved quit rates (Fiore et al, 1996).

ARRANGE: Schedule follow-up contacts.
● Telephone call on quit date.
● Follow-up within 1 week of quit date.
● Additional follow-up at 3, 6, and 12 weeks after quit date.
● If a slip or relapse occurs, schedule a visit as soon as possible.
● Provide office contact number for support.
Follow-up is a very important step in the intervention. One follow-up contact is associated with a 10% cessation rate and 4 to 7 follow-up contacts improve the cessation rate to ≥22%.

Bill for services: These services are reimbursable and can be applied to every clinical practice immediately. A simple office intervention can make a major difference for many individuals and begin to help smokers with PAD improve their survival and quality of life. Every clinician has a critical role to play in this long-term process. ■

BIBLIOGRAPHY

Ameli FM, Stein M, Provan JL, Prosser R. The effect of postoperative smoking on femoropopliteal bypass grafts. Ann Vasc Surg 1989;3:20–5.

Burghuber OC, Punzengruber C, Sinzinger H, et al. Platelet sensitivity to prostacyclin in smokers and non-smokers. Chest 1986;90:34–8.

Centers for Disease Control and Prevention. Smoking cessation during previous year among adults — United States, 1990 and 1991. MMWR 1993;42:504–7.

Chen C, Loo G. Inhibition of lecithin:cholesterol acyltransferase activity in human blood plasma by cigarette smoke extract and reactive aldehydes. J Biochem Toxicol 1995;10:121–8.

Covey LS, Glassman AH, Stetner F. Depression and depressive symptoms in smoking cessation. Compr Psychiatry 1990;31:350–4.

Cromwell J, Bartosch WJ, Fiore MC, et al. Cost-effectiveness of the clinical practice recommendations in the AHCPR guideline for smoking cessation. JAMA 1997;278:1759–66.

Faulkner KW, House AK, Castleden WM. The effect of cessation of smoking on the accumulative survival rates of patients with symptomatic peripheral vascular disease. Med J Aust 1983;1:217–9.

Fiore MC, Bailey WC, Cohen SJ, et al. Smoking Cessation: Clinical Practice Guideline #18. Rockville, Md: US Department of Health and Human Services, Public Health Service, Agency for Health Care Policy and Research; 1996. AHCPR Publication No. 96-0692.

Fiore MC, Bailey WC, Cohen SJ, et al. Treating Tobacco Use and Dependence. A Clinical Practice Guideline. Rockville, Md: US Department of Health and Human Services, Agency for Healthcare Research and Quality; 2000. AHRQ Publication No. 00-0032.

Freund KM, Belanger AJ, D'Agostino RB, Kannel WB. The health risks of smoking. The Framingham Study: 34 years of follow-up. Ann Epidemiol 1993;3:417–24.

Gardner AW. The effect of cigarette smoking on exercise capacity in patients with intermittent claudication. Vasc Med 1996;1:181–6.

Hirsch AT, Treat-Jacobson DJ, Lando HA, Hatsukami DK. The role of tobacco cessation, antiplatelet and lipid-lowering therapies in the treatment of peripheral arterial disease. Vasc Med 1997;2:243–51.

Hurt RD, Sachs DP, Glover ED, et al. A comparison of sustained-release bupropion and placebo for smoking cessation. N Engl J Med 1997;337:1195–202.

Hutchinson S. Smoking as a risk factor for endothelial dysfunction. Can J Cardiol 1998;14(suppl D):20D–22D.

Ingolfsson IÖ, Sigurdsson G, Sigvaldason H, et al. A marked decline in the prevalence and incidence of intermittent claudication in Icelandic men 1968-1986: a strong relationship to smoking and serum cholesterol—the Reykjavik Study. J Clin Epidemiol 1994:47:1237–43.

Jonason T, Bergström R. Cessation of smoking in patients with intermittent claudication. Effects on the risk of peripheral vascular complications, myocardial infarction and mortality. Acta Med Scand 1987;221:253–60.

Joseph AM, Norman S, Ferry L, et al. The safety of transdermal nicotine as an aid to smoking cessation in patients with cardiac disease. N Engl J Med 1996;335:1792–8.

Kalra VK, Ying YY, Deemer K, et al. Mechanism of cigarette smoke condensate induced adhesion of human monocytes to cultured endothelial cells. J Cell Physiol 1994;160:154–62.

Lassila R, Lepäntalo M. Cigarette smoking and the outcome after lower limb arterial surgery. Acta Chir Scand 1988;154:635–40.

McGill HC Jr. Smoking and the pathogenesis of atherosclerosis. Adv Exp Med Biol 1990;273:9–16.

Quick CRG, Cotton LT. The measured effect of stopping smoking on intermittent claudication. Br J Surg 1982;69S:S24–S26.

Reinders JH, Brinkman HJ, van Mourik JA, de Groot PG. Cigarette smoke impairs endothelial cell prostacyclin production. Arteriosclerosis 1986;6:15–23.

Reunanen A, Takkunen H, Aromaa A. Prevalence of intermittent claudication and its effect on mortality. Acta Med Scand 1982;211:249–56.

Diabetes and Peripheral Arterial Disease

Francis J. Kazmier, MD, FACP, FACC
Section Head, Vascular Medicine
Medical Director, Vascular Laboratory
Department of Surgery, Ochsner Clinic
New Orleans, Louisiana

Objective: To examine the relationship between DM and PAD.

The prevalence of diabetes mellitus (DM) in the United States exceeds 6% of the general population and appears to be increasing rapidly. DM will develop in many patients with impaired glucose tolerance and an additional 3% of the population is thought to have undiagnosed DM (Harris et al, 1998). The San Antonio Heart Study indicates that unlike certain cardiovascular (CV) risk factors, for example, hyperlipidemia, smoking, and hypertension, which are being ameliorated by better management, obesity and diabetes are increasing in incidence, particularly among minorities (Burke et al, 1999). Both type 1 and type 2 diabetes increase CV disease prevalence and severity, and about 80% of patients with DM die of some form of heart or blood vessel disease. Although in part, this reflects the comorbidity of other traditional CV risk factors, DM is an independent risk factor that itself accelerates atherosclerosis and ischemic events (Stamler et al, 1993). The risk of coronary heart disease is increased 2- to 4-fold in DM patients compared with nondiabetics. Diabetics are 2- to 4-fold more likely to have a stroke and the risk of developing peripheral arterial disease (PAD) increases >4-fold (Kannel and McGee, 1979). Atherosclerosis is a systemic process with vascular bed specificity and occurs principally in large- and medium-sized elastic and muscular arteries and is increasingly recognized as an inflammatory process (Ross, 1999). Traditionally, diabetic management of atherosclerotic risk has been principally focused on its coronary and cerebrovascular manifestations, with much less attention offered to the relationship between DM and PAD, in spite of the growing public health importance of the association.

DIABETES AND ATHEROSCLEROTIC COMORBIDITIES

Major atherosclerotic risk factors for DM include smoking, hypertension, dyslipidemia, hyperglycemia, and insulin resistance. The importance of tobacco smoking was addressed in the first article of this monograph. Hypertension commonly complicates type 2 diabetes, and the results of both the Hypertensive Optimal Treatment (HOT) trial and the UK Prospective Diabetes Study (UKPDS) strongly support protection against major CV events with tighter blood pressure control (Hansson et al, 1998; UKPDS, 1998b).

Aggressive normalization of serum lipids reduces ischemic CV risk. Subgroup analysis for DM in the Scandinavian Simvastatin Survival Study (4S) and the Cholesterol and Recurrent Events (CARE) trial demonstrated that lowering cholesterol levels in type 2 diabetics reduces the risk of recurrent coronary events. Correlation between the achieved lower low-density lipoprotein and risk reduction was poor, however, suggesting that additional nonlipid mechanisms may contribute to the benefit of 3-hydroxy-3-methylglutaryl coenzyme A reductase therapy (Pyorala et al, 1997; Sacks et al, 1996).

Initiated in 1977, the UKPDS was designed to evaluate the effect of intensive blood glucose control on macrovascular or microvascular complications in 3,867 newly diagnosed patients with type 2 DM. Patients were randomly assigned to intensive control with a sulphonylurea, insulin, or conventional therapy with diet, with the conventional group aiming for the best glycemic control with diet alone. The patients were followed for a mean of 10 years for development of microvascular complications or cardiovascular disease–related events (macrovascular complications).

Although trial data confirm the benefit of tight blood glucose control on microvascular complications, the trend toward a reduced incidence of macrovascular complications has not been statistically significant (UKPDS, 1998a).

Unlike the microvascular complications of DM, large-vessel atherosclerosis can precede the development of diabetes. Reaven (1988) described a cluster of conditions, including elevated insulin levels in the presence of normal blood glucose (insulin resistance), impaired glucose tolerance, a specific dyslipidemia (low high-density lipoprotein, elevated triglycerides), and hypertension. Subsequent research now suggests that prothrombotic risk factors are also associated with insulin resistance (the dysmetabolic syndrome). These prothrombotic factors include suppression of fibrinolysis due to high plasma concentration of plasminogen activator inhibitor type 1 (PAI-1), along with alterations in other clotting factors (Juhan-Vague et al, 1991; Fuller et al, 1979). Angiotensin II has been considered to potentially be particularly atherogenic (Dzau and Re, 1994). Angiotensin (AI) activates oxidative enzymes and promotes oxidative stress, which contributes to endothelial dysfunction, vasoconstriction, inflammation, vascular lesion remodeling, plaque rupture, and thrombosis. AI enhances thrombosis by activation of PAI-1, which in turn inhibits endogenous vascular wall tissue plasminogen activator (Dzau and Re, 1994). In a substudy of the Heart Outcomes Prevention Evaluation (HOPE) trial, the Microalbuminuria, Cardiovascular, and Renal Outcomes (MICRO-HOPE) study, use of tissue-specific angiotensin-converting enzyme inhibition was associated with significant reduction in all major clinical endpoints in diabetics, including vascular death, myocardial infarction, heart failure, revascularization, nephropathy, and a 30% reduction in new-onset diabetes (HOPE, 2000). Taken together, there is abundant evidence that patients benefit from glycemic control and that patients with PAD and diabetes should be aggressively treated to achieve this benefit.

DIABETES AND PAD

PAD is several times more likely to occur in patients with type 2 diabetes than in age- and gender-matched controls (Beach et al, 1982). Although the histology of the atherosclerotic lesion does not appear different in the diabetic, the distribution of disease in the lower extremity arteries is rather distinct. Patients with diabetes, compared with nondiabetic controls, generally have a lower incidence of aorto-iliac disease and about the same incidence of occlusive disease in the superficial femoral artery.

In contrast, the profunda femoris and the major calf arteries below the knee are more frequently and severely affected by PAD in diabetics. More often than not, the foot vessels are spared. Large-vessel atherosclerosis precedes the diagnosis of DM and often progresses more rapidly (Strandness et al, 1964; Akbari and LoGerfo, 1999).

Based on the microvascular renal and retinal complications peculiar to DM, there has been speculation for decades that such "small vessel disease" might be more widespread and underlie clinical events in other arterial circulations. This concept was based, in part, on histologic evidence of nonatheromatous PAD that was observed in amputation specimens (Goldenberg et al, 1959), and that led to the concept of diffuse end-arteriolar luminal occlusion in the diabetic patient. From these minimal histopathologic observations, there has developed a "therapeutic nihilism." Neither Strandness et al (1964), in a prospective blinded histologic study, nor Conrad (1967) could confirm these premises that clinically significant "small vessel disease" was prevalent, and blood flow studies actually demonstrated normal functional reactivity in the distal resistance vessels of diabetics (Barner et al, 1971). Thus, there does not appear to be any more end-artery obliteration in diabetic than in nondiabetic limbs.

The bedside vascular examination of the diabetic patient can occasionally be challenging for all clinicians. Not all physicians are equally adept at detecting and grading distal extremity pulses. The ankle-brachial index (ABI), as an extension of the physical examination, is simple to perform and usually reliable, but diabetes presents a challenge to the sensitivity of this diagnostic method, as calcific medial sclerosis is common in diabetic patients. First differentiated from atherosclerosis by Johann Monckeberg (1903), medial calcinosis results in noncompressible vessels and falsely elevates ankle pressures measured by sphygmomanometry. Though not common in the general population, 15% to 20% of patients referred to our vascular laboratory for testing have medial calcinosis due to both a high prevalence of DM and end-stage renal disease in our referral population. Pulse volume recordings (PVR) are plethysmographic tracings that record pulsatile volume changes in the limb. In contrast to the ABI, these tracings remain reliable in the context of medial calcification. Although the PVR is helpful, especially when normal, it is, however, neither precise nor quantitative. Toe pressures and the toe-brachial index measurements can be useful alternative tests when performed by experienced clinicians, as the digital vessels are usually spared from medial calcinosis. These measurements may be difficult to perform in patients with infarcted, infected, or edematous toes. The arterial duplex ultrasound technique remains an extremely useful and accurate diagnostic tool for patients with diabetes, because it accurately localizes arterial stenoses. In the diabetic patient facing limb salvage, arteriography will usually be needed to assess PAD in the entire lower extremity (reflecting the high degree of calf vessel involvement).

THE DIABETIC FOOT AND PAD

DM is a contributing factor in about half of limb amputations unrelated to trauma, undoubtedly due to the severity of associated PAD, and more rapid PAD progression to critical limb ischemia. The relative risk for limb amputation is 40 times greater for diabetics than nondiabetics (Nathan, 1993). Simply stated, major factors in limb loss in diabetics are PAD, neuropathy, and infection. The interplay among them is, however, far from simple. Foot ulcers typically begin in patients with neuropathy and altered foot biomechanics. Classic signs of infection are often absent in a diabetic foot infection and evaluation for ischemia and arterial compromise may require special studies (Akbari and LoGerfo, 1999). When arterial occlusive disease plays a role in a diabetic foot, a vascular specialist should be consulted. The best defense against amputation is prevention of ischemia, and distal arterial reconstruction is often effective.

Key Points

● The prevalence of DM in the United States is >6% of the general population with an additional 3% thought to have undiagnosed DM.

● Approximately 80% of DM patients die of some form of heart or blood vessel disease.

● The risk of coronary heart disease increases 2- to 4-fold in DM patients.

● The risk of developing PAD increases >4-fold in DM patients.

● Because the calcific medial sclerosis of most diabetics can make ABI readings nonreliable and PVR are not precise, duplex ultrasonography and occasionally arteriography may be more frequently needed to assess PAD in diabetic patients, especially in those with a threatened limb.

SUMMARY

For the office-based physician, there is now evidence-based support for blood glucose control, cessation of smoking, control of elevated blood pressure, and control of dyslipidemia. Patients with DM should leave the office with clear instructions on how to prevent disease progression, with specific educational material to outline the risks of all atherosclerotic syndromes, including PAD, and with a medical plan to reduce this risk. This plan will usually include suggested lifestyle interventions as well as pharmacotherapies, including where indicated, antihypertensives, lipid-lowering agents, medications to improve glycemic control, and an antithrombotic agent. The vascular bed specificity of DM and its implications for the diabetic foot need to be more widely appreciated. The outcome for the diabetic foot need not be uniformly poor. ■

BIBLIOGRAPHY

Akbari CM, LoGerfo FW. Diabetes and peripheral vascular disease. J Vasc Surg 1999;30:373–84.

Barner HB, Kaiser GC, Willman VL. Blood flow in the diabetic leg. Circulation 1971;43:391–4.

Beach KW, Brunzell JD, Strandness DE Jr. Prevalence of severe arteriosclerosis obliterans in patients with diabetes mellitus. Arteriosclerosis 1982;2:275–80.

Burke JP, Williams K, Gaskill SP, et al. Rapid rise in the incidence of type 2 diabetes from 1987 to 1996: results from the San Antonio Heart Study. Arch Intern Med 1999;159:1450–6.

Conrad MC. Large and small artery occlusion in diabetic and nondiabetics with severe vascular disease. Circulation 1967;36:83–91.

Dzau VJ, Re R. Tissue angiotensin system in cardiovascular medicine. A paradigm shift? Circulation 1994;89:493–8.

Fuller JH, Keen H, Jarrett RJ, et al. Haemostatic variables associated with diabetes and its complications. Br Med J 1979;2:964–6.

Goldenberg SG, Alex M, Josti RD, et al. Nonatheromatous peripheral vascular disease of the lower extremity in diabetes mellitus. Diabetes 1959;8:261–73.

Hansson L, Zanchetti A, Carruthers SG, et al. Effects of intensive blood-pressure lowering and low-dose aspirin in patients with hypertension: principal results of the Hypertensive Optimal Treatment (HOT) randomised trial. Lancet 1998;351:1755–62.

Harris MI, Flegal KM, Cowie CC, et al. Prevalence of diabetes, impaired fasting glucose, and impaired glucose tolerance in U.S. adults. The Third National Health and Nutrition Examination Survey, 1988–1994. Diabetes Care 1998;21:518–24.

Heart Outcomes Prevention Evaluation (HOPE) Study Investigators. Effects of ramipril on cardiovascular and microvascular outcomes in people with diabetes mellitus: results of the HOPE study and MICRO-HOPE substudy. Lancet 2000;355:253–9.

Juhan-Vague I, Alessi MC, Vague P. Increased plasma plasminogen activator inhibitor 1 levels. A possible link between insulin resistance and atherothrombosis. Diabetologia 1991;34:457–62.

Kannel WB, McGee DL. Diabetes and cardiovascular disease. The Framingham study. JAMA 1979; 241:2035–8.

Nathan DM. Long-term complications of diabetes mellitus. N Engl J Med 1993;328:1676–85.

Pyorala K, Pedersen TR, Kjekshus J, et al. Cholesterol lowering with simvastatin improves prognosis of diabetic patients with coronary heart disease. A subgroup analysis of the Scandinavian Simvastatin Survival Study (4S). Diabetes Care 1997;20:614–20.

Reaven GM. Role of insulin resistance in human disease. Diabetes 1988;37:1595–607.

Ross R. Atherosclerosis — an inflammatory disease. N Engl J Med 1999;340:115–26.

Sacks FM, Pfeffer MA, Moye LA, et al. The effect of pravastatin in coronary events after myocardial infarction in patients with average cholesterol levels. Cholesterol and Recurrent Events Trial investigators. N Engl J Med 1996;335:1001–9.

Stamler J, Vaccaro O, Neaton JD, et al. Diabetes, other risk factors, and 12-yr cardiovascular mortality for men screened in the Multiple Risk Factor Intervention Trial. Diabetes Care 1993;16:434–44.

Strandness DE Jr, Priest RE, Gibbons GE. A combined clinical and pathologic study of diabetic and non-diabetic peripheral arterial disease. Diabetes 1964;13:366.

UK Prospective Diabetes Study Group. Intensive blood glucose control with sulphonylureas or insulin compared with conventional treatment and risk of complications in patients with type 2 diabetes (UKPDS 33). Lancet 1998a;352:837–53.

UK Prospective Diabetes Study Group. Tight blood pressure control and risk of macrovascular and microvascular complications in type 2 diabetes: UKPDS 38. Br Med J 1998b;317:703–13.

Dyslipidemia in Peripheral Arterial Disease: Insights and Advances in Therapy

John P. Cooke, MD, PhD
Associate Professor of Medicine
Director, Stanford University School of Medicine
Stanford, California

Roberta K. Oka, RN, DNSc
Assistant Professor of Nursing
UCLA School of Nursing
Los Angeles, California

Objective: To examine the relationship between PAD and dyslipidemia, and the efficacy of risk-factor modifications for patient longevity and quality of life.

Peripheral arterial disease (PAD) is underestimated and undertreated. PAD patients often have concomitant coronary artery disease (CAD), carotid or aneurysmal disease that is silent, unrecognized, and deadly. Accordingly, they deserve aggressive risk-factor modification and antiplatelet therapy. Despite the compelling need for aggressive medical intervention, preliminary results from the PAD Awareness, Risk, and Treatment: New Resources for Survival (PARTNERS) study indicate that only one third of PAD cases are diagnosed. The large number of undiagnosed cases may explain the observation in PARTNERS that only 60% of these individuals were receiving antilipid therapy. An earlier study found that almost 90% of PAD patients have dyslipidemia (Olin et al, 1992) based on the 1988 National Cholesterol Education Program (NCEP) guidelines. These guidelines are less aggressive than current ones, under which nearly all PAD patients would likely be candidates for some form of lipid-reduction therapy.

FORMS OF DYSLIPIDEMIA IN THE PAD PATIENT

In PAD, several lipid fractions determine the presence and progression of disease. Independent risk factors for PAD include elevations of total cholesterol, low-density lipoprotein cholesterol (LDL-C), triglycerides, and lipoprotein(a) [Lp(a)] (Johansson et al, 1993; Hiatt et al, 1995; Murabito et al, 1997). For every 10 mg/dL increase in total cholesterol concentration, the risk of PAD increases approximately 10% (Hiatt et al, 1995). Increases in high-density lipoprotein cholesterol (HDL-C) and apolipoprotein A-I are protective (Johansson et al, 1993).

In patients with vascular disease, there has been an appropriate focus on the role of LDL-C in the pathophysiology of the disease. Epidemiological studies indicate that elevations in LDL-C impart a greater risk of developing vascular disease. Aggressively reducing LDL-C with statin therapy reduces both cardiovascular and overall mortality in patients with atherosclerosis or at high risk of developing atherosclerosis. Based on the available clinical trials, many experts are now recommending that LDL-C should be reduced below 100 mg/dL in patients with CAD or PAD.

Although this approach is appropriate and evidence-based, a recent study by Mowat and colleagues found that, in their sample of PAD patients and patients without cardiovascular disease, mean plasma total cholesterol concentration was similar between groups, while triglyceride and very low-density lipoprotein concentrations were higher in the PAD group. A low HDL concentration (rather than an elevated LDL) was the primary lipid abnormality in these patients (Mowat et al, 1997). These results suggest that low HDL levels contribute to the pathophysiology of PAD.

Lp(a) is a newly recognized independent risk factor for CAD and PAD (Lupattelli et al, 1994; Bostom et al, 1996; Valentine et al, 1996). Critical levels are ≥30 mg/dL. In PAD patients with only modest exposure to traditional risk factors, screening for elevated Lp(a), as well as hyperhomocysteinemia, is indicated.

ANTILIPID THERAPY

Dietary restriction of cholesterol and saturated fats

modestly reduces LDL-C levels. However, caloric restriction and weight loss can substantially decrease triglyceride levels, which are important in the management of PAD. Low-cholesterol diets can also be supplemented with high intakes of soluble fiber. When fiber is ingested in the form of psyllium, there are further decreases in total cholesterol and LDL-C levels in the range of 5% to 7% (Jenkins et al, 1993). Newly released food products containing stanol esters (such as Benecol®) are useful adjuncts to nutritional therapy. These agents increase cholesterol excretion, and augment the effect of statins.

Statins cause large decreases in LDL-C, and some of the newer agents also favorably affect triglycerides and HDL-C. Bile acid binding resins such as colestipol can further augment the effect of statins to reduce LDL-C. High-dose niacin also reduces LDL-C and increases HDL-C. In one study, controlled-release niacin reduced LDL-C levels by 24% and increased HDL-C levels by 6%. Unfortunately, almost half of the patients discontinued therapy because of side effects (Gray et al, 1994). Thus, while niacin is an effective agent, side effects limit its usefulness. Another class of antilipid agents to consider are the fibrates, specifically gemfibrozil. Gemfibrozil is effective at reducing triglyceride levels, with the added benefit of increasing HDL-C concentration.

In patients with refractory elevations in LDL-C levels, stepped care should include a statin drug such as pravastatin, together with niacin, or a bile acid binding resin such as cholestyramine. The practicality of this approach has been well established and may be necessary in a minority of patients, but significant side effects may occur (Pasternak et al, 1996). The combined use of statins with gemfibrozil increases the risk of myositis, and should generally be avoided.

EFFECT OF CHOLESTEROL LOWERING ON CARDIOVASCULAR EVENTS

Several large trials have been conducted in patients with underlying coronary disease, or at increased risk for coronary events, to determine the benefits of cholesterol lowering. The Scandinavian Simvastatin Survival Study (4S) was a secondary prevention trial and the first trial to demonstrate a very significant decrease in both total mortality and CAD mortality due to a lipid-lowering agent (Kjekshus and Pedersen, 1995). More than 4000 patients participated in this secondary prevention trial for >5 years. Simvastatin reduced LDL-C by 35%, increased HDL-C level by 8%, and reduced major coronary events and total mortality by 42% and 30%, respectively.

The investigators of the Cholesterol and Recurrent Events (CARE) trial studied pravastatin in >4000 patients with a previous myocardial infarction (MI) and lipid values in a normal range (Sacks et al, 1996). The benefit of pravastatin was seen in patients with reductions in LDL-C levels down to 125 mg/dL, with not much additional benefit at levels lower than 125 mg/dL (Sacks et al, 1998).

Results of CARE notwithstanding, meta-analyses of the lipid trials support the view that patients with cardiovascular disease should have target LDL-C levels of ≤100 mg/dL (Gould et al, 1998; Grundy, 1998). For every 10 percentage points reduction in total cholesterol, coronary mortality risk is reduced by 15% and total mortality risk by 11% (Gould et al, 1998). This benefit is also observed in women and in elderly patients (Miettinen et al, 1997).

CHOLESTEROL REDUCTION IN PAD

Antilipid therapies favorably impact PAD. In the carotid circulation, antilipid therapy slows the progression of carotid wall thickness (Furberg et al, 1994; Hodis et al, 1996). The combination of colestipol and niacin stabilized or reversed femoral atherosclerosis in the Cholesterol Lowering Atherosclerosis Study (Blankenhorn et al, 1991). The Program on the Surgical Control of Hyperlipidemias (POSCH) study revealed that ileal bypass surgery reduced lipid levels and reduced progression of PAD (Buchwald et al, 1996). In POSCH, ileal bypass surgery reduced the risks of developing an abnormal ankle-brachial index by 44% or symptoms of PAD by 30%. In the 4S study, simvastatin reduced the risk of new or worsening intermittent claudication by 38% (Pedersen et al, 1998). Thus, cholesterol lowering reduces cardiovascular morbidity and mortality, and symptomatic progression of PAD.

Whereas statins are very effective in reducing LDL-C, they do not affect Lp(a) levels. Patients with CAD and elevations in total cholesterol and Lp(a) were randomized to receive either simvastatin therapy alone or simvastatin with biweekly apheresis (Kroon et al, 1996). Simvastatin alone had no effect on Lp(a) levels whereas the combination of simvastatin with apheresis reduced Lp(a) levels by about 20%. Simvastatin therapy alone did not prevent an increase in the number of occlusive lesions in leg vessels over time. In contrast, simvastatin plus apheresis decreased the accumulation of lesions. Although apheresis is not a practical means to treat hyperlipidemia, this study suggests that lowering Lp(a) concentration improves peripheral circulation. Accordingly, in the case of the patient with elevated levels of Lp(a), it is reasonable to use agents that are known to reduce Lp(a) such as high-dose niacin therapy (ie, 1.5 g to 3 g daily). In the postmenopausal woman with elevated Lp(a), estrogen replacement therapy lowers

Lp(a) levels. This recommendation is made with the caveat that in postmenopausal women at risk for CAD, hormonal replacement did not reduce coronary events in the Heart and Estrogen/Progestin in Replacement Study (HERS) nor the Estrogen Replacement and Atherosclerosis study (ERA).

In summary, patients with PAD are at high risk for MI and ischemic strokes. Cholesterol-lowering therapy reduces cardiovascular events. Further, there may be positive effects on peripheral circulation. Therapy should be targeted to reduce the LDL-C level to <100 mg/dL, and should include a combination of diet, exercise, and antilipid agents, with statins usually required to achieve the target LDL-C value.

ADJUNCTIVE THERAPIES: NUTRITION AND SUPPLEMENTS

Nonpharmacologic therapies such as diet and exercise can be effective in reducing LDL-C (Superko and Krauss, 1994). The Heidelberg study examined the efficacy of a 1-year regimen of a low-fat diet (protein 15%; carbohydrates 65%; fat <20%; cholesterol <200 mg) and moderate physical activity (30 minutes daily at 75% maximum heart rate) in men with documented CAD. Coronary arteriography revealed that lesion progression was less in the diet/exercise group (23% vs 48%). Regression of lesions was greater in the treated group (32% vs 17%). Thus, an aggressive diet and exercise regimen can reduce coronary disease (Schuler et al, 1992).

The Lyon Diet Heart Study examined the efficacy of a Mediterranean-type diet: more bread, root vegetables, fruit, and fish, less meat (replaced with chicken), cream, and butter (replaced with margarine) than the conventional American diet in reducing recurrent MI events. After about 4 years, cardiac death and nonfatal MI were significantly reduced. Thus dietary modification, independent of cholesterol lowering, can reduce the risk of all-cause and CAD mortality in patients at risk (Leaf, 1999; de Lorgeril et al, 1994; de Lorgeril et al, 1999).

The Dietary Approaches to Stop Hypertension (DASH) trial examined the effect on blood pressure of a diet rich in fruits, vegetables, and low-fat dairy products with reduced saturated and total fat. The diet effectively lowered systolic and diastolic blood pressure in hypertensive patients by about 11 mm Hg and 6 mm Hg, respectively. Therefore, a diet rich in fruits, vegetables, and low-fat dairy is at least as effective as drug monotherapy in lowering blood pressure (Moore et al, 1999).

In PAD there is a severe impairment of vasodilation in the peripheral vessels. In part, this is due to arteriosclerosis, fibrosis and calcification of the conduit vessels with fixed lesions that impede blood flow and

Key Points

● Dyslipidemia is undertreated in patients with PAD.

● Aggressive antilipid programs reduce cardiovascular mortality, morbidity, and overall mortality by about 30% in patients with atherosclerosis, or at high risk.

● Antilipid therapy reduces the anatomic and clinical progression of PAD.

markedly reduce vasomotion. However, there are also vasodilator defects in the collateral vessels and microvasculature that further contribute to ischemia. The most salient of these abnormalities is an impairment of endothelium-dependent vasodilation. This abnormality is multifactorial, but partly due to abnormalities of the nitric oxide (NO) synthase pathway.

Nutritional supplements that act on the NO synthase pathway, such as extracts of *Ginkgo biloba*, may be beneficial in PAD, in the absence of an effect on lipid levels. The mechanism of benefit is thought to be due to the antioxidant effects of this agent, and improvement in vascular relaxation, due to preservation of endothelium-derived NO. Additional studies are needed to confirm the benefit in PAD.

L-arginine is another promising supplement, a semi-essential amino acid that is the precursor of the potent vasodilator, endothelium-derived NO. This agent also is effective in the absence of an effect on the lipid profile. Individuals with hyperlipidemia and/or PAD appear to synthesize less NO, possibly due to elevated levels of asymmetric dimethylarginine, the endogenous NO synthase inhibitor (Cooke, 2000). Infusions of L-arginine increase limb blood flow and increase walking distance in patients with PAD (Bode-Böger et al, 1996; Böger et al, 1998). In patients with CAD, oral L-arginine (6 to 9 g/d) improves coronary blood flow response, reduces angina, and significantly increases walking time on the treadmill prior to ST-segment depression (Lerman et al, 1998; Ceremuzynski et al, 1997). In a single randomized clinical trial, an arginine-enriched medical food improved exercise capacity in patients with PAD, relieved claudication, and improved quality of life. A supplemental dose of 3 g to 9 g oral L-arginine/d may be useful in PAD patients. Additional studies are under way to confirm the benefit of an arginine-based therapy. However, the data for exercise, cilostazol, and revascularization are stronger.

CONCLUSIONS

Contrary to popular belief, there is much that the skilled internist or primary care practitioner can do to relieve symptoms for PAD patients and to increase their longevity. Interventions include risk-factor modification, antiplatelet therapy, exercise and diet, and nutritive approaches to relieve claudication pain and to improve quality of life. ■

BIBLIOGRAPHY

Blankenhorn DH, Azen SP, Crawford DW, et al. Effects of colestipol-niacin therapy on human femoral atherosclerosis. Circulation 1991;83:438–47.

Bode-Böger SM, Böger RH, Alfke H, et al. L-arginine induces nitric oxide-dependent vasodilation in patients with critical limb ischemia. A randomized, controlled study. Circulation 1996;93:85–90.

Böger RH, Bode-Böger SM, Szuba A, et al. Asymmetric dimethylarginine (ADMA): a novel risk factor for endothelial dysfunction : its role in hypercholesterolemia. Circulation 1998;98:1842–7.

Bostom AG, Cupples LA, Jenner JL, et al. Elevated plasma lipoprotein(a) and coronary heart disease in men aged 55 years and younger. A prospective study. JAMA 1996;276;544–8.

Buchwald H, Bourdages HR, Campos CT, et al. Impact of cholesterol reduction on peripheral arterial disease in the Program on the Surgical Control of Hyperlipidemias (POSCH). Surgery 1996;120:672–9.

Ceremuzynski L, Chamiec T, Herbaczynska-Cedro K. Effect of supplemental oral L-arginine on exercise capacity in patients with stable angina pectoris. Am J Cardiol 1997;80:331–3.

Cooke JP. Does ADMA cause endothelial dysfunction? Arterioscler Thromb Vasc Biol 2000;20:2032–7.

de Lorgeril M, Renaud S, Mamelle N, et al. Mediterranean alpha-linolenic acid-rich diet in secondary prevention of coronary heart disease. Lancet 1994;343:1454–9.

de Lorgeril M, Salen P, Martin JL, et al. Mediterranean diet, traditional risk factors, and the rate of cardiovascular complications after myocardial infarction: final report of the Lyon Diet Heart Study. Circulation 1999;99:779–85.

Furberg CD, Adams HP Jr, Applegate WB, et al. Effect of lovastatin on early carotid atherosclerosis and cardiovascular events. Asymptomatic Carotid Artery Progression Study (ACAPS) Research Group. Circulation 1994;90:1679–87.

Gould AL, Rossouw JE, Santanello NC, et al. Cholesterol reduction yields clinical benefit: impact of statin trials. Circulation 1998;97:946–52.

Gray DR, Morgan T, Chretien SD, Kashyap ML. Efficacy and safety of controlled-release niacin in dyslipoproteinemic veterans. Ann Intern Med 1994;121:252–8.

Grundy SM. Statin trials and goals of cholesterol-lowering therapy. Circulation 1998;97:1436–9.

Hiatt WR, Hoag S, Hamman RF. Effect of diagnostic criteria on the prevalence of peripheral arterial disease. The San Luis Valley Diabetes Study. Circulation 1995;91:1472–9.

Hodis HN, Mack WJ, LaBree L, et al. Reduction in carotid arterial wall thickness using lovastatin and dietary therapy: a randomized controlled clinical trial. Ann Intern Med 1996;124:548–56.

Jenkins DJ, Wolever TM, Rao AV, et al. Effect on blood lipids of very high intakes of fiber in diets low in saturated fat and cholesterol. N Engl J Med 1993;329:21–6.

Johansson J, Egberg N, Johnsson H, Carlson LA. Serum lipoproteins and hemostatic function in intermittent claudication. Arterioscler Thromb Vasc Biol 1993;13:1441–8.

Kjekshus J, Pedersen TR. Reducing the risk of coronary events: evidence from the Scandinavian Simvastatin Survival Study (4S). Am J Cardiol 1995;76:64C–8C.

Kroon AA, van Asten WN, Stalenhoef AF. Effect of apheresis of low-density lipoprotein on peripheral vascular disease in hypercholesterolemic patients with coronary artery disease. Ann Intern Med 1996;125:945–54.

Leaf A. Dietary prevention of coronary heart disease: the Lyon Diet Heart Study. Circulation 1999;99: 733–5.

Lerman A, Burnett JC Jr, Higano ST, et al. Long-term L-arginine supplementation improves small-vessel coronary endothelial function in humans. Circulation. 1998;97:2123–8.

Lupattelli G, Siepi D, Pasqualini L, et al. Lipoprotein(a) in peripheral arterial occlusive disease. Vasa J Vasc Dis 1994;23:321–4.

Miettinen TA, Pyorala K, Olsson AG, et al. Cholesterol-lowering therapy in women and elderly patients with myocardial infarction or angina pectoris: findings from the Scandinavian Simvastatin Study (4S). Circulation 1997;96:4211–8.

Moore TJ, Vollmer WM, Appel LJ, et al. Effect of dietary patterns on ambulatory blood pressure: results from the Dietary Approaches to Stop Hypertension (DASH) trial. DASH Collaborative Research Group. Hypertension 1999;34:472–7.

Mowat BF, Skinner ER, Wilson HM, et al. Alterations in plasma lipids, lipoproteins and high density lipoprotein subfractions in peripheral arterial disease. Atherosclerosis 1997;131:161–6.

Murabito JM, D'Agostino RB, Silbershatz H, Wilson WF.

Intermittent claudication: a risk profile from The Framingham Heart Study. Circulation 1997;96:44–9.

Olin JW, Cressman MD, Young JR, et al. Lipid and lipoprotein abnormalities in lower-extremity arteriosclerosis obliterans. Cleve Clin J Med 1992; 59:491–7.

Pasternak RC, Brown LE, Stone PH, et al. Effect of combination therapy with lipid-reducing drugs in patients with coronary heart disease and "normal" cholesterol levels. A randomized, placebo-controlled trial. Harvard Atherosclerosis Reversibility Project (HARP) Study Group. Ann Intern Med 1996; 125:529–40.

Pedersen TR, Kjekshus J, Pyorala K, et al. Effect of simvastatin on ischemic signs and symptoms in the Scandinavian Simvastatin Survival Study (4S). Am J Cardiol 1998;81:333–5.

Sacks FM, Moye LA, Davis BR, et al. Relationship between plasma LDL concentrations during treatment with pravastatin and recurrent coronary events in the Cholesterol and Recurrent Events trial. Circulation 1998;97:1446–52.

Sacks FM, Pfeffer MA, Moye LA, et al. The effect of pravastatin on coronary events after myocardial infarction in patients with average cholesterol levels. Cholesterol and Recurrent Events Trial investigators. N Engl J Med 1996;335:1001–9.

Schuler G, Hambrecht R, Schlierf G, et al. Regular physical exercise and low-fat diet. Effects on progression of coronary artery disease. Circulation 1992;86:1–11.

Superko H, Krauss R. Coronary artery disease regression. Convincing evidence for the benefit of aggressive lipoprotein management. Circulation 1994;90: 1056–69.

Valentine RJ, Kaplan HS, Green R, et al. Lipoprotein(a), homocysteine, and hypercoagulable states in young men with premature peripheral atherosclerosis: a prospective, controlled analysis. J Vasc Surg 1996; 23:53–61.

Newer Risk Factors and Peripheral Arterial Disease

Killian Robinson, MD
Associate Professor
The Department of Internal Medicine/Cardiology
Wake Forest University
Baptist Medical Center
Winston-Salem, North Carolina

Objective: To understand the role and interrelationship of biochemical and hematologic markers as potential risk factors for PAD.

Several nontraditional risk factors for peripheral arterial disease (PAD) have now been identified. These include elevated levels of lipoprotein(a) [Lp(a)] and triglycerides as well as low levels of high-density lipoprotein cholesterol (HDL-C). High plasma levels of homocysteine, low levels of vitamin B_6, and elevated fibrinogen and plasminogen activator inhibitor (PAI) levels may also be important. The roles of chronic infection and inflammation in the development of vascular disease are also being studied.

LIPOPROTEIN(a)

Lp(a) consists of a low-density lipoprotein (LDL) particle containing apolipoprotein (apo) B-100 linked to the apo(a) protein (Rader and Rosas, 2000), which has an amino acid sequence similar to plasminogen. The function of Lp(a) remains unclear. Concentrations in plasma range from 1 to 100 mg/dL, but most values are <20 mg/dL. Levels do not bear any clear relationship to age or gender, but rise following menopause and with the concentrations of LDL cholesterol (LDL-C). Concentrations are also higher in both American and African blacks than in whites, and in patients with nephrotic syndrome, chronic renal failure, and diabetes (Rader and Rosas, 2000).

Many studies have shown a relationship between Lp(a) and coronary artery disease (CAD) in prospective and nested case-control studies. In the Helsinki Heart Study (Jauhiainen et al, 1991) and the US Physicians Health Study (Ridker et al, 1993), however, no relationship was noted between baseline levels of Lp(a) and risk of CAD. High levels of Lp(a) combined with high LDL-C, however, may confer a particularly high risk of CAD (Rader and Rosas, 2000). In patients with PAD, levels of Lp(a) were higher than in controls (Valentine

et al, 1996, Figure 1). Among patients, 40% had levels ≥30 mg/dL compared with only 16% of controls, giving a greater than 3-fold risk of vascular disease. Lp(a) was directly related to vascular risk (P = 0.003) with an odds ratio for each 1 mg/dL Lp(a) increase of 1.03 (CI 1.0 to 1.1). Wollesen et al (1999) studied patients with type 1 and type 2 diabetes mellitus and showed that the toe systolic blood pressure index, a measure of PAD, was independently related to Lp(a) levels in diabetic patients.

The mechanism of thrombosis and atherosclerosis in patients with elevated Lp(a) is unknown. The structural similarity of apo(a) to plasminogen, however, suggests that high levels of Lp(a) could inhibit endogenous fibrinolytic activity; unlike plasminogen, apo(a) cannot be converted to a plasmin-like molecule. In addition, owing to its kringle-like domains, apo(a) binds and displaces plasminogen from sites on fibrin and fibrinogen.

Various drugs may lower Lp(a) levels including niacin, the only lipid-lowering agent that does this reliably (Rader and Rosas, 2000), and estrogen. The clinical benefit of Lp(a) reduction is speculative, especially since higher levels may not confer greater cardiovascular risk even when LDL-C is lowered considerably.

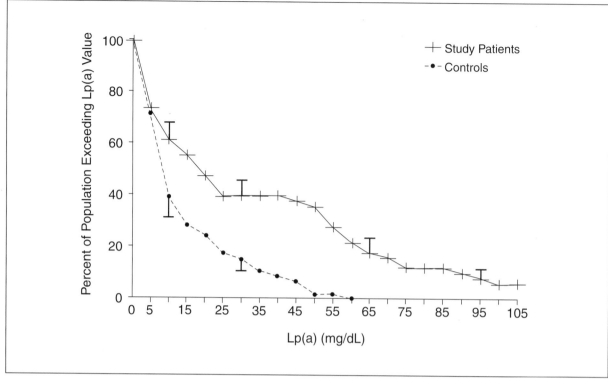

Figure 1. Negative cumulative lipoprotein(a) [Lp(a)] distribution of symptomatic patients with vascular disease and randomly selected controls without symptoms. Each point represents percent (±SEM) with Lp(a) levels exceeding given value on the x-axis. Reproduced with permission from Valentine RJ, et al. J Vasc Surg 1996;23:53–61, discussion 61–3.

LOW HDL-C AND HIGH TRIGLYCERIDES

Low levels of HDL-C and high triglycerides are commonly seen in patients with CAD. Drexel et al (1996) studied patients with PAD referred for angioplasty, and age-matched controls with normal coronary and peripheral angiograms. PAD was associated with LDL-C, triglycerides, and smoking and decreased HDL-C. LDL-C, triglycerides, smoking, and systolic blood pressure independently predicted disease while its extent correlated negatively with HDL-C and positively with smoking and fasting blood glucose. Thus, hypertriglyceridemia and low HDL-C may confer an increased risk of PAD.

HOMOCYSTEINE

Homocysteine is an important metabolite of methionine (Refsum et al, 1998; Seshadri and Robinson, 2000). The normal reference range for fasting plasma homocysteine is 5 to 15 μmol/L although some now feel that the upper limit of normal should be 10 to 12 μmol/L. About 30% to 40% of patients with vascular diseases have levels >15 μmol/L. Concentrations rise with age, are higher in men than in women, and increase after menopause. In some individuals, fasting

homocysteine levels may be normal but may rise abnormally after a methionine loading test. The rise may be considered abnormal if the postload homocysteine level exceeds the 90th percentile for normal subjects. The test may detect the presence of high homocysteine levels after loading despite normal fasting levels, but its role in clinical practice remains unclear, as it is labor-intensive, time-consuming, and expensive.

Metabolism of homocysteine (Figure 2) requires vitamin B_6, vitamin B_{12}, folic acid, and several enzymes (Refsum et al, 1998; Seshadri and Robinson, 2000). Thus, deficiencies of either vitamins or enzymes may result in accumulation of homocysteine. Serious enzyme deficiencies are rare, although a common variant of the methylenetetrahydrofolate reductase gene, with a prevalence of ~10% to15% in the general population, predisposes to mild to moderate hyperhomocysteinemia, especially in the presence of low plasma folate levels. Other causes of a high homocysteine level include smoking, coffee consumption, chronic renal insufficiency, some malignancies, hypothyroidism, and inflammatory bowel disease. Drugs that may elevate homocysteine levels include

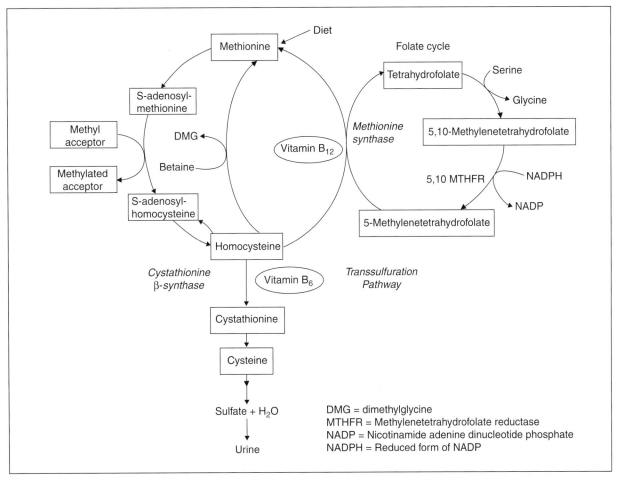

Figure 2. The metabolic pathways for the metabolism of methionine and homocysteine (see text for discussion). Reproduced with permission from Robinson K. Heart 2000;83:127–30.

cholestyramine, folate antagonists, theophylline, niacin, and gemfibrozil. Conversely, exogenous estrogen and tamoxifen may lower homocysteine. Many of these drugs are commonly used in patients with vascular disease and should be considered when evaluating an increased homocysteine level in patients with vascular diseases.

In case-control studies, a high homocysteine level has been seen consistently in patients with vascular disease although data from prospective studies are conflicting (Refsum et al, 1998; Seshadri and Robinson, 2000). In one study, Malinow et al (1989) found levels of homocysteine in patients with PAD were significantly higher than in apparently healthy controls. The authors concluded that an elevated plasma homocysteine concentration was an independent risk factor for PAD. Not all studies are positive, however, and Valentine et al (1996) found that mean total plasma homocysteine level in patients was not significantly different from controls. The relationship between plasma

homocysteine and PAD was investigated in the Homocysteine and Progression of Atherosclerosis Study (Taylor et al, 1999). This prospective, blinded study investigated the influence of homocysteine and other atherosclerotic risk factors on the progression of disease in patients with symptomatic PAD. After a mean follow-up period of 37 months, deaths from cardiovascular disease increased and progression of coronary disease was worse in those with homocysteine concentrations >14 µmol/L. After adjustment for age, smoking, hypertension, diabetes, and cholesterol, a 1.0-µmol/L increase in plasma homocysteine resulted in a 3.6% increase in the risk of death (all causes) at 3 years and a 5.6% increase in the risk of death from CAD.

Despite these epidemiologic links, the mechanism, if any, of atherosclerosis induced by hyperhomocysteinemia is unknown, although endothelial damage and/or an increased tendency to thrombosis are possible (Refsum et al, 1998; Seshadri and Robinson, 2000). Physiologic models in both animals and humans have demonstrated that elevated homocysteine concentrations are associated with an impaired vasodilator response. In hyperhomocysteinemia, the vascular endothelium may be susceptible to injury, perhaps mediated by hydrogen peroxide, a product of auto-oxidation of homocysteine. Homocysteine may also inhibit nitric oxide or affect clotting. Hajjar et al (1998) found that homocysteine formed a stable disulfide bond with N-terminal Cys_9 of annexin II, inhibiting its binding to tissue-type plasminogen activator (t-PA) on endothelial cells.

Folic acid decreases plasma homocysteine level by 25% to 30% (Refsum et al, 1998; Seshadri and Robinson, 2000). Doses as low as 0.4 mg/day are successful in most cases. Vitamin B_{12} alone only modestly reduces fasting homocysteine levels, while vitamin B_6 may be effective in reducing levels after methionine loading. Recently, fortification of cereal grain products with folic acid has been undertaken in the United States to reduce the incidence of neural tube defects, and population homocysteine levels have already fallen by ~10%. Conceivably, this may have beneficial effects on the prevalence of atherosclerosis. Several large, controlled, intervention studies are now in progress to study the effect of B vitamins on clinical endpoints in patients with documented atherosclerosis.

The American Heart Association recommends measurement of a fasting plasma total homocysteine as a screening tool in certain high-risk individuals such as those with arterial or venous thrombotic disease or those with a strong family history of vascular disease. Such individuals may benefit from increased folate intake either in the form of supplements or fortified food products (Malinow et al, 1999). This is of speculative benefit, however, until ongoing trials have been completed. Caution should be exercised in using folic acid alone in those at risk of cobalamin deficiency, as symptoms of this may be unmasked leading to adverse neurologic sequelae.

VITAMIN B$_6$

Vitamin B_6 is inversely related to the concentration of plasma homocysteine. In studies of homocysteine and vascular disease, a low concentration of vitamin B_6 has been shown to be a risk factor for atherothrombotic disorders. One large case-control study included patients with CAD, stroke, and PAD. Vitamin B_6 deficiency was seen in 15% to 20% of cases and was independently associated with increased risk of atherosclerosis, including PAD (Seshadri and Robinson, 2000). The mechanism for this increased risk is unclear but may involve an effect on coagulation. It is also unknown if supplementation with this vitamin will improve prognosis, although this is currently the subject of clinical trials.

FIBRINOGEN

The circulating concentration of fibrinogen is usually between 200 to 400 mg/dL. Levels are higher in blacks than in whites and in women than in men. Concentrations rise with age, menopause, body weight, LDL-C, Lp(a), smoking, hypertension, diabetes mellitus, stress, and physical inactivity. In a meta-analysis of prospective studies, the overall odds ratio for cardiovascular events for the upper versus the lowest tertiles of fibrinogen concentrations was 2.3 (Ernst and Resch, 1993).

In the Edinburgh Artery Study (Smith et al, 2000), patients were followed prospectively to detect the onset of, and deterioration in, PAD in relation to fibrinogen. After 5 years, 5.5% of study subjects developed the disease while 14% of those with established disease deteriorated. After adjusting for cardiovascular risk factors and baseline ischemic heart disease, the association between fibrinogen and development of disease was significant (Figure 3). A high level of von Willebrand factor was also associated with PAD. In the same study, the 455AA polymorphism of the P fibrinogen gene was associated with an increased risk of peripheral atherosclerosis (Lee et al, 1999).

Although fibrinogen may increase risk, whether it causes atherosclerosis or secondary thrombosis is unknown. Reduction of plasma fibrinogen concentrations is feasible using some β-blocking agents, platelet inhibitors, and fibric acid derivatives (especially bezafibrate), but lifestyle interventions such as increased exercise may be the most satisfactory initial choice.

PLASMINOGEN ACTIVATOR INHIBITOR

The most extensively investigated PAI in relation to atherothrombosis is PAI type 1 (PAI-1). Levels increase with other risk factors including age, systolic blood pressure, triglycerides, insulin concentrations, and body-mass index.

High levels have been reported in patients with venous thrombosis and myocardial infarction (MI), but plasma levels do not correlate with the extent of atherosclerosis, and its relationship to other risk factors confounds the issue. Furthermore, PAI-1 is also an acute phase reactant. Although high levels of both t-PA and PAI were seen in patients with PAD, its contributions to atherosclerosis risk disappeared when data were adjusted for smoking and hypertriglyceridemia (Smith et al, 1995). More work is needed to unravel the relationship between these hemostatic factors and vascular disease.

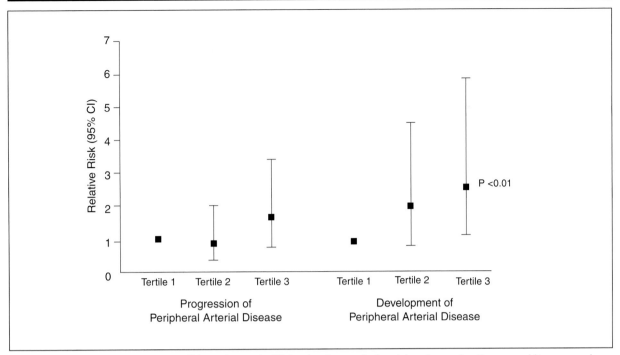

Figure 3. Relative risk with 95% confidence intervals (CI) for development of peripheral vascular disease and its progression across tertiles of fibrinogen, adjusted for age, sex, cigarette smoking, systolic blood pressure, low-density lipoprotein cholesterol, and ischemic heart disease. Tertile cut-points were <2.53 g/L, 2.53 to 3.09 g/L, and >3.09 g/L. Reproduced with permission from Smith FB, et al. Blood Coagul Fibrinolysis 2000;11:43–50.

INFECTION

Chronic infections are associated with the development of atherosclerotic disease states, including unstable angina, MI, cerebrovascular disease, and PAD (Muhlestein, 2000). The infectious agents with the most evidence to support a causal role in atherosclerosis are *Chlamydia pneumoniae* and cytomegalovirus, but others have also been implicated, including *Helicobacter pylori* and hepatitis A. Possible mechanisms include vessel wall colonization or exacerbation of preexisting plaque by enhancement of T-cell activation. Clinical trials of antibiotic treatment are ongoing. In one, patients were treated with roxithromycin to eradicate C *pneumoniae* from carotid artery plaques. C *pneumoniae* DNA was seen in 12 of 16 nontreated patients but was detected in only 5 of 16 treated patients. Larger studies will help determine whether antibiotic therapy is of long-term benefit in patients with atherosclerosis.

Chronic inflammation is an integral part of atherosclerosis and infections of the endothelium are one dimension of this process. The inflammatory marker C-reactive protein (CRP) helps identify future risk of vascular morbidity and mortality independent of traditional risk factors. In one study (Ridker et al, 1998), CRP was measured in men who later developed PAD and in controls who did not. Levels were higher in those who subsequently developed disease (relative risk 2.1 for the highest quartile of CRP compared with the lowest). It is still unclear, however, if elevation of CRP reflects plaque burden or vulnerability, ongoing inflammation or activity of disease, or simply the effects of other risk factors. Clinically, however, CRP might help stratify patients in terms of disease severity and/or activity and monitor the effects of treatments in specific clinical situations (Morrow and Ridker, 2000). ∎

REFERENCES

Drexel H, Steurer J, Muntwyler J, et al. Predictors of the presence and extent of peripheral arterial occlusive disease. Circulation 1996;94(9 Suppl):II 199–205.

Ernst E, Resch KL. Fibrinogen as a cardiovascular risk factor: a meta-analysis and review of the literature. Ann Intern Med 1993;118:956–63.

Hajjar KA, Mauri L, Jacovina AT, et al. Tissue plasminogen activator binding to the annexin II tail domain. Direct modulation by homocysteine. J Biol Chem 1998;273:9987–93.

Jauhiainen M, Koskinen P, Ehnholm C, et al. Lipoprotein(a) and coronary heart disease risk: a nested case-control study of the Helsinki Heart Study participants. Atherosclerosis 1991;89:59–67.

Key Points

● Nontraditional risk factors for vascular disease include elevated levels of Lp(a), low HDL-C, and high triglycerides.

● Other risk factors include a high plasma homocysteine concentration, although data from prospective studies are conflicting, and low concentrations of vitamin B_6. Trials are ongoing in this area.

● High levels of fibrinogen and PAI are also associated with vascular disease although the latter may be a proxy for other risk factors.

● Chronic infections with some microorganisms have been associated with the development of atherosclerosis, and trials of antibiotic therapy are currently in progress.

● Chronic inflammation markers are now available that may help in monitoring disease activity and in targeting patients or treatments more specifically.

● Clinical trials are now under way to determine if treatment of these abnormalities has long-term benefit in patients with PAD.

Lee AJ, Fowkes FG, Lowe GD, et al. Fibrinogen, factor VII and PAI-1 genotypes and the risk of coronary and peripheral atherosclerosis: Edinburgh Artery Study. Thromb Haemost 1999;81:553–60.

Malinow MR, Bostom AG, Krauss RM. Homocyst(e)ine, diet, and cardiovascular diseases: a statement for healthcare professionals from the Nutrition Committee, American Heart Association. Circulation 1999;99:178–82.

Malinow MR, Kang SS, Taylor LM, et al. Prevalence of hyperhomocyst(e)inemia in patients with peripheral arterial occlusive disease. Circulation 1989;79:1180–8.

Morrow DA, Ridker PM. C-reactive protein, inflammation, and coronary risk. Med Clin North Am 2000;84:149–61.

Muhlestein JB. Chronic infection and coronary artery disease. Med Clin North Am 2000;84:123–48.

Rader DJ, Rosas S. Management of selected lipid abnormalities. Med Clin North Am 2000;84:43–61.

Refsum H, Ueland PM, Nygard O, Vollset SE. Homocysteine and cardiovascular disease. Annu Rev Med 1998;49:31–62.

Ridker PM, Cushman M, Stampfer MJ, et al. Plasma concentration of C-reactive protein and risk of developing peripheral vascular disease. Circulation 1998;97:425–8.

Ridker PM, Hennekens CH, Stampfer MJ. A prospective study of lipoprotein(a) and the risk of myocardial infarction. JAMA 1993;270:2195–9.

Robinson K. Homocysteine, B vitamins, and risk of cardiovascular disease [editorial]. Heart 2000;83:127–30.

Seshadri N, Robinson K. Homocysteine, B vitamins, and coronary disease. Med Clin North Am 2000;84:215–37.

Smith FB, Lee AJ, Hau CM, et al. Plasma fibrinogen, haemostatic factors and prediction of peripheral arterial disease in the Edinburgh Artery Study. Blood Coagul Fibrinolysis 2000;11:43–50.

Smith FB, Lee AJ, Rumley A, et al. Tissue-plasminogen activator, plasminogen activator inhibitor and risk of peripheral arterial disease. Atherosclerosis 1995;115:35–43.

Taylor LM Jr, Moneta GL, Sexton GJ, et al. Prospective blinded study of the relationship between plasma homocysteine and progression of symptomatic peripheral arterial disease. J Vasc Surg 1999;29:8–19; discussion 19–21.

Valentine RJ, Kaplan HS, Green R, et al. Lipoprotein(a), homocysteine, and hypercoagulable states in young men with premature peripheral atherosclerosis: a prospective, controlled analysis. J Vasc Surg 1996;23:53–61, discussion 61–3.

Wollesen F, Dahlen G, Berglund L, Berne C. Peripheral atherosclerosis and serum lipoprotein(a) in diabetes. Diabetes Care 1999;22:93–8.

Subject Index

A

Abdominal aorta
    examination of, 15–16, 128, 132
    small syndrome of, 43–44, 113, 164
Abdominal aortic aneurysm (AAA)
    diagnosis of, 148
    general considerations of, 13, 15, 147–148, 151
    imaging of, 148–149
    as incidental finding, 148–149
    noninvasive examination of, 132–133
    rupture of, 147–148, 150–151, 166
    screening programs for, 148–149
    surgical repair of, 150–151
        complications of, 150
        preoperative medical evaluation for, 149–151
    symptomatic, 148, 151
    in women, 163, 165–166
ABI. *See* Ankle-brachial index
Absolute claudication distance (ACD), 90–92
Accelerometers, for claudication evaluation, 92
ACD (absolute claudication distance), 90–92
Acetylcholine, vasomotor tone and, 33, 182
Activity. *See* Physical activity
Acute arterial occlusion. *See* Embolism; Thromboses
Acute arterial occlusive disease, chronic *vs.*, 52, 55–57, 63, 77
Acyl coenzyme A (acyl-CoA), in claudication, 77
Adjunctive therapies, 110, 194
AFB (aortofemoral bypass), 121–122
Age and aging
    as mortality factor, 7–8, 21
    population trends in, 120–121
    as risk factor, 5–6, 9, 96, 100, 120
        in women, 157–160
    as symptomatology factor, 12, 20, 42–43
Agency for Healthcare Research and Quality (AHRQ), 185
Alternative medicine, 110, 194
Ambulation. *See* Walking
American Heart Association, risk-factors per, 22, 25, 162, 200
Amputation
    coordination of, 97–98, 100–101, 115
    for critical limb ischemia, 52, 57, 59, 61, 64, 68–70
    late incidence of, 12–13, 18
    level of, clinical determinants of, 68–69
    rehabilitation potential with, 68, 100–101
    risk factors for, 22, 98–99
Anatomic assessment, noninvasive, 129–133, 141
Aneurysms. *See also specific anatomy*
    noninvasive examination of, 130, 132–133, 148–149, 151
    as testing indication, 130
    in women, 155, 163, 165–167
Angina

in diagnosis and treatment, 36
    epidemiology of, 6, 15, 21
Angiogenesis, therapeutic, 65, 110
Angiography. *See* Arteriography
Angioplasty. *See* Percutaneous transluminal angioplasty
Angiotensin, as atherogenic, 189
Ankle-brachial index (ABI)
    calculation of, 16, 129, 136, 142
    as cardiovascular event predictor, 20–21, 25, 193
    in critical limb ischemia, 53–57
    diagnostic applications of, 16, 18, 82, 138
    diagnostic reliability of, 5–6, 9, 12, 15, 20, 136
    disease prevalence per, 76, 96–97
    disease severity correlation with, 8–10, 13, 16, 24–25
    electrocardiogram correlations with, 6–7, 99
    with exercise testing, 141–144
    in functional status assessment, 24–25, 90–91, 93
    indications for, 69, 131
    limitations of, 136–137, 189
    lower extremity function and, 24–25, 108, 113
    with moderate claudication, 108, 113
    in prevention strategies, 98–100
    in women, 42–43, 158–160, 164
Antibiotic therapy, for infection risks, 201
Anticoagulation therapy
    following revascularization, 40, 60
    long-term, 39
    for thromboses, 39–40
Antidepressant agents, for smoking cessation, 184
Antihypertensive agents, for women, 164
Antiplatelet agents
    for claudication, 83, 99, 108–110, 165
    coordination of, 97–98
    for graft patency, 60
    trial results, 6, 37–40, 165
Antiplatelet Trialists' Collaboration, 39, 108, 165
Antithrombotic therapy
    anticoagulants for, 39–40
    aspirin as, 22, 36–37, 40
    for critical limb ischemia, 63–65
    following revascularization, 36, 39–40, 60
    intra-arterial, 64, 115
    intraoperative, 39–40, 116
    other platelet inhibitors as, 6, 37–40
    risks with, 37–39
AOD. *See* Arterial occlusive disease
Aorta. *See also* Abdominal aorta
    ultrasonography of, 15, 148–149, 151, 163
Aortofemoral bypass (AFB), 121–122
Aortogram, applications of, 16
Aortoiliac angioplasty, indications for, 84, 114–118, 122
Aortoiliac bypass surgery, 60–61, 122
    in women, 43–44